❀ STORY LINE ❀

STORY LINE

Exploring the Literature of the Appalachian Trail

Ian Marshall

University Press of Virginia

Charlottesville and London

The University Press of Virginia
©1998 by the Rector and Visitors of the University of Virginia
All rights reserved
Printed in the United States of America

First published 1998

ⓧ The paper used in this publication meets the minimum requirements
of the American National Standard for Information Sciences—
Permanence of Paper for Printed Library Materials, ANSI Z39.48-1984.

Library of Congress Cataloging-in-Publication Data

Marshall, Ian, 1954–
    Story line : exploring the literature of the Appalachian Trail /
Ian Marshall.
        p.   cm.
    ISBN 0-8139-1797-2 (alk. paper). — ISBN 0-8139-1798-0 (pbk. :
alk. paper)
    1. American literature—Appalachian Region—History and criticism.
2. Appalachian Region—In literature.   3. Appalachian Trail—
Historiography.   4. Appalachian Trail—In literature.   5. Mountain
life in literature.   6. Nature in literature.   I. Title.
PS286.A6M37   1998
810.9'3274—dc21
                                                                97-44616
                                                                    CIP

For Jacy and Kira

❁

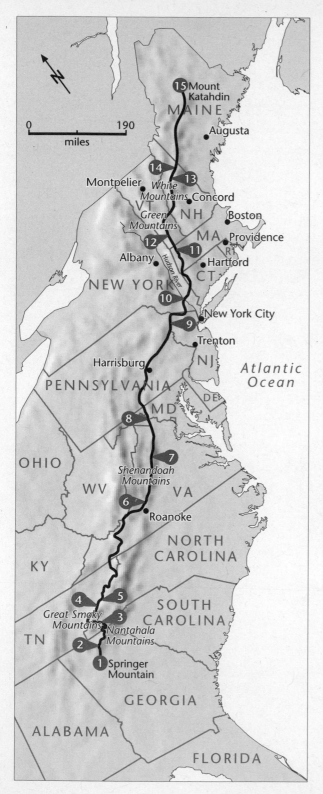

Appalachian Trail

Selected Sites

1. Springer Mountain
2. Blood Mountain
3. Wayah Bald
4. Clingmans Dome
5. Mount Kephart
6. Tinker Cliffs
7. Swift Run Gap
8. Harpers Ferry
9. Delaware Water Gap
10. Bear Mountain
11. Mount Greylock
12. Stratton Mountain
13. Mount Lafayette
14. Mount Washington
15. Mount Katahdin

CONTENTS

Acknowledgments   *ix*

Introduction: Walking the Line   *1*

1

Cherokee Myths and the Pleasures of Geopiety   *10*

2

Puc Puggy in the Nantahalas:
The Turning Point of William Bartram's *Travels*   *35*

3

Mary Noailles Murfree:
Ecofeminist of the Great Smoky Mountains   *51*

4

Horace Kephart's "Man's Game" and the
Community of *Our Southern Highlanders*   *70*

5

Pilgrim at Tinker Cliffs   *88*

6

From Imperialism to Nationalism: The Knights of the
Golden Horseshoe Cross the Blue Ridge   *103*

7

Confluences: The View from Jefferson Rock   120

8

From Wind Gap to Water Gap:
On the Trail of *Edgar Huntly*   131

9

Where the Open Road Meets Howl   151

10

Greylock and the Whale   162

11

Synecdoche and Ecology:
Frost in the Greens and Whites   180

12

Democracy and Ecology:
Hawthorne's White Mountain Stories   203

13

Contact! Contact! A Walk to Thoreau's Ktaadn   226

Notes   251

Index   271

ACKNOWLEDGMENTS

For their company and friendship, and their part in my stories, thanks to my hiking partners — to name a few, Pesch, Joe Dunes, Gerry Wade, Duane Loeper, Wolverine, Just Jane, Tiger Lily, and David "Pathfinder" Taylor. For scholarly companionship and inspiration, thanks to Mike Branch, SueEllen Campbell, Cheryll Glotfelty, Sean O'Grady, Suzanne Ross, Don Scheese, Mark Schlenz, Scott Slovic, and other friends and colleagues in the Association for the Study of Literature and the Environment. For financial support, thanks to the Penn State Altoona Advisory Board. For their advice and encouragement as they read drafts or portions of the manuscript, thanks to my colleagues Dick Caram, Dinty W. Moore, and Sandy Petrulionis, my editor Boyd Zenner, and, especially, Judy McKelvey.

For the map, thanks to Thad Lenker and David DiBiase of the Deasy GeoGraphics Laboratory, Penn State University, University Park, Pa.

Portions of chapter 6 appeared in different form as "Landscape Aesthetics and Literary History: The Knights of the Golden Horseshoe in Journal, Poem, and Story," *Mississippi Quarterly* 44, no. 1 (1990–91): 69–82. Chapter 10, "Greylock and the Whale," appeared in similar form in a Japanese translation in *Environmental Approaches to American Literature: Toward the World of Nature Writing*, ed. Scott Slovic and Ken-ichi Noda (Kyoto: Minerva Press, 1996), 153–83.

Robert Frost excerpts: From *THE POETRY OF ROBERT FROST* Edited by Edward Connery Lathem, Copyright 1951 by Robert Frost, Copyright 1923, © 1969 by Henry Holt and Company, Inc. Reprinted by permission of Henry Holt and Company, Inc.

Allen Ginsberg excerpts: From "Howl" FROM *COLLECTED POEMS*

❧ STORY LINE ❧

The wild requires that we learn the terrain,
nod to all the plants and animals and birds,
ford the streams and cross the ridges,
and tell a good story when we get back home.

Gary Snyder, *The Practice of the Wild*

INTRODUCTION

Walking the Line

As I sit in the train station in Wilmington, Delaware, backpack at my side, I am just finishing Bruce Chatwin's book *The Songlines*. Chatwin writes of his quest to learn about the Dreaming-tracks of the aboriginal peoples of Australia. These Dreaming-tracks — the "Songlines" of Chatwin's title — are trails walked by the "Ancestors," who in the "Dreamtime" long ago fashioned themselves out of clay and sang the earth into existence, naming items in the landscape as they progressed on their journeys, recording their paths in songs whose melodic contours echo the geologic forms of the land. To this day aboriginals learn the songs of their ancestors, and every so often they set out on ritual journeys called walkabouts, following in the footprints of their ancestors and recreating in song the emergence of the land.[1]

When my train arrives, I leave Chatwin's book on the bench, wishing it well on its journey, wherever it may wander. I'm headed for Gainesville, Georgia, where a friend will pick me up tomorrow morning, the last day of April, and drive me to Amicalola Falls State Park. There a trail will take me (or I will take it, I'm not sure which) to Springer Mountain, southern terminus of the Appalachian Trail. The northern terminus is 2,150 miles away, on Mount Katahdin in Maine. My destination this trip is Hot Springs, North Carolina, about 270 miles north of Springer, but I expect that I'll encounter quite a few "thru-hikers" intending to walk the full length of the trail. Those I meet will be the tail end of this year's herd of several hundred thru-hikers, mostly young adults just out of college looking to find themselves or the meaning of life. But there will also be middle-aged folks taking a career break or trying to sort out their lives or searching for adventure, and even some retirees seeking lost youth or setting out on the stroll of a lifetime. All, it occurs to me, will be embarking on an American version of a walkabout, a ritual journey of some sort. The Appalachian Trail is itself a kind of songline, a path of verbal creations on the land. In America, though, these stories of the land are more often recorded in books than in songs. These are my subject—the literary works set in locales along the Appalachian Trail.

❀   ❀   ❀

The A.T., as the trail is often called, was the brainchild of Benton MacKaye, a regional planner who in the early twentieth century considered himself engaged in the work of "geotechnics." As opposed to the descriptive work of the geographer, who studies the land as it is, the geotechnician prescribes— and plans—how it ought to be. MacKaye believed that in our increasingly urban society, Americans needed restored access to the "primeval." And so in 1921 he outlined his idea for "An Appalachian Trail: A Project in Regional Planning." His proposed trail would run on federal, state, and private lands from Mt. Washington in New Hampshire to Mt. Mitchell in North Carolina, the highest point in the Northeast to the highest point in the Southeast.[2] Almost immediately volunteers from hiking clubs north and south set to work on the proposed trail, connecting existing trails and extending the plans northeastward to Mt. Katahdin and southward to Mt. Oglethorpe in Georgia. In 1937 the trails were completed and linked up, only to be disconnected a year later by the construction of the Blue Ridge Parkway in Virginia and, subsequently, by disputes with landowners. Not until 1951 did the trail again become a continuous path. Then in 1958, as a result of urban pressures, the southern terminus was moved twenty miles north, from Mt. Oglethorpe to Springer Mountain.

Today about three million people a year walk at least a portion of the Appalachian Trail. According to records kept by the Appalachian Trail Conference (ATC), the governing body of the A.T. headquartered in Harpers Ferry, since its founding over four thousand people have hiked the entire trail, either as thru-hikers (one trip, end to end) or section hikers (a bit at a time). As MacKaye intended, the trail conserves some wilderness within a day's drive of the nation's most populous areas. But it is a cultural as well as natural treasure. A hike along the Appalachian Trail is a walk into the heart of America, not just north or south as the compass settles, nor into the soul of the hiker, nor "away from it all," but into America's past.

Although MacKaye is often considered the "father" of the Appalachian Trail, in truth its ancestry predates 1921. As the *Member Handbook* of the ATC points out, the Appalachian Trail idea was a logical extension of the long-distance trails proposed by trail club leaders in New England and New

York in the first two decades of the twentieth century.[3] But even before there was an Appalachian Trail—in the dreamtime before it became a reality, before it was even conceived of—the Appalachian Ridge was called into cultural being by our literary ancestors.

The Appalachians are the only American mountain chain for which we have written accounts of encounters with the land from the earliest days of European settlement to the present. As a result, in the body of literature set in the Appalachians one can trace our evolving legacy of landscape aesthetics and our changing attitudes toward nature and the wild. The "story line" that emerges from that tracing runs something like this: in general, appreciation for nature in America shifts from evaluations based on economic, imperialistic, and theologic preconceptions (in colonial America) to a nationalist aesthetic whereby the land becomes associated with the American character (in the nineteenth century), to an appreciation incorporating ecological awareness (in the twentieth century).

If I were writing a literary history of the Appalachian Trail, that story line would be my thesis. To some extent I do employ the tactics of traditional literary history by considering the aesthetics of the writers I look at in the context of the cultural values and historical events of their time. And so that thesis emerges in several places—in the chapters on the Knights of the Golden Horseshoe and Hawthorne's White Mountain stories, for instance. But I'm not concerned only with change through time. I am also interested in exploring the influence of place. Not so much place as political entity, demarcated by state lines, but as geographic entity, identifiable by common geology. Might not the people of the Appalachian Range, all the way from the deep South to the upper reaches of New England, have as much or more in common with one another as they do with the flatlanders of their own states? Might not their literature reflect their shared geographical heritage—its unifying themes being a heightened regard for place and a sense that their place is (for better, not worse) out of step with the march of time? Geologically, the Appalachians are the ancient, erosion-resistant remnants of a once much larger range. Culturally, too, the Appalachian Mountains have been remarkably resistant to the incursions of the surrounding civilization.

In this sense, what I am embarking on here is more a literary geography than a literary history. Or maybe it's a literary geohistory, the "geo" referring in part to geology since that is the unifying principle of the literature of the Appalachian Trail, its starting point, and in part to geography, because that is my organizing principle. In exploring the literature of the Appalachian

Trail, I progress from south to north, from Georgia to Maine — as most thru-hikers do, starting in spring, ending in autumn.

❦   ❦   ❦

Riding the train south, I've got plenty of time to think about the attractions of the songlines myth as described in Chatwin's book. As someone who makes a living talking about books to university students, I am delighted by the myth's implicit privileging of aesthetic concerns, sanctifying as it does the arts of music, poetry, and narrative. It is also a wonderful story in itself, this story about the creative power of stories. But as Chatwin points out, the myth of the songlines appeals on more than "mere" aesthetic grounds. It served several practical purposes in the Australian outback. In such an arid environment, people needed the freedom to move to where the food and water were. A land-tenure system of boundaried territory would lead inevitably to border conflicts. But the songlines gave every person property rights in territory that could stretch hundreds, even thousands, of miles. A member of the wallaby clan ("I have a wallaby dreaming," he would say) was free to follow the full length of his wallaby ancestor's songline. Along the way he was welcomed by neighboring peoples, perhaps even invited to share his song. Even where those he met spoke another language, his wallaby song — and the right of access that it gave its singer — would be recognized by its melodic mapping of shared lands.

In a similar way the Appalachian Trail crosses social and political borders, running from the deep South through the Mid-Atlantic states to New England, through parts of Georgia, North Carolina, Tennessee, Virginia, West Virginia, Maryland, Pennsylvania, New Jersey, New York, Connecticut, Massachusetts, Vermont, New Hampshire, and Maine. En route, hikers are granted right of way into all the American cultures along its length. And everywhere the walker is welcomed. Not just on the trail, where the hikers form a tight-knit community of their own, but in towns along or near the trail — in Hot Springs, North Carolina; in Damascus, Virginia; and Harpers Ferry; in Port Clinton, Pennsylvania; Cheshire, Massachusetts; and Monson, Maine — places where locals shower hospitality upon hikers, as if they mean to spread across the land via hiker hotline the proud word about their town, their place. For the A.T. is not just a means of access — it is a connecting thread, stitching together the patchwork geography of eastern America. There is no better way to see the country than this — to place one foot in front of the other on Springer Mountain, then repeat, about five million times, until you're on top of Katahdin.

❀   ❀   ❀

Sources of information about the Appalachian Trail abound. There are, of course, the trail guides issued by the Appalachian Trail Conference and several how-to books, such as Dan "Wingfoot" Bruce's *Thru-Hiker's Handbook*. There are numerous accounts of individual hikes, among the best of them Earl Shaffer's *Walking with Spring: The First Thru-Hike of the Appalachian Trail*, an account of his 1948 hike, and David Brill's *As Far as the Eye Can See: Reflections of an Appalachian Trail Hiker*. There is a book about the "History, Humanity, and Ecology" of the A.T. and a study of its geology. There is a fine anthology of varied writings about the trail.[4] Many of these books are excellent, and some make occasional mention of literary works associated with the trail. Some, such as the accounts by Shaffer and Brill, even display a linguistic and narrative artistry that might qualify them as literary. My concern, though, is not with books specifically about the Appalachian Trail but with the literature of places that now happen to be crossed or touched by the trail. There lies a literary heritage of interest to scholars and hikers alike, both seekers of a sort.

Hence this book—part guidebook, part exploration into uncharted territory. It's a guide to the literary history and geography of the Appalachian Trail and an exploration into the theory and practice of "ecocriticism"—the emerging field of literary scholarship informed by ecological awareness.[5] Its boundaries have yet to be determined, but the starting point of ecocriticism is to take seriously the importance of place. I try to suggest the breadth of possibility for ecocritical practice—from traditional methods of literary criticism (textual explication, history of ideas, influence study) to the postmodern (cultural studies, Bakhtinian dialogics, and ecofeminism—a branch of ecocriticism that at present is bigger than the rest of the tree). I share the traditionalist's view that literature, especially literature that concerns itself with the solid earth and its inhabitants, is about a real world that deserves our attention. But it is a mistake, I think, for the ecocritic to reject and belittle the insights of poststructuralist literary theory. For all its emphasis on the contingent nature of reality and its preoccupation with human culture, poststructuralist ideology has much in common with ecological thought, primarily in its decentering tendencies. The deep ecologist contends that the human being is not the center or source or end of all value and meaning, that there are other living things that ought to be considered. Similarly, the poststructuralist says we should recognize that there is no single authority for determining literary value and meaning, not even the author; rather, there are cultural (and literary and historical) contexts that affect what authors write and how we read.[6]

Borrowing as it does from other modes of literary scholarship, perhaps ecocriticism is more a state of mind than a packaged set of critical tools. If there is a methodology that sets ecocriticism apart from other modes of literary scholarship, it is its inherent interdisciplinary nature. Ecology itself, at the heart of ecocriticism, is interdisciplinary. To study the interrelationships between living things, and between them and their habitat, requires some acquaintance with such fields as biology, physics, geology, anthropology. Though I am no scientist, I am curious about how the world works, and science piques and sometimes satisfies that curiosity. And I find that science can indeed be a useful tool for the study of literature, at times helping to resolve critical problems, often clarifying my understanding of a principle of life that once engaged a writer's attention. But ecological awareness, based on the principle of interconnectedness, can take spiritual as well as scientific form—witness, for example, the popular sense of the word *ecology* to mean something like "love of nature." So in places I emphasize the belief systems of various American cultures—from native American theology to Enlightenment faith in natural law. And in places I emphasize the values of my own belief system, my own sense of the sacred, for these too are a part of my ecological understanding.

The literary works I have chosen to focus on are diverse but roughly balanced in terms of genre, chronology, and geography. Five chapters deal primarily with works of nonfiction, five with fiction, two with poetry, two with myth. Three chapters focus mainly on works from the eighteenth century, four on works from the nineteenth, four on works from the twentieth, one on works from both the eighteenth and nineteenth centuries, and one on works from the nineteenth and twentieth centuries. Seven chapters are set in the South, six in the North. In order, from south to north, Georgia to Maine: James Mooney's *Myths of the Cherokee* (1900); William Bartram's *Travels* (1791); Mary Noailles Murfree's *Prophet of the Great Smoky Mountains* (1885); Horace Kephart's *Our Southern Highlanders* (1913); Annie Dillard's *Pilgrim at Tinker Creek* (1974); John Fontaine's *Journal* (kept from 1710 to 1719, published in 1972), George Seagood's "Expeditio Ultramontana" (1729), and William Caruthers's *Knights of the Golden Horseshoe* (1841); Thomas Jefferson's *Notes on the State of Virginia* (1785); Charles Brockden Brown's *Edgar Huntly* (1799); Walt Whitman's "Song of the Open Road" (1860) and Allen Ginsberg's *Howl* (1955); Herman Melville's *Moby-Dick* (1851) and "The Piazza" (1856); Robert Frost's *New Hampshire* (1923);

Nathaniel Hawthorne's "The Ambitious Guest" (1835), "The Great Carbuncle" (1836), and "The Great Stone Face" (1850); and Henry David Thoreau's *The Maine Woods* (1864).

I do not pretend that my survey is comprehensive. I could have included many other works—for example, *Song of the Chattahoochee* by nineteenth-century Georgia poet Sidney Lanier, or his novel *Tiger Lilies*, which opens in the Smoky Mountains; or John Muir's *Thousand Mile Walk to the Gulf* (1916), which includes a glowing description of the southern Appalachians; or Harry Middleton's *On the Spine of Time: An Angler's Love of the Smokies* (1991); or stories from the Davy Crockett almanacs of the mid-nineteenth century, some set in the mountains of eastern Tennessee; or the contemporary Blue Ridge fiction of Lee Smith; or Jonathan Edwards's eighteenth-century theological notes *Images or Shadows of Divine Things*, many of which reflect his interest in the Berkshires; or Thoreau's journal accounts of his climbs in the White Mountains; or the contemporary New England essays of Noel Perrin or Edward Hoagland; or some Maine tall tales collected in Richard Dorson's *Jonathan Draws the Long Bow* (1946); or some of the Abenaki tales collected in Joseph Bruchac's *Native American Stories* (1991)—and on and on. Suffice it to say that the literary heritage of the Appalachians is rich. But I want to leave a few trees standing. I have chosen to explore what seem to me works that best represent my subject's range, the most closely associated with recognizable landmarks, maybe not always the most renowned but the best of the literature of the Appalachian Trail.

❧   ❧   ❧

I have hiked all but a couple of hundred miles of the A.T., walking it in sections over the past twenty years. My trips began in the summer of 1977, when two friends and I, all of us recent college graduates, hiked from Delaware Water Gap at the Pennsylvania–New Jersey border to Katahdin. That autumn we hiked from the Water Gap to Harpers Ferry. A few years later I hiked from Harpers Ferry down through Shenandoah National Park. In the 1980s I returned numerous times to favorite spots on the trail in Pennsylvania, and for the last four years I have spent several weeks each spring and summer hiking stretches of the trail commemorated in literary works. In my critical explorations of those works, I have included descriptions of my own experiences of the setting, practicing what has been called "narrative scholarship." That's a term coined by Scott Slovic, referring to literary criticism enlivened with stories. Slovic urges ecocritics to "encounter the world and literature together, then report about the conjunctions."[7]

The subjective approach seems compatible with much contemporary literary theory. Neohistoricists, for instance, assume that all readings are somehow "situated," so true objectivity requires clarifying your position in terms
of its historical or cultural context. Feminist scholars claim that the "personal
is political," so larger cultural implications are always embedded in individual experience.[8] The subjective approach also seems entirely compatible
with ecocritical ideas. Narrative scholarship is a way of putting into practice
the ecological principle of interconnectedness. To look at something from
some objective distance implies that you are outside it, not part of it. To be
aware of our role not just as observer but as participant, as part and parcel of
the world, is a healthy attitude to apply not just to studies of the natural world
but to explorations of the literary world as well. In Kenneth Burke's phrase,
literature is "equipment for living," meaning that literature matters in our
lives, maybe even gives our lives meaning or helps us understand the meaning of our lives. But so too are our lives equipment for understanding literature, helping us appreciate and understand what we read.[9] The same holds
true for the scholarly study of literature. Its purpose is not simply to help us
understand literature but to help us understand our lives, and sometimes our
lives and the literature we read help us understand critical theories. What
I'm attempting to practice is an ecology of reading, where life, literature, and
theory interconnect and merge in a meaningful way, everything hitched to
everything else.

I practice narrative scholarship, too, because it seems true to the spirit of
the writers I am studying. Nature writers typically use the first person to situ-
ate themselves in the natural world, to place themselves, to make apparent
where they stand in the world. In exploring and responding to the conjunctions between my experiences in the mountains and the stories set there, I
am following their models—not just their way of writing but their way of
being in the world. I am also offering testimony to the infusive spirit of a
place that has inspired some of America's finest writers. I suppose that that's
one more way in which narrative scholarship meshes with an ecocritical
approach. If we believe that writers are influenced by places as well as texts,
it makes sense that a careful scholar, as a matter of credibility and authority,
should check those sources, making use of what Simon Schama calls "the
archive of the feet."[10]

But ultimately my highlighting of subjective experience is not motivated
by theoretical considerations, ecocritical or otherwise. My defense rests on
grounds more personal than theoretical. I write in the first person and check
out original sources in the landscape because the things I'm writing about,

well-turned words and a line of elevated earthen verse, have moved and touched me. It seems to me odd to write about things you love as if they're only objects of study.

❀　　❀　　❀

My friend Gerry picks me up at the train station in Gainesville and hikes with me to the top of Springer. We knew each other in high school, and now we can't believe how far we've come: she's a doctor, I'm a professor. We talk of careers, marriages, old friends. We touch on politics. As it turns out, she's conservative, I'm liberal. We disagree about most national issues. Seeking a safer topic, Gerry asks about my research. "My purpose," I tell her, "is to unearth a story line written by our literary ancestors." I had intended no pun by saying "unearth," but I like it — as if the stories are literally wrapped within these mountains, contained by them. Then again, maybe what I'm trying to do, by walking the terrain I've known mainly through the pages of books, is bring the stories *back* to earth.

Near the summit Gerry points out the two broad, low-lying leaves of a lady's slipper, not yet in bloom. I tell her that the Cherokee called that a "partridge moccasin," something I've learned from my reading. She sees some tiny yellow-eyed blue-petaled flowers, kneels to get a better look, gently touches. I take a picture. Here, at least, is common ground.

At the top, after admiring the vista for a few moments, I see the first white blaze on a nearby tree, pointing the way north. I remember something else from *Songlines*. In the Australian outback, aboriginals consider preservation of the land a religious act, for it is through the land and the song-stories associated with it that one connects with the Ancestors. So too the Appalachian Trail. It is sacred ground whose stories tell something of where we came from and how we came to be who and what we are.

1

Cherokee Myths and the Pleasures of Geopiety

On my third day of hiking, descending Justus Mountain, anticipating a good long foot-soak in Blackwell Creek before climbing again, I meet a southbound hiker. He sticks his hand out, introduces himself—he's Wayne Wright. We exchange the usual information—where ya headed? where'd ya start? I ask where he stayed last night, and he says, "Oh, I stayed in a great place! And have I got a story for you!"

Two days before he had stopped to chat with a woman who escaped a rainstorm by camping under a large overhanging rock about fifty feet off the trail near Henry Gap. She heard voices all night long, which she attributed to "Indian spirits." We are, after all, in what has historically been Cherokee country. In fact, for about its first four hundred miles or so, from northern Georgia up through western North Carolina and eastern Tennessee and into southwestern Virginia, the Appalachian Trail travels through Cherokee country. Alone among the native peoples of eastern America, the Cherokee were mountain dwellers.

"She struck me as a religious fanatic," says Wayne Wright, still talking about his encounter. "Me, I'm a retired Green Beret and I'm not the kind to hallucinate." I wonder for a moment why an ex-marine should be less prone than anyone else to having visions or why a "religious fanatic" would be attuned to Cherokee spirits. Then I realize that to me the term connotes Christian fundamentalism, while to Wayne Wright it suggests new age spiritualism. While I'm figuring that out, and while I'm trying to remember what a *wainwright* is (a maker of wagons, a dictionary tells me much later), Wayne is telling me about his own stay under that rock. He not only heard voices— "as if they were close by, but just out of earshot, so you couldn't make out the words"—but all night long he kept thinking he saw flashlights, as if someone was coming up the trail. But nobody ever came.

I reach the rock early next afternoon. It's immense, maybe thirty feet in diameter, with the front lip a good ten feet high, the overhang slanting back another ten feet. I sit by the remains of a campfire under the overhang, leaning back against my pack, eating granola bars, listening, listening. I hear birdsong, but I can't tell what kind of bird, and I hear occasional rustles of leaves being stirred by the breeze, but I can't say that they sound much like whispers. After a while I take from my pack the book I've chosen to carry for the first few weeks of my hike—James Mooney's *History, Myths, and Sacred Formulas of the Cherokees*, a recent reprint of two works first published in 1891 and 1900.[1] In the section headed "Local Legends of Georgia," there is a reference to a "Talking Rock," but it's about a different rock, one in a streambed that sends out echoes.

I tell Wayne's story to several hikers for the next few days, but they've all heard it already, from Wayne. His voice, at least, has been heard.

❀ ❀ ❀

Later that afternoon, on the way up Blood Mountain, the shadows of large birds keep crossing my path. Each time, I look directly overhead to find the source of the shadows, but of course I should have looked toward the sun. By the time I correct my eye-aim, the birds are usually lost above treetop foliage. Only once do I actually see the birds—vultures, as it turns out. I was stopped at a spring, talking with a middle-aged couple from New Jersey, Art and Sue, who had just sold their house. Art was out of work, and they were hiking the trail until they decided what to do next. Homeless, but they seemed quite content with their lot. The bird-shadows crossed the clearing, and we saw three buzzards. "One for each of us," said Art, and we all laughed.

That evening I find several references to buzzards in Mooney. Unlike me and the Jerseyites, the Cherokee admired vultures, considering them "good medicine." Since vultures can eat carrion, they were assumed to be immune from sickness. A buzzard's flesh was said to prevent smallpox, and gunshot wounds were treated by blowing medicine through a buzzard quill onto the wound and then covering it with buzzard down. A buzzard feather above a door was believed to keep out witches. Like many pharmaceuticals, though, it had side effects. If worn, its feathers were thought to cause baldness. In the buzzard's own baldness lies a story warning against excessive pride. Long ago, says Mooney, "the buzzard used to have a fine topknot, of which he was so proud that he refused to eat carrion." He told the other birds that such fare was not good enough for him. To teach him a lesson, they removed the buzzard's head-feathers. Mooney comments, "He lost his pride

at the same time, so that he is willing enough now to eat carrion for a living"
(293).

The buzzard plays a crucial role in the Cherokee creation myth. Once,
all the animals lived in Galunlati, their abode in the heavens. These animals
were larger and in every way superior to those that we know, since the animals of earth were mere imitations of the animals of Galunlati — just as modern humans are inferior to the hero-gods of Cherokee myths. The earth itself, at the time, was water, until a water beetle dived down and brought up
some mud, which began to spread over the surface. Since Galunlati was
crowded, every so often an emissary was sent down to earth to see if there
was enough solid ground to support animal life yet. On one of these mis-
sions, a buzzard flew so low that his wings touched the muddy ground,
leaving valleys where he flapped downward, creating mountains on the up-
draft. "The Cherokee country remains full of mountains to this day," says
Mooney (239).

In some more recent versions of the story, the Creation Bird is an eagle.
I wonder, though, if that change does not reflect the influence of Euro-
American sensibilities. I mean, after all, the eagle is the national bird —
proud, strong, soaring, emblem of freedom. To contemporary eyes, the vulture is a harbinger of death, a scavenger without respect for the dead. Is it
not the height of incongruity to make the vulture a key player in a creation
myth? Besides, seen up close, with its bald head and face of crinkled ruddy
flesh, it's a remarkably ugly bird.

❀   ❀   ❀

The trail up Blood Mountain leads through Slaughter Gap, site of a fierce
battle between the Cherokee and the Creek long ago. Blood Mountain itself
is a reputed home of the Nunnehi, the immortals, who, explains Mooney,
"were invisible except when they wanted to be seen" and who cared for wan-
derers lost in the mountains (331). They were friendly to the Cherokee, and
fought for them on occasion. Once, a legend goes, four Nunnehi women
attended a dance and impressed all the young men. When the women left,
the young men followed to see which way they went, but the women mysteriously disappeared near a river, "although it was a plain trail, with no
place where they could hide. Then the watchers knew they were Nunnehi
women" (332).

The Nunnehi are said to drum at night on Blood Mountain. I stay in a
four-sided stone shelter up there, a cabin really, complete with fireplace,
built by the Civilian Conservation Corps in the 1930s. According to the trail

register in the shelter, nightly visits are made by numerous mice, an immense rat, and a skunk. My fellow hikers and I draw up battle plans. We close all the shutters and doors and lash them down with nylon cord. We hang our packs from the rafters. We agree not to shriek if the skunk gets in — we don't want to scare it. I sleep with a flashlight and my hiking stick next to me, ready to beat away whatever rodent shows his insolent face. Only one does — a rat (not as large as rumored) in my boots, dangling from a nail in the rafters over my head. Before dawn I hear a thumping and squealing from the front of the shelter. I think skunk, and have trouble sleeping. But by dawn's early light we figure out that it was just the wind pushing on the creaky door.

Nobody mentions anything about immortals or spirits.

❧ ❧ ❧

Coming off Blood Mountain, the trail descends into Neel's Gap, crosses a highway, and then goes through the archway of a building, a camping supply store and hostel called Walasi-yi — Cherokee for "Frog Place." The story goes that on a mountain near here a hunter once saw a frog as big as a house. I resupply at the store, call home, then head up the trail to Levelland Mountain. Fully laden with five days' worth of food, my pack is too heavy. It rains like hell that day, and it's windy and cold, with sleet up on the ridge. I put wool socks on my hands to try to keep warm. It's weather only an amphibian could love. But me — I'm miserable. And I'm ready to leave the cold and rain to the house-high frogs of legend.

❧ ❧ ❧

I suppose one could say that I'm just not getting it — "it" being the spiritual belief system of the Cherokee. True, I'm having some fun looking up stories in Mooney's book that have something to do with places I've passed on the trail or wildlife I've seen. But I can view the stories only ironically, as amusing but inconsequential tales whose supernaturalism is very much at odds with the actual experiences of my day. Mine is, I suppose, the skepticism of a rationalist confronting the mystical. I discount what is not demonstrable based on the evidence of my senses. That's the sort of empiricism we consider "down to earth." But so-called primitive peoples, those who live a whole lot closer to the earth than us "civilized" folk, are anything but averse to the mystical. Why then do we consider our rejection of the supernatural "down to earth"? Why do we consider nature the realm of the empirical? How is it that science has laid claim to the wild?

I could learn something from James Mooney's story. As a young man, an aspiring anthropologist from Indiana who was fascinated by American Indian cultures, Mooney applied for a job with the U.S. Government's Bureau of Ethnology three times over the course of three years, and was rejected each time. Finally, in 1885, he showed up at the bureau's office in Washington, D.C., and managed to arrange an interview with the bureau's founder and director, Maj. John Wesley Powell, famed for his river trips through the Grand Canyon. Powell was impressed with Mooney's ten years' worth of notes and maps on American Indians, but asked him to work as a volunteer for a year before hiring him in a salaried position. Mooney first visited the Cherokee of western North Carolina in 1887, and he returned several times through 1890, then again in 1900. Seeking to preserve traditions that were already being lost, Mooney learned to speak, read, and write Cherokee (using the syllabary invented by Sequoyah in the 1820s), and he conducted numerous interviews. Most of his material came from Ayunini, or "Swimmer," whom Mooney describes as "a priest, doctor, and keeper of tradition. . . . a genuine antiquarian and patriot, proud of his people and their ancient system." Much of the rest he heard from Itagunahi, or John Ax, a centenarian "authority upon all relating to tribal custom . . . of a poetic and imaginative temperament" (236–37).

What impresses me most about Mooney's rendering of the myths told him by Swimmer and John Ax is his respectful attitude. There is no irony or rational skepticism in his treatment of these men or the legends they passed on to him. Instead, there is sensitivity, empathy, admiration. Mooney claims that his collected material demonstrates that

> the Indian is essentially religious and contemplative, and it might almost
> be said that every act of his life is regulated and determined by his religious
> belief. It matters not that some may call this superstition. The difference
> is only relative. . . . Christianity itself is but an outgrowth and enlargement
> of the beliefs and ceremonies which have been preserved by the Indian in
> their more ancient form. When we are willing to admit that the Indian has
> a religion which he holds sacred, even though it be different from our own,
> we can then admire the consistency of the theory, the particularity of the
> ceremonial and the beauty of the expression. (SF, 319)

Such overt pleas for cross-cultural understanding are but one way Mooney makes apparent his esteem for the Cherokee. Even more convincing is the language he uses to record their stories. The Cherokee myths as told by Mooney are conveyed in the language of an intelligent adult, not the childlike pidgin of Hollywood Indians. While the stories are fantastic, in Mooney's treatment they read more like parables than fairy tales. Brought up in an Irish-Catholic home, Mooney must have doubted their literal truth. But there is no hint of any disbelief or value judgment in his renderings of Cherokee myths. There are stories, good stories many of them, well told.

Mooney's career ended unhappily, in large part, ironically, precisely because of his ability to set aside and see beyond the norms of his own culture. When he studied the Plains Indians, he took two unpopular stands that ran counter to the beliefs and values of white America — and to the policies of his governmental employer. First, he contended (correctly) that the ghost dance movement of the 1890s was a religious revival, not preparation for war. Second, he defended the Plains Indians' ritual use of peyote as a religious sacrament. Mooney argued that the government's attempt to squelch these practices was misguided. For these heresies, the Commissioner of the Bureau of Ethnology forbade Mooney to do fieldwork on any Indian reservation. For the last few years of his life, from 1918 to 1921, Mooney's work with the bureau was restricted to the study of manuscripts.

✿   ✿   ✿

It takes a while, but Mooney and the Cherokee stories and the Cherokee country have an effect on me. The process begins with my choice of a trail name.

Most long-distance hikers on the Appalachian Trail go by some name of their own creation. The names range from the cartoonish ("Green Lantern," "The Heroes of the Beach") to the literary ("Puck," "Piglet," "Tigger," "Ancient Mariner," "The Lorax"). They can be descriptive about one's appearance ("Daddy Longlegs," "Bill the Hat," "Lady Di") or background ("Catoctin Nomad," "Dixie Dynamite," "Tom the Vet," a guy named "Nurse without Purse"), or they can be whimsical ("Weathercarrot," "Thunderspoon," "Zen Bootist," "Tuna Finch," "Forest Gimp," "Dances with Skunks" — and a dog dubbed "Worthless Bert, the Emergency Stew"), or evocative ("Foxfire," "Riverwind," "Moonchild," "Moonflower," "Night Sprite"). Flora and fauna are often the source: "White Pine," "Thistle," "Indigo" (a guy whose last name is Bunting), "Turtle," "Snake," "Human." The names, I suppose, serve several functions. A trail name is part of the process of self-discovery or self-(re)invention that so many hikers engage in on the trail, akin to the naming ritual that is part of the rite of passage in many cultures. A chosen name can reflect one's character as it is or as one hopes it will become. Trail names also help separate the hiking community from the "real world"—where a name is neither earned nor selected and so does not serve as an indicator of personality or accomplishment.

I started hiking with several possibilities for a trail name in mind, among them "Muck," an old nickname that seemed appropriately and unpretentiously down-to-earth. Ultimately, though, I decided to let my trail name emerge from my experiences on the trail. The day I was caught in the rain and sleet coming out of Neel's Gap, I reached the shelter at Low Gap (aptly named in light of my spirits) in the late afternoon. I was shivering so much I had trouble lighting my stove. Wrapped in my sleeping bag, I cooked hot chocolate, soup, and a noodle dinner, but still it took me hours to get warm. It was not just the cold and rain getting me down. My feet had erupted in blisters, I was lonely, and I was disappointed about seeing so little wildlife—just those buzzards, a salamander, and a bluebird after four days of hiking. I thought about packing it in and going home. Then I read Mooney's version of the Cherokee account of "How the World Was Made":

> When the animals and plants were first made—we do not know by whom—they were told to watch and keep awake for seven nights, just as young men now fast and keep awake when they pray to their medicine. They tried to do this, and nearly all were awake through the first night, but the next night several dropped off to sleep, and the third night others were asleep, and then others, until, on the seventh night, of all the animals only the owl, the panther, and one or two more were still awake. To these were given the power to see and to go about in the dark, and to make prey of the birds and animals which must sleep at night. Of the trees only the cedar, the pine, the spruce, the holly, and the laurel were awake to the end, and to them it was given to be always green and to be greatest for medicine, but to the others it was said: "Because you have not endured to the end you shall lose your hair every winter." (240)

I'd found my trail name—Evergreen. I wanted "to be always green," with its connotations of environmentalism and still-growing youth. But mostly, like the cedar, the pine, the spruce, the holly, and the laurel, I wanted to be able to endure, even through a hard season—or a cold and rainy day. And I began to understand what these Cherokee myths are all about, and what they're for.

❀   ❀   ❀

In a 1966 book called *Human Nature in Geography*, John Kirtland Wright coined the term *geopiety*, which he defined as "pious emotion evoked by the wonder and the terror of the earth in all its diversity." Wright focuses on early

American Christian versions of geopiety, whereby geography is seen as evidence of God's glory, and "geoteleologic forces" (geographic forces that reveal God's purposes) serve humanity in three possible ways: "awardatively," by rewarding virtuous behavior either in advance or after the fact; "punitively," by punishing immoral behavior; and "correctively," seeking to change behavior via awards and punishments.[2] Wright gives many examples from early Anglo-American theologians, scientists, and philosophers who found cause for reverence in geographical forces. But I'm struck by how abstract their geography is. They describe mountains in general, not any specific mountain. One sign of their reverence was the frequent drawing of parallels between New World topography and biblical terrain—America as Eden or Canaan—but that's exactly what makes their descriptions so lacking as geography. They impose on the land their preconceptions, seeing what they've read about rather than what's right before their eyes.

I'm also troubled by the limited kind of piety expressed. The term *geopiety* suggests a form of nature worship, but in the examples from early America given by Wright it is not nature itself that is revered but its Creator. The word *piety* comes from the Latin *pietas*, which translates as "dutiful conduct," but the examples in Wright express only reverence and devotion to God and make no suggestions about human conduct in regard to anything other than God. The only "corrective" function geography seems to have among the early Anglo-Americans quoted by Wright is to remind us, through punishment, to be more devout. But does not piety involve being *good* as well as devout?

Wright himself anticipates that there is more to the concept of geopiety than he outlines, saying that his examples "fall far short of representing all of the many kinds of geopiety there are and have been among different religions."[3] Yi-Fu Tuan expands the dimensions of the concept, in part by considering the root connection between the words *piety* and *pity*. Piety requires reverence for something that is strong—a God, for instance, capable of rewarding or punishing human behavior, or interested in correcting it—while pity calls for compassion for something that is weak. Among its many connotations, piety involves reverence for one's parents. But when parents grow old and weak, they need our compassion and service as well as our reverence. According to Tuan, geopiety demands recognition of the need for reciprocity, as illustrated by the Roman temple erected to the goddess Pietas: "The story goes that on the site of the temple a mother had been imprisoned and was kept alive by the milk from her own daughter's breast." The lesson in ecological terms: "nature nurtures men and men owe it reverence"—and care.[4]

In moving beyond Wright's original exclusively Christian conception of the idea of geopiety, Tuan suggests that geopiety should consist of compassion as well as awe, virtue as well as reverence. He tells us how we ought to treat the land, why we should respect it and care for it. But both Wright and Tuan remain rather vague about the other side of our reciprocal arrangement with our environment. Besides giving us physical sustenance or aesthetic pleasure, how does nature make us better? How does it teach us proper behavior?

Though he never uses the term *geopiety*, Keith Basso, in an essay entitled "'Stalking with Stories': Names, Places, and Moral Narratives among the Western Apache," gets to the heart of this element of the concept. Basso explains that "losing the land is something the Western Apache can ill afford to do, for geographical features have served the people for centuries as indispensable mnemonic pegs on which to hang the moral teachings of their history."[5] Quite literally, their land tells the Apache how to be good, how to behave, how to be. Stories associated with particular features of the landscape—a tree, a rock, a mountaintop—become a means of relating Apache history and conveying moral lessons. A spring where a man drowned after mistreating his wife, for instance, serves as a constant reminder about proper marital relations. The landscape, then, becomes a text, not just because it is the work of a creator, but because it tells, or at least initiates, a story.

The metaphor of the land as a sacred text is a notion I've read about in reference to the Puritan settlers of the New World, those who reverenced the land, as Wright describes, as God's creation. Their purpose seemed to be to read geography in order to discover God's meaning or intent—what formalist literary critics used to call the "intentional fallacy," since guesses about an author's intention may distract readers from the evidence of the actual text before them. Such an approach to landscape makes sense in a culture that prizes literacy. A people accustomed to the written word, after all, are used to respecting *author*ity, he who controls the wor(l)d. But here's the irony—if the world is a form of scripture, why did devout Christians in early America, and since, do so little to preserve it? Is it because they had God's word intact in another form, the written word, page-bound and typeset? Ultimately, through the word—and *not* the world—lay the Christian's path to God, the way to spritual understanding.

But there's another explanation for the Christian's lack of respect for topographic scripture in America. Geopiety may be inherent in the origins of all religions—but perhaps it is the distance from its place of origin that has made Christianity so spectacularly insensitive to natural values in America and, sometimes it seems, so ineffective a moral guide. The sacred sites of

Christianity are in the middle East. Americans can't look up at Mt. Sinai every day to be reminded of God's immanence and his decalogical guidelines for appropriate behavior — principles so firm, about which God is so unyielding, that they were written in stone.

Amid the arid climate of the middle East, perhaps the ritual of baptism made special sense, for water was viewed as a blessed thing, a gift of God occasionally withheld in time of drought to show his displeasure. And in the middle East, perhaps the Old Testament's view of wilderness as hostile makes equal sense. If the land is an antagonist, it needs to be converted, made into something useful. One way to do that is to read the land as parable, a clue to the author's intent. Another is to make it arable, symbol of God's approbation. Thus the misplaced land ethic of early European settlers in lush eastern America, worshipping the geography of a distant and different place.

I'm leery of suggesting that the Cherokee view of nature is precisely that of the Apache, as described by Basso. I don't want to commit the common error of assuming that all native American cultures are alike. But, as Joseph E. Brown argues, they have in common "a metaphysic of nature . . . a reverence for the myriad forms and forces of the natural world specific to their immediate environment." J. Baird Callicott contends that the shared "metaphysic of nature" among native Americans was incipiently ecological.[6] The lush southern Appalachians and the arid Southwest could not be more different, and the Cherokee and Apache developed very different cultures in response to their particular environments. But the strong attachment of a people to their place is the same, and so is the attachment of story to place. For Cherokee and Apache both, for Iroquois and Sioux and Lenni Lenape as well, scripture is all around us. Mooney notes that "almost every prominent rock and mountain, every deep bend in the river, in the old Cherokee country has its accompanying legend. It may be a little story that can be told in a paragraph, to account for some natural feature, or it may be one chapter of a myth that has its sequel in a mountain a hundred miles away. As is usual when a people has lived a very long time in the same country, nearly every important myth is localized, thus assuming more definite character" (230).

This is akin to what Basso was told by one of his Apache informants: "All these places have stories."[7]

❁   ❁   ❁

The Appalachian Trail through northern Georgia passes through long tunnels of overhanging rhododendron. A few days earlier I had noticed only that the rhododendron were not yet in bloom. Now, recalling the origin myth about how conifers came to be ever green, I ponder the rhododendrons' hardiness, I savor the welcome cool they offer on warm afternoons, and I notice the twisted grain of their stalks. Each day as I walk, each evening as I read, I see how the myths of the Cherokee, and in turn the values they held, are products of the particular piece of land they inhabited — or, to use a less manufacturing-oriented metaphor, how their stories emerge from the land. Not a "product" of the land — more like a plant from a seed.

Mooney recognized the importance of their bioregion to the Cherokee, saying that

> their old country is a region of luxuriant flora, with tall trees and tangled undergrowth on the slopes and ridges, and myriad bright-tinted blossoms and sweet wild fruits along the running streams. The vegetable kingdom consequently holds a far more important place in the mythology and cere- monial of the tribe than it does among the Indians of the treeless plains and arid sage deserts of the West, most of the beliefs and customs in this connection centering around the practice of medicine. . . . In general it is held that the plant world is friendly to the human species, and constantly at the willing service of the doctors to counteract the jealous hostility of the animals. (420)

The friendship of the plants is demonstrated in a story about the origin of disease. "In the old days," says Mooney, "the beasts, birds, fishes, insects, and plants could all talk, and they and the people lived together in peace and friendship." But then humans became many, and arrogant, and they devised weapons with which they slaughtered game, while "smaller creatures, such as the frogs and worms, were crushed and trodden upon without thought, out of pure carelessness or contempt" (250). Among the retributions devised by the animals were various diseases. The deer demanded that hunters first ask pardon of the deer before killing one; failing to do so, hunters would be stricken with rheumatism. The birds, insects, and small mammals, led in council by the grubworm, invented the numerous other diseases that afflict human beings; one even proposed that menstruation be fatal, a thought that so tickled the grubworm that he fell over backward, and "had to wriggle off on his back, as the Grubworm has done ever since." Upon hearing what the animals had done, the plants got together and volunteered their services as cures. "Thus came medicine," writes Mooney, "and the plants, every one of which has its use if we only knew of it, furnish the remedy to counteract the evil wrought by the revengeful animals. Even weeds were made for some good purpose, which we must find out for ourselves" (252). Sounds like the premise for the 1992 movie *Medicine Man,* a not-so-subtle plea for the pres-

ervation of the Amazon rain forests in which the character played by Sean
Connery discovers a cure for cancer in the flora and fauna of the jungle
canopy. But the Cherokee story brings the lesson closer to home.

A few days earlier I had complained in a trail register that I wasn't sure if
rhododendron or poison ivy should be the Georgia state flower. While I'm
still wary of anything with three leaves, I feel properly abashed for my fear
and loathing of poison ivy. The Cherokee, I learn, propitiate poison ivy by
addressing it as "my friend" (425). Perhaps its "medicine" is to discourage
those who are untutored in the ways of the woods, so that the woods receive
less trampling under human feet. Despite my general ignorance about botany, I begin to notice more of what's growing — those delicate little blue and
yellow flowers that I'd first seen on Springer Mountain, some upturned
leaves with purple veins running through them, a flower with a fleshy spike
overhung by a flaplike leaf. From talking to other hikers and, later, riffling
through a guide to wildflowers, I even learn names to go with what I've
seen — bluets, rattlesnake weed, jack-in-the-pulpit.

A phrase from the 1960s comes back to me, invested now with new meaning: Flower Power.

A trail guide tells me that in the southern Appalachians there are more
species of plants than in all of Europe.

                    ❧   ❧   ❧

I don't want to pretend that I somehow became steeped in Cherokee philosophy or spirituality in any sort of life-changing way — even if I did one day find
a hawk feather and stick it in the back of the bandana wrapped around my
forehead. Along the ridge just before descending into Bly Gap at the North
Carolina line, I see a knee-high pile of stones out on a ledge about twenty
feet off the trail. I'm hungry and thirsty and the view is nice, so I stop to rest
on the ledge. The stones look like a small, trail-marking cairn, pyramiding
from large stones to small. I think about leaving an M&M on top, a red one.
It might make a nice decorative touch and amuse or puzzle the next hiker
to come along. But something tells me not to.

That night I'm standing around a small fire with David, a Georgia police
sergeant who is part-Cherokee. He asks if I saw the prayer stones, and I remember the cairn. David explains that the stones are typically placed high
up on a mountain. The stones hold the prayer, uttered aloud, so winds can
later carry it to the spirits. I tell him about the candied chocolate contribu-
tion I had thought about adding to the stones. "That would have been sacri-
lege," says David. I protest, "But wouldn't I have been making an offering?

And of something pretty darn valuable, too, at least in a hiker economy. I mean, I was thinking of leaving a *red* M&M!"

David doesn't laugh. I'm glad I didn't desecrate the prayer stones, and not just because I have no M&Ms to spare. Especially red ones.

❀ ❀ ❀

Our fire is built primarily of dead rhododendron. Mooney points out that the Cherokee never burned rhododendron or laurel, because fire would destroy the medicinal properties of those plants and would bring cold weather. The legend arose, says Mooney, because the hissing sound they make when burning is "suggestive of winter winds and falling snow" (422). That night we hear a grouse thumping. One story about drumming grouse is that during a winter famine, a grouse found a holly tree loaded with red berries. He called the other birds, and they circled around the tree, "singing, dancing, and drumming with their wings in token of their joy" (290). As part of the green-corn dance of the Cherokee, dancers imitate the grouse's drumming with their feet.

After several minutes of the drumming, we hear a new sound, the call of an owl, sonorous and haunting. Then we hear a loud, outraged squawk, and more hooting. But no more drumming. Next morning it's cold, in the thirties.

❀ ❀ ❀

While I'm climbing Standing Indian Mountain, rain threatens. I don't want to get caught on top in a lightning storm, so I move fast. The *Appalachian Trail Companion* for 1994 gives this explanation for the mountain's name: "According to Cherokee legend, a great winged monster once inhabited the mountain, and, during the monster's reign, warriors were posted on the mountain as lookouts. A tremendous bolt of lightning shattered the mountain and killed the monster. During the strike, a lone Cherokee sentinel also was hit by the bolt and turned into stone, supposedly for being a poor sentry." [8] This seems to be a powerful topo-lesson about attention to duty, but I suspect something bogus in the story. Attention to duty, after all, is more a virtue in the eyes of the American WASP, imbued with the philosophy of the work ethic, than to the Cherokee. Mooney hints at the spurious legends that have grown up around this mountain. He says, "The name is a rendering of the Cherokee name, Yun wi-tsulenun yi, 'Where the man stood,' . . . given to it on account of a peculiarly shaped rock formerly jutting out from the bald summit, but now broken off. As the old memory faded, a tradition grew up of a mysterious being once seen standing upon the mountain top" (409). The legend in the *Trail Companion* is more romantic than Mooney's matter-of-fact account, and I suppose even if the *Trail Companion's* story is a recent creation, it tells us something of the continued vitality of the oral folktale. But I don't know — it sounds like a story designed to tell mainstream America what it wants to hear. I'm put off, too, by the "supposedly" in the *Trail Companion's* rendering of the story. It sounds snide, like a polite, verbalized snicker. Not that I believe in the literal truth of the stories in Mooney, but I am willing to suspend disbelief in order to get at the gist of the story, the moral meat, in the same way that many good Christians ultimately don't seem too concerned about whether evolutionary science calls into question the Bible's literal or historical accuracy. It's still a good book, one you can live by, even if a few scientific or historical facts are askew.

If the moral lessons of Cherokee myths are not about duty or devotion, what are they about? Mostly, it seems, about respect for other living things and regretful humility for human separation from the natural world. In his introduction to his section on "Quadruped Myths," Mooney explains:

> In Cherokee mythology, as in that of Indian tribes generally, there is no essential difference between men and animals. In the primal genesis period they seem to be completely undifferentiated, and we find all creatures alike living and working together in harmony and mutual helpfulness until man, by his aggressiveness and disregard for the rights of the others, provokes their hostility. . . . Henceforth their lives are apart, but the difference is always one of degree only. The animals, like the people, are organized into tribes and have like them their chiefs and townhouses, their councils and ballplays, and the same hereafter in the Darkening land of Usunhi yi. Man is still the paramount power, and hunts and slaughters the others as his own necessities compel, but is obliged to satisfy the animal tribes in every instance. (261)

The Cherokee version of the Fall stresses the need to recognize our separation from the natural world and to try to repair it. Fear of the wild does not preclude respect.

❁   ❁   ❁

Crossing Wayah Gap I've got my eye out for yellowjackets, warned about them by the story of the Ulagu, a giant insect that lived in a "secret hiding place" near here and used to swoop down into settlements and carry away children. The people baited the Ulagu with a squirrel and a turkey, each with a string attached so they could follow the Ulagu to its nest. But it was so fast and flew so high that they could not follow it, so they tied a longer string to a deer, so the Ulagu could not fly so high or fast, and this time they followed it along a ridge to its cave in the rocks near the site of Franklin, North Carolina. Where they spotted its nest, they let out a shout, and so that place, Wayah Gap on my map, was called "Atahita," or "Where they shouted." The Ulagu was surrounded by thousands of smaller creatures of its kind—yellow-jackets. The people built fires all around and the smoke filled the cave and killed the Ulagu and many of the smaller bees—"but others which were outside the cave were not killed, and these escaped and increased until now the yellow-jackets, which before were unknown, are all over the world" (260). In a footnote Mooney gives another version of the story, from Charles Lanman's *Letters from the Alleghany Mountains*. In this version the Cherokee tracked the Ulagu by posting sentries on mountaintops. When they could not reach the monster-hornet's cave, they prayed to the Great Spirit. Lightning destroyed half a mountain in one stroke, chasing the hornet out of his cave to be slain by the people. The Great Spirit was pleased with the courage and cleverness of the Cherokee and "willed it that all the highest mountains in their land should thereafter be destitute of trees, so that they might always have an opportunity of watching the movements of their enemies."[9] Hence the grassy open "balds" of the southern Appalachians.

Lanman's version of the Ulagu story sounds a lot like the myth about Standing Indian Mountain in the *Appalachian Trail Companion*, but without the warning about attending to sentry duty. Lanman calls the lightning-struck summit "Bald Mountain," which could be any of a number of mountains besides Standing Indian. Since he heard the story near the Nantahala River, it could be Wayah Bald. Quite likely he heard a blending of two different stories.

The supernatural explanation about the origin of the balds attempts to account for something that has baffled scientists. Timberline in the southern Appalachians is theoretically about seven thousand feet, higher than any of the summits, so it's not that the balds are above timberline. Some possibilities: fire, wind, insects, disease. According to Ann and Myron Sutton, some scientists believe that a warm spell after the last period of glaciation eliminated conifers, and then when the climate cooled again there were no seeds nearby to refoliate the mountaintops.[10] However the balds first became so, the baldness was maintained by sheep grazing. Now, without the grazing, trees and bushes are returning to the summits, and many are no longer bald—just a little thin on top.

Atop Wayah Bald I see a grand panorama of the Nantahalas, but no yellowjackets. Descending, I'm questioning the myth's usefulness as a biotic
guide, but I soon have reason to take to heart, or keep in mind (a strange
duality there), the moral lessons of the Ulagu story, about ingenuity and
perseverance. At a shallow, mud-bottomed spring not far from the top of
Wayah Bald, the filter of my water pump gets clogged. At first, I think it is
broken, and cussing, strangely enough, does not seem to solve the problem.
I consider using my toothbrush to clean the filter, but don't relish the thought
of sacrificing dental hygiene for the next couple of weeks. Spruce needles
might substitute for toothbrush bristles, but no evergreens are in sight. There
are other ways besides brushing, though, to dislodge the dirt. I try smacking
the filter against a rock, and it works—mud splatters onto the rock. I pump
some more, smack out more mud, pump some more. While I'm so engrossed, a yellowjacket lands on my pack. I barely notice at first, but then the
story of the Ulagu comes back to me and I am stung by realization.

It has been over a hundred years since Mooney copied down the story of
the Ulagu—but I feel as if Swimmer has just spoken to me.

        ❁   ❁   ❁

Every day I've got my eye out for snakes, and every night I indulge my timid
fascination by sifting through Mooney. It seems to me that the snake is an
excellent test case for determining the depth of one's appreciation for nature.
How far people go in respecting snakes' rights usually says a lot about how
committed they are to the idea of wilderness.

Mooney's collection is full of delightfully fantastic stories about snakes.
They are "regarded as . . . supernaturals, having an intimate connection with
the rain and thunder gods, and possessing a certain influence over the other
animals and plant tribes." One who kills a snake will see lots of other snakes,
and if he kills another, he will soon see so many that he will become "dazed
at the sight of their glistening eyes and darting tongues." A rattler can be
killed only if absolutely necessary, and only if the killer asks pardon of the
snake's ghost; otherwise its relatives will track the killer down and bite him
dead (294–95). Like most long-distance hikers, though, I've got a not-so-
secret weapon. According to Mooney's story of "The Hunter and the Uksuhi," snakes cannot stand the stench of perspiration. The Uksuhi was a giant
black racer that chased a great hunter over the mountains, caught him and
was crushing him to death, until the hunter rubbed his hand in his armpit
and then on the Uksuhi's nose. The Uksuhi writhed in olfactory agony, and
the hunter escaped.

Mooney relates numerous stories about monster snakes, two of them rumored to frequent Nantahala Gorge, where the trail crosses the Nantahala River and "where, by reason of its gloomy and forbidding aspect, Cherokee tradition locates more than one legendary terror" (459). Several stories concern the Uktena (also said to inhabit the Smokies), a fearsome creature about the diameter of a tree trunk with a great crystal in its forehead and "scales glittering like sparks of fire" (297). The crystal in its head is called the Ulunsuti, or the "Transparent," and it possesses great powers. A person gazing at it would be so dazed that he would rush towards the Uktena, to be devoured—and at the same time his family would die. But despite the risks the fabulous Ulunsuti was much sought after.

Mooney reports that "whoever owns the Ulunsuti is sure of success in hunting, love, rainmaking, and every other business, but its great use is in life prophecy. When it is consulted for this purpose the future is seen mirrored in the clear crystal as a tree is reflected in the quiet stream below" (298). The Ulunsuti is a two-inch pyramid, transparent except for a red streak running through it; Mooney theorizes that the stone is "a rare and beautiful specimen of rutile quartz" (460). Similar but smaller crystals, also endowed with magic, are said to be scales of the Uktena.

One story about the Ulunsuti says that it was given to the white man at the creation, while the Indian received a piece of silver. But both despised their gifts and threw them away, to be found by the other. The Ulunsuti is the Indian's talisman, "as money is the talismanic power of the white man" (351). Putting the two stories about the origin of the Ulunsuti together, I wonder at the conflation of white man and Uktena as its source. Are we the monstrous snake in the garden of the southern Appalachians? But the parallel to the Eden story does not hold. If the Ulunsuti is a source of wisdom, our sin, according to the Cherokee story, is in rejecting it. That's almost the opposite of the biblical account of what happened in Eden. Then again, perhaps the Cherokee and the Christian stories of origin simply refer to different sorts of knowledge. To the mind of a rational skeptic, the Ulunsuti sounds like a combination of good luck charm and crystal ball. To say we don't believe in such things may be another way of saying we reject that kind of knowing.

Nantahala Gorge is also home to the Uwtsunta, or "bouncer," a snake that "moved by jerks like a measuring worm, with only one part of its body on the ground at a time." *Nantahala* translates as "noonday sun," a reference to the steepness of the mountain slopes, for only at midday could the sun penetrate to the valleys. But the shadows are also accounted for by the story of the Uwtsunta. At Nantahala Gorge, it is said, the shadow of the immense Uwtsunta would darken the valley when it crossed the gorge. Surprisingly, the people did not realize the snake was there for a long time; when they did, they were afraid to live there, and so the valley was deserted (303–4).

After crossing the Nantahala River, on the hard climb up Swim Bald, I consider how the story of the Uwtsunta typifies Cherokee myths. I'm a bit puzzled at first about the moral lesson in the story, but I guess it suggests the powerful presence of animals in our lives, there even when we don't know it, right over our heads sometimes, affecting us in ways that we don't always recognize immediately. It's also a cautionary tale, I suppose, teaching its hearers to watch out for large snakes. And it's a story that is intertwined with place, giving information about the nature of a place, in this case the shadowy Nantahala Gorge.

But there's something else, too—the sheer creative joy of a story, the pleasures of the imagination. Obviously anybody can see that the real reason the gorge is dark is that the mountains above it are steep. But that fact alone doesn't make for any kind of story. With a story attached to it, the fact becomes memorable—and in a culture that relies on oral transmission to disseminate information, memorability is of paramount importance. The stories relate history, geography, and morality in a narrative nutshell.

I imagine stories like that functioned to educate, and I think of the advantages of that form of education. If I were out walking with my little boy on Mt. Nittany, a few miles from our home, what could I tell him about whatever wildlife we might see? Precious little. Most likely I could at best identify it and tell Jacy what to be careful of ("That's a yellowjacket—watch out! it could sting you!"). Then when we got home we could look it up, whatever it was, in our field guide, and we'd learn a few facts about habitat or mating habits. But there would be none of the joy of extravagant narrative in such information. My warnings about bees or snakes would be mere remonstrance or command—they would be discourses devoid of pleasure, an authoritarian setting up of rules to govern behavior ("Don't touch that!"). But a story—there's some delight in the lesson, and rather than a command, it's a demonstration, exaggerated, yes, but that's what makes it memorable, the appeal to fantasy as well as fact. And the lessons about more abstract concepts—on vigilance, ingenuity, perseverance—inherent in the stories of the Uwtsunta and Ulagu lie embedded in the story, waiting to be discovered by the young adult long after the surface warning about snakes and bees and their habitat has been unearthed by the child. That's a lot to get out of the sight of a reptile or insect—a lot more than the paucity of information we get from a field guide.

It occurs to me that in the very playfulness of the story of the Uwtsunta lie more implicit lessons. The story tells us that the natural world, though worth knowing well for what it is, is also a fantasy land, a place where things are not always as they seem, where you can find something new every day, where not all the shadows in the valley are cast by mountains. And so we should not be too quick to stop looking around and above us, too quick to assume that today's shadows must be caused by the same thing that caused them yesterday. The story instructs us not to let accepted knowledge interfere with our powers of observation, not to assume that what was true in the past will always be true. It tells us too that the natural world is a changeful, magical place, made anew every day—in a word, supernatural.

❁   ❁   ❁

After a tiring three-thousand-foot climb out of Nantahala Gorge, out of the mountain's shadows to the upper reaches of Swim Bald, I read another anecdote in Mooney "illustrating the steepness" of the Nantahalas. A famed hunter used to toss the liver of the deer he had killed off a cliff and onto the roof of his house, "so that his wife could have it cooked and waiting for him by the time he got down the mountain" (408).

Recuperating over a Nantahala vista—contrary to idiom, it gives my breath back rather than takes it away—I see a greenish-gold lizard, hear unidentified birds twittering, and I read one more Nantahala story. Long ago there lived here an old woman, an ogress who had skin of stone and a pointy forefinger like a spear and who fed on human livers. She was called "Stone-dress" or "Spear-finger," and she "had such powers over stone that she could easily lift and carry immense rocks, and could cement them together by merely striking one against another." She roamed the Nantahalas, "always hungry and looking for victims." Once she built a bridge of rock over the mountains, but lightning shattered it, and now the fragments of rock are found along the whole ridge.

The old woman would approach children with her deadly finger hidden under her robe, sometimes appearing as a member of the child's family. Often, she would stroke the children's hair before taking out her spear-finger and stabbing the children through the heart or neck. At a council meeting, the people devised a plan. They trapped the witch in a pit, but their arrows could not penetrate her stony skin. While she jeered at them, they heard a

titmouse on a nearby tree singing "un, un, un," which they took to be a
reference to unahu, the heart. So they aimed there—"but the arrows only
glanced off with the flint heads broken." Since then, the titmouse has been
known as a liar.

Then a chickadee, Tsi-kilili, lit upon the witch's spear-finger hand—indi-
cating where her heart was. An arrow there killed the witch. "Ever since,"
says Mooney, "the tsi kilili is known as a truth teller, and when a man is away
on a journey, if this bird comes and perches near the house and chirps its
song, his friends know he will soon be safe home" (317–19).

I'm disturbed momentarily that I don't think I can tell the difference between a titmouse and a chickadee. All I know is that they are both small
brownish birds. What does that say about my ability to recognize truth? But
truth can be heard as well as seen. I remember something: a chickadee goes
"chick-a-dee-dee-dee." Or, put another way, "tsi-ki-li-li." The beauty of ono-
matopoeia: The names of things can tell a lot about them.

❁   ❁   ❁

The trail leaves the Nantahalas for the Great Smoky Mountains. Here, in
1838, about a thousand Cherokee hid out when the rest of their people, fourteen thousand strong, were rounded up for the death march now called The
Trail of Tears. The forced evacuation commenced just south of the Smokies,
and some four thousand died on the way to Indian territory in Oklahoma,
where there was already a settlement of western Cherokee previously evicted
from their home in the Appalachians.

It may seem peculiar that the U.S. government should have treated the
Cherokee so cruelly, for the Cherokee had done as much as any tribe to
accept the ways of the whites. Hundreds of Cherokee had fought under
Andrew Jackson against the Creek nation in 1814, and they were largely responsible for the federals' success in the crucial battle of Horseshoe Bend.
In the next couple of decades, the Cherokee set up a republican form of
government, a court system, a tax agency, a constitution, a newspaper—all
made possible by the spread of reading and writing in the Cherokee syllabary
invented by Sequoyah. Christian missionaries were busy among the Cherokee; the syllabary was used to translate the Bible and hymnbooks, and many
Cherokee came to accept the white man's God. There was a widespread
temperance movement, and the sale of whiskey was strictly regulated. In
short, the Cherokee were exemplars of all that Americans (at that time, no
native persons qualified for citizenship) claimed to hope for from Indians.
And yet, and yet—still the diaspora.

The issue, of course, was land, the means for taking it broken treaties. The same old story. Not that the Cherokee were singled out. In 1828 newly-elected President Andrew Jackson—he whom the Cherokee had fought under at Horseshoe Bend—sponsored the Indian Removal Act, giving the federal government and its troops the power to drive all native peoples to the lands west of the Mississippi.

Not all whites of the time were blind to the horror of what was being done to the Cherokee. In his *Letters from the Alleghany Mountains*, written just a decade after the removal, Charles Lanman tells the stories of two Cherokee heroes, Yonaguska and Tsali, who resisted deportation. In each account, Lanman climaxes the story with an expression of geopiety.

Yonaguska, Drowning Bear, was a peace chief who died in the year of the deportation. "In power of oratory," says Mooney, "he is said to have surpassed any other chief of his day" (162). Yonaguska had led the temperance movement among the Cherokee in the Smokies, circulating an abstinence contract after emerging from a dream vision brought about by a severe illness—perhaps a wicked hangover, according to at least one version of the story.[11] But he resisted Christianity. After hearing some of the Bible read to him, he once commented, "Well, it seems to be a good book—strange that the white people are not better, after having had it so long" (163). When the Cherokee ceded their lands in the Smokies by an 1819 treaty, he refused to relocate. For the rest of his life he resisted numerous "invitations" from the government to "emigrate." Here, according to Lanman, is how he responded to one of those requests: "You say the land in the West is much better than it is here. That very fact is an argument on our side. The white man must have rich land to do his great business, but the Indian can be happy with poorer land. The white man must have a flat country for his plough to run easy, but we can get along even among the rocks on the mountains. We never shall do what you want us to do. I don't like you for your pretended kindness. I always advise my people to keep their backs for ever turned towards the setting sun, and never to leave the land of their fathers."[12]

Yonaguska's argument is echoed by Tsali, an old man who was to become a martyr of the Trail of Tears. Angry at the way soldiers treated his family on the march west, Tsali led a small uprising, killing two soldiers and wounding one in making his escape to the mountains. When General Winfield Scott found it difficult to track down the refugee Cherokee hiding in the mountains, he singled out Tsali as a basis for a face-saving compromise. Scott was willing to call off pursuit of the mass of fugitive Cherokee hiding in the

mountains if they would agree to turn in Tsali and his party. He sought help
from Will Thomas, a trader who so enjoyed the confidence of the mountain
Cherokee that he was adopted by Yonaguska. Approached by Thomas, Tsali
agreed to sacrifice himself for the benefit of his people. Facing a firing squad
of his own people, whom Scott had recruited for that purpose, Tsali made a
last request: "You know that I had a little boy, who was lost among the mountains. I want you to find that boy, if he is not dead, and tell him that the last
words of his father were that he must *never* go beyond the Father of Waters,
but die in the land of his birth. It is sweet to die in one's own country, and to
be buried by the margin of one's native stream." [13]

Today there is a Cherokee reservation at Quallah, on the North Carolina
side of the Smokies. It is on land procured by Will Thomas, who after the
removal made several extended trips to Washington to secure governmental
permission for the Cherokee to remain in the Smokies. He purchased the
land with money that was due the Cherokee for "improvements"—the
buildings—they had left behind on their usurped land. As I hike through
the Smokies, several people who see me reading a book of Cherokee myths
say that I really ought to go down to the town of Cherokee, on the reservation, and see "Cherokee Frontier Land" and the outdoor pageant *Unto these
Hills*, an enactment of Cherokee history. But others scoff, saying that it's all
a depressing sellout. The town is full of fast food joints and sleazy, overpriced
motels with names like the "Indian Inn" and the "Redskin Motel," I'm told,
and Cherokee Frontier Land has been called in print "a classic form of tourist blight—a tawdry amusement park." [14] Rumor has it that the Cherokee
dress up in Sioux-style feather headdresses because that pleases the tourists,
who see it as appropriately "Indian" looking.

❦   ❦   ❦

On Clingman's Dome the day is gloomy and grey. At 6,643 feet it's the highest point on the Appalachian Trail, and the trees, all evergreens, are stunted
and skeletal-looking. The terrain reminds me of Maine. There's an observation tower up here, but today the only view is an up-close look at the insides
of clouds, and I understand why these are called the Smokies. I can't see any
of the surrounding mountains—and I can certainly forget about catching a
glimpse of nearby Atagahi, the legendary enchanted lake that cannot be seen
by humans. People have heard the sound of many ducks there, but only the
animals know how to reach it. Says Mooney, "It is the medicine lake of the
birds and animals, and whenever a bear is wounded by the hunters he makes

his way through the woods to this lake and plunges into the water, and when he comes out upon the other side his wounds are healed. For this reason the animals keep the lake invisible to the hunter" (322).

The Cherokee called Clingman's Dome "Kuwahi," or Mulberry Place, and below the summit was the townhouse of the bears—who came from people. Once, the story goes, a boy who spent all his days in the woods began to grow hair all over his body. When his worried parents begged him to stop going to the woods, he told them that there was plenty of food there, "better than the corn and beans we have in the settlements," and he did not have to work for it. If they were willing to fast for seven days, said the boy to his parents, they could come too. The word spread, a council was held, and all the clan fasted and went to the woods, with hair already growing on them en route because "they had not taken human food and their nature was chang-ing." On the way, they told the people of other towns, "when you yourselves are hungry, come into the woods and call us and we shall come to give you our own flesh. You need not be afraid to kill us, for we shall live always" (325–26). Then they taught the people special songs that would call the bears to the hunters. The lesson seems to be that if people can transmogrify into animals, their souls are kindred.

But other stories suggest enmity between bears and humans, and empha-size the necessary distinction between our respective natures. When all the other animals got together to find ways to punish men for their arrogance, the bears gathered at their townhouse. Their solution to the problem of man was not to invent disease but to start a war. And they decided that to succeed they must use man's own weapons. One bear, an ursine version of Tsali (or perhaps the mythic model for Tsali's martyrdom), sacrificed himself so that his entrails could be made into bowstrings. But when the bears tried to shoot with a bow, they found that their claws got in the way. Some proposed trim-ming their claws. "But," reports Mooney, "here the chief, the old White Bear, objected, saying it was necessary that they should have long claws in order to be able to climb trees. 'One of us has already died to furnish the bow-string, and if we now cut off our claws we must all starve together. It is better to trust to the teeth and claws that nature gave us, for it is plain that man's weapons were not intended for us'" (250).

It is good, I think, that the bears, at least, still have their nature.

Several hundred bears still roam the Smokies. Hikers on the Appalachian Trail are required to stay in stone-walled shelters, all of which have chain-link fence in front to keep out the bears. Several hikers joke about feeling as if they're on display in a store window, or imprisoned. They all seem excited rather than fearful about the prospect of seeing a bear. Maybe we've seen too many Yogi Bear cartoons to be properly respectful, or maybe the protective enclosures dissolve our fears. Whatever the reason, I'm delighted to be in a place where there's an animal large enough to be a potential threat to people, a place where stripped of our machines we're not so sure that we are superior to the beasts. I feel just timid enough to keep a whistle in my pocket while I hike, in case I surprise a bear. But I'm disappointed. Though I think I hear a bear off the trail near Siler's Bald, I never see any.

❦ ❦ ❦

At Cosby Knob shelter, my last night in the Smokies, a thru-hiker named Blackberry Bob tells a story about a retired DEA agent who attempted to make a big score. He rented a Piper Cub, loaded up some duffel bags with confiscated cocaine, and flew over the hills of north Georgia. He dropped some duffel bags in places that he figured he could locate, then jumped out with the last one. But his parachute didn't open, and he ended up splattered in someone's driveway. One of the cocaine-filled duffel bags landed in the woods, and a bear found it and ate most of its contents. In a newspaper snapshot of the dead bear, the surrounding trees are scratched and clawed to smithereens, the damage presumably done by the coked-up bear.

I don't believe a word of it, but it's a good story. Blackberry Bob has more of them, and he keeps us entertained past dark. In front of the shelter, the trees are dark shadows losing themselves in the moonless night. After I snuggle into my sleeping bag, I check the index of Mooney for references to stars.

Once, some boys stayed out late playing ball, and their mothers grew angry and yelled at them. The boys did a defiant whirling dance that lifted them into the air, and they became the Pleiades, except for one who was grabbed by the heel and pulled down to earth by his mother. Where he landed, a pine tree grew, the first pine tree (258–59).

I blow out the candle I'm reading by, walk out of the lean-to. The gate of the fence creaks. The night is clear. I find the big dipper, Ursa Major, the only Big Bear I'll see in the Smokies, I guess. I follow the line of the dipper's outside edge five times its length to find Polaris. There is north—where the trail goes. The Milky Way is a blaze in the sky. I find the big "W" of Cassiopeia, "the lady of the chair," with her big toe sticking out from under the hem of her skirt. And there is the small cluster of the Pleiades, just above tree line.

With darkness wrapping itself around them, only up near their tops are the trees distinguishable from one another. I find the triangular apex of a conifer. I look at it closely, seeing it anew, seeing it point like an upward aimed arrow, a symbol of yearning for something higher. It occurs to me that the Appalachian Trail symbol, an A and a T with the crossbar of the A resting on the crossbar of the T (like this — A̱), sketches the outline of a pine.

2

Puc Puggy in the Nantahalas:
The Turning Point of William Bartram's *Travels*

AMONG THE BARTRAM FAMILY PAPERS at the Historical Society of Pennsylvania is an 1808 broadside catalog of plants from the Bartram Gardens, near Philadelphia. On the back, in close script, is an antislavery essay written by William Bartram, son of John Bartram, founder of the gardens and one of America's first and most famous botanists. Addressed to his fellow citizens, William's essay asserts that "God is no respecter of Persons & that the Black White Red & Yellow People are equally dear to him & under his protection & favour." One critic has termed this a plea "on behalf of the 'Universal Family of Mankind.'"[1] Perhaps it seems like an innocuous enough civil rights statement now, a religious version of "All people are created equal." But in the early nineteenth century, while slavery was still a going concern in the South and before the abolitionist movement was much of a force for reform, Bartram's position would have been considered radical.

A statement in similarly impassioned language in another unpublished manuscript among the Bartram papers might still, to this day, strike some as radical. This one was written, in part, over some delightful artistic doodles. On the back of one sheet, in the lower right, is a small house. To the left of it, appearing larger than the house, is a top-hatted figure carrying a walking stick, striding away from the house and toward a high hill with trees on it in the lower left. In the middle of the page is a prancing horse. In that essay Bartram writes, "I cannot believe; I cannot be so impious; nay my soul revolts, is destroyed by such conjectures as to desire or imagine that man, who is guilty of more mischief and wickedness than all the other animals together in this world, should be exclusively endued with the knowledge of the Creator, and capable of expressing his love and gratitude and homage to the Great Author of Being who continually feeds and delights us and all his

creatures with every good and enjoyment."[2] While readers today would have
no trouble accepting Bartram's statement of racial equality, his defense of
the sanctity of all living things would undoubtedly prove less palatable.
Bartram claims not just that God loves all his creatures but that all have mind
and soul.

Inherent in both statements is the assumption that all living things have
value—*equal* value, even. I find it telling that Bartram's antislavery essay was
written on the back of a plant catalogue—a celebration of floral diversity, a
plea for respecting human diversity, two sides of the same thing. And I wonder: did Bartram progress from accepting the value of people of all races and
then to valuing nonhuman living things, or did he move from respect for
plants and animals to respect for nonwhite people? Did his sense of social
justice lead him to the incipiently ecological understanding that interrelationship is the binding force of the natural world, or was it vice-versa? Judging from the structure of his most famous work, the *Travels* of 1791, I suspect
that the ecological understanding came first. For the *Travels*, which is both
a natural history of the American South and a narrative of Bartram's sojourns
there, begins as a study of nature and ends as a defense of native Americans.
Where the shift of emphasis begins, the socioecological epiphany, the moment when the connection between nature and culture became apparent to
Bartram, may have been his meeting with a Cherokee chief in the Nantahala
Mountains.

❦   ❦   ❦

Climbing mile-high Albert Mountain in the southern Nantahalas, I pass
through a tunnel formed by overarching rhododendrons, the leaves still dripping from last night's rain. Streaks of early morning sun pour through, looking almost palpable. Farther up the trail, the rock face on the uphill side of
the trail is covered with greenish-gold moss, streamlets of water spilling off it.
From the summit, I see cottonballs of clouds piled in the valleys, glaringly
white in the sun. It's a cool day, and I hike the twelve miles to a road crossing
at Wallace Gap by early afternoon. At a campground a mile or so down the
road, I resupply, shower, and do laundry. I've been out ten days. I call home,
and my wife tells me about our kids' adventures at the park that morning.
She also tells me that yesterday our little boy asked the babysitter, "Does
Daddy still live here?" Ouch.

Next day I'm missing my family so much that at first I can take little joy
in my hike. I climb out of Wallace Gap, descend into Winding Stair Gap,
up Siler Bald, into Wayah Gap, up Wine Spring Bald. I'm disappointed at

the cartographic false advertising there, since Wine Spring Bald is now tree-covered. Just past Wine Spring the Appalachian Trail joins for a couple of miles with the Bartram Trail, a sixty-eight-mile trail from Rabun Gap in Georgia to the Nantahala River, approximating the route across the mountains taken by William Bartram in 1775. I follow the Bartram Trail up Wayah Bald, possibly the site where Bartram described seeing "a sublimely awful scene of power and magnificence, a world of mountains piled upon mountains."[3] The view jolts me out of my homesick sorrow. Mountains recede into the horizon till they are engulfed by haze. I take a picture, knowing even then that contained in a three-by-five colored glossy, or on a screen in a darkened room, the picture will convey little of the scene's grandeur. In the actual terrain before me, it is the very lack of containment that awes, the unboundedness, the fact that I can look around and see on all sides more mountains than can be captured within a single frame, or a gaze. It is the amplitude of mountains that impresses in a panorama, and any attempt to enclose it within borders diminishes that amplitude.

It's not just the scenery that's making an impression on me. It's the presence of Bartram, my sense that I'm following in his footsteps. I felt the same awe in the Historical Society reading room in Philadelphia, trying to make out his two-hundred-year-old scrawl. I remember the doodle, of the man leaving home and heading for the hills. Was it this particular hill that Bartram had in mind?

I stare long from Wayah Bald, trying to fix the fullness of the vista in memory if not on film. Then I hike down to Licklog Gap, where I have been planning to stay the night. The campsite is a bare patch of ground surrounded by gray oaks just coming into leaf. There are several good flat places to pitch a tarp, but the place looks lonely, or I feel lonely there, so I push on another three and a half miles to Cold Spring shelter, hoping to find company. Nobody's there. I soak my feet, tend to some blisters, then read the shelter register. A hiker named Moonchild, about a week ahead, has left a quote from Wendell Berry's *The Unforeseen Wilderness*:

Always in big woods, when you leave familiar ground and step off alone to a new place, there will be, along with feelings of curiosity and excitement, a little nagging of dread. It is the ancient fear of the unknown, and it is your first bond with the wilderness you are going into. What you are doing is exploring; you are understanding the first experience, not of the place, but of yourself in that place. It is an experience of our essential loneliness, for nobody can discover the world for anybody else. It is only after we have discovered it for ourselves that it becomes a common ground and a common bond and we cease to be alone.[4]

Moonchild's thought for the day is propitious. I'm not sure yet what sort of discovery or common bond my own solitude might lead to, but I consider how Berry's observation applies to William Bartram. For Bartram too was bedeviled by loneliness here in the Nantahalas, and it was here that he made what may have been his most important discovery.

❧   ❧   ❧

Bartram was commissioned in 1772 by John Fothergill of London, a physician and amateur botanist who owned England's largest private garden, to draw and collect plants in the American South. Setting out the following spring, Bartram spent the next five years traveling in South Carolina, Georgia, Florida, North Carolina, and Alabama, covering about six thousand miles in all. A Seminole chief named Cowkeeper dubbed him Puc Puggy, or "The Flower Hunter." Bartram's trip proved a zoological and botanical success, as he was one of the first to study American bird migrations and was the first to discover or describe numerous species of plants and animals. Of course, he "discovered" those plants and animals in the same sense that Columbus "discovered" America, a place where there were already plenty of people living. What Bartram actually did was catalog the things he saw, claim them in the name of science, and publish their existence to European and Euro-American readers.

Despite its scientific significance, Bartram's excursion has earned more acclaim for its literary value. The record of Bartram's journey, entitled in full *Travels through North & South Carolina, Georgia, East & West Florida, The Cherokee Country, the Extensive Territories of the Muscogulges, or Creek Confederacy, and the Country of the Choctaws; containing An Account of the Soil and Natural Productions of those Regions, together with Observations on the Manners of the Indians*, was converted from journal to travel narrative in the 1780s and published in 1791. Almost immediately, it caught the attention of romantic writers in Britain and America. Traces of Bartram's descriptions have been found in several of Samuel Taylor Coleridge's poems, including "The Rime of the Ancient Mariner" and "Kubla Khan," and in Wordsworth's *The Prelude, The Recluse*, and *The Excursion*.[5] Thomas Carlyle in recommending the *Travels* to Ralph Waldo Emerson admired its "wondrous kind of floundering eloquence" and said that "all American libraries ought to provide themselves with that kind of book; and keep them as a kind of future *biblical* articles."[6] More recently, in the introduction to the 1988 Penguin edition of the *Travels*, James Dickey praised its "visionary quality" and "the passionate, wonderstruck, daring and very personal scientism, the repeated acts of rapt, total absorption" in the natural world.[7]

Alone in Cold Spring shelter, I am particularly enthralled by the portion of the narrative describing Bartram's excursion into the Nantahalas, at Wayah Gap. In May of 1775 Bartram passed through the Cherokee town of Nikwasi, then northwest to another Cherokee settlement in the valley of Cowee. On an afternoon jaunt there in the company of a trader named Galahan, Bartram saw young Cherokee women gathering strawberries, swimming, and in various ways "disclosing their beauties to the fluttering breeze." Bartram and his friend shared in a basket of strawberries proffered by "the innocent jocose sylvan nymphs" (289–90).

Back at the settlement in Cowee, he waited a couple of days for a guide, then decided to proceed alone, despite recalling advice that the trip was dangerous because of resentments arising from the latest series of white intrusions into Cherokee territory. In Bartram's words, recent "blood being spilt" left the native inhabitants "extremely jealous of white people travelling about their mountains, especially if they should be seen peeping in amongst the rocks, or digging up their earth" (270). There were also, of course, tensions arising from the recent outbreak of the Revolutionary War, in which the Cherokee would eventually side with the British.

Wandering alone, Bartram felt the absence of companionship, terming the mountains "dreary," wondering if "mankind feel in their hearts a predilection for the society of each other," comparing himself to Nebuchadnezzar, "expelled from the society of men, and constrained to roam in the mountains and wilderness, there to herd and feed with the wild beasts of the forest" (292). Soon afterward Bartram met a young Cherokee man, apparently a hunter out with his rifle and dogs, to whom he gave "some choice Tobacco." After Bartram asked about the way through the mountains, he and his new acquaintance shook hands and "parted in friendship," the Cherokee man singing as he left (293).

Bartram climbed to the "most elevated peak" of what he called the "Jore mountains" (293), a peak that scholars have variously identified as Wesser, Wayah, or Wine Spring Bald. The most thorough reconstruction of Bartram's route is Frances Harper's in his naturalist's edition of the *Travels*; Harper claims that Bartram's grand view was from Wine Spring Bald, which is closer to Wayah Gap than Wayah Bald.[8] But Wayah Bald is just a mile and a half further and is higher than Wine Spring Bald—and hence is the "most elevated peak" in the area. Since the summit of Wine Spring is now forested, wherever Bartram was, today the view from Wayah certainly gives more of a sense of what he saw.

Bartram descended down the western side of Wayah Gap, along Jarret Creek. The following day he crossed the Nantahala River and saw approaching "a company of Indians, all well-mounted on horse-back." They were led by Attakullakulla (Bartram spells it Ata-cul-culla), "the Little Carpenter, emperor or grand chief of the Cherokees" (230). Attakullakulla was one of seven Cherokee chiefs who had traveled to England in 1730, where they went to the theatre, sat for a portrait by William Hogarth, and presented the king with gifts of scalps and eagle tails.[9] Renowned as an orator and statesman, Attakullakulla was the friend and savior of John Stuart, the superintendent of Indian Affairs in the southern colonies. Stuart had been second in command at Fort Loudon when the garrison surrendered to the Cherokee in 1760. Rescuing him from the attack, Attakullakulla led Stuart through the wilderness for nine days and delivered him to the royal forces at Fort Patrick Henry. Later Attakullakulla was instrumental in negotiating an end to the Cherokee War. On the day he met William Bartram, he was on his way to see Stuart in Charleston. But before he got there, Stuart, a loyalist, had been forced to flee.

As Attakullakulla's party neared, Bartram stepped aside, "in token of respect." Attakullakulla shook hands with Bartram, who told the chief that he "was of the tribe of white men, of Pennsylvania, who esteem themselves brothers and friends to the red men, but particularly so to the Cherokees, and that notwithstanding we dwelt at so great a distance, we were united in love and friendship." Presumably Bartram was alluding to his pacifist Quaker faith. He also told the chief that Stuart, whom Bartram had seen in Charleston, had asked that he be given "the friendship and protection of the Cherokees." Attakullakulla responded favorably, telling Bartram he "was welcome in their country as a friend and brother" (295).

In essence Bartram had been granted safe passage. Nevertheless, later that day he "suddenly came to a resolution to defer [his] researches." The reason he gives is concern for his safety, but considering the success he always had in earning the friendship of native Americans he met in his travels, and considering the permission he had just received from Attakullakulla, there may have been something more to his decision. Loneliness, to which Bartram had given such poignant expression after Galahan's departure two days earlier, must have been part of it. One critic, in fact, contends that Bartram's loneliness in the Nantahalas profoundly altered his view of nature. Calling the ascent of the mountains "the psychological turning point of [the] trav-els," Robert Arner notes that from that point on Bartram never again traveled alone. And from then on, claims Arner, Bartram tends to depart from his usual celebratory descriptions of nature and increasingly perceives the natu-ral world as "unpleasant and sinister," "threatening and chaotic." [10]

My own experience on Wayah Bald makes me skeptical of Arner's argu-ment. Being lonely may actually make one more sensitive to natural beauty rather than less so. It is shortly *after* he gives vent to his melancholia that Bartram gives his ecstatic description of the panorama he beheld from Wayah (or Wine Spring) Bald. Arner himself observes that "ambivalence characterizes Bartram's response to nature throughout the book," so his read-ing of the change in the tone of the *Travels* is a matter of "emphasis, not . . . any absolute shift in attitude." [11]

Was Bartram fearful and lonely as he crossed the mountains? Undoubt-edly. But I am less inclined than Arner to take such a dim view of those feelings. Taking a cue from Wendell Berry, I wonder if fear and loneliness are not an essential part of the process of exploration that leads to discov-ery—of both the self and the world. And I wonder if in Bartram's case those discoveries might have involved finding common ground and a com-mon bond with the indigenous peoples he had come to know in the course of his journey. Why did Bartram turn back? Ultimately, perhaps the answer has to do with ecology, and with the cultural implications of ecological understanding.

❦   ❦   ❦

To suggest that Bartram was some sort of incipient ecologist calls for imme-diate qualifications. The word *ecology* was not even coined until almost a century after Bartram visited the South, and Bartram was heir to all the philosophic, theologic, aesthetic, and scientific assumptions of his era that run counter to anything approaching ecological understanding. [12] In the first paragraph of the *Travels* he sets forth the proposition that "men and manners undoubtedly hold the first rank," echoing, even in a study of the natural world, Alexander Pope's neoclassical dictum that "The proper study of man-kind is man." Bartram goes on to expound the doctrine of use in defending his interest in the natural world. He says that plants and animals are valuable only insofar as they "promote the happiness and convenience of mankind." Those that don't "contribute to our existence" in economic terms at least offer aesthetic attractions, which Bartram records in the well-worn language of the beautiful, the picturesque, and the sublime. In all these ways, living things serve to illustrate the glory of the Creator, "who was pleased to endow them with such eminent qualities, and reveal them to us for our sustenance, amusement, and delight" (15–17). Evidently God had only human well-being in mind in creating everything else. This is the height of anthropocentrism and seemingly the antithesis of a deep ecologist's ideal of biocentrism.

It's also hard to speak of Bartram's ecological bent since he was writing within the constraints of his chosen genre, natural history. In a recent study called *Describing Early America*, Pamela Regis explains what that meant in the late eighteenth century. Essentially, natural history was the study of anything not made by humans. It included botany, zoology, geography, geology — even anthropology and ethnology, since native peoples were often subjects of study in natural histories. That sort of interconnection between various sciences seems vaguely ecological, but the eighteenth-century natural historian focused on things in nature pretty much in isolation from each other, describing and classifying living things by employing the Linnaean system of taxonomy. Linnaeus's widely disseminated system was essentially static, assigning each thing its own immutable place in the natural order. It was a hierarchical system entirely compatible with the concept of the Great Chain of Being, the neoclassical pecking order that placed God at the top, above angels, humans, animals, plants, and inanimate objects — in that order. Purely descriptive, Linnaean taxonomy offered no means for explaining interconnections between living things or for considering evolutionary changes in living things, both of which are implicit in an ecological conception of the world.[13]

What, then, *was* ecological about Bartram's view of nature? Though he worked within the constraints of the aesthetic, theologic, and scientific conceptions of his time, Bartram was a perceptive enough observer to test the boundaries of those conceptions. Bartram uses Linnaean nomenclature, but rather than describe plants in isolation from each other, he tends to describe whole communities, often listing all the plants that coexist in one place — plants that would be far separated in a taxonomic list, notes Regis.[14] Bartram also describes how species are adapted to their habitats. In the introduction, for instance, he describes, in detail, the physiology of a pitcher plant. Its pitcher-shaped leaves can hold about a pint of water, he notes, but it is also equipped with a lid that turns over "to prevent a too sudden and copious supply of water from heavy showers of rain, which would bend down the leaves, never to rise again." That's a valuable adaptation "since these plants naturally dwell in low savannas liable to overflows, from rain water." Bartram also concludes that the short hairs on the leaves funnel moisture down to the funiculum and at the same time prevent insects from escaping the plant once they are lured in by the pool of water at the heart of the plant (18). By noticing such adaptations to the circumstances of climate and prey, Bartram recognizes a basic principle of ecology: the dynamic connection between a living thing and its environment. Rather than simply label and catalog and classify the object of study, Bartram's descriptions offer insights as to how it works and how it lives.

His scrupulous and sympathetic observations of plants and animals led Bartram to at times articulate a conservationist agenda that sounds strikingly modern in its ecological awareness and environmental concern. In a study of Bartram's ideas about "the moral sensibility of brute creation," Kerry Walters claims that Bartram was a "pioneering environmentalist," chastising his contemporaries for "destructively short-sighted slash and burn [agricultural] techniques" in the savannas of Georgia and Florida.[15] Bartram also warns that abuses of the land and animals will have economic and moral consequences. Such conservationist impulses suggest a recognition of the inherent value of things in nature and of the dependence of all things, including human beings, on the health of the biosphere.

In his studies of nature, then, Bartram was able to move beyond the limitations of the science of his day. Similarly, he was able to move beyond the conceptions of the dominant natural theology of his time. Bruce Silver points out that although Bartram initially relies on the premise that the natural order reflects heavenly design, he does not attempt to justify every natural fact as evidence that the system of creation must reflect the Creator's beneficent plan. Thus when Bartram describes a lake where various fish and crocodiles peacefully coexist, he does not conclude that "such happiness and tranquility are the basis for arguing that divine benevolence extends to every living creature."[16] Rather, he concludes that the exceptional clarity of the spring-fed water makes predation difficult: "It places them all on an equality with regard to their ability to injure or escape from one another" (151). By seeing how habitat affects behavior (again calling into question the Linnaean conception that the character of a species is fixed and constant), Bartram does not necessarily reject the argument from design, but his observations focus on the immediate details of place that contribute to the characteristics of the species he is studying rather than on the overall design. The system may be God's creation, but it is also consistent with what we would call an ecosystem.

Even aesthetically, Bartram's view of nature passed beyond the norms of his day and approached something akin to ecological understanding. Hugh

Moore points out that Bartram's descriptions rely in large part on the conventions of the sublime as it was defined by eighteenth-century aestheticians — appreciation for vastness, magnitude, dramatic light or sound, anything in nature that could contribute to a sense of awe. But Bartram added to the prevailing sense of the sublime an appreciation for "variety" and "diversity," as opposed to the typically "more unified sublimity . . . dependent upon one grand and overwhelming impression."[17] "Variety" and "diversity," the keys to Bartram's aesthetic appreciation of nature, are also the keys to ecological understanding.

His varied language, too, seems compatible with a protoecological view. At times Bartram employs a style stripped to the bare bones of scientific fact, in the form of Linnaean nomenclature, the lists of Latin names of plants and animals; at other times the text soars in the exalted language of the sublime. On occasion the combination can be comical, as when Bartram rhapsodizes regarding the Venus flytrap, "But admirable are the properties of the extraordinary Dionea muscipula!" (19). Critics of the Travels have expended much of their energy trying to account for the mixture of discourses and addressing the problem of classification that arises from the multiplicity of language styles. Just what sort of textual creature, they've wondered, is Bartram's Travels? Is it natural history or natural theology or political science or travel narrative? History or sociological study? Scientific report or poetic effusion? Neoclassic or romantic? Deist or Quaker? A sly commentary on the political situation of the United States or a defense of American Indians? "Religious quest" or "practical handbook on gardening"?[18] Or is it, as most critics eventually conclude, some combination of any number of these? For the most part critics have tended to argue that the Travels seems scientific but it's really artistic, influenced by the aesthetic categories of the time and in turn influencing the romantic movement that would follow on the heels of the Travels.[19] Regis's study of the Travels in its natural history context counters the critical tendency to ignore the book's scientific bent and to read it as predominantly a work of belles lettres. But as Charles Adams notes in a review of Regis's book, she still assumes that it must be one or the other, science or art.[20]

Adams's own take on the "dizzying succession of discourses" in the Travels — from "the language of Romantic primitivism" to "poetic apostrophe" to "moral lesson" to "scientific language reminiscent of the Linnaean list" — is that such diversity reflects his subject: "a commitment to natural 'variety' implies a corollary commitment to rhetorical complexity." The blending of the "theological, didactic, metaphorical, affective, [and] scientific" languages, says Adams, creates the "polyphonic effect" esteemed by the literary theorist Mikhail Bakhtin. The *Travels* offers "a sort of *dialogics of nature*," an interplay of the multiple voices of nature. Adams contends that "from a contemporary perspective," Bartram's recognition of nature's "diversity and interrelatedness," as reflected by his mixture of discourses, "might be called ecological."[21]

❦   ❦   ❦

At the university where I teach, a "cultural diversity" requirement was mandated a few years back, part of the nationwide educational movement to recognize the intellectual contributions of women and minorities in our culture and to promote "tolerant cooperation," as a Penn State handbook puts it, "within a complex and increasingly interdependent global community." Diversity, interdependence, community—these are the catch phrases of both ecology and multiculturalism. The common linguistic ground suggests a link between the social ideal of cultural diversity and the ecological ideal of biodiversity. In both, the chief article of faith is that everything is connected. It is this link that Murray Bookchin has forged and tempered in his studies of "social ecology," which premises that "the ecological principle of unity in diversity" can serve as the grounding for an "ethics of freedom." Typically our views of nature, says Bookchin, are projections of the current social order. We see hierarchies in nature (the kingly lion, the lowly ant) in order to justify the institutionalized hierarchies that pervade our social relations. Bookchin urges us to reconsider the nature of nature in order to save both it and ourselves, to recognize that an ecosystem—or "ecocommunity," as he prefers—is more symbiotic than competitive, ordered more on the principle of interdependence than on hierarchy. The ant is as necessary to the health of a particular ecosystem as the lion. Biodiversity makes stability possible, rendering an ecosystem better able to withstand blight or trauma or climactic shifts or environmental change.[22]

Perhaps the insights of ecology could do more to advance the cause of multiculturalism than any amount of politically correct preaching about tolerance and respect for others. I'm not just talking about ecology's value as metaphor. "Touchy-feely" as it may sound, the basic principle of ecology is interconnectedness, and writers like Bartram who paid close attention to the natural world perceived that principle even before there was a science of ecology. To recognize the advantages of diversity and the verities of interrelationship and interdependency—that is the ecological way of knowing. And it is a habit of mind that translates to the human realm, involving a movement out of the self and toward consideration for others, both other living things and other people. But as the situation exists in our universities, human cultures are in the domain of the humanities, and ecology is a subject of the natural sciences, and the twain not only don't meet in the classroom, they're not even invited to the same parties.

Bartram's *Travels* could serve as an instructive text for the advocates of multiculturalism and social ecology. For if Bartram's views of nature in a variety of ways moved beyond the assumptions and conventions and norms of his time and toward ecological awareness, so too did his views of race move toward a respect for cultural diversity. In the introduction to the *Travels* Bartram devotes four paragraphs to the Indian nations of the Southeast, recommending that Anglo-Americans study native languages, customs, political systems, traditions, and history. Even to perceive that Indians had such things as legislative systems, traditions, and history, Bartram had risen above the prejudices of his time. In the introduction he still accepts the ethnocentrism of his culture in assuming that assimilation of Indians into Anglo civilization would be to their benefit. But in the final part of the *Travels*, beyond saying that whites should study Indians and respect their ways, Bartram suggests that we can even learn from them—not just about how to get along with nature (by adopting native agricultural practices) but how to get along with each other. Their (unwritten) constitution, he contends, "produces a society of peace and love, which in effect better maintains human happiness, than the most complicated system of modern politics" (488). A statement like that would have had special force in the politically turbulent 1780s and 1790s, when the United States was coming into being amid bitter disputes about the Constitution.

Bartram's tolerance, respect, and admiration for the ways of native Americans were remarkable considering the mores of his social era. They are even more astounding considering his family history. Bartram's paternal grandfather had been killed by Indians, and his grandmother had been a captive for almost a year. William's father, John, was a confirmed Indian hater. He called native Americans "the most barbarous savages on earth," whose violence should never "be forgot by our childrens children."[23] What accounted for the difference in attitude between John and his son? Undoubtedly, first-hand experience had a lot to do with it. William says he associated with Indians on his travels "that I might judge for myself, whether they were deserving of the severe censure which prevailed against them among the white people, that they were incapable of civilization" (26). Taught by his culture and his father to hate, William delayed judgment until he could find out for himself.

To immerse himself—that was how William learned about the native peoples of the South. That was also how he studied the natural world of the South, and in that matter, too, he differed from his father, who was, according to one critic, apparently "squeamish" about touching things in nature. John Bartram was a perceptive and thorough observer, enough so for Linnaeus to call him "the greatest living botanist in the world." But William was more of a hands-on expert, "closer to nature and more intimate with it." [24] Whether it was plant, animal, or human, William believed in making direct contact with his subject.

Perhaps we can only intuit that there is some connection between Bartram's practice as a naturalist and his cultural sensitivity. Nowhere does he claim that one results from the other. But both seem to arise from the same kind of thinking, the same awareness of the connectedness of all things to each other and to their place. The parallels are most suggestive in Bartram's *Observations on the Creek and Cherokee Indians*, written in 1789 but not published until 1853. Bartram notes that the Creek and Cherokee "seem to consider all the Indians of the earth as one great family or community, who have separated themselves as convenience or necessity have directed, and formed innumerable nations,—climates, situations, revolutions, renovations, or other unknown causes, having marked the different nations and tribes by different stature, color, complexion, manners, customs, language, etc." [25] What Bartram says here is essentially an ecological insight, seeing that differences between human beings are attributable to different environmental conditions and historical circumstances. But all are still part of the same human "family"—the family being a social construct of connectedness akin to the biological concept of an ecosystem. Bartram goes on to say that in the Creek and Cherokee moral system, even white men are perceived as members of the human family, being treated with full hospitality and addressed as "brothers." If a white man were in Indian country, says Bartram, "alone in the dreary forest, naked, hungry, bewildered, lost, the Indian would give him his only blanket, half his provisions, and take him to his wigwam, where he would repose securely and quietly, and in the morning conduct him safe back to his own frontier—and all this even though he had been the day before beaten, bruised, and shot at by a white man." [26] Clearly the lessons of social ecology have been better learned by some people than others.

To suggest a link between attitudes to nature and attitudes to native

Americans makes many contemporary critics uncomfortable. Regis, for one, though she concedes that Bartram was more sympathetic to Indians than most whites of his day, is troubled by the dehumanizing inclusion of human beings in a study of flora and fauna: "The American Indians are treated as just one more item of natural history. . . . A tree is clearly Other. So is a bird. Transfer the method to describe the tree or bird to another human being, and he becomes Other too."[27] But as Bartram's introduction makes clear, he does not conceive of tree or bird, spider or bear, as Other; they all exhibit recognizably human traits. The Venus flytrap has senses, the power of loco-motion — even, Bartram claims, volition. Bears show emotion, as he illus-trates by a story of a cub crying over its slain mother. A spider hunting a bee exhibits planning and cunning — in short, the power of reason. Birds have social structures, a language, even the art of music. Regis says that Bartram simply moves everything up a notch in the Great Chain of Being, so that plants are like animals and animals are like people (and Indians are like whites). But one could also say that he is seeing something human — or something in common that is not exclusively human — in plant, insect, bird, mammal, Nantahala Cherokee, Philadelphia Quaker, all. Perhaps this is why, as Christopher Looby points out, Bartram habitually describes "groups of animals and even plants as social groups" — "communities" of flowers, "nations" of fish, "tribes" of butterflies, deer, turkeys, and cranes.[28] Scientists tend to dismiss the projection of human constructs, traits, or emotions onto nature as naive anthropomorphism, reflecting an inability to see nature in anything other than human terms; literary critics disparagingly refer to it as the "pathetic fallacy." But one can also argue that such anthropomorphizing is profoundly ecological since it expresses the interrelatedness, the sense that humanity and the natural world are one, that constitutes a premise of ecol-ogy.[29] If the pathetic fallacy is not good science, it does bespeak an intuited sense of connection to nature. That sense that we are more like other living things than unlike them is a valuable corrective to the impression we gener-ally get from science or religion. There is nothing insulting, then, about including human beings in a study of the natural productions of a place, for they too are part of the ecosystem, and no living thing is the Other.

Regis also contends that Bartram focuses mainly on native peoples as a group, offering generalizations rather than writing about individual Indians, and that he excludes them from the narrative portion of his travel account and relegates them to the purely descriptive section at the conclusion of his book. The movement of narrative, says Regis, is at odds with the static de-scription at the heart of the Linnaean system, and unfortunately, in her

view, Bartram forsakes narrative in his treatment of native Americans and
falls back on atemporal, ahistorical description in part 4 of the *Travels*. But
Bartram does not wholly deport his material on native Americans to the
purely descriptive section of ethnology that concludes the book. Throughout parts 1 to 3, Bartram's encounters with Indians constitute some of the
most dramatic moments of his narrative — among them his meeting with
Attakullakulla.

In stepping off the trail for Attakullakulla, Bartram says he was showing
respect. Let us not underrate the magnitude of that step, for it was the first
step in his decision to withdraw from Cherokee land. Might not Bartram's
yielding of all the country west of the Nantahalas have been the natural
product of his respect for the Cherokee? Alone among his kind, perhaps
Bartram recognized the obtrusiveness of his presence — and he decided not
to violate the territorial prerogative of a native people. On a very personal
level, he chose not to invade. Out on the trail, feeling lonely, welcoming and
cherishing the encounters with the berrying Cherokee women, the singing
hunter, the noble Attakullakulla, maybe Bartram came to recognize his common bond with the Cherokee, not just their shared humanity but their
shared love for the natural world. And maybe in respect of that bond he
decided to give ground. Or rather, not to take it.

❦　　❦　　❦

The Nantahala portion of Bartram's hike took place in 1775, but in the *Travels* he states that it was 1776, when events of some historical importance
were taking place, about which Bartram has nothing overt to say. Is the mis-
dating a careless error or, as some critics suggest, a subtle way of linking his
Travels with contemporary political affairs and offering some sly comment?
Christopher Looby and Douglas Anderson believe that Bartram's cataloging
of species might be a way of expressing his yearning for order amid chaotic
times.[30] Perhaps Bartram feared that such sentiments might seem antirevolu-
tionary in early America and so needed to be expressed covertly. But maybe
he says nothing because he had some inkling that the Revolution was not
going to effect any real change in the dominant culture on the American
continent. Whoever won the war, American or British forces, the Cherokee
would be losers. The tactical retreat he made in the Nantahalas would not
be the way of the victors. America would follow a different path.

The year following Bartram's crossing of Wayah Gap was eventful. Like
most native American tribes, the Cherokee sided with the British, whom
they hoped could regulate incursions of white American settlers into their

territory. The Cherokee raided white settlements east and west of the mountains. In August of 1776 the North Carolina army, 2,400 men under Gen.
Griffith Rutherford, retaliated, cutting through Cherokee country, burning
crops and villages. Thirty-six towns were destroyed. Many of the Cherokee
retreated to the Great Smoky Mountains, but a large force gathered at Wayah
Gap. There the fighting was brutal and bloody, but eventually the Cherokee
were beaten back. Among the dead Cherokee was a woman, in war paint
and battle dress.

Following the Revolutionary War, a series of treaties shrank the Cherokee
lands. The first Treaty of Tellico in 1798 guaranteed "the remainder of their
country forever." As Michael Frome points out, "forever" lasted only a few
years, until the second and third treaties of Tellico in 1804 and 1805 further
reduced Cherokee lands.[31] In 1815 gold was found in north Georgia, and in
1828 the state of Georgia passed laws annexing all Cherokee lands within its
chartered limits, declaring Cherokee laws and customs null and void, out-
lawing Cherokee councils, and forbidding any Indian from being a witness
or party to any suit where the defendant was a white male. According to
James Mooney, "The purpose of this legislation was to render life in their
own country intolerable to the Cherokee by depriving them of all legal protection."[32] It worked. Armed whites swarmed into Cherokee lands, asking for
and receiving the protection of the U.S. government. In 1838 the bulk of the
Cherokee nation was deported on the Trail of Tears. So much for Bartram's
"Universal Family of Mankind."

❁   ❁   ❁

On Wayah Bald a display case at the summit explains that Wayah is the
Cherokee word for wolf. Wolves were common on Wayah Bald until the
middle of the nineteenth century. But in the 1860s a bounty was placed on
them. Within twenty years, they were wiped out.

I remember when my wife and I were first getting to know each other,
and asking each other such things as "if you were an animal, what would
you be?" I had said I'd be a wolf—according to the popular image a loner,
but in reality a social creature, devoted to his family. Judy's first gift to me
was an origami wolf head. Years later, playing with my little boy, I sometimes,
to his endless delight, put it on and howl.

3

Mary Noailles Murfree:
Ecofeminist of the Great Smoky Mountains

Aт Mollies Ridge Shelter, just a few miles into the Great Smoky Mountains, I'm talking with a young man, recently graduated from the University of North Carolina, who's hiking with his father. They've been out for about three weeks, heading south from Damascus, Virginia. I'm curious about their father-and-son adventure, and I suppose I'm also projecting about eighteen years into the future and thinking I'd like to do a hike like this with my son someday. I learn that the parents are divorced, but the guy from UNC regularly gets together with his father for camping trips. His father, in fact, used to be his scoutmaster.

As we fire up stoves to make dinner, other hikers show up. It looks like the shelter will be full this night. As it happens, all the hikers are male. "Good," says the guy from UNC, "we don't have to deal with any women tonight!"

"What have you got against women?" I ask.

"I come out here to get away from them," he says. "I see too much of them at home. There are some up ahead of you, though. The Granola Girls about a week ahead. There's a cute girl hiking by herself just a day or so ahead. She must be crazy."

I'm a little shocked at his misogyny, but I don't say anything. His father laughs.

    ❧   ❧   ❧

For the next day or so I'm hiking through the literary high ground of Mary Noailles Murfree, better known in the late nineteenth century by her pen name, Charles Egbert Craddock. The male pose, intended to gain a fair reading for her work, was a familiar one for women writers, which led Elaine Showalter to propose the term *Georgics*, in honor of George Eliot and

George Sand, for works written by women under male pseudonyms.[1] Perhaps, too, Murfree found the craggy sound of "Charles Egbert Craddock" appropriate to her highland subject matter.

Murfree was born in 1850 near Murfreesboro, Tennessee (named for her great-grandfather). From 1855 to 1870 her family summered at Beersheba Springs in the Cumberland Mountains, and then in the 1870s they made several visits to the Smokies. Writing as Craddock, she began in 1878 to publish her short stories about the Cumberlands and Smokies in the *Atlantic Monthly*, collecting them under the title *In the Tennessee Mountains* in 1884. The next year her best-known novel, *The Prophet of the Great Smoky Mountains*, was serialized in the *Atlantic* and then published in book form. Both went into numerous reprintings and were highly praised, with Craddock, or Murfree (she revealed her identity the same year *Prophet* appeared), being compared with such literary lights as Bret Harte, Nathaniel Hawthorne, and Henry James. Fiction poured from her pen for the next thirty years, but her reputation began waning well before her death in 1922. Today, only one of her twenty-five books, *In the Tennessee Mountains*, remains in print.[2]

Murfree's stories were part of the local color movement of the late nineteenth century, American regional fiction concerned with life in rural areas of the country. Marked by a preoccupation with dialect and setting, local color was a field dominated by women writers. Foremost among them was Sarah Orne Jewett, whose story "A White Heron" is a masterpiece of ecofiction. Many of the women local colorists have received increased attention from feminist critics in the last couple of decades, and their literary reputations have been restored. Certainly that has been the case with Jewett, and so too with such writers as Rose Terry Cooke, Mary Wilkins Freeman, and Kate Chopin. But not so with Murfree.

Joining me for my hike through the Smokies is a friend named David, a Thoreau scholar who has just recently accepted a teaching position at a women's college in South Carolina. We leave the shelter early and follow the ridgeline, North Carolina on our right, Tennessee to the left. All morning we catch glimpses of a cleared vale a few miles away on the Tennessee side, a patch of lighter green where forest makes way for fields. That's Cades Cove, the setting for most of Murfree's Smoky Mountain stories, called "Eskaqua Cove" in *The Prophet of the Great Smoky Mountains* and "Piomingo Cove" in an 1887 novel, *In the Clouds*, but in many stories identified simply as "The Crossroads," "The Settlement," or "The Cove." When Murfree visited Cades Cove in the 1870s, the community was past its prime. Perhaps her fiction set there was a deliberate attempt to preserve a way of life already passing as American civilization rumbled toward the twentieth century. In a study of the decline and fall of Cades Cove, Durwood Dunn shows that until the Civil War, Cades Cove was a thriving community with close economic ties to other towns and a constant influx of settlers from the outside. But a series of Confederate raids during the war left the townsfolk bitter and suspicious of outsiders. A regional depression further weakened economic ties between communities, and the westward movement passed by many mountain settlements. Even then, the isolation of Cades Cove was hardly absolute — crops were sold in other towns, for instance — but an always strong sense of community became even more pronounced. As a result, says Dunn, "an indigenous folk culture developed which compensated the cove people in part for their economic losses." That folk culture was defined in part by a unique dialect and in part by "interpretation of the culture by outsiders" — outsiders such as Mary Noailles Murfree.[3] When Smoky Mountain National Park was established in the 1930s, the people of Cades Cove were bought out. Now the village, accessible via a side trail off the A.T., is maintained by the Park Service as an example of Appalachian backwoods life — like Murfree's fiction, a historical curiosity, a testament to the past, a fading portrait of a way of life that even a hundred years ago was seen as backward.

Often the action of Murfree's stories ranges out of Cades Cove, west to the county seat of "Shaftesville," based on Maryville, and even more often into the mountains, west to Chilhowee Mountain and east into the Smokies. In the mountains, it is less easy to identify her settings with precision. Often the mountains are nameless, referred to simply as "the mounting." In *The Prophet of the Great Smoky Mountains* the title character, Hiram Kelsey, is said to roam around "Great Smoky" or "the Dome" — probably Clingman's Dome, which was once commonly called Smoky Mountain or Smoky Dome. But not necessarily. Since the descriptor *dome*, in Smoky Mountain parlance, can refer to any mountain with a rocky summit, it may refer to one of the mountains immediately above Cades Cove, like Gregory's Bald or Parson's Bald. *In the Clouds* begins with a sheepherder's view of Thunderhead as seen from a nearby peak to the northeast that Murfree calls Piomingo Bald. On the map that would be Derrick Knob, where there was indeed a herder's hut in her day, now the site of a shelter. Or if her sense of direction is confused, the novel may be set at Spence Field, a bit to the southwest of Thunderhead, where another herder's hut was once located and where Thunderhead lowers over the scene in a way that accords with the novel's opening description.[4]

David and I take a lunch break at Spence Field, lounging in the grass. Deer approach within twenty feet of us. On Rocky Top we sing an obligatory chorus of the bluegrass tune, then on the way up Thunderhead see a tiny ring-necked snake. We stay the next night at Derrick Knob, where views are limited by trees encroaching on the bald. The next day we set off in rain and are enshrouded with mist on Clingman's Dome.

Throughout the Smokies the shelters are crowded, but on only one night is there a woman in the party. Hannah is a student at the University of Colorado, hiking with her boyfriend, Chris. He's from Colorado, and he can't help but compare the Smokies to the Rockies. He finds the Smokies "quieter" mountains, less spectacular than the Rockies, but surprisingly rugged once you start walking. For Hannah, the trip is a return to her home ground. She's from Tennessee and has missed these mountains. She prefers them over the Rockies. The Smokies seem to her more intimate, not so much because they're smaller, but because the foliage restricts views and makes you pay more attention to what's right in front of you.

Also sharing the shelter with us is a fellow from Florida named Adam, also a college student, majoring in environmental studies. When he finds out that David and I are English professors, he shows us an excerpt from Thoreau that he has copied down into his journal. It's the "I went to the woods because I wished to live deliberately" section from *Walden*. Adam is impressed that David and I know it by heart. He wonders if we memorize everything we read. "No, just the good stuff," says David.

In the course of our conversation, we learn that Hannah is a women's studies major. Adam asks what that is all about. Hannah gives a good one-sentence explanation: "It has to do with who wrote history and what they thought was important." I tell Hannah about Mary Noailles Murfree, and I ask if she has done any reading in ecofeminism. Adam, ever curious it seems, asks what that is. In a nutshell, I say, it's the idea that women are closer to nature, or that in our culture women and nature are associated with one another, and that the oppression of women and the despoliation of the environment and the mistreatment of animals are related problems.

I'm not so satisfied with my own attempt to sum up vast fields of intellectual inquiry in one sentence, and I want to go on to explain that, from an ecofeminist viewpoint, women and nature both suffer from the hierarchical, binary thinking that is dominant in our patriarchal culture. We tend to think in terms of opposites—good/evil, reason/instinct, mind/body, civilization/nature, human/animal, man/woman—and one side of those opposing concepts is "privileged," or considered the norm, and the other side is not and becomes the Other. Women have been associated with the nonprivileged side of things in our culture, and especially with nature — think of such concepts as "Mother Earth" and the "rape of the land." Another tenet of ecofeminism, I'm ready to tell Adam, grows out of psychological studies of gender differences. Growing up, little girls can identify with their prime nurturer, the mother, and can see her as a model for their own identities. Little boys, though, must at some point in their egodevelopment grapple with the recognition of their difference from the mother. They establish an identity based on separation and difference. The result is that men tend to put a great premium on individualism, and they accept alienation — from others and from the world — as given, while women are more likely to feel a strong sense of relationship with others. That predisposes women to appreciate the essence of ecology — everything is connected.[5]

Before I can get into any of that, though, Adam stops me with a logical objection: "If women are closer to nature, then where are they? Why aren't they here?"

Hannah, David, and I wrestle with answers. Hannah says, partly defensive and partly proud, "I *am* here!" David offers the conjecture that *fear* keeps women out of the wilderness, fear of men, and if it's true that women are by nature more closely attuned to the natural world, then just think of the devastating effects of that fear. The violence perpetrated by men on women who leave the safety of civilization works in effect to deny women their essential nature, which involves contact with nature. Now *that's* oppression, he says. I point out that ecofeminists don't necessarily argue that women *are* closer to nature, but that they are *perceived* as closer to nature, and that nature is perceived as feminine.

I'm still not quite satisfied with our responses. In both Adam's healthy skepticism and the haughty assumption of the guy from UNC that the wild is a male domain, there's a challenge to the most basic premise of ecofeminist thinking. Judging from the demographics of the trail, women do not as a rule seem closer to nature than men. But the literature of the trail may tell a different story. If there is validity to ecofeminist propositions, then the association of women with nature should be apparent even in literature that predates the contemporary feminist movement or the development of ecological awareness. In the stories, for example, of Mary Murfree.

❀   ❀   ❀

The recurring plot of Murfree's fiction features a woman who enjoys a special kinship with the land and who sacrifices herself in some way for a man.

Often there is some sort of conflict between her moral values and legal codes. In "Drifting down Lost Creek," the first story of *In the Tennessee Mountains* (and arguably Murfree's best), a mountain girl named Cynthia Ware is in love with the local blacksmith, Evander Price. When he is falsely accused of murder, Cynthia ventures into town to work for his freedom. She feels out of place in town, barked at by dogs and mocked by children, barely able to speak. Eventually she succeeds in convincing the authorities that Evander is innocent. But Evander, unaware that Cynthia was the agent of his freedom, stays in town, marries someone else (unhappily), and becomes a success marketing his inventions. Cynthia, meanwhile, stays in the mountains. He is associated, then, with civilization and technology, she with nature. The story ends with an implied comparison of her life to Lost Creek, which meanders aimlessly before disappearing in the mountains.

Though "Drifting down Lost Creek" is set not in the Smokies but in the Cumberlands to the west, the pattern of that story holds for many of the Smoky Mountain stories: men are associated with towns and civilization, women are associated with nature and sacrifice themselves or their chance at love for men. I find the most interesting and complex of her stories, at least from an ecofeminist perspective, to be *The Prophet of the Great Smoky Mountains*. The title suggests that the hero is Parson Hiram Kelsey, a tortured soul who takes up religion and takes to the mountains in search of salvation after his wife and baby die—the baby as a result of Hiram's misreading the label on some medication, the wife out of sorrow for the baby. In truth, though, the protagonist is Dorinda Cayce, whose family makes a living off moonshine.

Early in the novel Dorinda refuses help, or rather fails to volunteer information, to a sheriff hunting an admirer of hers, Rick Tyler, wanted for murder. The charge is unjust, for Rick was simply in the company of a friend who did the shooting. When the Cayce clan learns that the frustrated sheriff threatened to jail Dorinda for withholding information, they vow to take his life. Rick is eventually caught through the machinations of blacksmith Gid Fletcher, who is after the reward. Rick escapes, and everyone thinks Parson Kelsey is responsible, so he is wanted for aiding and abetting. When Rick is cleared of the charges against him, Dorinda begs him to clear Kelsey's name. But because he is jealous of the high regard in which Dorinda holds Kelsey, Rick refuses to sign an affidavit attesting to the facts on the parson's behalf. So Dorinda gives him up. The novel concludes when the Cayce men attempt to kill the sheriff in retribution for his earlier insult to Dorinda, but in the middle of the melee, on a dark night, Kelsey lets himself be

taken in place of the sheriff and drowned — sacrificing himself, achieving his
martyrdom.

In some ways the story follows the ecofeminist story line of much of
Murfree's fiction. Dorinda feels protective of things in nature, finds solace
there, and is associated with nature in ways that most of the male characters
are not. When she finds a raccoon family, she is careful not to tell her youngest brother about it, fearing that he would trap it. Her favorite spot is a spring
in a deep mountain cleft that "reminded her of the well-springs of pity." And
when she spurns Rick's love late in the novel, he finds her "as immovable,
and as infinitely remote from his plane, as the great dome of the mountain." [6]

Men, on the other hand, tend to be destroyers of nature. Rick Tyler escapes from his confinement amid the hubbub of a gander pull, a ritualistic
torture that passes for sport among the men, in which they ride past a goose
tied to a tree and try to break its neck. Women are not allowed to participate.
Least attuned to nature is Sheriff Green. While searching for Rick, the sheriff
kicks a dog that's making too much noise. And he has no appreciation for
"the supreme dignity" of the mountains: "Their awful silence," we are told,
"like the unspeakable impressiveness of some overpowering thought, affected him not. The vastness of the earth which they suggested, beneath the
immensity of the sky, which leaned upon them, found no responsive large-
ness in his emotions." To him, "the splendors of the landscape were not
more seemly or suggestive than the colors of a map on the wall" (216–17).

Even the Cayce men demonstrate the opposition of men and nature. In a
way, they seem close to nature, since they have to know the land well in order
to hide their still, and at times they seem to see the mountains as a protective
fortress that keeps out intruders. But at other times they perceive nature as
antagonistic. When the family patriarch John, a.k.a. "Groundhog" Cayce, is
expressing outrage at Sheriff Green's treatment of Dorinda, he recites the
family history as a series of contests in which battle has been waged against
a number of foes, among them the land: "Me an' mine take no word off'n
nobody. My gran'dad an' his three brothers, one hunderd an' fourteen year
ago, kem hyar from the old North State an' settled in the Big Smoky. They
an' thar sons rooted up the wilderness. They crapped [cropped, I assume].
They fit the beastis; they fit the Injun; they fit the British; an' this last war o'
ourn they fit each other" (33). Their relationship to nature is essentially one
of conquest. Their claim to the land is based on a sense that they have subdued the wilderness, conquered it, when they "rooted it up." And "crapped"
on it.

What complicates the apparently straightforward opposition of men to

nature is the figure of the Prophet himself, Parson Kelsey, the character most
closely associated with nature. He spends most of his time riding the ridge
and has become something of an expert naturalist: "He was learned in the
signs of the weather, and predicted the mountain storms; he knew the haunts
and habits of every beast and bird in the Great Smoky, every leaf that bur-
geons, every flower that blows" (81). Like Dorinda, he is associated with
animals—he believes that Satan hunts him "like a pa'tridge on the mounting" (79), and Gid Fletcher says the Parson is "more like a wild beastis 'n
a man" (288). And like Dorinda he seeks to protect animals from human
cruelty. At the gander pull, Kelsey puts a stop to the proceedings, saying,
"The pains o' the beastis he hev made teches the Lord in heaven; fur he
marks the sparrow's fall, an' minds himself o' the pitiful o' yearth!" (110).

Kelsey senses the presence of God not just in the miracle of life but in the
majesty of the mountains as well. While Rick Tyler and most of the other
men of the Settlement feel they "kin pray in the valley . . . ez peart ez on
enny bald in the Big Smoky" (8–9), the Prophet feels that the mountains are
sacred:

> Infinity was expressed before the eye. On and on the chain of mountains
> stretched. . . . They breathed solemnities. They lent wings to the thoughts.
> They lifted the soul. Could he look at them and doubt that one day he
> should see God? . . .
>
> Somehow, the mountains had for his ignorant mind some coercive in-
> ternal evidence of the great truths. In their exalted suggestiveness were
> congruities: so far from the world were they,—so high above it; so inter-
> linked with the history of all that makes the races of men more than the
> beasts that perish, that conserves the values of that noble idea,—an im-
> mortal soul. On a mountain the ark rested; on a mountain the cross was
> planted; the steeps beheld the glories of the transfiguration; the lofty soli-
> tudes heard the prayers of the Christ; and from the heights issued the great
> sermon instinct with all the moralities of every creed. How often He went
> up into the mountain! (168–69)

At the end, Kelsey quite literally becomes one with nature as the mountain
becomes his tomb. The Cayce men mistakenly push the Prophet instead of
the sheriff into a pond, and they roll a huge boulder over it to seal off any
escape route. Dorinda ever after believes the Prophet mysteriously disappeared, perhaps being "caught up into the clouds," even closer to heaven
than the mountains could bring him (308).

Does the association of the Prophet with nature negate an ecofeminist reading of the book? I don't think so, for in many ways Kelsey *is* a female figure, a counterpart to Dorinda, a representative of traits associated with women in the nineteenth century, and a spokesperson for Murfree. Though Dorinda is said to have "no religion," she shares Kelsey's perception that the mountains are the abode of the sacred. There's quite a bit of humor at Dorinda's expense since she consistently assumes that the terrain of the Bible must refer to local geography. She believes that Kelsey speaks with "'Lijah an' 'Lisha, an' them men" up on the ridge of the Smokies—and she's not thinking metaphorically. When Rick informs her that the parson only "meets the sperits o' them men on the bald," she can only believe that biblical characters *used* to live up there, even if it was as far away as the other side of the ridge, across the state line (10). Similarly, at her favorite spring, she is reminded by the surrounding cliffs of "that rock which Moses smote," even though she knows, or thinks she knows, that Mount Horeb is a distant place—located far off "in Jefferson County." Literally, of course, Dorinda's sense of biblical geography is laughably askew. But in a higher sense, a spiritual sense, she's right—the Smokies are God's country, and the mountains are appropriately in "close communion with the heavens" (143). Despite her lack of acquaintance with the Bible, or maybe precisely *because* her religion comes from nature and not from a book, Dorinda's faith stands on even firmer ground than Kelsey's. He is tormented by doubts, and he roams "the desert places to upbraid the God in whom he believed because he believed that there was no God" (79). She sees the majesty of the mountains and believes. Or knows.

The suggestion that Dorinda has some sort of natural religious faith and that the Prophet's religious faith allies him with feminine traits is entirely in keeping with nineteenth-century American notions about gender and religion. As American civilization grew, women were regarded as the caretakers of moral and religious values. Barbara Welter points out that the "traditional religious values . . . [of] humility, submission, and meekness [were deemed] incompatible with success" in a male-dominated society that prized aggressiveness and competitiveness in the political and economic spheres. Since women were denied meaningful participation in those realms anyway, they were expected to maintain the "more soft and accommodating" traits associated with both religion and femininity. The association of women and religion is not something perceived only by twentieth-century scholars. Nineteenth-century feminist leader Sarah Grimke wrote in an 1856 newspaper article that "the strength of the moral world lies in woman . . . in her heart religion has found its home."[7]

It is not just in his appreciation for nature and in his religion that Kelsey embodies traits that Murfree might have associated with the feminine. He is renowned as a Prophet because he possesses the "female" gift of intuition, which the Settlement people take to be a sign of supernatural power but which really derives from close observation and empirical knowledge. He can foretell weather because he knows and observes nature. He knows without being told that blacksmith Gid Fletcher took Rick Tyler prisoner because he knows and observes *human* nature—only Fletcher would be powerful enough and greedy enough to take Tyler into custody. Similarly, he knows that Groundhog Cayce will live to regret his quest for vengeance on Sheriff Green because he knows something about the workings of conscience.

What most allies Parson Kelsey with Dorinda is their mutual resistance to the values of the law, their shared regard for morality in preference to justice. In this respect too Kelsey exhibits traits associated with the feminine. In her landmark study of gender and psychology, *In a Different Voice*, Carol Gilligan claims that in assessing disputes men try to sort out who's right and who's wrong by applying abstract principles of justice, aiming at the ideal of impartial rationality, whereas women express more concern about how conflicts might have been avoided in the first place and what the human consequences of any action might be. Theirs is an ethic based on care and concern for others. Women are less likely to see a given situation as reducible to an abstract principle involving issues of rights; instead, their ethical reasoning tends to be contextual.[8] But civil law, which can be seen as the codification of male-centered ethics, is anything but contextual or personal.

Kelsey's scorn for the law is most evident when he chastizes Gid Fletcher for capturing Rick Tyler. Fletcher protests that he's doing his duty in turning Tyler over to the law. And he justifies his greed by citing the law as a higher authority than morality; he is not ashamed of receiving a two-hundred-dollar reward because, he says, "it air lawful fur me to yearn it." In other words, he has a right to it. Kelsey says, contemptuously, "Lawful! . . . . Judas war a law-abidin' citizen. He mos' lawfully betrayed *his* frien' ter the law" (67). Kelsey relies on a higher standard than law for moral guidance, an unwritten code based on concern for others rather than arbitrary rules of societal justice. In Dorinda's actions, that moral standard first leads her to protect and then later reject Rick Tyler. When Rick is on the run from Sheriff Green, she treats him with kindness and gives him succor despite the legal ramifications. Later, when Rick refuses to clear Kelsey of charges that he aided Rick's escape, he protests that he is under no legal obligation to do so. But that is not the point. He owes his word not to the law but to another human being.

It's hard to say which came first for the Prophet and Dorinda, their association with nature or their shared ethic of care, but the two concerns are linked in some way. Perhaps it is their ethics of care that makes them sensitive to natural beauty and sanctity, or perhaps their sensitivity to nature gives rise to their ethic of care. It is telling that the only representative of the law in the book, Sheriff Green, is also the most oblivious to natural beauty.

Of course, the Cayce men reject the law as well. In defending their support for Rick Tyler, one of the Cayce sons says, "I dunno ez he air a offender agin the law, an' 't ain't my say-so. I ain't a judge, an' thar ain't enough o' me fur a jury" (164). But the Cayce men do not reject the male preoccupation with justice that the law is intended to uphold. When they declare vengeance on the sheriff, it is because he has violated *their* code of justice; when they break the law by moonshining, it is because they feel they have a right to, a right based on a sense of their individual rights and their ancestral claim to their land. While nature seems a morally beneficial influence on Dorinda, so that her reliance on some sort of "natural law" guides her to virtue, it leads the men of her family to violence. Their relationship with nature is based on the patriarchal logic of domination, on principles of self-interest, and on assumptions about their right to the land. They deserve to be above the law, they believe, because their family has cleared the land and lived on it for a long time — since before the law came. They have a right to make a living and to be left alone, and so they are justified in seeking to kill the sheriff. In essence, the Cayces have constructed their own laws, basing them on the same premises as the laws of the settlement — the protection of individual rights. Without a change in their value system, nature is an uncertain moral guide for men; they become what we call *wild*, a loaded term that connotes a sort of frightening recklessness that goes beyond the borders of socially approved conduct. They seem to require some sort of codified law in order to behave morally.

Some might argue that even Hiram Kelsey goes astray when he dispenses with codified law in favor of natural instinct. He becomes confused about his values and beliefs while frequenting the mountains, and his self-sacrifice is a kind of suicide, which could be construed as a sin. In an early review of *Prophet*, William Dean Howells found Kelsey's death one of the few flaws in an otherwise exemplary work of American realism: "If Kelsey's substitution of himself for Micajah Green . . . was insanely voluntary, it was not interesting, for no act of lunacy is so, except pathologically; if it was voluntary, it was romantic, which is worse than uninteresting; if it was accidental, it was insignificant."[9] Howells seems to miss the obvious point that even the Cayce men grasp—that Kelsey's death was indeed a voluntary sacrifice. The suggestion is not that he's insane but that he's Christ-like, a martyr dying for the sins of others. Kelsey plays the role of sacrificial victim usually reserved for women in Murfree's stories. Of course, Dorinda too sacrifices something of herself, giving up her romantic prospects with Rick Tyler, knowing that there's no one else likely to engage her affection—and so she will end up alone. Perhaps the pattern of sacrifice so common in Murfree's stories arose from the circumstances of her life. Like her solitary protagonists who consistently forfeit or relinquish their chances at love, she never married. Like Kelsey, she roamed the mountains on horseback, since a childhood illness left her partially lame and so not very mobile afoot. Perhaps that association between author and character is what led an early reviewer to hail Murfree as the "Prophetess of the Great Smoky Mountains." But more likely, that perception of some link between Kelsey and Murfree arose from the recognition that both see something sacred in the land.

☙   ☙   ☙

Even critics generally sympathetic to Murfree seem able to muster only half-hearted praise for her, paying more attention to her faults than her strengths as a writer. In a 1967 critical biography—the only major study of Murfree done in the last half century—Richard Cary condemns her work for its "pedantry . . . and sermonizing," its "extravagant characters and implausible coincidence," its "excess of sentiment and pathos," its "persistent iterations of incident and plot," Murfree's "massive doses of panchromatic landscape, her ponderous Latinate diction," and her overelaborate sentence constructions. But these are the least of her problems, according to Cary. The "major contemporary objection to her works," he says, is Murfree's restricted focus on "the crudities of mountaineer life." He wonders if she would not have been better off writing about "the world of fashionable society, . . . the atmosphere of women's drawing rooms and polite rapier thrusts." He claims that "her most grievous misstep may have been when she turned away from the garden party and took the long path up the mountain."[10] All this from someone claiming to appreciate her work!

Some of Cary's judgments ring true, but some are troubling. To some extent his criticism seems to reflect the same attitude espoused by the fellow from UNC, specifically the idea that woman's place is decidedly *not* in the wild, neither in life nor in literature. Among Cary's criticisms is a scornful reference to her "constricted feminist perspective on society," illogically accompanied by his complaint that she dared to write about a world beyond the constraints of polite society where women were expected to dwell. But his concern is not just that Murfree as writer is out of place in terms of gender. Her very subject matter seems to constitute grounds for suspicion. Cary seems to consider writing about the mountains an inherently limited kind of endeavor, assuming that there is not enough material in the mountains for any kind of sustained literary endeavor. At the same time, he suggests that there is plenty to say, enough for a library full of stories, about the life of a twenty-foot square drawing room—which is, after all, a woman's proper place. In short, Cary is no ecofeminist.

Cary's bias against nature and women may also be the source of his complaint about Murfree's "massive doses of panchromatic landscape." His charge pinpoints the issue that most seems to preoccupy critics of Murfree: whether her extensive descriptions are justified. One camp claims that the descriptions, although powerful, are excessive, digressive, distracting, repetitious, monotonous, affected, and florid. Too often, they believe, descriptions interrupt the plot. For example, when Groundhog Cayce is about to issue the family death warrant for Sheriff Green, he pauses after outlining the ancestral history that he feels justifies his indignation, and Murfree inserts this apparently irrelevant description: "The moon, still in the similitude of a silver boat, swung at anchor in a deep indentation in the summit of Chilhowee that looked like some lonely pine-girt bay; what strange, mysterious fancies did it land from its cargo of sentiments and superstitions and uncanny influences!" (33). In the next sentence Groundhog orders his daughter to notch his rifle in honor of the sheriff, a sort of counting coup before the fact. Dorinda is horrified. She had been asking only for her family's sympathy, not their vengeance. Nevertheless, her brother marks the rifle barrel. The chapter concludes: "The moon had weighed anchor at last, and dropped behind the mountain summit, leaving the bay with a melancholy waning suffusion of light, and the night very dark" (34).

This is the sort of descriptive detail that has earned Murfree much critical abuse. Cary sums up the case against her, charging that Murfree "injects mountain vignettes into the midst of crucial action, between sentences in a conversation, into the thoughts and vision of characters—usually in terms they would not understand." (Presumably none of the Cayces had ever seen any ships or seaports.) Way back in 1889 Horace Scudder (who was generally sympathetic to Murfree and in fact intended to praise her descriptions) had commented on Murfree's "overworked landscape," noting especially that "she works her moon too hard." [11]

Those who have sought to defend Murfree's descriptions have tried to show that the descriptions are somehow relevant to the story — that they serve symbolically or thematically to further plot, develop character, or establish a mood. In those terms, the description of the moon mooring itself in Chilhowee could be considered justifiable because it builds suspense leading up to the climactic action of the chapter. Or because it reflects Dorinda's spirits. Another example: later in the story, after Dorinda has rejected Rick Tyler, Murfree offers this haunting description of seasonal change:

> All the leaves were falling. Crisp and sere, they carpeted the earth and fled before the wind. They seemed in some wise to illumine the slopes as they lay in long yellow vistas under the overhanging black boughs. Many a nest was revealed, — empty, swinging on the bare limb. The mountains near at hand were sad and sombre, the stark denuded forests showing the brown ground among the trees, and great jutting crags, and sterile stretches of outcropping rocks, and fearful abysmal depths of chasms — and streams, too, madly plunging. All the scene was stripped of the garb of foliage, and the illusion of color, and the poetry of the song birds and the flowers. More distant ranges were of a neutral vagueness, and farther still they seemed a nebulous gray under a gray sky. (286)

Clearly in this instance setting is used as a kind of objective correlative to Dorinda's psyche — it is the fall of her spirits. This is the sort of prose that defenders of Murfree's descriptive bent seize on. Harry Warfel, for example, praises Murfree's ability to "adapt the setting to present the metaphor and the mood of the story. All scenes are emotionally toned, so that they serve both as setting and as images interpreting the characters' thoughts and actions." What is striking about arguments like that is that even Murfree's advocates share the assumption that description for its own sake, mere "word-painting" (a pejorative description repeated by many early reviewers) is indefensible. Even those who admire Murfree's descriptions do so by contending that the descriptions serve some larger purpose, contributing to mood or character development. The objection of those who do not admire the descriptions is that they add little to plot development. [12]

To some extent, the same criticism of purposeless description is directed at local color writing in general. The premise is that descriptions of place must be justified by their contributions to what really matters in literature:

character or plot. Setting should somehow advance the story line; the first things we learn about stories are that they are based on some sort of conflict and that the plot must progress in a linear way toward some sort of climax. But that may be only one kind of story, a male story, an outgrowth of the patriarchal tendency to think in terms of implicitly conflictive binary oppositions. It may be that the critical insistence that everything contribute to the forwarding of plot reflects a cultural bias that in turn reflects a gender bias. Perhaps women, freed of literary traditions based on male narrative models, would tell different kinds of stories, based on the dynamics of connection instead of conflict.

In a study of "The Female Geography of Sarah Orne Jewett's *The Country of the Pointed Firs*," Elizabeth Ammons contends that the dramatic structure of Western narratives typically reflects patriarchal thinking—"grounded in separation and aggression" and proceeding in a linear way toward a climax. (No sexual pun intended by Ammons, but French feminists like Hélène Cixous do make the point that male narrative practice, with its emphasis on progression to climax, is related to male sexual behavior.) In contrast, says Ammons, Jewett's novel is grounded in connection and structured like a web rather than a line, moving out and back again from a central point rather than progressing ever onward and upward in its plot.[13]

Murfree did not forsake traditional plot line to the extent that Jewett did. In fact, the charge that her plots were hackneyed suggests that she relied too much upon traditional narrative forms. But I can see in her digressive descriptions evidence that she was not wholly committed to the premise that everything must contribute to the forwarding of the plot line. Murfree typically uses place description to communicate feeling, in part as a means of revealing character (which her defenders have found acceptable), but in part too, I suspect, because setting matters to her for its own sake, and because she is interested in exploring connections between humans and their environment as well as presenting intrahuman conflict. As Scudder wrote in defense of Murfree's descriptive powers, "For her, it is not a landscape with figures, nor a group with a landscape background. By a unity of impression nature and human nature are constantly present to her, and even when some bold action is in progress she cannot help feeling that the mountains, the trees, the sun, moon, and stars, are not merely spectators, but participants."[14] Murfree's finest writing appears when she suspends plot to allow herself some momentary indulgence in scenic absorption. The way to enjoy Murfree's prose is to slow down and savor the descriptions rather than hurry through them to find out what happens next—what happens next, that is, to the human characters. For to Murfree, "what happens"—the plot, the story line—involves nature as well as people.

❧   ❧   ❧

So is Murfree an ecofeminist? It seems to me that in *The Prophet of the Great Smoky Mountains* she achieves a synthesis of sorts, creating a narrative that pursues an advancing plot line toward a climax, founded on conflict—while also telling, concurrently, another story, where place matters as much as plot and connectedness matters as much as conflict. And she clearly approves of her protagonists' sensitivity to nature and their sense of the natural world's spiritual value. But Murfree does not seem optimistic about how such attitudes fare in the world. Her protagonists' stories are not happy ones. The Prophet dies, the heroine pines away. One prominent contemporary critic speaks of "the power and promise of ecofeminism," suggesting that it can revolutionize human behavior and save the planet.[15] Murfree has a bleaker ecofeminist vision. In a culture that devalues nature, those who are associated with nature are similarly devalued. They suffer, the oppressors triumph.

In its bleak view of the consequences of an association with nature, Murfree's work might be seen as anticipating the objections of many feminists to ecofeminist ideas. Ynestra King points out that while ecofeminists see "the woman/nature connection [as] potentially liberating," others see it as "simply a rationale for the continued subordination of women." The latter argument dates back to Simone de Beauvoir's *The Second Sex* in the 1950s. Beauvoir said that to achieve full status in society—to become liberated—women must sever their association with nature and, in Linda Vance's words, seek "full integration . . . into the 'man's world'" of culture.[16] That integration into patriarchal culture is something that the women in Murfree's stories (or characters like Kelsey who are associated with female traits) are consistently denied. But that's not really the source of the sorrow. The real tragedy is not that women are denied entrance to the world beyond the mountains but that their relationships with men are not sustainable in the mountains. The fault for that does not lie in the mountains, which continue to provide the attractions of natural beauty and psychic solace. Even if her female protagonists forsake marriage, they still have their life in the mountains, and that too is a consummation devoutly to be wished. For Dorinda Cayce, nature is her companion, and it is home. The greater loss is that of her male characters, who also lose their chance at love but in addition cannot find comfort or moral guidance in nature.

Another objection to the ecofeminist association of women and nature is that it may have a negative impact on our valuing not just of women but of nature as well, for, as Patrick Murphy points out, "designating an entity [the earth] female in a patriarchal culture guarantees its subservient status." [17] In Murfree's case, according to one critic, the ecofeminist bent of her fiction may have led to the devaluing of Appalachia that persists in the American mind. Allen Batteau in *The Invention of Appalachia* argues that Murfree's associations of women with nature played a "pivotal role" in codifying the southern mountains as a "domestic preserve" separate and distanced from mainstream American civilization, untouched by progress.[18] But that devaluing seems more the work of later writers who saw nature as a force of mental and moral deterioration whose end product is the hillbilly. For Murfree, nature remains valued to the end, despite all that is relinquished or sacrificed for its sake.

❁   ❁   ❁

In the morning David and I say goodbye to Hannah, Chris, and Adam. We won't see them again. Up and on the trail early, we walk five miles through morning fog by 9 A.M. Two hours later we reach the Snake Den Ridge trail junction, where David and I split up. He's headed home, I'm trying to cover a few more miles on this, my last full day in the Smokies. Onward, upward, following that pine-shaped arrow on the Appalachian Trail markers, following the line of the trail northward along the Appalachian Ridge.

Thinking about narrative, I'm beginning to understand why so few women are out hiking long stretches of the A.T. If the trail is a story line, it's a linear narrative. A male narrative about escaping from social constraints in order to search for identity, to find oneself, to test oneself, to contest against the elements, to conquer, to reach the end. It is a story line in which the protagonist self must display certain qualities of character in order to succeed: determination and fortitude and perseverance get the hiker up a steep climb or through a long, hard day. The preoccupation with individual identity, the structure of opposition and conflict, the sense of progress through time and space, the emphasis on strength and endurance — these are ways of being that in our culture are associated with the masculine.

It strikes me that the universal symbols for male and female suggest something about gender differences in narrative. Emerging from a central circle (the body? earth?), the male symbol is an arrow, implying outward movement, progression. The female symbol is a cross emerging from the same circle. The outward movement is not perpetual, it is bounded, and the crossbar partially deflects the outward movement in other directions, to either side.

Perhaps there's more there than simply some suggestion about narrative structure. Something about male versus female experiences of the world, the kinds of gender differences out of which narrative differences grow. In his essay "A Land of One's Own: Gender and Landscape," Stephen Trimble tries to sort out why nonfictional nature writing has been a genre dominated by men. He suggests that in part it's because writing by women in general has been undervalued and because the natural history essay is a specialized pursuit and women may prefer the "more creative synthesis of human and landscape concerns" that is possible in fiction (like Murfree's *Prophet*). But Trimble says the explanation also has to do with differing experiences of nature in childhood. Boys are given plenty of freedom to roam, gaining knowledge about their environment and confidence in their abilities to cope with it. Girls on the other hand are encouraged to develop a relationship with the land close to home and as part of a social experience — by gardening or gathering berries or flowers, for example.[19] When my wife wants to get outside, she takes the kids out into the backyard, to fill the birdfeeders and feed the cats, or they go up the road to the neighboring farm, to see the sheep and cows. I'd rather drive an hour or so to a state park and a bona fide hiking trail, in the slim hope of spotting a beaver or a coyote.

Trimble makes a case that neither relationship to nature is complete. In their encounters with nature, catching snakes and torturing bugs, boys learn the logic of domination and fail to develop a sense of connection — to either the earth or other people; girls are discouraged from testing themselves in natural environments as a way of developing a strong sense of self. Trimble hopes to make available to his own children the best of both approaches to the world, "integrating sensitivity and strength, turning to the earth as a setting and source for both."[20]

I suppose that ultimately I'm not an ecofeminist. In my maleness I value nature for the sense of freedom I get from it, for the feeling of liberation from the constraints of human communities, for the sense of self I find there, and for the opportunity for self-development that it affords me. I value the attributes of fortitude that the trail builds in me. And in others. Entering the Smokies, I'd dreamed of someday hiking the trail with my son. But surely my daughter could stand to gain something from that sort of adventure, too. To look at a map and get a sense of where she is and where she's going, to feel those miles passing by, to be free of expectations about how young women ought to behave, and to simply be herself, to devote herself for a few months to the project of clarifying for herself who she is, to show herself and the world that she has the wherewithal to accomplish whatever task she sets for herself—these are things that might be especially beneficial to a girl growing up in a society that would seek to contain her spirit within the rigid boundary lines of restrictive codes governing female behavior.

But if I am no ecofeminist, I surely could learn something from ecofeminist values. Something about stopping to smell the laurel, or to watch the play of shadow on rock, or to examine the intricate patterns of a wildflower in bloom, or to feel coldstreamwater drip from my beard. To interrupt my forward progess, forget about where I'm headed, and linger in the now. To enjoy the setting as well as to trace a developing story line. To explore the world but also to discover it close at hand and underfoot.

4

Horace Kephart's "Man's Game" and the Community of *Our Southern Highlanders*

In *Backpacker Magazine's Guide to the Appalachian Trail*, Jim Chase says that many A.T. thru-hikers are engaged in a "vision quest." It's a concept he's borrowed from native American traditions describing an initiation into adulthood via the ritualistic journey of an individual heading off alone into the world in search of spiritual enlightenment.[1] The other main purpose of a thru-hike, says Chase, is to seek adventure. Both of these are individualistic motives, where some sort of self-gratification is the goal. But whether they're embarked on a pilgrimage or an exploration, often what thru-hikers discover en route is a society of kindred spirits. They speak of the trail as a "linear community," with its own communication system (the trail registers), its own lingo, a shared set of values (much preoccupation with blister care, water purification techniques, mileage, and yearnings for pizza, beer, and ice cream), even a shared sense of identity that differentiates its members from outsiders — often with some haughty scorn for the outsiders.

In the registers one gets word of the hikers ahead, of their experiences, of their state of mind and soul. From Georgia through the Smokies I've been following the adventures of a group of hikers who were at first hiking separately but by the Smokies were together most nights, apparently enjoying a traveling party. At each shelter, I seek out the jottings of the most articulate, especially those who seem to appreciate literature. Back on Tray Mountain, in Georgia, a woman named Pigpen, one half of the Granola Girls, kept up her spirits on a miserably cold rainy day by copying down E. E. Cummings's "in Just- / spring when the world is mud- / luscious" and "puddle-wonderful." Moonchild is carrying a book of literary quotations and he copies one into a register every evening, words for the world from Thoreau, Wendell Berry,

Chief Seattle, Harriet Beecher Stowe, Robert Frost. Other hikers respond to Moonchild's quotes, discussing how they explain or reflect the experiences of their hike, or at times quarreling with the sentiments expressed. It's real-world literary criticism.

The registers are also full of banter and information. Pigpen's partner Puck complains good-naturedly about "PUDS" in northern Georgia—Pointless Ups and Downs—to viewless summits and streamless gaps. Northbounders leave notes for southbounders, telling them where to get off the trail for a good meal, or supplies, or a shower. Many write knowledgably and with sensitivity of things they've seen and heard and felt that day—a bluebird in the laurel, says one, or was it an indigo bunting? The delicate bells on the underside of a Solomon's seal, the snowflake-bloom of Queen Anne's lace. Fiery azalea splattering red in the woods. A bear off to the side of the trail, chasing a dog. Churned-up earth, sign of wild boar. An owl in the night, the squawk of its prey. Exhilaration on a summit. Loneliness. Appreciation.

Pack finally off after a long, sweet day on the trail, perspiration cooling on their backs, taking a swig of water while scanning the register, their readers understand.

It is this sort of communal connection that distinguishes the Appalachian Trail from other long-distance hiking trails. It also makes some die-hard outdoorsy types scornful of an A.T. hike as a wilderness experience. But the assumption that wilderness must or should be equated with human solitude (or absence) is open to challenge. For most of our history, human beings have lived in the wild and been part of it. Poet and wilderness philosopher Gary Snyder writes that "it has always been part of basic human experience to live in a culture of wilderness. . . . Nature is not a place to visit, it is *home*." [2] If there is a central theme of Snyder's important book *The Practice of the Wild*, that's it. And he does not mean people are at home in the woods only when they are alone. Traditionally, the wild has been the setting for human societies.

It's a large claim that Snyder makes, for the compatibility of community and the wild, and I'd like to believe in it. But I'm not sure about the permanency of the trail as community. I mean, if its residents are constantly in motion, and if its citizenry changes every year, what kind of community can it be? The obvious answer: only a temporary one. A community is supposed to give us some kind of grounding in the world, some sense of belonging to something larger than ourselves. I'm not sure if the typical hiker's preoccupation with matters of the self can be compatible with the commitment to place and one's neighbor that are an essential part of belonging to a community. These same challenges to the concept of community apply not just to the Appalachian Trail but to any place we might consider wilderness. It's the place where we go to get the measure of our selves, or where we go to get away from the constraints upon our freedom that are inherent in our responsibilities to the communities we've left behind. Then again, the wild might indeed be the best place for humans to negotiate the conflicting claims of self and community, a neutral setting where both solitude and companionship can be found, both to a degree that is not always possible in civilization.

A search for the self, the discovery of a community—this is the sort of exploration that most A.T. hikers are engaged in. And it has its literary precedent in the life and works of the most famous writer of the Smoky Mountains, Horace Kephart.

❁   ❁   ❁

Kephart's great-great-grandfather was an early settler in the Allegheny Mountains in central Pennsylvania, west of the Susquehanna, at the turn of the nineteenth century.[3] After the Civil War, when Horace, an only child, was five, his family moved to central Iowa. Kephart grew up roaming the prairie and reading a lot; *Robinson Crusoe* was a favorite. As a teen, he went to Western College in Iowa, Lebanon Valley College in Pennsylvania, and Boston University, and in 1880 he began a career as a librarian, working at Cornell, Yale, and the St. Louis Mercantile Library, where he developed a superb collection of western Americana. Kephart was writing articles while he worked as a librarian, mostly on bibliographical matters of interest mainly to other librarians. But after 1897 he stopped publishing scholarly works and began to write on American history and guns and outdoor life. He also began to neglect his library work and to take frequent camping trips to the Ozarks, often alone. A drinking problem developed. When he was forced to resign in 1903, his wife, Laura, took their children to her family in Ithaca. Kephart later told friends that he had caught Laura in the midst of an act of adultery. Though his youngest son reported that his parents had an understanding and real affection between them, they never reconciled.

Trying to sort out his life, Kephart returned to his family cemetery in Pennsylvania. Looking at the weathered inscriptions, he apparently longed for the frontier life his ancestors had lived. According to one story, he took out a map and compass while visiting his father's home and drew a series of concentric circles, with Dayton, Ohio, at the center, trying to find the nearest blank space. He said he was looking for "a Back of Beyond," "terra incognita." He found it in the Smokies.

Kephart arrived in the mountains west of Asheville in the summer of 1904, living in a tent by a tributary of the Tuckaseegee from August through October. Then he moved on to a cabin by an abandoned copper mine on the Little Fork of the Sugar Fork of Hazel Creek. He arrived in the area ill (or drunk, according to one source), but he soon recovered and began to make a living publishing articles in outdoor magazines like *Sports Afield* and *Field and Stream*.[4] A couple of years later he reworked these articles and gathered them under the title *Camping and Woodcraft*, which he revised and expanded several times. Enormously and enduringly popular throughout the twentieth century—"the camper's bible," Michael Frome calls it—*Camping and Woodcraft* is still in print, having been reissued, in various forms, about sixty times.[5]

Much of the book's information on equipment is dated, but it's still a good read, inspiring in its evocation of camping's spiritual attractions and interesting stylistically. Kephart deftly weaves technical information and practical advice with quotations from literature (he opens with a pertinent epigraph from Chaucer: "So priketh hem Nature in hir corages,—/ Thanne longen folk to goon on pilgrimages"), philosophical musings on the attractions of the outdoors, and anecdotes and adventures drawn from history, literature, and his own experience.

For all its attractions, *Camping and Woodcraft* is not Kephart's most famous work. Almost from the time he arrived in the Smokies he began taking notes for a book on the people of the mountains. In 1907 he began to travel to other parts of the southern Appalachians, to see if his observations in the Smokies held true for other parts of Appalachia. Three years later he returned to the Smokies to live in Bryson City and continued his copious notetaking. *Our Southern Highlanders* came out in 1913, then was revised and expanded in 1922. Just as *Camping and Woodcraft* has remained perenially acclaimed as a guide to the backwoods, *Our Southern Highlanders* has proved to be, still, the most popular account of the people who *live* in the backwoods of the southern Appalachians. "The most vigorous and honest book written on the Appalachian South," one critic calls it. George Ellison, the editor of the most recent edition of the book, goes further, terming it "the finest regional study yet written by an American." Though it's a very different book from *Camping and Woodcraft*, it is similar in its blending of genres and styles. Ellison calls it "a literary work that is at once historical, sociological, and autobiographical."[6] Ostensibly a descriptive piece, it is enlivened by humor, character sketches, dialogue, and stories of Kephart's adventures. His particular talent is to make what he writes about seem personal and immediate and familiar, rather than some dry object of study regarded from a safe and neutral distance.

After publishing his two great works, Kephart continued writing for outdoor magazines. In the 1920s he worked on a novel, *Smoky Mountain Magic*, as yet unpublished. The last years of his life were devoted to writing articles supporting the establishment of Great Smoky Mountain National Park and letters supporting the development of the Appalachian Trail. He helped plan the trail's route through the park. Just a few weeks before he died, in an automobile crash in 1931, a peak on the main divide of the Smokies was named for him. After his death, a local Boy Scout troop erected a monument to him at one of his favorite campsites, on Deep Creek. The plaque hails him as the "Dean of American Campers and one of the principal founders of the Great Smoky Mountains National Park."

❧   ❧   ❧

On the northeast side of Mt. Kephart, David and I get water at Icewater Spring and rest while paging through the register in the shelter there. Walking on, we soon come to Charlie's Bunion, where the trail winds around a rocky outcropping that seems on the brink of tumbling down the steep mountainside. It's a long, long way down, with only a few feet of trail between the rock and the green abyss of the valley below. One hiker said that if you fell you'd have to pack a lunch to keep from starving to death before you hit bottom.[7] The name of this landmark too can be traced back to Kephart. The story goes that he and a friend named Charlie discovered this formation shortly after a landslide created it in 1929 and named it in honor of Charlie's aching feet.

David and I hike on as the Trail threads along the ridgetop. David tells me about his visit, on an earlier hike, to the site of Kephart's cabin. There's no sign or historical marker, just two rusted buckets to mark the place. A couple of nights ago we stayed at another of Kephart's hangouts, Derrick Knob, where a shelter now stands on the site of a herder's hut that Kephart used to stay in on hunting trips.

We talk about what brought Kephart to these mountains. Was he getting away from something—an unhappy marriage, an unsatisfying career, the velvet-lined trap of the bottle? Or was he going *to* something? Was he running away from home or finding it?

❧   ❧   ❧

From *Camping and Woodcraft*:

First, and above all, be plain in the woods. In a far way you are emulating those grim heroes of the past who made the white man's trails across this continent. We seek the woods to escape civilization for a time, and all that suggests it. Let us sometimes broil our venison on a sharpened stick and serve it on a sheet of bark. It tastes better. It gets us closer to Nature, and closer to those good old times when every American was considered "a man for a' that" if he proved it in a manful way. And there is a pleasure in achieving creditable results by the simplest means. When you win your own way through the wilds with axe and rifle you win at the same time an imperturbability of a mind at ease with itself in any emergency by flood or field. Then you feel that you have red blood in your veins, and that it is good to be free and out of doors. It is one of the blessings of wilderness life that it shows us how few things we need in order to be perfectly happy. (1:109–10)

Woodcraft may be defined as the art of finding one's way in the wilderness and getting along well by utilizing Nature's storehouse. When we say that Daniel Boone, for example, was a master woodsman, we mean that he could confidently enter an unmapped wilderness, with no outfit but what was carried by his horse, his canoe, or on his own back, and with the intention of a protracted stay; that he could find his way through the dense forest without man-made marks to guide him; that he knew the habits and properties of trees and plants, and the ways of fish and game; that he was a good trailer and a good shot; that he could dress game and cure peltry, cook wholesome meals over an open fire, build adequate shelter against wind and rain, and keep himself warm through the bitter nights of winter—in short, that he knew how to utilize the gifts of Nature, and could bide comfortably in the wilderness without help from outside. (2:16)

The man who goes afoot, prepared to camp anywhere and in any weather, is the most independent fellow on earth. He can follow his bent, obey the whim of the hour, do what he pleases whenever he pleases, without deference to anybody, or care for any beast of burden, or obedience to the course of any current. He is footloose and free. (2:97)

From a selfish standpoint, the solitary camper revels in absolute freedom. Any time, anywhere, he can do as he pleases. There is no anxiety as to whether his mates are having a good time, no obligation of deference to their wishes. Selfish? Yes, but, *per contra*, when one is alone he is boring nobody, elbowing nobody, treading on nobody's toes. He is neither chiding nor giving unasked advice. Undeniably he is minding his own business — a virtue to cover multitudes of sins. (2:148)

These excerpts reveal the recurring themes of *Camping and Woodcraft* —
the emphasis on freedom, simplicity, independence, self-reliance, and manliness; the idealization of the frontier life and the frontiersman; the yearning for the past; the rejection of civilization. In a way, the extent to which
Kephart stresses individualistic values is surprising, since the first volume,
Camping, is intended for well-equipped *groups* of outdoorsmen; only the
Woodcraft volume is ostensibly written with solitary backpackers in mind,
"those who travel light, in the real wilderness, rove about a good deal, and
sometimes scatter, every man for himself, with his life in his own hands" (2:
17). Even when he describes the makeup of the ideal group, Kephart em-
phasizes the virtues of the individualist: "There are other qualities in a good
camp-mate that are rarer than fortitude and endurance. Chief of these is a
love of Nature for her own sake — not the 'put on' kind that expresses itself
in gushy sentimentalism, but that pure, intense, though ordinarily mute affection which finds pleasure in her companionship and needs none other."
He recommends "good-hearted, manly fellows, who will take things as they
come, do their fair share of the camp chores, and agree to have no arguments
before breakfast. There are plenty of such men, steel-true and blade-straight"
(1:27–28). In short, the strong, silent type who doesn't really need anybody
else and wouldn't say so if he did and certainly wouldn't spoil the beauty of
a moment by talking about it — that's Kephart's ideal camper. John Wayne
with a walking stick.

Our Southern Highlanders begins in the same vein. In the first chapter
Kephart explains that what he saw as the chief allure of the southern Appalachians was that they were far outside the mainstream of American civilization. He could find almost no information on the area in libraries, other than
Murfree's fiction and a Poe story, apparently "A Tale of the Ragged Mountains," which Kephart says depicts Appalachia's people as "an uncouth and
fierce race of men, inhabiting a wild mountain region little known" (13).
They live "ghettoed in the midst of a civilization that is aloof from them as
if it existed on another planet." Or as if it existed in another era: "Time has
lingered in Appalachia. The mountain folk still live in the eighteenth century. The progress of mankind from that age to this is no heritage of theirs."
They "are still thinking essentially the same thoughts, still living in much
the same fashion as did their ancestors in the days of Daniel Boone." Their
mountain environment is "a labyrinth that has deflected and repelled the
march of our nation for three hundred years" (18–19).

Clearly, Kephart buys into the image of Appalachia as the backwards
backwoods. But for him that is precisely the attraction, for he is searching for

some place remote from contemporary civilization, a remnant of frontier where he can match his mettle against the woods. Here is his own description of what he was looking for in the Smokies: "When I went south into the mountains I was seeking a Back of Beyond. . . . With an inborn taste for the wild and romantic, I yearned for a strange land and a people that had the charm of originality. . . . I had a passion for early American history; and, in Far Appalachia, it seemed that I might realize the past in the present, seeing with my own eyes what life must have been to my pioneer ancestors of a century or two ago. Besides, I wanted to enjoy a free life in the open air, the thrill of exploring new ground, the joys of the chase, and the man's game of matching my woodcraft against the forces of nature, with no help from servants or hired guides" (29–30).

This is the "man's game" that he gives sporting tips about in *Camping and Woodcraft*, a contest of the lone man against nature, where the Hall of Famers are Daniel Boone and Davy Crockett. Kephart admits that he initially saw the playing field as being devoid of other contestants: "For a long time my chief interest was not in human neighbors, but in the mountains themselves—in that mysterious beckoning hinterland which rose right back of my chimney and spread upward, outward, almost to three cardinal points of the compass, mile after mile, hour after hour of lusty climbing—an Eden still unpeopled and unspoiled." At first he played his man's game in solitude: "I loved of a morning to slip on my haversack, pick up my rifle, or maybe a mere staff, and stride forth alone over haphazard routes, to enjoy in my own untutored way the infinite variety of form and color and shade, of plant and tree and animal life, in that superb wilderness that towered there far above all homes of men" (50).

In his emphasis on manliness and solitude, and in his rejection of emotion (or at least any outer expression of it) and civilization, Kephart borrows from a story line once considered the essence of American literature—the story of the rugged individualist outcast from society, finding solace in the woods, displaying those good old American virtues of independence and freedom. The male bias of this story line has been exposed by Nina Baym in her important study of canon formation, "Melodramas of Beset Manhood: How Theories of American Fiction Exclude Women Authors." What has been seen as the classic American story, says Baym, typically involves an individual's alienation from a "society [that] exerts an unmitigatedly destructive pressure on individuality." Society is the "adversary" in the individual's quest for "self-definition," and the wild is the arena where that quest can be fulfilled: "The essential quality of America comes to reside in its unsettled wilderness and the opportunities that such a wilderness offers to the individual as the medium on which he may inscribe, unhindered, his own destiny and his own nature." Baym's objection to this story line is that it favors the individualistic traits and geographic mobility more common to male than female experience, and it has consistently associated women with the forces of civilization that must be rejected or overcome — its "social conventions and responsibilities and obligations," all those things that might tend to restrict one's freedom.[8] In selecting this sort of story as the classic representation of American values, critics and editors systematically (if not consciously) deem stories reflecting values associated with female experience — community, communication, commitment to one another — as of lesser importance. But there's something else to wonder about in the story of the individual alone in the woods — the assumption, shared even by critics like Baym, that the wild is the domain of alienation, antithetical to human society.

❧   ❧   ❧

On my last night in the Smokies, after David has returned home, I meet up with a hiker who goes by the name of Wolverine. Turns out that he had started out from Springer Mountain the same day I did, and he's been about half a day behind me for the past three weeks. He gives me news of people I'd met and passed. Wolverine has a ready laugh and a hoard of Snickers bars that he's glad to share. We make a fire that night, one that Wolverine calls a "white man's fire — lots of smoke. Indian's fire small," he says, "but Indian gets warm." I enjoy his company.

As it happens, we hike at the same pace, so Wolverine and I spend much of the next few days walking and talking together. He helps me fix a peeling boot sole with some shoe glue that he's carrying. We pass a couple named Phil and Sarah — the Trail Snails, they call themselves. Phil's a grad student in history working on a study of the Pan-Indian movement (of intertribal alliances) in the late eighteenth century. Sarah makes funky hats that she sells at craft fairs. Together they play old-timey music; she plays banjo, he fiddle. That night, Wolverine and the Trail Snails and I share a shelter. Sarah writes in the register that they'd been passed on the trail that day by "some larger species of flora and fauna — Evergreen and Wolverine." No wonder we hike at the same pace — we even rhyme.

Next day, on an expansive grassy bald called Max Patch, Wolverine and I spend several sunny hours basking and betting Snickers bars on small things like whether we'll see a hawk up there, or whether the Trail Snails will catch up to us while we're up on the bald. Since only Wolverine has any Snickers

Bars (the legal tender of the Trail), he lets me win most of the bets. When we get more personal in our conversation, he tells me of his years-long, country-crossing search for his birth mother, of his marriage that lasted only a couple of months, a coupling inspired by pregnancy rather than love. We talk about our kids and bring out pictures from our packs. In the shelter register that night we read about the fun the group ahead of us had up on Max Patch. The Granola Girls, Green Lantern, Avalon, Mad Markham, and Moonchild spent an afternoon on the bald tumbling and rolling down the hillsides.

I feel like I am surrounded by friends. Some of them I have not even met.

After a couple of hundred miles, it's almost like the trail changes direction, no longer leading only onward, or inward. The change in direction is more metaphoric than geographic. The trail begins in a wilderness, a testing ground for the self, the unbounded territory of individual freedom. But it turns out that it leads to a friendly town where Main Street is about a foot wide and two thousand miles long and where folks still say hello to strangers. Maybe it's home.

But sometimes the companionship gets in the way. Wolverine tells me that he had attempted a thru-hike the year before. He hooked up with a group of about a dozen people that generally shared shelters each night. They had a lot of fun, but Wolverine said he did not have much time to be alone. He was with people, establishing relationships with *them*, and not with nature or with himself. Some sexual liaisons sprang up, and dissolved, and jealousies and tensions followed. Since they were all headed in the same direction, it was difficult to separate from the pack. Somewhere in the Shenandoahs, Wolverine tired of the squabbling and hitched home.

❁   ❁   ❁

In the course of *Our Southern Highlanders*, Kephart tries to negotiate a middle ground between his enthusiasm for the wild, which he sees very much as the realm of individual freedom, and his desire to join the human commmunity of the mountains. He had left family and attachments behind in the North, soothed his isolated soul in the Appalachians, and then found himself on the outskirts of a community that shared many of his values, like his respect for nature, his love of hunting and moonshine, even the premium he put on individual freedom. The book explores the inherent tension between the competing attractions of individualism and community in the wild, and it traces his own fluctuating status as sometimes member of the community and sometimes outright outsider.

Kephart's advances toward membership in the community of the southern highlanders begin in the fourth chapter, "A Bear Hunt in the Smokies."
Set in the herder's hut on Derrick Knob—with one room in Tennessee, the
other in North Carolina—the chapter is essentially about Kephart's initiation into a fraternity of hunters. It also serves to introduce topics that will be
discussed later in the book—those things that he says make the "mountaineers of the South" a distinct culture: their dialect, customs, character, and
"self-conscious isolation" (16). Surprisingly, Kephart plays the role of green-
horn, the least competent hunter of the group, unfamiliar not just with the
vocabulary of his fellow hunters but with the lay of the land. That's a surprising role for Kephart to play since he was undoubtedly more adept at outdoor
skills than his companions and more knowledgable about the woods despite
being an admitted outsider. In *Camping and Woodcraft* he boasts that not
long after moving to the Appalachians he "was going even 'farther back'
than the native woodsmen themselves," identifying more edible plants than
the locals could and improving their ways of "dressing and keeping game
and fish" (2:14). Perhaps his pose as novice shows that this story occurred
before he learned his way around the Smokies; perhaps even if he was
knowledgable it shows his willingness to keep learning. Perhaps he is consciously playing a role his readers could relate to, inexpert and curious, eager
to learn directly from the more experienced locals. But I wonder too if he is
not downplaying his skills and sublimating his ego in an attempt to make
friends. Conscious of his status as an outsider, maybe Kephart hesitated to
show off his woodsmanship, knowing that good will comes from allowing
others to give, to show their kindness.

Though it is nonfiction, Kephart arranges the chapter as a story—one
critic calls the chapter "found fiction"—full of dialogue, details of characterization, and an elegiac theme on the passing of a way of life.[9] The story
begins with four dogs and five men huddled in the cabin amid a fierce windstorm. The men pass around "a bottle of soothing-syrup that was too new to
have paid tax" (81), making plans for their hunt the next day and trading
stories. Doc Jones tells of another windstorm, a "turrible vyg'rous blow," that
ripped his coat off and lifted him off Thunderhead and into the sky: "About
half an hour later," he says, "I lit *spang* in the mud, way down yander in
Tuckaleechee Cove—yes, sir: ten mile as the crow flies, and a mile deeper
'n trout-fish swim." One of his companions, going along with the yarn, asks
which "buryin'-ground" he was "planted" in. To which Doc replies that he
didn't die, he just had "one tormentin' time" finding his hat (78).

This little tall tale is certainly amusing, and it gives us some indication of the linguistic flavor of the mountaineers, but it also says something about Kephart's place in the group. In an article titled "In the Name of Wonder," Henry Wonham shows that tall tales predicate a sense of insider status to listeners who go along with the joke, and can even be used to "initiate new members" who can understand "how the rhetorical game is played." [10] Initiates demonstrate their understanding by accepting the tall tale on its own terms. They should not be duped by the lie, but neither should they challenge it. And they join the insiders by sharing in the cultural reference to common experience in a common environment. In the case of Doc Jones's story, the understood message is that it sure is windy up here in the Smokies.

In the bear hunt chapter Kephart learns much more about the customs and lore of the culture he is being initiated into — learning, for instance, that dreams foretell the success of a hunt, but that he must not tell what he dreamed of until the hunt is over "or it'll spile the charm" (83). A dream of stealing an overcoat, for instance, means you'll get a bear's hide. Kephart learns the lingo, asking what words mean even when his questions evoke the response, "*Good* la! whar was you fotch up?" (94) "Brigaty," for instance, means "stuck on hisself and wants to show off" — an adjective which Kephart works hard not to deserve. He is so well accepted by the hunters that they give him the best stand on the final day of the hunt.

Kephart further allies himself with the mountaineers by taking a stand with them against the incursions of civilization. When Kephart hears a train from a lumbering operation, he complains, "Slowly, but inexorably, a leviathan was crawling into the wilderness and was soon to consume it. 'All this,' I apostrophized, 'shall be swept away, tree and plant, beast and fish. Fire will blacken the earth; flood will swallow and spew forth the soil. The simple-hearted native men and women will scatter and disappear. In their stead will come slaves speaking strange tongues, to toil in the darkness under the rocks. Soot will arise, and foul gases; the streams will run murky death. Let me not see it!'" (104)

At the end of the story, Kephart tells of the death, two years later, of the dog Coaly, who before the hunt had been as green as Kephart but who earns renown for his part in taking down a bear. Coaly dies from a shot from a .30-.30 carbine that went right through a bear. Kephart precedes this anecdote with a conversation from a local hunter who complained about the overkill potential of "power-guns." Though Kephart himself was a gun enthusiast who later wrote a book called *Sporting Firearms* and designed a popular high-powered rifle bullet,[11] in the context of the story he suggests that these newfangled guns are part of the invasion of values from the outside that spells death to the way of life in the southern highlands. He may have come from the outside, but in his regard for the land he stands with the community in opposing the values of the outside.

In several subsequent chapters Kephart reenacts his progress from outsider to at least a peripheral member of the community as he investigates the topic of moonshining. Kephart confesses that he knew beforehand he was moving into moonshine country and that, to him, "this prospect was not unpleasant" (115). At first his inquiries about still operations are rebuffed, until he lets a neighbor know that he is merely curious about the process (and, presumably, a potentially valuable customer). The word spreads that Kephart is safe—"There is no telegraph, wired or wireless, in the mountains," he says, "but there is an efficient substitute" (124)—and therafter several moonshiners agree to be interviewed, even allowing him to take notes. Kephart vouches for their integrity, saying he "never met with any but respectful treatment from these gentry," and he defends their business on economic terms, against the prejudices of outsiders, saying bad roads necessitate the transport of their crops in the condensed form of corn whiskey (125). He speaks admiringly of the moonshiner's code, each "blockader" fighting fairly if single-handedly "against tremendous odds" (127). Though he professes to be an objective reporter whose "duty [is] to collect facts, whether pleasant or unpleasant, regardless of my own or any one else's bias," as he traces the history of the mountaineers' resistance to government taxation of the trade, he clearly sides with his moonshining neighbors. His ultimate complaint about Prohibition is that it damages "the moral fiber of the whole community" by increasing the profit margin so that some distillers become affluent and others jealous of that affluence and so willing to turn informer, until both sides become "mean, treacherous, dishonorable" (189). What he regrets most is the disruption of harmony in the community that he apparently considers himself part of. Deploring the "war between enforcement agents and blockaders," he complains that "*we* who live in the mountains are fairly within gun-crack of it" (189, emphasis mine).

His taste for moonshine is not all that gains Kephart admittance into the community of those he studies. His book itself gives him an "in." A chapter added to the book for the 1922 edition, "A Raid into the Sugarlands," describes Kephart's experience helping a friend, a federal officer, on a manhunt in the mountains. When he seeks lodging and a dinner at the home of a man named Jasper Fenn, Kephart is at first regarded with cool suspicion. Until, that is, he mentions another friend, whose photo the Fenns had seen in an early copy of *Our Southern Highlanders*. Kephart mentions, proudly, that the people of the mountains regard his book as accurate and fair, and when the Fenns learn that he is the author, they give him a warm welcome and a fine meal.

Kephart clearly develops respect for the people of Appalachia, at times identifies with them, and often seems almost protective of them in defending their way of life. He is especially passionate about defending their linguistic inventiveness. In a chapter on "The Mountain Dialect," he expresses his admiration for the range and creativity of their idioms, their "picturesque and pungent diction," its humor, "irreverence," and "scorn of sentimentalism" (372, 376). He sees in the language of the mountain folk evidence of their quick wit. But his discussion of the language of Appalachia reveals that ultimately Kephart is writing as an outsider, one who is impressed with the dialect but who does not speak it himself. It's a key distinction. Kephart can admire the culture of the southern highlanders, even side with it in opposition to the values of the outside world—but he can never be fully integrated into it. Even in the bear hunt chapter, Kephart realizes that he has not actually become one of the highlanders. He confesses that he got the best hunting stand precisely because he is perceived as an outsider: "Neighborly kindness moved them to do their best for the outlander," he says (98). Tellingly, his best friend seems to be the federal agent who took him on the manhunt, an employee of the Bureau of Indian Affairs who is trying to track down the source of liquor on the reservation. Their friendship is based in part upon a shared love of literature, a cultured appreciation that sets them apart from their neighbors in the mountains.

By chapter 12, "The Outlander and the Native," Kephart seems reconciled to his outsider status. He is treated well, he points out, but that's because hospitality is part of the highlander's code. For the last third of the book Kephart elaborates on the peculiarities of that code, on the unique way of life of the people, and on their distinctive history. And more and more he adopts an objective stance, no longer a participant in what he describes, and more willing to judge. He calls the subjects of his study a "strange race," repeatedly describing them as "primitive" and "feral," "unstarted" on the road to civilization (286, 349). More and more he relies on negative stereotypes and generalities in his descriptions. Example: "Many wear habitually a sullen scowl, hateful and suspicious, which in men of combative age, and often in the old women, is sinister and vindictive" (288). Theirs is a patriarchal culture, where the men exhibit "an indifference to woman's weakness, a disregard for her finer nature, a denial of her proper rank"—a line that tells us even more about Kephart's sexism than that of the mountaineers (331–32).

Kephart claims that he includes this sort of information as part of his pursuit of the truth, and it's not as if he suddenly becomes blind to any good in the people he's writing about. But he's observing from the outside, and maybe looking down. Whether he can become part of that society has been decided. He is not. What is left for Kephart to explore is the question of whether the community of the southern highlanders is a viable one.

❧   ❧   ❧

Wolverine remembers reading my entry in the register at Icewater Spring. The Granola Girls had been through just a few days before, gloating about their successful "yogi-ing" of some Snickers bars from some day hikers. "Yogi"—that's trail talk for relying on the esculent kindness of strangers, in other words for cadging food, à la the famous bear of Jellystone Park. In the register Puck left a hilarious description of a pack of binocular-eyed, field-guide-toting, polyester-panted day hikers, trail tourists. Even though I was amused, I added a note accusing her of acting "greener than thou"—just because day hikers don't have six months to devote to the trail doesn't mean they are unappreciative or undeserving of what's here. Perhaps I was being oversensitive, aware that I would not long be part of the community of thru-hikers. Perhaps I was disturbed that she was drawing the boundaries of the hiking community pretty narrowly. Thru-hikers, dressed in funky T-shirts and their worn wool socks drying on their packs—they're in. All others, especially those wearing checked pants and deodorant and who drove most of the way up the mountain—they're out.

I'm reminded of another Gary Snyder piece called "Why Tribe." It's about the counterculture, those who subvert the "hierarchy and specialization" of contemporary civilization, who believe that "man's natural being is to be trusted and followed" and "suspect that civilization may be overvalued." Who's in? "Men, women, and children—all of whom together hope to follow the timeless path of love and wisdom, in affectionate company with the sky, winds, and clouds, trees, waters, animals and grasses—this is the tribe." [12] The truth is that lots of those who seek and keep "affectionate company with the sky, winds, and clouds" are anything but subversive in their lifestyle and beliefs. It's not just the counterculture who are out here in the woods—it's mainstream America, and here is maybe the one place where we listen to each other. Out here I've got something in common with a cop who's interested in Cherokee myths, an elder in a fundamentalist church who can teach me about wildflowers, a business major with bad grammar who helps me fix my boots. They can all be part of my tribe. They may even wear Bermuda shorts.

❀   ❀   ❀

While Kephart finds fault with much in the social codes of the southern highlanders, he remains impressed by them for exhibiting the "manly" virtues that he celebrates in *Camping and Woodcraft*: self-reliance, independence, individualism, stoicism, freedom. They are a people formed by the wilderness, and they know it "for a tyrant, void of pity and of mercy, from whom nothing can be wrung without toil and the risk of death." Life is "one long, hard, cruel war against elemental powers," and to succeed demands skill in "warlike arts" and self-reliance (379). But as a "reward to those who endured," from this harshness emerged "the most outright independence to be had on earth. No king was so irresponsible as the pioneer." Their independence is "haughty," their individualism "intense." Isolated by geography, they willingly do without whatever society can offer: "To be free, unbeholden, lord of himself and his surroundings—that is the wine of life to a mountaineer" (380–81). But it is also the source of the threat to community values: "The very quality that is his strength and charm as a man—his staunch individualism—is proving his weakness and reproach as a citizen." The southern highlanders "recognize no social compact" (383). In short, it would seem that every fiber of their being revolts against the idea of community. To the extent that there is loyalty to others at all, it is limited to the clan, a tendency Kephart traces back to Scotland (via Pennsylvania and northern Ireland). But clan loyalty, because it takes precedence over social law, gets in the way of the establishment of any sort of community bonds. The highlander defends his kin no matter what crime he may have committed against any member of the community—any one of whom, if not a member of the clan, is an outsider.

Kephart wishes it were otherwise. He argues that there are strong common bonds that ought to be the essence of a community feeling among the southern highlanders: "Not only are they all closely akin in blood, in speech, in ideas, in manners, in ways of living; but their needs, their problems are identical throughout this vast domain" (385). The urge for freedom and independence is itself a common bond. Kephart makes a case for the southern mountaineers as exemplars of American virtues, perhaps in an attempt to make them members of a larger American community: "The strong and even violent independence that made them forsake all the comforts of civilization and prefer the wild freedom of the border . . . blazed forth at a happy time for this country when our liberties were imperilled" (439). He's referring, of course, to the Revolutionary War—the War for *Independence*—when most Americans shared the backwoodsmen's distrust of centralized authority. To treasure freedom and independence, to be self-reliant—hostilities with Great Britain made these part of the American way.

As much as Kephart admires these virtues, he also believes that the result in the southern mountains has been dissolution. Their geographic isolation and their attachment to home have left the people of Appalachia behind. Surprisingly, Kephart suggests that nature is partly to blame: it stifled ambition and "begat laziness and shiftless unconcern." Connected to nature as they are, they fell prey "to a law of Nature that dooms an isolated and impoverished people to deterioration" (445).

If Kephart confesses to being conflicted about nature's influence and about the ultimate value of individualism, he is similarly at odds with himself about the prospects for the future as progress makes its inroads into the mountains. For the most part, by the end of *Our Southern Highlanders*, he welcomes the prospect: "The mighty waterpower that has been running to waste since these mountains rose from the primal sea is now about to be harnessed in the service of man. . . . The highlander, at last, is to be caught up in the current of human progress" (451). Sometimes he views the change with resignation: "Commercialism has discovered the mountains at last, and no sentiment, however honest, however hallowed, can keep it out. The transformation is swift. Suddenly the mountaineer is awakened from his eighteenth-century bed by the blare of steam whistles and the boom of dynamite" (454). Sometimes he laments the change: "The curse of our invading civilization is that its vanguard is composed of men who care nothing for the welfare of the people they dispossess" (457). Among the causes for despair when civilization displaces the community of southern highlanders is their loss of identity: "Then it is 'good-by' to the old independence that made such characters manly" (457).

To become part of civilization, then, evidently means to lose the qualities of independence that make the highlanders distinct. But then a few pages later Kephart says that in the highlanders there are "certain sterling qualities of manliness that our nation can ill afford to waste" (465). It's a catch-22: civilization needs their virtues, the classic American virtues that arise from contact with the wild. But once civilization arrives, those virtues disappear.

Freedom and independence seem incompatible with civilization and difficult to accommodate within a community.

❧   ❧   ❧

Descending into Hot Springs, Wolverine and I move from early to late
spring. In the lower elevations, laurel is abundantly abloom. Approaching
town, I offer him a piece of gum — "to sweeten your breath," I say. Wolverine
says he could really use some in his armpits, and we book on down the trail
flapping our arms, working on imaginary gum. In town, we run into some
other hikers in a cafe, Green Lantern and Moonflower and the Lucky Bitch.
Later that day, a friend from Knoxville picks me up, and the next day I'm on
a Greyhound heading north. Later that summer I get a few postcards from
Wolverine. A couple of days north of Hot Springs, he writes, he caught up to
the Granola Girls. By the time they reached the Shenandoahs in Virginia,
he and Puck had a romance going.

When they reach Pennsylvania, I go to meet Wolverine and hike with him
for a day. I'm curious about meeting Puck as well as excited about seeing
Wolverine. I bring them a six-pack of Snickers Bars, but they're sick of them
by now. Puck just graduated from college with a degree in anthropology, and
she's planning to move west when she's done hiking. She laughs almost as
much as Wolverine, and they seem to get along great. I take a picture of
them resting by a spring, grinning. When I tell Puck that I chastised her in a
register for putting down day hikers, she says I misunderstood what she was
trying to say. But she does not take offense. We hike that day past a place
called the Pinnacle, and find four copperheads in a crack between two boulders at the summit, bundled and twined together in a sinuous snaky mass.

Though Puck and Wolverine do not plan to stay together all the way, that
autumn I get a postcard from them in Maine — they're about to climb Katahdin. In December, Wolverine sends a Christmas card and confesses that he's
having trouble adjusting to the civilized world. He feels out of place, can't
find a job, but isn't much concerned. The next spring I get a postcard from
him in Georgia. He says he and Puck lived together for a while in Seattle,
but it didn't work out. Now, for the third consecutive year, Wolverine is back
on the trail, heading north, alone.

5

Pilgrim at Tinker Cliffs

L EGS DANGLING over several hundred feet of Blue Ridge air, I'm resting on the jutting sandstone overhang of McAfee Knob, perhaps the number one photo-op of the whole Appalachian Trail. Below is a Virginia valley sprinkled with a few lovely farmhouses. From somewhere down there, from everywhere down there, comes the weird, wired sound of periodical cicadas. This is the year when they emerge from their grublike state underground, grow hard bodies and bulbous eyes, keen in unison like electricity seething, mate, lay eggs, and die. I search the valley, unsuccessfully, for a particular gleaming line of running water. My eye travels along the ridge of Tinker Mountain and across the valley to Tinker Cliffs. Beyond that, not yet visible, lies Tinker Creek.

Ordinarily, the sixteen miles along the ridge of Tinker Mountain from McAfee Knob to Tinker Creek would take about a day to walk. But I'm taking five days, so I can spend (or invest) time on the knob and the cliffs to observe the workings of nature and to ponder Annie Dillard's 1974 Pulitzer Prize–winning book, *Pilgrim at Tinker Creek*. I'm setting for myself a task I once gave a class that I took out to a stream on our campus. I asked them, after we'd read *Tinker Creek*, to "do an Annie Dillard"—to sit and think and look and write, to read and absorb and to let the reading infiltrate the seeing and thinking. Before I descend to the creek she wrote about, I want to savor Dillard's book and consider its chief mystery. Dillard's title proclaims that she's on a pilgrimage. A pilgrimage is a journey to a sacred place, a journey of exalted moral significance, a journey in search of spiritual enlightenment—whatever its goal, a pilgrimage involves a journey of some sort. I can see that Dillard is seeking enlightenment. I can see that she finds something sacred at Tinker Creek. But where's the journey? For the most part she stays at home, by the banks of Tinker Creek, occasionally wandering a few miles up and down its banks. She wrote much of the book while holed up in a windowless library carrel at nearby Hollins College. Hers is a pilgrimage that involves no grand peregrination.

The quick and easy answer to my question is that Dillard is on a pilgrimage of the soul. But there's a spiritual element to any pilgrimage, and by definition it is arrived at by means of a physical journey. A journey like one, say, on the Appalachian Trail. When they reach Tinker Mountain, northbound thru-hikers have come seven hundred miles from Springer Mountain, one-third of the way through their trip. If their walk is a pilgrimage, here is a good place to take spiritual stock. Though it's not the ultimate destination, the Mecca of Maine, it is one of the sacred places along the way, if for no other reason than that the views are outstanding. But it's also been sanctified, for a few hikers at least, by Dillard's literary presence.

A garrulous eighty-four-year-old man climbs to the knob, bellows a hearty hello, and doesn't stop talking while he takes out a foot-long hunting knife from its sheath and notches his hiking stick for the eighty-seventh time. One notch for each successful climb of the knob. A rufous-sided towhee splashes in a pool that has collected on the rocks from last night's rain. A reddish beetle with stripes of yellow and black on its rounded back totters down the avenue of my walking stick. Some thru-hikers reach the top of the Knob, gasp at the view, glory in the sunshine, and settle down for an extended lunch. They decorate a spruce with wet clothes. They see me reading, I say I'm working, doing research, they say they want my job. Dillard describes shadow "pooled in the valley," shadow that "washes up the sandstone cliffs on Tinker Mountain and obliterates them in a deluge; freshets of shadow leak into the sky." [1] And there it is, on the page and in the world before me, light effects like water, pouring upwards, defying gravity.

After a while Tapeworm and Sleeping Bear and Holiday leave, putting in another seven miles that day. The old man and the towhee are gone too, and I'm alone, reading. That's mostly what I do for the next few days, sit and read and watch. I spend a couple of days on McAfee Knob, a couple more on Tinker Cliffs, a day at Tinker Creek. While camping below the high points, while sauntering from point to point, I see things—a muddy pool of still water with resident bullfrog and hundreds of black tadpoles, the frothy spittle of praying mantis eggs nestled at the juncture of leaf and stem on some knee-high weeds, the rump of a deer blending in with forest duff, trailside fire pinks and mountain laurel abloom, ladybugs that are golden rather than the

orangish ones I'm used to. Always I hear the cicadas, in the distance when
I'm up on the knob or the cliffs, all around when I descend to camp or to the
creek.

These things I hear and see, some of nature's details — these are the stuff
of *Pilgrim at Tinker Creek*. Reading Dillard's book up on Tinker Cliffs is a
good way to learn about the particulars of this place. It never occurred to
me, until Dillard alerted me, that the globs that look like spit in weeds could
be praying mantis eggs. I'd never before heard of such a thing as the giant
water bug, common in freshwater ponds, that sucks out all the juices and
internal organs and life essence from a frog so that it deflates before her eyes
like a leaking balloon. I watch the bullfrog and tadpoles in the muddy pond
in anticipation of some such event. No luck.

And the cicadas I'm hearing. I find out, in the chapter of *Tinker Creek*
called "The Present," that they appear every thirteen years down south, not
every seventeen as they do further north. The eggs are laid in bark, and when
the nymphs hatch they drop to the ground and burrow, living underground
off the sap of roots, for thirteen years, until they all emerge together in spring,
as many as eighty-four per square foot (96). On the trail I see the holes where
they've come up from underground. It looks like rain hit the riddled earth
with a vengeance.

Even as I'm learning from Dillard about the flora and fauna of Tinker
Mountain and environs, I'm aware that she is engaged in something more
than natural history. She's using nature in order to get at something else,
which is why so many critics consider her some kind of new transcendentalist, reading nature as symbolic of something spiritual, as Thoreau does, but
doing so from the perspective of a Christian well-acquainted with twentieth-
century science, one who finds in nature grounds for more ambivalence
than optimism.[2] It's the ambivalence that sets her book apart. Dillard is trying
to reconcile nature's beauty and life's unending creativity with the appalling
nature of parasitism and death. She's trying to get beyond a naive appreciation for nature and for God, for the beautiful and good, to an appreciation
that recognizes the sometimes brutal and bizarre facts of the natural world.
An appreciation that incorporates knowledge, minute and detailed and rig-
orous, as well as faith. An appreciation that is also understanding.

It's quite a balancing act that she's engaged in. In a study of Dillard's "dialectical vision," Margaret Loewen Reimer says the book's dichotomies include "the material and the spiritual, the natural and the transcendent," science and religion, "the beauty and the horror within the natural world," the
particular and the universal. Dillard's genius is in holding these opposites

"in constant tension," without trying to resolve or remove the mystery of either the natural world or the spiritual world by finding easy answers.[3] Scott Slovic contends that Dillard's ultimate concern is with neither the natural nor the spiritual world but with the self and the "psychology of awareness." Still, there is a "dialectical tension" at work, common to nature writers, between "two opposing modes of response to nature: disjunction and conjunction." One response leads to our perception of nature as alien, as Other; the other response leads us to feel that we can achieve harmony or oneness with it.[4] Dillard herself observed in an interview that her book is structured by the opposition of two traditional approaches to God: the *via positiva*, the positive way, assuming that God is knowable through contemplation of the glories of creation, and the *via negativa*, the negative way, a more complex concept. It means not just taking into consideration the horror and apparent senselessness of nature but also conceiving of God as unknowable through the rational mind. To approach God through the *via negativa* one must empty the mind.[5]

I see in *Pilgrim at Tinker Creek* other dichotomies as well, introduced early in the book, when Dillard describes her geographic (and philosophic?) position:

> I think of this house clamped to the side of Tinker Creek as an anchor-hold. It holds me at anchor to the rock bottom of the creek itself and it keeps me steadied in the current, as a sea anchor does, facing the stream of light pouring down. It's a good place to live; there's a lot to think about. The creeks — Tinker and Carvin's — are an active mystery, fresh every minute. Theirs is the mystery of the continuous creation and all that providence implies: the uncertainty of vision, the horror of the fixed, the dissolution of the present, the intricacy of beauty, the pressure of fecundity, the elusiveness of the free, and the flawed nature of perception. The mountains — Tinker and Brushy, McAfee's Knob and Dead Man — are a passive mystery, the oldest of all. Theirs is the one simple mystery of creation from nothing, of matter itself, anything at all, the given. Mountains are giant, restful, absorbent. You can heave your spirit into a mountain and the mountain will keep it, folded, and not throw it back as some creeks will. The creeks are the world with all its stimulus and beauty; I live there. But the mountains are home. (2–3)

This passage is Dillard's overture, introducing topics for later chapters ("Seeing," "The Fixed," "The Present," "Intricacy," "Fecundity") and what I see as the book's key oppositions — the active versus the passive, the fluid versus the fixed, creek versus mountain. But here's the apparent irony: living by the creek, seeing nature as essentially fluid, she acts like a mountain. Immobility is the paradoxical means she chooses to come to know something fluid and mobile. In her chapter called "Stalking," Dillard says that whether you're tracking game or enlightenment, there are two ways to proceed: to wait patiently or to pursue. In that chapter, she sits motionless on a bridge waiting to see a muskrat, but in larger terms she waits for the creek itself, for the whole natural world and its attendant grace. The creek is the poetry of creation in motion, "an active mystery," which she explores by the passive means of sitting and watching, a process of meditation that Dillard associates with the *via negativa* (184). According to Sandra Humble Johnson, Dillard doesn't need to travel far to find God. She finds illumination unexpectedly, as it comes to her in small details, small moments, in the close-at-hand.[6]

Johnson contrasts Dillard's passive approach, her "openness to spirit" based on calm, centered observation, with the practice of most writers in the tradition of wilderness literature. They are the chasers, in pursuit of epiphany through "high-powered physical forays into wilderness." Citing John Muir as the exemplar of that tradition, Johnson points out that Muir actively seeks out enlightenment in high, grand places, where people generally expect to encounter God. Then, Moses-like, Muir returns with his good news of the world's essential harmony.[7] That's the way of the thru-hiker, active questing in pursuit of the sacred on high. The world is there, rock-solid, "a passive mystery," and they go to it, they track it down, they track it up, crossing summits, following blazes, constantly moving. It's almost like each, creek and mountain, active and passive, implies its opposite, or its complement, like yin and yang.

❁   ❁   ❁

In his chapter of *The Practice of the Wild* entitled "Blue Mountains Constantly Walking," Gary Snyder points out that the Chinese term for landscape translates as "mountains and waters." In eastern conceptions, mountains symbolize "spirit, . . . transcendence, hardness, resistance, and masculinity. For the Chinese they are exemplars of the 'yang': dry, hard, male, and bright. Waters are feminine: wet, soft, dark 'yin' with associations of fluid-but-strong, seeking (and carving) the lowest, soulful, life-giving, shape-shifting." Together, says Snyder, "mountains and waters are a dyad that . . . make wholeness possible," both for human beings ("wisdom and compassion are the two components of realization") and for the natural world ("'Mountains and waters' is a way to refer to the totality of the process of nature"). Mountains and waters create each other, waters, of course, being "precipitated by heights," but also forming mountains when they "carve and deposit landforms in their flowing descent, and weight the offshore continental shelves with sediment to ultimately tilt more uplifts." The wholeness created by mountains and waters includes everything from the sound of cicadas to "farms, fields, villages, cities, and the (once comparatively small) dusty world of human affairs."[8]

Snyder's comments about landscape are on my mind (and in my notebook) as I savor the wholeness created by the mountains and waters of Tinker Cliffs. It's a pretty picture. Even the world of human affairs as seen from the cliffs looks nice — lush and spacious and green. My gaze trickles down the mountainside to the valley. I wouldn't mind living down there, maybe in that white house with the red roof. My imagination settles there.

I'm also wondering, though, about the notion of the mountains "constantly walking." Snyder is quoting the zen master Dogen, who in turn is quoting another master. I'm thinking of all the ways in which mountains may be walking — because they are still moving, geologically speaking, still caught in the act of creation; because they are the place for pilgrimage, for walking to and on and over; because they shift as our perspective shifts. Dogen says, "If you doubt mountains walking you do not know your own walking."[9] As Dolores LaChapelle explains it, "As you walk toward the mountains, the nearby hills rise up and cover the distant ones. If you change your direction, the nearby hills sink and the mountains behind them rise up. If you walk to the right or left, the mountains slide in front of and behind one another; so do the rocks and trees. . . . There is a continuous interaction between you and the environment."[10] That sounds nicely ecological, human and earth connected, the mountains moving because we do. But is there a sense in which mountains move independent of our shifting perspective — other than in the geological sense? If we stop moving, do the mountains stop too?

Up on Tinker Cliffs, reading, butt to rock and nose to book, I meet a stream of thru-hikers — Tiger Lily, Rainwater, Dixie Dynamite, Geezer, White Pine, Wild Goose. They stop to chat, ask what I'm reading. A few are reading *Pilgrim at Tinker Creek* themselves, and we talk about such matters as what Dillard might mean when she says such things as the "lover" and the "knowledgable" can see in nature what others cannot. Then they move on. I feel the urge to join them, to put in some miles, to move. But I resist, and read some more, hoping nature comes to me. I'm taking the passive approach in the realm of the passive. Atop the cliff I see an indigo bunting, some vultures wheeling. Between slabs of rock I discover some surprisingly ripe blueberries. Have I really stopped traveling? Has the mountain?

Moving through the "Stalking" chapter, I encounter Dillard's discussion of quantum mechanics, which she claims is "a world symbolically similar to my world at the creek" (202). She's particularly interested in the "Principle of Indeterminacy," the tenet of physics that "says in effect that you cannot know both a particle's velocity and position" (202). If one is measured or determined, the other slips away, and the world is ultimately unknowable. There's motion and there's position, journey and home, pursuit and patient waiting, and you can't know or do or have one without losing the other.

I try to reconcile the principle of indeterminacy with the wholeness Snyder speaks of, symbolized by mountains and waters. They say you can't step in the same river twice. Can you step in the river at all if you're on the mountain? We can perceive the wholeness of a landscape, the mountains and rivers together, only from a distance, an aesthetic distance that renders nature into picture, which, as Paul Bryant observes, automatically separates us from the scene.[11] To put ourselves into the scene, to experience nature, in Bryant's term, as "milieu," to interact with it in some meaningful way—that's the ideal pursued by pilgrims and nature writers and thru-hikers. But to enter the picture means to pick a territory. It's mountains *or* waters, it seems— choose one, lose the other.

Here is what I'm wondering, then: Can our experience of nature, or of ourselves in nature, be only a kind of half-knowledge, forever and inevitably partial? Are we forever denied access to the all by the inevitable act of choosing? Does Annie Dillard, engaged in passive stalking amid nature in its active phase, the creek, miss half the creation? And a thru-hiker, actively following the ridgeline, traversing nature in its passive phase, the static stone of mountains—is that too only a partial experience of nature? Is each unable to see what lies on the other side of the thin curved borderline between yin and yang?

And if so, is that necessarily a loss? Whether you're moving or still, there's always something else to look forward to. Home awaits the wayfarer, the journey entices the homebody. The stream comes to us, we go to the mountains. I recall the title of Snyder's long-awaited poem-cycle, several decades in the making—*Mountains and Rivers without End*.

❁   ❁   ❁

It's easy to overlook mountains in *Pilgrim at Tinker Creek*. Clearly Dillard is preoccupied with the yin of waters, with the creek world of motion, fluidity, continuity, life, light, freedom, flux, evanescence, the dashing and vanishing present moment, the rush of time. The motion of the stream is like life, and that's what she's studying: "It has always been a happy thought to me that the creek runs on all night, new every minute, whether I wish it or know it or care, as a closed book on a shelf continues to whisper to itself its own inexhaustible tale. So many things have been shown me on these banks, so much light has illumined me by reflection here where the water comes down, that I can hardly believe that this grace never flags, that the pouring from everrenewable sources is endless, impartial, and free" (68). Eventually, inevitably, she comes to explore the physical and spiritual sources of waters in the mountains above, where the waters come from. But she challenges the archetype of the sacred mountain: "I have never understood why so many mystics of all creeds experience the presence of God on mountaintops," she says. "Aren't they afraid of being blown away? . . . It often feels best to lay low, inconspicuous, instead of waving your spirit around from high places like a lightning rod" (89). Seeking enlightenment in the here and now, she seems to reject the cosmic realm of mountains, referring to them mainly as points of contrast with moving water: "The physical world as we understand it now is more like the touch-and-go creek world I see than it is like the abiding world of which the mountains speak" (204). Mountains are shadow, the fixed, transcendence, forever. "Living this way by the creek," says Dillard, "where the light appears and vanishes on the water, where muskrats surface and dive, and redwings scatter, I have come to know a special side of nature. I look to the mountains, and the mountains still slumber, blue and mute and rapt. I say it gathers; the world abides. But I look to the creek, and I say: it scatters, it comes and goes" (201).

But there's a dark side to the stream, a side that she calls Shadow Creek. Like the polyphemous moth that hatched in a mason jar, its wings hardening inside the jar, wings essentially glued to its back so that when it was released all it could do was walk—like the beetle pinned on a collection board not quite dead so that days later it still wriggles its tiny legs in an attempt to swim away—like the praying mantis devouring its mate, the young of the ichneumon devouring their mother—the creek too partakes of the "horror of the fixed." She describes fixity not as pure stasis but as "motion without direction, force without power," fecundity without apparent purpose. Though she usually finds delight in Tinker Creek's unending activity, one night it strikes her as sinister, a "dumb dead drop over rocks . . . a hideous parody of real natural life, warm and willful. It was senseless and horrifying; I turned away. The damned thing was flowing because it was *pushed*" (68). Presumably the mountain, or the natural law of gravity, is giving the Sisyphean push. "The pure trickle" of the creek "leaks from the unfathomable heart of Tinker Mountain" (101). Here, if mountains and waters are part of a whole, mountains are the source of the world's relentless flow of shadow.

There is terror, too, in the creek world because it fosters life so exuberantly, for nature's extravagance, its constant experiments in new and strange forms of life, not only requires the controlling force of death, the ultimate in fixity, but depends on it, is driven by it, is caused by it. For "the faster death goes, the faster evolution goes" (175). At first Dillard finds all this hard to handle, and she questions her devotion to the ways of the creek world: "I had thought to live by the side of the creek in order to shape my life to its free flow. But I seem to have reached a point where I must draw the line. It looks as though the creek is not buoying me up but dragging me down." She feels she "might have to reject this creek life unless I want to be utterly brutalized" (176). But ultimately she comes to reconcile herself to the world as it is, seeing that both beauty and horror, life and death, "are two branches of the same creek, the creek that waters the world" (180). The creek contains shadow as well as light, a kind of fixity as well as the visual trill of nature dancing. But that is as it should be, for we need shadow to "define the real," to make "some sort of sense of the light" (62). This is her defense of the horrors of the world, of death, of the *via negativa*. This is Snyder's wholeness.

"Its source is freedom," she says. Freedom makes possible nature's beautiful intricacy and its horrifying death-driven fecundity. But don't streams come down from mountains? Aren't mountains the essence of the fixed? Ah, here's the other side of Dillard's equation. Just as the stream contains the fixed as well as the fluid, so too does the mountain contain the fluid and the free as well as the fixed. I'm not just talking about the process of erosion, which Dillard points out takes place at the rate of about "one thousandth of an inch a year" (98). She's describing something more dynamic. Celebrating the play of light and shadow around Tinker Creek, she says "the mountains are going on and off like neon signs," glowing one moment, disappearing the next, as if "some sort of carnival magician has been here, some fast-talking worker of wonders" (10–11). An epiphany arrives at a "moment when the mountains open and a new light roars in spate through the crack, and the mountains slam" (34). Later she says moments of insight arrive when "occasionally the mountains part" (205). Resting at a gas station she watches the Blue Ridge: "Shadows lope along the mountain's rumpled flanks. . . . The ridge's bosses and hummocks sprout bulging from its side; the whole mountain looms miles closer . . . the bare forest folds and pleats itself like living protoplasm before my eyes, like a running chart, a wildly scrawling oscillograph on the present moment" (78). Trying to track the present, capture the present, which is gone the moment she becomes conscious of it, she says, "I repeat a phrase: the thin tops of mountains. Soon the thin tops of mountains erupt, as if volcanically, from my brain's core" (93). In short, mountains too are part of the "touch-and-go creek world," where everything is motion, the future rushing to the present where the perceiver waits on a bridge, passing under our feet and downstream to the past. Mountains are not just symbols of eternity, the source of shadow and creek and time's flow—they are part of the current of life and light, part of the dance.

Maybe the movement of her mountains is simply a function of Dillard's energetic, verb-filled prose. I tell my students in writing classes that good writing is driven by strong verbs. I illustrate. "There is a chair," I say, and I point out that that's dull language, nothing's happening, who cares if there's a chair. Then I get a running start and lash out at the chair, hurt my toe, scream once samurai-style in preparation for the kick and a second time in pain, send the chair crashing to the floor, it bounces, loud on the tile. Shock snaps into my students' faces, they jerk forward in their seats, the instructor in the room across the hall looks over startled and frowning, birds outside lift to sudden flight. "Now that's the active voice," I say, leaving the downed chair in the middle of the room as a reminder. And if they still don't get it, I read a passage from Dillard.

Maybe the energy of her writing constitutes the movement of Dillard's pilgrimage. It is her prose as well as her soul that travels, and it is her prose by which we know her. I know I am moved by her writing. But Dillard's verbal vigor is attuned not just to her persona or the affective response she seeks, but to her subject. Ideally, critics say, form should follow content. One says Dillard's style is "exuberant and baroque" in imitation of the "lush Virginia valley" she's writing about, living in.[12] What I'm getting at is that Dillard's energetic style echoes her discovery that we live in a world of flux and change and motion, where even mountains are caught up in the stream. Her verbs move mountains along with everything else in the universe.

❊   ❊   ❊

I leave the cliffs, descend to Scorched Earth Gap, so named for the supposed effects of the "exuberant" language of a hiker distressed by the difficult terrain. I'm in the thick of the cicadas there. Up close, I note that the sound, like the whine of an alien spacecraft, is not at a constant volume and pitch. It rises and falls. The cicadas seem to sing—or whatever it is they're doing—together.

In truth, the singing cicadas are all males, and far from harmonizing, they are competing to attract females.

I camp at Lambert's Meadow, next to Sawmill Brook, along with Palouche, the Dutchman, Wild Goose, Timber Pixie, and (really) a guy going by the trail name of Pilgrim. I watch crayfish for a while, stalk them, see them scuttle backwards under rocks when I lean toward them, watch the mud burst into a brown cloud that rises in the water and then falls, dissolves, glides away. "You have to stalk everything," I read. "Everything scatters and gathers; everything comes and goes like fish under a bridge. You have to stalk the spirit, too" (205).

It's Dillard's book I'm stalking now, its meaning my prey. Right about when darkness drops its first hint, I'm starting chapter twelve, "Nightwatch." That much is planned, but what happens next is pure coincidence, it's the mountains parting unsought for.

From above where I'm camped, where the trail descends a hillside to the creek, I hear my name. "Evergreen!" It's Thistle, a woman I'd met weeks earlier, back in North Carolina, who'd taken her name from a passage in *Pilgrim at Tinker Creek*, a passage just a few pages ahead of where I'm reading. It's the passage where freedom and fixity meet, an exultant description of a goldfinch tugging at the seedcase of a thistle, "sowing the air with down." The thistledown, says Dillard, "strayed like snow, blind and sweet, into the pool of the creek upstream, and into the race of the creek over rocks down. It shuddered onto the tips of growing grasses, where it poised, light, still wracked by errant quivers." It's one of the book's epiphanic moments, and it is the here and now where, when, Dillard sees that "the same fixity that collapses stars and drives the mantis to devour her mate eased these creatures together before my eyes: the thick adept bill of the goldfinch, and the feathery, coded down." It's all perfect. The reliance of one creature on another is not always or purely depredation or parasitism, it's not just the horror of fixity. It's also the beauty of the free, the wonderfully bearable lightness of being. Knowing that "the thistle is part of Adam's curse," Dillard feels fully that "the fall was happy indeed. . . . Creation itself was the fall, a burst into the thorny beauty of the real" (216).

Back in North Carolina, Thistle and I had hiked together on a drizzly morning, and she told me that an old boyfriend had been her goldfinch, freeing her in a way. But part of that freedom meant leaving him, being taken by the wind. She said it's funny, though, even when she's out here hiking, she doesn't really think of herself as a free spirit. She likes to be grounded, to put down roots, to be at home. She's like Dillard, trying to reconcile freedom and fixity, finding the two interpenetrating.

Now Thistle is crossing Sawmill, hopping on boulders. She's hiking with Snake and Beaver, it's her birthday tomorrow, and they've brought the makings for s'mores. We roast the marshmallows over a fire, marry them to chocolate bars, and house them between graham crackers.

Dillard asks of the goldfinch tugging at the thistle: "Is there anything I could eat so lightly, or could I die so fair?" (216)

If she'd had some s'mores, she needn't have asked.

❃　　❃　　❃

Next day the other hikers are off early, headed north. By midmorning they'll be at Tinker Creek. Months later Thistle sends me a photo of Pilgrim—at Tinker Creek, naturally. Meanwhile, I'm backtracking to a shelter a third of a mile back, where Thistle had left me a note in a register, responding to a request I'd made weeks earlier. Like all Thistle's entries, this one is dated "A Day":

> Evergreen,
>
> I'm sure I'll see you this evening at the campsites [a ridgerunner had told her there was an English professor ahead reading Annie Dillard], but I wanted to write down some of my thoughts on this 4th day of June upon hiking over Tinker Cliffs. It's been a year tomorrow, my birthday, since I received a copy of *Pilgrim at Tinker Creek*, the book from which I chose my Trail name. And here I am, thru-hiking the AT. No, let me rephrase that. Today, I am hiking on the AT, ever attempting to enjoy every moment, take my time, see, hear, touch, smell, and taste the world. So today, I slackpacked, doing what I can to make my hike on the AT non-linear, non-goal-oriented, and always new. Pretty inspiring to be on the cliffs on a sunny day with blooming mountain laurel. Moreso even to see three lizards, a frog, a high-flying hawk, some bumblebees, and the boulders, to smell fresh oranges (one of my birthday treats), and yes, to hear the buzzing, so unnatural and yet so soothing, of the locusts. The fullness of life overwhelms me, makes me feel lucky, a little privileged even, to be out here. There's so much more to see at every step.
>
> Thistle

In her attention to the here and now, to the details of living things, to the particulars of the senses as a means of tasting the world, in her apprehension of the constant freshness of existence, even in feeling overwhelmed by it all, Thistle has caught, I think, the gist of *Pilgrim at Tinker Creek*. She's understood it, found her meaning in it. Even while traveling ever onward, northward, she has adopted Dillard's passive means of stalking, the *via negativa*, the emptying of self to let in the world. I note the paradox—to reach her goal of living in the present moment, she must be "non-goal-oriented." When she succeeds, is her pilgrimage done, though her trip is not? Or does the pilgrimage end with the trip? Neither, I guess. For Thistle and for Dillard, for all of us, these moments of intense presentness—call them enlightenment—come and go, mostly go, says Dillard, and all we can do is seek out—or wait for—the next one. So our pilgrimages are never done, whether we move or stand still, and that is as it should be, for to arrive would mean stasis, fixity, like a squirming beetle or J. Alfred Prufrock "formulated, sprawling on a pin."

I follow the trail along the ridge of Tinker Mountain, with views opening up of the valleys on either side, Carvin's Cove to the south. I figure out just where on Tinker Creek Dillard's book is set—east of the mountain, I think, downstream from where I'll hit the creek. A thought occurs to me: early in *Tinker Creek*, Dillard invites her readers to "drive across the country and over the mountains, come into our valley, cross Tinker Creek, drive up the road to the house, walk across the yard, knock on the door and ask to come in and talk about the weather, you'd be welcome" (49). I could do that, and without the driving! But I know better. The truth is, Annie doesn't live there anymore. She moved.

❊   ❊   ❊

At Tinker Creek I sit on a concrete bridge to read the last two chapters. The cicada-sound shrills intensely here. I figure something out about their lives, something that strikes me as entirely compatible with the wonder that Dillard takes in nature's intricacy and fecundity. If the cicadas emerged and mated and laid eggs every year, the predator population would increase accordingly—and they'd wipe out the cicadas. But because the cicadas transmogrify from nymph to locustlike form only once every thirteen years, the predators are not numerous and cannot keep up with the supply. So most of the cicadas get to mate and lay their eggs. It's a strange but wonderful and effective way to propagate a species. Aren't they all.

Yellow ladybugs cling to the side of the bridge, hundreds of them. Each has whitish eyes, ten black spots per wing, and six tiny legs. When I blow one off my hand, its wing parts stick out like a tail. The creek is slow-moving, the water muddy. On the upstream side of the bridge a logjam spans the creek, but the water slides under it.

"Northing" is the penultimate chapter. It could be the credo of the thru-hiker. In this chapter Dillard abandons her anchored position along the creek banks and climbs the cliffs. And there she feels the urge of the long-distance hiker: "I could go. I could simply angle off the path, take one step after another, and be on my way. I could walk to Point Barrow, Mount McKinley, Hudson's Bay" (248). I can't help but wonder if the path she's on is the A.T., if she's imagining it leading her so far north that a quick bushwhack would take her to Alaska or Canada. She mentions the trail earlier in the book, complaining that on a spring day it is "probably packed with picnickers" (111). So she's aware of the trail, maybe reminded of it as a boreal avenue now that she's reading accounts of Arctic adventure. "Shall I go northing?" she asks. "My legs are long" (249). Enumerating the spiritual qualities that she associates with "northing," she echoes the philosophy of the pack-toting, weight-conscious thru-hiker: "reduction, a shedding, a sloughing off" (251).

In her talk of northing, Dillard is feeling the draw of the active form of stalking. But still she rejects it. "I'll stalk that floating pole and frigid air by waiting here," she says. Some feel the restless Odyssean urge to seek, to find, but they also stalk who only sit and wait. "The North washes down the mountains like a waterfall, like a tidal wave, and pours across the valley; it comes to me" (251). She recalls the advice of Abba Moses to a disciple: "'Go and sit in your cell, and your cell will teach you everything'" (257). Tinker Creek, maybe even a library carrel — anywhere, everywhere, can contain the world, with all its light and dark.

A knee-braced thru-hiker named Robo stops to chat, sees me reading *Tinker Creek*, and asks, "So what's so special about this creek that's got everybody reading all these books about it?" It's all one book, I say, this one. And the creek? It's not so special, except they're all this special.

The last chapter is called "The Waters of Separation." A half-mile away, the trail crosses a highway. My car waits there, parked at a Pizza Hut. Soon enough I'll be thinking I can already taste a large pie with extra cheese, and the cold of a beer. But not just yet. Tinker Creek bubbles over a dam below where I sit on the bridge. I read: "Come on, I say to the creek, surprise me; and it does, with each new drop. Beauty is real. I would never deny it; the appalling thing is that I forget it. . . . These are the waters of beauty and mystery, issuing from a gap in the granite world. . . . And these are also the waters of separation: they purify, acrid and laving, and they cut me off" (266).

There are still some mysteries to consider. Clearly, Tinker Creek's are the "waters of separation" for me, marking the border between woods and home, trail and highway—but what do the waters cut Dillard off from? And why, way back on page 2, does she say that the creek world is where she lives, but the mountains are home?

Dillard looks to the mountain, sees a maple key twirling downward. From where I sit I see no maples, and no maple keys, and the brush blocks my view of Tinker Mountain. But I've got Dillard's book, just a couple of pages left, to turn the keys, and the creek itself, its waters, and the trail, its earth, lead up the mountain, connect me to it.

"The gaps are the thing," says Dillard. "The gaps are the spirit's one home, the altitudes and latitudes so dazzlingly spare and clean that the spirit can discover itself for the first time like a once-blind man unbound. The gaps are the clifts in the rock where you cower to see the back parts of God; they are the fissures between mountains and cells the wind lances through, the icy narrowing fiords splitting the cliffs of mystery. Go up into the gaps. If you can find them; they shift and vanish too. Stalk the gaps. Squeak into a gap in the soil, turn, and unlock—more than a maple—a universe" (268–69). These gaps—on one level they are the passes in the mountains, where streams begin their gravity-driven downdance. But she's also talking about the spaces, the moments, where we see through the matter of existence. I stalk them here, I stalk them there. I stalk them up on Tinker Cliffs and in the creek and in between the lines of Dillard's book.

Mountains and waters. The mountains and the creeks are one. Discovery, enlightenment can take place on either, each implying its opposite, each creating the other, each partaking of the active and passive mystery, each accessible by either means of stalking—but only in part. If you stop to rest and read and watch and wait, you see the world moving. If you move, you find the world waiting.

The joyful mystery of creation persists because you can't do both at once.

6

From Imperialism to Nationalism:
The Knights of the Golden Horseshoe
Cross the Blue Ridge

O N S EPTEMBER 5, 1716, the colonial governor of Virginia, Alexander
Spotswood, accompanied by four Meherrin Indian guides, a dozen aristocratic gentlemen, and about fifty soldiers and servants, reached the crest of
the Blue Ridge. According to a diary kept by one John Fontaine, the explorers "drank King George's health, and the Royal family's at the very top of the
Appalachian Mountains." [1] Later that day they proceeded down the western
side of the ridge to the Shenandoah River, which they called the Euphrates.
The next day they forded the river and, at this far point of their journey, again
"drank some healths." Back on the eastern side of the river, Fontaine went
swimming, then "got some grass hoppers" and caught "a dish of fish." Others
spent the afternoon hunting for deer and turkey. Spotswood, meanwhile,
proclaiming imperial dominion, buried a bottle "with a paper enclosed in
which he writ that he took possession of this place in the name and for King
George of England" (106).

That evening the party celebrated their accomplishment with plentiful
and varied libations: "After dinner," writes Fontaine, "we got the men all
together and loaded all their arms and we drunk the King's health in Champagne, and fired a volley; the Prince's health in Burgundy, and fired a volley;
and all the rest of the Royal Family in Claret, and a volley. We drunk the
Governor's health and fired another volley. We had several sorts of liquors,
namely Virginia Red Wine, and White Wine, Irish Usquebaugh [whiskey],
Brandy, Shrub, two sorts of rum, Champagne, Canary, Cherry punch, Ci-
der, Water &c." (106).

Miraculously, no one was shot amid all the toasting and volleying.

On September 7 the explorers headed back home, recrossing the mountains. Shortly thereafter Spotswood rewarded the gentlemanly members of the expedition with tiny golden horseshoes studded with garnets. These jeweled trinkets commemorated the fact that the party's seventy-four horses had been shod before ascending the mountains, a circumstance memorable because in the soft soil of Virginia's lowlands horses did not need shoeing. On one side of the horseshoe mementos an inscription read "Sic juvat transcendere montes," or "Thus does he rejoice to cross the mountains," and on the other, "The Tramontane Order." So began the legend of the so-called "Knights of the Golden Horseshoe." [2]

❧   ❧   ❧

From Hightop Mountain in Shenandoah National Park, the Appalachian Trail descends to Swift Run Gap, where it crosses Route 33. Just south of the crossing stand three monuments honoring the Knights of the Golden Horseshoe. The first is a sign giving the basic facts of the expedition and claiming that it was on this spot that Spotswood and his men crossed the mountains. The expedition, claims the sign, "paved the way for the settlement of the west." I'll say — on the paved way the cars are hitting seventy, and almost hitting me as I back up to take a picture.

The second monument, a plaque set in a pyramidal rock, gives the names of some of the members of the Golden Horseshoe venture. Spotswood's name is there, of course, and Fontaine's, and so is that of Robert Beverley, author of the 1705 account of *The History and Present State of Virginia*, which praised the Blue Ridge Mountains "for their Height and Bigness: which by their difficulty in passing may easily be made a good Barrier of the country against Incursions of the Indians, etc." [3] The plaque also mentions, in passing, the "rangers and Indians and servants, about 50 in all," the hoi polloi who accompanied the aristocratic gentlemen.

The final monument, erected in 1934, has another plaque, this one set in a large boulder, featuring a poem by someone named Gertrude Claytor. Entitled "Alexander Spotswood Discovers the Valley of the Shenandoah," it's forgettable stuff, for the most part, but I admire bits and pieces: a clever metaphor describing the hills as "a deep blue ocean with living spars / Of pine to catch the clouds and spread white sail"; a description of God hiding his "handicraft behind a silver veil / That welded earth and sky"; a line about a native American guide whose "ear had caught the music under ground / Made audible in water"; the party's thirst slaked by the "crystal courage of the hills." The poem ends with the expedition's climax:

We stumbled on, up scarp and jagged boulder
And down the wet ravines, and up again we fought
Until one dawn we stood upon a Titan's shoulder,
And saw—beyond the blue unchallenged hills
That bore no trace of sorrow or of wars—
The Shenandoah, Daughter of the Stars.

I don't know who Gertrude Claytor was, but I recognize the impulse be-hind her work. Like many writers before her, she has found the epic pre-tensions and self-consciously romantic nature of the Golden Horseshoe ex-pedition irresistible. Within a few months of the explorers' return from the mountains, a humanities professor at the College of William and Mary, Arthur Blackamore, presented a Latin poem to Spotswood praising their ex-ploits. That poem is lost, but still extant is a 1729 translation of it by George Seagood, entitled "Expeditio Ultramontana." Over a century later William Caruthers returned to the subject in a historical romance called *Knights of the Golden Horseshoe: A Traditionary Tale of the Cocked Hat Gentry*.[4] Ad-mittedly, none of these is considered a classic of our literature, but the ac-counts by Fontaine, Seagood, Caruthers, and Claytor suggest something about the changing politics of American landscape aesthetics, tracing a path from imperialism to nationalism.

In her classic study of images of mountains in English literature, *Moun-tain Gloom and Mountain Glory*, Marjorie Hope Nicolson describes the development of the sublime, the "aesthetics of the infinite," in the eigh-teenth century.[5] Before then, the grand and the vast and the awe-inspiring elements of nature were regarded with terror and revulsion rather than ap-preciation. It was only when aesthetic appreciation for sublime objects de-veloped that to be "full of awe" at the sight of something like a mountain meant something connotatively different from "awful." But in America the situation was different. Even before the rise of the sublime sensibility in America, mountains were not necessarily denigrated as excrescences upon the face of the earth. The settlers' economic, theologic, and imperial precon-ceptions made possible an appreciation for mountain scenery in America even before aesthetic appreciation developed. Mountains were regarded as a possible source of mineral wealth (maybe there was gold and silver in them thar hills), or as natural scripture, untarnished by civilization and fresh from the hand of God, or as new territory to be claimed for one's sovereign. When aesthetic appreciation for mountains did develop in America, it incorporated those other modes of landscape appreciation and was accompanied by a rise in nationalistic fervor.

That's the path of development we can trace in the accounts of Fontaine, Seagood, Caruthers, and Claytor.

❦   ❦   ❦

Contrary to legend, the Knights of the Golden Horseshoe were not the first white men to reach the top of the Blue Ridge. Governor William Berkeley had planned expeditions beyond the Appalachians throughout his tenure from 1641 to 1676. John Lederer in 1669, probably acting at the behest of Berkeley, was the first white man to record an ascent of the Blue Ridge, though even he saw evidence (in the form of initials carved on trees) of earlier exploration. Two years after Lederer's expedition, Robert Fallam and John Batts also reached the top of the Blue Ridge. After Batts and Fallam, exploration slowed until Spotswood arrived in Virginia. He approved an expedition that explored the mountains in 1710 and helped establish an iron-works at Germanna that became the gateway to later excursions into the Blue Ridge, including the Golden Horseshoe expedition.[6]

John Fontaine, the expedition's diarist, had served in the British military and traveled to Virginia to buy land for his family. For the most part, his journal offers a matter-of-fact progress report on the journey to the mountains, given neither to excessive complaint nor grandiose rapture. The Knights killed bears, deer, and rattlesnakes, but even in describing the strange and, one would think, unsettling incident where a "prodigious snake" emerged from their firewood, Fontaine's prose remains solidly down to earth. This partial entry from September 4 is typical in its recognition of the difficulties and attractions of the trip: "The sides of the mountains are so full of vines and briars that we were forced to clear much of the way before us. We crossed one of the small mountains this side the Appalaches. From the top of it there is a fine prospect of the plains below" (105). The last line suggests some aesthetic appreciation for mountains, but notice that Fontaine praises the view *from* the mountains, and not the view *of* the mountains. And what we would consider an aesthetic impulse to climb to the top of something to take in a vista, Fontaine attributes to mere curiosity: "I being somewhat more curious than the rest went on a high rock on the top of a mountain to see fine prospects and I lost my gun" (106). If his motivation was aesthetic, the impulse is lost in the preoccupation with a more practical, material concern—the loss of his gun. Mostly, Fontaine's enjoyment of mountains stems from a sense of accomplishment after climbing them, the satisfaction of overcoming a significant obstacle.

The Knights named the highest mountain above the pass Mount George, in honor of the king, and the next highest Mount Alexander, in honor of Spotswood. This Adamic naming suggests some association between mountain and royalty, but Fontaine never elaborates on the metaphoric associations. He declines to give the landscape a symbolic or allegoric reading, leaving it to the reader to interpret the facts as recorded. But certainly the overall impression we get from Fontaine's account of the expedition is that a roaring good time was had by all. With all the liquor and the gunplay, the expedition seems like a glorified camping trip. Celebrating their successful ascent, exhilarated at being away from civilization and its attendant codification of conduct, the Knights of the Golden Horseshoe apparently felt the freedom of the hills that still attracts hunters and campers today, many of whom emulate Spotswood's party in bountifully stocking their larders with booze.

❁   ❁   ❁

From Swift Run Gap you can't really see the surrounding mountaintops, but if Spotswood's expedition did indeed cross here, then what they called Mount George is Hightop, and Mount Alexander is Saddle Back. There's been some debate, though, over just where the Golden Horseshoers crested the ridge. In a 1965 article Delma Carpenter challenged the accepted wisdom and argued that the expedition followed a route to Milam's Gap, about fourteen miles to the north.[7] The trail parallels Skyline Drive, and I camp between Swift Run Gap and Milam Gap, at Lewis Mountain Campground, which has a store, laundry facilities, and drive-in campsites. After pitching the tent, I explore my territory. In the site next to mine, nobody's home, but there's a black pickup truck parked there, and what looks like a horse trailer. On the trailer are bumper stickers for Pink Floyd, Harley Davidson, and "New Jersey and You—Perfect Together." Uh-oh, I think. These could be signs of noisy, obnoxious neighbors. But there are also bumper stickers for the World Wildlife Federation, the Sierra Club, the ASPCA, "Support the Gray Wolf," "Virginia Is for Lovers." Ah, well, I guess they're OK, I think.

While I'm eating a macaroni and cheese dinner my neighbors arrive on loud, spirited Harleys. They're a couple, dripping in flashy black leather. They open up the pickup's cap, revealing a clothes rack stretched across the back. Inside the trailer, tools and lanterns hang neatly on the walls. The floor is carpeted. The guy pulls the Harleys up a ramp and into the trailer, then changes into casual clothes—a full camouflage outfit, including the wide-brimmed hat. The woman connects a lantern and stove to a large propane tank and starts cooking dinner—vegetable shishkabobs and barbecued chicken wings. He shakes up a couple of martinis, selecting the ingredients and glasses from a well-stocked liquor rack. She sets the picnic table with cloth place mats and real silverware, pours herself some burgundy into a long-stemmed wineglass, and for him pops a Löwenbräu. After dinner, they light bucketed citronella candles to keep bugs away.

I'm impressed. I mean, these people are prepared! The two of them have launched an expeditionary force on the Shenandoah that would put the Knights of the Golden Horseshoe to shame. I just hope they don't start firing off drunken volleys.

I'm reminded of another early literary reference to the Knights of the Golden Horseshoe, from William Byrd's 1728 *Secret History of the Dividing Line*, an account of his exploration along the Virginia–North Carolina border. Byrd satirizes the mock-chivalric pretensions and bibulous exploits of Spotswood's expedition by calling his party the "Knights of the Rum Cask." Camped next to me, I think, are the Knights of Internal Combustion, with wineglass gules and Harleys rampant, on a field of asphalt, sable.

❧   ❧   ❧

The imperial metaphor associating mountains with royalty, only hinted at in Fontaine's on-the-spot account, is elaborated in George Seagood's "Expeditio Ultramontana." In this neoclassical poem, the Blue Ridge serves as the medium for praise offered to the king and his appointed representative in the Virginia colony, Governor Spotswood. But the use of conventional poetic rhetoric in describing the landscape leads to a willful misperception of the land being described.

Early in the poem the mountains are depicted as part of a hideous unknown wilderness, full of "thick Woods impervious to the Sun, / To poisonous Snakes and Monsters only known." Though the lines recall negative attitudes to mountains and wilderness typical of the preceding century, the loathing for mountain wilderness contradicts the admiration expressed later in the poem. As in Fontaine's journal, Seagood's purpose here is not so much to denigrate mountains as to elevate Spotswood. The governor's willingness to enter and explore the unknown points up his heroism.

Though Spotswood is the hero of the poem, the king gets most of the praise. Seagood spells out the association between the highest mountain and the king's grandeur:

When he from hence [civilization] a hundred Miles had pass'd
T'wards George's Hill a wishful eye he cast:
This mountain taller than the rest appears,
As to the Sky his stately Front he rears:
Which Spotswood, mindful of his Sov'reign's Fame,
Grac'd with the Title of his Royal Name,
As Proud Olympus above the Hills does rise,
And nearer views the Starry Pole and Skies;
So much thy Mountain Upwards does aspire,
And o'er the Highest thrusts his Shoulders higher;
As Thou, great GEORGE, the Monarchs dost surpass,
In vertuous Deeds familiar to thy Race.

Despite the unfortunate and presumably unintended pun that has the mountain, a symbol of the mighty sovereign, *rear*ing a stately *Front* (a metaphor
that confuses the kingly visage with the royal buttocks), this passage intends
to offer a compliment. The mountain is personified as something powerful
(the country of big shoulders), its senses and spirit concerned with elevated
matters (it "views the Starry Pole and Skies" and "Upwards does aspire"). To
the extent that the mountain is a mountain, not a person, it bears little resemblance to the real mountain that the explorers saw. It's not just that there is
little precise or detailed description, but that the operative assumption is that
mountains are by definition grand and imposing. What's described is not
the rounded, rolling Blue Ridge, but something more like the pyramidal
Alps, or more to the point the epic mountains that rise above the plains in
poetry. Since King George had never seen America, nor had Seagood seen
the Blue Ridge, the mountain that serves as the basis for comparison to the
king is borrowed from something all literate men knew, classical literature.
"George's Hill" is like Olympus, home of the Greek gods, and George, by
implication, attains godlike stature. Later in the poem Seagood boasts that
the grandeur of George's mountain exceeds even Parnassus, home to the
Muses. All noble mountains that have previously inspired encomia, it seems,
fall short of this one named for King George.

By the end of the poem Seagood says of Spotswood that "a beauteous
Landskip charm'd his ravish'd Sight," a far cry from the foreboding early
description of dark, snake-infested woods. The shift reflects the rise of aesthetic appreciation for mountains taking place in the eighteenth century.
Granted, the appreciation is not purely aesthetic, praise for nature's beauty
for its own sake. Rather, the appreciation for mountains serves the imperial

purpose, not because they are an economic boon or a protective barrier against invasion or even a springboard for further conquests to the west, but because of their symbolic properties, their ability to represent the virtues of royal personages. It's still, in a way, an appreciation based on the doctrine of use — nature is good insofar as it is useful, even if only as storehouse for symbolism. This tactic of interpreting the landscape metaphorically derives from the theological practice of reading landscape as natural scripture. Still, mountains would not possess such positive value as metaphoric vehicles if they were not also beginning to be appreciated aesthetically.

❦   ❦   ❦

In an essay called "The Cycle and the Roots," Robert Spiller traces the typical passage of a society through four stages of cultural development on its way to becoming a mature civilization.[8] Fontaine's journal represents the first stage, a period of exploration when mainly journals and letters are produced. Next comes a stage where a culture develops its own political and religious ideas, which Spiller identifies in American culture as the era from 1750 to the late eighteenth century. In stage three the leisure arts are cultivated but imitate familiar forms. Seagood's poem, though it falls chronologically into the era that Spiller identifes as stage one, and though it certainly precedes the rise of any distinctly American political ideas, seems to fit the description of stage-three art. In its use of tidy heroic couplets, classical allusion, and descriptive attention to the ideal world as opposed to the real, "Expeditio Ultramontana" mimics English neoclassical poetry. Other critics have noted that this imitative quality is typical of eighteenth-century American poetry. Kenneth Silverman sees in poems like Seagood's a "lapse between language and experience," pointing out that "the abstract language of much eighteenth-century English poetry resisted immediate naked experience. . . . Eighteenth-century meter and diction bespoke a sense of harmony, or moral and philosophical certainty, that settlers on a raw frontier could hardly feel." Eugene Huddleston makes similar observations. American poets of the early national period, he says, focused on nature as one way to form an indigenous poetry, but their descriptions borrowed from the styles and forms and diction of English descriptive poetry and thus create "an incongruity between convention and experience," a "discrepancy between their environment and the literary tradition in which they felt compelled to work." He explains, "The environment was new, democratic, and undisciplined; the tradition aristocratic, moralistic, and orderly."[9]

In Spiller's stage theory of cultural development, the period of culmination is reached when "a new literature steps out with its new experience wrapped about it in natural folds."[10] Though America had won political independence in 1776, American writers and critics in the early nineteenth century were still fighting for their cultural independence. Reviewers cried incessantly in print for a national literature to reflect America's character, many suggesting that attention to nature could be the source of both inspiration and distinction for our artists. When Ralph Waldo Emerson proclaimed in "The American Scholar" that "our day of dependence, our long apprenticeship to the learning of other lands, draws to a close," he was expressing a wish that had been in the cultural air for half a century.[11]

It's hard to pinpoint the beginning of literary independence in America, but many critics propose James Fenimore Cooper's Leatherstocking tales as a likely starting point. Though he borrowed the form of the historical romance from Sir Walter Scott, Cooper focused on American history, described American settings, and created in Natty Bumppo a democratic American hero—a common man, close to nature, with uncommon skills and heart. Though not as well known as Cooper's Leatherstocking tales, William Caruthers's *Knights of the Golden Horseshoe: A Traditionary Tale of the Cocked Hat Gentry* is working the same vein, resurrecting the Golden Horseshoe expedition as a means of celebrating America's landscape and its history. Actually, the novel plays fast and loose with history, as Caruthers exaggerates the size of the party, saying it consists of a small army, and the nature of the difficulties they face, inventing an Indian fight to bring the action to climax.[12] And in true romance fashion he introduces a love plot. His greatest alteration, though, is his imposition of nineteenth-century political views and landscape aesthetics on events of over a century before. By comparison with the earlier accounts of the expedition, this 1841 historical romance suggests how the imperialist landscape aesthetics of colonial America evolve into the nationalist aesthetics of the independent United States of the nineteenth century.

That evolution from imperialism to nationalism comes late in the novel. First, Caruthers reproduces an authentic colonial landscape aesthetic. In the early going, his explorers find little to appreciate, aesthetically or otherwise, in the mountains. Caruthers portrays the Blue Ridge as an obstacle to be overcome. Hungry and weary, the explorers are dismayed by views of "a continuous pile of mountains behind mountains, seemingly interminable in their breadth" (209). The rugged terrain lames the horses and exhausts the soldiers. The Knights must also deal with hostile Indians, who are at home in the mountains and throughout the novel are closely associated with them.

In fact, what knowledge the governor has of the route through the mountains and into the valley beyond comes from the Indians, especially the devious, white-educated Chunoluskee.

As the whites advance into the mountains, they fear the Indians, wondering "what might not be done among their own mountain fastnesses, whose intricate defiles were known only to themselves" (175). The Indians can be regarded not only as human obstacles but also as personifications of the geographic hardships. Ultimately the conflict of white man versus red man provides a more stirring climax than that of man against mountain, but the battles against land and Indian are related. Significantly, when the whites defeat the Indians in battle, they do so by using the landscape to their advantage. Part of the Golden Horseshoe party circles around behind the Indians and assumes position atop an eminence. At the same time, a fire started by the Indians, intended to entrap the whites, reveals the gap in the mountains that the whites had sought. Through the gap they escape the trap and pursue the retreating Indians. The mountains' topography ultimately works to the advantage of the whites. In triumphing over the land, they triumph over the Indians, and vice-versa.

The motivation for the conquest of the Blue Ridge, according to Caruthers, runs the gamut of colonial perspectives on mountains; scientific curiosity, economic expectation, and theological justification all play a part. Spotswood's scientific curiosity is aroused by accounts of natural phenomena such as salt springs or the natural bridge of Virginia, which he terms "a noble arch of solid rock—extending from mountain to mountain" (58). More often the governor's interest is sparked by economic considerations rather than by a thirst for knowledge. He refers several times to an "El Dorado beyond the mountains" (195; also 7, 122), and he foresees that the region will become a flourishing valley full of "rich meadows, and neat farm houses, and . . . gilded spires," a vision that, from Caruthers's nineteenth-century perspective, fulfills Thomas Jefferson's agrarian ideal.

In Caruthers's story, theological preconceptions also tint Spotswood's vision. Like America's early settlers, he refers to the new land both as Eden ("a perfect terrestrial paradise, abounding in deer elk, buffalo, and game of every sort—the land teeming with wild fruits of every kind, and bright with the purest fountains of water that ever gushed from the solid rocks" [57]), and Canaan ("a finer country than that promised land which Moses beheld but never reached" [122]). The Blue Ridge is the Promised Land, and Spotswood is Moses. God's approbation of his endeavor is suggested by the support offered by the minister, Dr. Blair. At one point the preacher chooses as text for

a service the Sermon on the Mount. Later he blesses the expedition, implying that the cavaliers go forth on behalf of God and exhorting them to deliver
a message of "peace, and mercy, and good will" to the "benighted inhabitants" of the mountains (174). His justifications (empty as they may be in
light of Euro-American contacts with native American peoples) echo sentiments offered by religious-minded settlers since the early Puritans.

Though Caruthers's Knights hope to find scientific and economic treas-
ures, and though they profess to do God's work, clearly their exploration is primarily motivated by imperialist impulses. In part their concern is to defend
against the threat of the French, who are trading west of the mountains. In trying to gather the General Assembly's support for his expedition, Spotswood
proposes a sneak attack on the "rascally Frenchmen" who have established
military outposts on the far side of the mountains. So Spotswood values the
mountains not as land to be developed nor as a barrier to rebuff would-be at-
tackers but as a pathway into the enemy's backyard and to unclaimed territory
beyond. The governor boasts that he will "plant the British Lion on the most
commanding position which it has ever occupied" (39). In a rousing speech
before the House of Burgesses, intended to win political backing and to en-
courage volunteers, he says that the Blue Ridge Mountains are "the pass, the
key, the gates of the mightiest empire ever conceived of by the most towering
ambition. . . . It is not merely to explore a few insignificant water-courses, and
thread an unknown mountain pass, that I would urge you, but it is to enter
upon that grand inheritance which Providence opens to our acceptance"
(123). In short, the military motive is not defensive but expansionist.

Caruthers's version of Spotswood's rhetoric is consistent with what histo-
rians tell us inspired the Golden Horseshoe expedition and other forays westward.[13] Seeking to extend the realm of God and king and country, early
American explorers were inspired by their vision of a vast and fruitful domain, their conviction that God supports their enterprise, and their loyalty
to the imperialist cause. But this imperialist enthusiasm takes on a different
meaning when we consider Caruthers's perspective. Writing in 1841, he
commits his loyalty to a democratic and independent America, not to the
British throne. So he has Spotswood and company praise the land not for
the glory it brings to its rulers — as Seagood did — but for the glory of the
future civilization that will take root there. Spotswood's future is Caruthers's
past and present, and so Spotswood's vision of a glorious future serves to
congratulate America, from Caruthers' and his readers' nineteenth-century
point of view, on what it has achieved. The novel celebrates America's history
and present state as fulfillment of a retroactive prophecy. The empire Spots-

wood envisions is America's, not Britain's. An imperialist landscape aesthetic has been nationalized.

As Davis suggests, Caruthers's nationalism, thinly disguised as Spotswood's imperialism, helped further the cause of America's trumpeted Manifest Destiny.[14] America's success in the territorial expansion initiated by the Knights of the Golden Horseshoe prepares the way for future endeavors of that kind — endeavors such as the Mexican War, fought within a decade of the appearance of Caruthers's book. Caruthers actively supports America's nineteenth-century sense of a territorial imperative throughout the novel. Here, for instance, is his comment on the initial gathering of the Tramontane Order: "Grand and enthusiastic as were the conceptions of Sir Alexander Spotswood and his young followers, they had little idea that they were about to commence a march which would be renewed from generation to generation, until, in the course of little more than a century, it would transcend the Rio del Norte, and which perhaps in half that time may traverse the utmost boundaries of Mexico" (161). By celebrating America's past history, Caruthers also justifies America's present (as of the mid-nineteenth century) expansionist policies. Though writers like Cooper and Caruthers may have told stories from America's past as a way to remedy the apparent lack of associations in the American landscape, they also celebrated bountiful wilderness as a landscape of the future, unbounded, laden with possibility, evoking hope rather than memory.[15]

Later in Caruthers's novel a subtle change in the symbolic properties associated with mountains indicates the shift from British imperialism to American nationalism. Early in the work, Caruthers stresses the sublimity of the mountains in order to reflect the nobility of Spotswood's character. His daughter Kate suggests the identification of her noble father with the mountains, saying that "his thoughts soar forever over those blue mountains, and that very passion will carry him one day to their summits, and does it not ennoble his character? Is he not elevated by it?" (30) This metaphoric use of the mountains' grandeur to reflect the great personage's stature is typical of the imperialist attitude as expressed in the accounts of Fontaine and Seagood. But American writers of the nineteenth century tend to stress that mountains reflect the character of the ordinary citizen, as in the Leatherstocking tales or Nathaniel Hawthorne's story "The Great Stone Face." Similarly, in the later stages of Caruthers's version of the Golden Horseshoe expedition, the mountains' democratizing influence is stressed. Insofar as the mountains serve to measure a man's true character, social rank and background are deemed insignificant en route up the Blue Ridge. While many of the Knights suffer and groan in distress, the rough-hewn and rough-speaking backwoodsman-scout Red Jarvis becomes a leader. And Jarvis makes no attempt to humble himself before his social betters. Early on, in conversation with the gentleman protagonist, Frank Lee, Jarvis notes with foresight, "You'll see who's the best man among us, when we get among the mountains, and when neither money nor larnin' can do much for a man" (186). As it turns out, Jarvis's knowledge of horses, Indians, and the wilderness saves the day for the Knights on several occasions. Of course, Caruthers was too much the southern gentleman himself to preclude the well-born from the ranks of "the best"; if Jarvis outshines many of the Knights in wilderness skills, still he lacks the native intelligence, social grace, and political leadership of Frank Lee and Governor Spotswood.

Besides becoming "democratized" in Caruthers's story, the landscape is also treated with conservationist sympathy, another attitude derived more from the author's time than the historical setting. Jarvis complains about the scarcity of game in the settled portions of Virginia, and, sounding much like an incipient environmentalist, he blames the dearth on the spread of civilization. That sort of awareness of the costs of progress would have been unusual in America when the Golden Horseshoe expedition actually took place. Jarvis sounds like Cooper's Natty Bumppo in *The Pioneers*, undoubtedly a source for Caruthers's novel.

Aesthetic appreciation in Caruthers's novel marks another change from accounts of the previous century. As the accounts of Fontaine and Seagood indicate, in the colonial era aesthetic appreciation for mountains sometimes grew out of economic, imperialist, or theological considerations, but it wasn't the starting point for valuing the wild. In the nineteenth century aesthetic appreciation comes first, and symbolic associations grow out of that. The nationalistic portrayals of mountains in the nineteenth century arise in part because aesthetic appreciation could be taken for granted. The mountains' magnificence, not the king's, is the basis in the familiar for any metaphoric associations. But now the mountains represent the grandeur of a whole nation rather than the glory of any royal individual. Natural beauty becomes a source of national pride and a symbol of it.

Another symbolic association inherent in natural beauty, or at least in the ability to perceive and appreciate natural beauty, was moral virtue. According to Scottish Enlightenment philosophers, who were influential in American education in the early 1800s, aesthetic taste and moral discernment were allied innate qualities, deriving from the same "common sense," so appreciation for natural beauty served as a measure of character.[16] In Caruthers's novel the heroine, all the gentlemanly protagonists, and most of all the narrator admire mountain scenery. The rhetoric of aesthetic appreciation reaches its highest point at the same time that the explorers reach the geographic high point. It's the same pattern as in Fontaine's account, a rise in rhetorical pitch accompanying the ascent, but here the climax of the narrative comes precisely at the geographic high point, and the psychic release involves not riotous high spirits but a more contemplative, purely aesthetic delight:

> What a panorama there burst upon the enraptured vision of the assembled young chivalry of Virginia! Never did the eye of mortal man rest upon a more magnificent scene! The vale beneath looked like a great sea of vegetation in the moon-light, rising and falling in undulating and picturesque lines, as far as the eye could reach towards the north-east and south-west; but their vision was interrupted on the opposite side by the Alleghanies. For hours the old veteran chief stood on the identical spot which he first occupied, drinking in rapture from the vision which he beheld. Few words were spoken by any one, after the first exclamations of surprise and enthusiasm were over. The scene was too overpowering — the grand solitudes, the sublime stillness, gave rise to profound emotions which found no utterance. Nearly every one wandered off and seated himself upon some towering crag, and then held communion with the silent spirit of the place. There lay the valley of Virginia, that garden spot of the earth, in its first freshness and purity, as it came from the hands of its Maker. Not a white man had ever trod that virgin soil, from the beginning of the world. What a solemn and sublime temple of nature was there — and who could look upon it, as it spread far out to the east and west, until it was lost in the dim and hazy horizon, and not feel deeply impressed with the majesty of its Author. (229)

The rhetoric may be too overblown for our tastes, but we need only compare the attempt to render excitement in this description with John Fontaine's matter-of-fact tone in the original account to see how far aesthetic appreciation for mountains had grown in a little over a century.

In a later passage Caruthers de-emphasizes the theological imperative as the basis for appreciation and specifically invokes patriotism as a reason for celebrating the mountains. "It has often been remarked," notes Caruthers, "how ardent is the attachment to home of every mountaineer, and as this homely feeling is the basis of all true patriotism, it is a feeling to be admired and cherished" (205). Caruthers has trouble explaining what it is that accounts for a people's attachment to its mountains; much of it surely has to do with symbolism. Besides their associations with economic possibility and divine presence, with freedom and the future, mountains are signs, memorable and prominent landmarks that help us identify where, and who, we are.

The changing politics of landscape aesthetics is evident still in the twentieth century, in that poem on the historic marker by Gertrude Claytor, for instance. Like Fontaine and Seagood and Caruthers, she accentuates the difficulties of the trek in order to highlight the heroism of the Knights, and like Caruthers she lovingly describes a scene of natural beauty. But the Indians in her account are not antagonists. They share in the aesthetic appreciation of the wild, and their inclusion in the landscape is signified by the adoption of the native name for this place, Shenandoah, "Daughter of the Stars." Let's not claim too much for Ms. Claytor—it was easy to be democratically inclusive as of 1934 when native American peoples had been safely contained on reservations and no longer posed a threat to American expansionism. And she still skirts the untidy little fact that some of the servants accompanying her heroes were probably slaves.[17] But at least in symbolic terms she's continued the progression from exclusive aristocracy to ever more inclusive democracy.

❀   ❀   ❀

The couple at the next campsite—I've taken to calling them the "Harleys" in my mind—are sipping snifters of some kind of liqueur. When they see me slapping at mosquitoes, they bring over one of their citronella candles. They introduce themselves as Don and Cheryl, and we talk. He's a UPS driver, she does something with computers, and they take their pickup and trailer and motorcycles on their vacations every summer, camping in national parks and exploring on their Harleys. "It's a good way to see the country," they say. Today they had ridden up and down Skyline Drive, parking at trailheads and walking in to see as many waterfalls as they could. They enthusiastically recommend some favorite spots.

Next day, I hike on to Milam Gap, over Bear Fence Mountain and Hazeltop, the highest point on the A.T. in the Park. At the summit, the sign giving the elevation figures has been wrapped in barbed wire, I guess to keep bears from mauling it. They lay claim to the land in their own way. At Milam Gap, marauding flies keep my lunch stop brief. Near Big Meadows I hike off the trail and through a campground to get a sandwich and milkshake at the Wayside Restaurant. The waitress calls me "Hon," and the people at the next table are talking about the Orioles. Looking out the window, I watch cars go by, see a flag waving on the lawn. A couple cross the highway hand in hand and start off down a trail, disappearing into the swells of tall grass in the meadows. According to Carpenter's account of the route, the Knights of the Golden Horseshoe may have topped the ridge right out there.

I'm trying to feel the presence of the Knights of the Golden Horseshoe, but it's just not coming. My milkshake is not the stuff for royal toasts. Then a moment from a few hours earlier comes back to me.

At Bear Fence Mountain, I had taken a side trail the Harleys told me about. A sign warned that the trail is a "strenuous scramble." At the top of some high rocks, with panoramic views, I scanned map and horizon for Fork and Doubletop mountains—the Knights' Mount George and Mount Alexander, according to Carpenter's reconstruction of their route. I struck a "conquest" pose, one foot planted on the highest rock as if atop a vanquished foe, all the visible world under my boot heel, my walking stick like a sword pricking the earth's granite Adam's apple. It's a pose I have struck for hundreds of summit photos, but on Bear Fence there was no one to see or record. If I had called out, "I claim this land in the name of . . .," who would I have claimed it for? For myself? My country? For the Marxist state of Fredonia? (Groucho, that is, not Karl—All Hail!)

It would have been an absurd gesture, of course, deliberately spoofing the Knights of the Golden Horseshoe. The truth is, my instinct is to mock the imperialistic and nationalistic appropriations of the land that crop up in all the accounts of the Knights of the Golden Horseshoe. In all these stories I hear the same old logic of domination, the kind of thinking that oppresses minority peoples and turns forests and fields into parking lots. Or Skyline Drive. I've been prepared to share the disdain of most thru-hikers for the whole Shenandoah stretch of the Appalachian Trail, never more than half a mile from that darn highway, constantly crossing it, being crossed by it. And I've been prepared to despise the Harleys, with their motorcycles and their propane tank and all the comforts of home, equipment enough for an army. Isn't that all part of the logic of domination, to bring our noisy, smelly civilization with us, to impose it on the woods, to blaze our trails with double-yellow lines so we can drive, not walk? Shouldn't we go to the wild not to conquer it but to attune our lives to its rhythms—and its silences?

But the fact is I have come to like the Harleys. With all their creature comforts—no, *human* comforts—they are unpretentious about it all. They enjoy themselves out here, and yes, that means enjoying their wine and beer and brandy, and their Harleys, but they also enjoy the place they're exploring. And I'm thinking back to Fontaine's journal. Weren't those original explorers also out for a good time, maybe even spoofing themselves a bit? In Fontaine's account, claiming the land for king and country is an act of drunken foolishness. It's the later writers, the ones who were not even there, who invest their claims with such grand import.

This is not to say that those original Knights were not also imbuing the land with symbolic properties, as an emblem of their king's magnificence. But I think I understand, and I think I understand how Caruthers or Claytor could see in this land some representation of the virtues and the promise of their country. Like Fontaine and Seagood, they sensed in the land something bigger than themselves — call it God, or king, or country. To make the association between the land and those large, abstract theological and political allegiances, they must appreciate the land. If the land also represents to them something else that they care about deeply, that's all the more reason to appreciate the land. Of course the land is more than just symbol, and of course we diminish it when we see it as no more than a representation of our moral or political virtues. But symbols do matter. And symbolic associations give us all the more reason to love our country. We may even love something for its symbolic value first, and then find the real value inherent in the thing itself. If the Harleys cruise the Shenandoah to "discover America," on their Made-in-America hogs, more power to them. At least they stop to read roadside signs, they are curious, and they follow some old trails. They love their country, not just in the abstract, but the actual country — the silhouette of distant mountains, the solid rock and green fern of this one, the blue haze in the valley viewed from on high where you've pulled off the road, the spot where spray from a waterfall touches your face gentle as a fragrance, the shade under a hemlock where you hear the chatter of a creek and an unidentified, unseen bird not too far away.

The waitress asks if everything's OK. It's fine, the milkshake is great, the Orioles, I hear, won last night but they still need pitching. The tall grasses of Big Meadows swirl with the shifting winds, a car pulls off to the side of the road, the driver pointing something out to her companion, something interesting off in the distance.

7

Confluences: The View from Jefferson Rock

JEFFERSON ROCK, on the cliffs above Harpers Ferry: On a Memorial Day weekend a parade of families comes by, kids climbing up on the rock, parents warning them to be careful or forbidding the clambering when a drizzle dampens the rocks. Most spend only a few moments here, just long enough to snap a scenic photo of kith and kin in the time-shadow of Thomas Jefferson, hoping to capture on film what Jefferson did in words.

Jefferson visited these cliffs in 1783, when there wasn't much more than a ferry service here, and left this description in his *Notes on the State of Virginia*:

> The passage of the Patowmac through the Blue ridge is perhaps one of the most stupendous scenes in nature. You stand on a very high point of land. On your right comes up the Shenandoah, having ranged along the foot of the mountains an hundred miles to seek a vent. On your left approaches the Patowmac, in quest of a passage also. In the moment of their junction they rush together against the mountain, rend it asunder, and pass off to sea. The first glance of this scene hurries our senses into the opinion, that this earth has been created in time, that the mountains were formed first, that the rivers began to flow afterwards, that in this place, particularly, they have been dammed up by the Blue Ridge of mountains, and have formed an ocean which filled the whole valley; that continuing to rise they have at length broken over at this spot, and have torn the mountain down from its summit to its base. The piles of rock on each hand, but particularly on the Shenandoah, the evident marks of their disrupture and avulsion from their beds by the most powerful agents of nature, corroborate this impression. But the distant finishing which nature has given to the picture, is of a very different character. It is a true contrast to the foreground. It is placid and delightful as that is wild and tremendous. For the mountain being

cloven asunder, she presents to your eye, through the cleft, a small catch
of smooth blue horizon, at an infinite distance in the plain country, inviting you, as it were, from the riot and tumult roaring around, to pass
through the breach and participate of the calm below. Here the eye ultimately composes itself; and that way, too, the road happens actually to
lead. . . . This scene is worth a voyage across the Atlantic. Yet here . . . are
people who have passed their lives within half a dozen miles, and have
never been to survey these monuments of a war between rivers and mountains, which must have shaken the earth itself to its centre.[1]

Jefferson's description of the confluence of the Potomac and Shenandoah
rivers is one of the two most renowned passages in the *Notes*, the other
being his description of Virginia's Natural Bridge. He began the *Notes* in
November of 1780, responding to queries from François Marbois, secretary
of the French delegation in Philadelphia. Marbois was seeking data about
America, about the land, the laws, customs, economy, history, and inhabitants. The impetus was more than idle curiosity. The French had chosen to
support the Americans in the Revolutionary War, so they were looking for
information about their political investment. Their concern was heightened
by the ideas of some noted French thinkers. The famed naturalist Georges-
Louis Leclerc, comte de Buffon, had proclaimed that nature existed in a
degenerate state in America, the animals being smaller and feebler than
their European counterparts, the number of species fewer, the climate cold
and wet. According to Enlightenment thought, as propounded in such works
as Montesquieu's *The Spirit of Laws*, the character of a nation is affected by
environmental conditions, and so Buffon's disparaging comments on nature
in America were soon extended to apply to the human sphere. The Abbé
Guillaume Raynal took the dearth of geniuses in America as evidence that
the people, too, had degenerated in the New World.

And these were our friends.

Jefferson's initial attempt to respond to Marbois's queries was interrupted
by the events of the war. British forces drove him from the seat of government
in Richmond and then from his home at Monticello. By the following summer, Jefferson was no longer governor, and the military failures of his admin-
istration prompted an investigation by the Virginia House of Delegates. One
of his children died in April, and his wife was gravely ill after the birth of
another child. Jefferson himself was laid up after a fall from a horse. Perhaps
in part to revive his spirits, in part as a retreat from governmental affairs, and
in part to defend his country from intellectual attack, Jefferson sat down in

the summer of 1781 to respond to Marbois. The *Notes* first circulated among friends, then was expanded and published in a limited edition in 1785, and finally made available to the public in a London edition in 1787. All that time Jefferson continued working on the manuscript, adding and revising material. His only published book, it has received extravagant praise as "the most important book written by a Southerner before the Civil War" and "America's first permanent literary and intellectual landmark."[2] In truth, much of it is pretty dry reading, full of tables and statistics and charts comparing the size of American and European animals, part of Jefferson's attempt to disprove Buffon's theories. But there are also scientific arguments that make the *Notes* a fascinating illustration of eighteenth-century natural history. To cite just one provocative example: Jefferson contends that the mammoth must not be extinct, because if it existed once, it has a place in the natural order, and so it must still exist. The *Notes* also contains passionate rhetoric condemning slavery and defending what has come to be called Jefferson's "agrarian ideal." But what has most attracted the attention of those who argue for the literary artistry of the *Notes* are the few instances of much-admired scenic description, such as his account of the view from Jefferson Rock.

❀   ❀   ❀

It's raining harder now, and I crawl under the rock, which is not the actual rock Jefferson stood upon. The original was pushed over the cliff by his political opponents. Now there's a different rock slab supported on sandstone pillars atop a larger boulder. The pillars were put there in 1860, to keep the top rock from tumbling down. There's plenty of room to sit under there. I worry that I'll be ruining people's photos — they want pictures of Sublime Nature, or of The Place Where Thomas Jefferson Stood, not some scruffy backpacker trying to stay dry. But the rain seems to have halted the flow of tourists up the shale steps cut out of the cliff. I'm alone. Looking out, beyond the spire of St. Peter's Church, I imagine that I'm hearing the rivers meeting each other with a rush, but it's really the hiss of rain spattering on rock and leaf not far from where I sit hunched under the rock and over a book.

Jefferson's boast that "this scene is worth a voyage across the Atlantic" makes his description part of his patriotic defense of American nature. If nothing else he shows that nature in America had not, despite early impressions, degenerated into chaos. Instead, it's an orderly setting, which bodes well for its social and political future. William J. Scheick calls Jefferson's description the classic example "of how the American landscape adumbrates the ideal of imaginative order," with the contrast of the "placid and delightful" landscape beyond the riotous slash of the rivers suggesting "the future imaginative order which would emerge from the discord of war and internal strife." So Jefferson is reading the land as symbol, suggests Scheick, seeing in geological forces not just the potential power of America but the political and social order to follow the disruptions of the Revolutionary War. In elaborating on the symbolism, Wayne Franklin associates the rivers with the American settlers, "ranged along the foot of the mountains," and the mountains with the British, who "have hindered the natural desire of the colonists for a freer movement and a more ample ground."[3]

Critics have offered numerous variations on the order-from-chaos reading of the Blue Ridge Gap passage. Some contend that the passage begins by echoing the disorder of Jefferson's personal crises. Gisela Tauber, for instance, in an interesting bit of psychohistorical analysis, sees the passage as an allegory of the "disrupture and avulsion of childbirth," recalling the difficult labor that had "cloven asunder" Jefferson's wife Martha, leading to her death just a few months before Jefferson visited Harpers Ferry. But labor results in new life, with a child emerging "through the cleft" to the "small catch of smooth blue horizon" that is the world. Others have seen the description as an aesthetic melding of the sublime and the beautiful, or of sublime terror and pastoral harmony. Stephen Cox sees another sort of aesthetic order at work, Jefferson's emotional attraction to the sublime in nature being tempered by scientific explanation, so that the description contains something of the head as well as the heart. The result, says Cox, is a "rationalistic sublimity," whereby Jefferson "discovers the sublime in geological forces."[4]

In truth, Jefferson usually took scant interest in geology. In a study called *Jefferson and Nature*, Charles A. Miller notes that in general Jefferson thought little of geology as a science, frustrated that it seems "unobservable in its processes and unverifiable as to most of its operations." Outlining an ideal curriculum for the University of Virginia, he said that he would devote to geology the "least possible time," complaining that conjectures about the earth's origins are "too idle to be worth a single hour of any man's life."[5] Perhaps it is not surprising, then, that Jefferson's guesswork about the geologic history of Harpers Ferry is off the mark. Rather than an ocean bursting through the ridge here, it is more likely that a small gap became larger as the river grew. Geologists now believe that the Shenandoah grew in size and strength through a process called "river piracy" or "stream capture." Once there were many water gaps through the Blue Ridge, but the Shenandoah gradually captured the headwaters of various streams and rivers that crossed the ridge and carried those waters with it on its northeasterly course. But if Jefferson has some of the details wrong, his perception that water has the power to carve mountains is accurate, and his description demonstrates his awed awareness of the vastness of the geological past. I'm less sure about his vision of the political future.

From my perspective, up on Jefferson Rock over two hundred years later, overlooking the quaintly preserved national historic site of Harpers Ferry, the symbolic reading that Scheick and others attribute to Jefferson's description of this scene rings horribly ironic. The peaceful future Jefferson foresaw was short-lived. For it was here that in October of 1859 abolitionist John Brown led twenty-one men in an attempt to take the federal arsenal, here where he hoped to spark a mass slave uprising, here that he was taken prisoner after ten of his fellow revolutionaries, including two of his sons, were killed by federal troops. Before being sentenced to hang for treason, Brown made himself into a martyr to the cause of freedom, declaring, "Now, if it is deemed necessary that I should forfeit my life for the furtherance of the ends of justice, and mingle my blood further with the blood of my children and with the blood of millions in this slave country whose rights are disregarded by wicked, cruel, and unjust enactments,—I submit; so let it be done."[6] On the day of his execution he spoke of the violence to come over the issue of slavery, prophesying that "the crimes of this *guilty, land: will* never be purged *away*, but with Blood."[7]

In his martyrdom Brown accomplished his object. In the North, his execution on December 2 brought sympathy for him and outrage at the peculiar institution of slavery. In the South, many became convinced by Brown's raid that there was no chance that they could ever reach any sort of agreement or understanding with opponents of slavery and concluded that secession was the only way to preserve their way of life. And so it was here that, in a way, the bloody Civil War began. America's future was a far cry from the placidity that Jefferson foresaw.

More ironies: the federal forces that quelled Brown's rebellion were led by Robert E. Lee. His lieutenant was J. E. B. Stuart. Among the U.S. soldiers at Brown's hanging was John Wilkes Booth.

Or maybe all of that is not so ironic. After all, Lee and Stuart did end up fighting for the South, and Booth too in his way, so it was appropriate that they'd oppose John Brown right from the start. Maybe the whole symbolic association that Scheick and others attribute to Jefferson is not so ironic either. Maybe the violence of the rivers cutting through the mountains represents not the Revolutionary War but the Civil War, a clash of forces, one from the South, one from the North, the Shenandoah and the Potomac, meeting here. And after the war, a new national order, where, as the historical story goes, this country was no longer *these* United States but *the* United States. I note that after the Shenandoah and Potomac clash — and join — here, they become one and continue on their, its, way eastward to the Chesapeake, past the nation's capital, as the Potomac. The northern current is victorious.

Of course Jefferson could not have been thinking of that particular symbolic association, for the Civil War was far in the future when he was here. But I can.

The question, maybe, is, why should I?

❧   ❧   ❧

I have environmentalist friends who object to the appropriation of nature to serve human ends — not just in the sense of using up natural resources, like gold, iron, coal, water, but even the use of natural facts and scenery as they are deemed valuable for what they can teach us about ourselves. The transcendental method, reading natural facts as symbols of spiritual facts, is just an intellectual adaptation of the doctrine of use, they say. Nature has value beyond its ability to serve human needs, whether those needs are economic or aesthetic or jingoistic or spiritual or moral.

In reading the confluence of the rivers as symbol, I am valuing nature not for itself but for its ability to speak to me, to suggest to me some understanding of history by tracing its course on the landscape with the stylus of geology. I'm constructing an analogy in which the meanderings of history are like the paths of streams, the events leading up to the Civil War like the hydrotectonics of the Shenandoah River. What, I wonder, were the forgotten breaches of the southern code that got caught up by the growing force of John Brown's raid, a revolt that tore a nation apart? Was it something like Frederick Douglass's *Narrative of the Life of an American Slave* (1845), Harriet Beecher Stowe's *Uncle Tom's Cabin* (1852), Henry David Thoreau's antislavery essays like "Slavery in Massachusetts" (1854) or "A Plea for Captain John Brown" (1859)? Was it an earnest discussion by lantern light, black faces illumined as they planned an escape, or by a different lantern, white faces pondering the loss of an escaped slave, lit by a sudden glimmer of understanding that broke through the bulwark of a lifetime of self-willed and culturally reinforced blindness? Perhaps these were not the streams assaulting the mountain to be captured by the mythos of John Brown's raid, but mere droplets in the course of history, droplets that became part of the rivulets and streams and rivers that tore at the granite bedrock of a civilization.

The analogy is not perfect. The Shenandoah comes from the southwest, John Brown came from the northeast, from Massachusetts. In terms of direction of origin, he's more like the Potomac coming in from the north, but it is not known for river piracy, for capturing the headwaters of other rivers. Then again, neither did Brown capture much, not on his actual raid. So I guess he's not the Shenandoah, but the Potomac.

This is the sort of analogizing that my environmentalist friends would say effectively reduces nature to metaphor, so that it can serve in the glorious cause of cultural reference. But there is another way to see the relationship between nature and human concerns, a way that Jefferson himself would have been more likely to adopt. He might have seen in the course of history and the course of rivers separate illustrations of the same natural law, occuring in history as well as geography. Rivers bursting through reluctantly yielding rock, leading to a placid and delightful arcadia beyond—that image was not just symbolic justification for a Revolution, that is the way of the world, in nature and in human society. In drawing some connection between the scene at Harpers Ferry and the events (and aftermath) of the Civil War, I see the same natural laws still at work. Only the context has changed since Jefferson's day.

In *American Incarnation*, a study of the effect of the American landscape on the developing national identity, Myra Jehlen notes that, in the beginning, "Americans saw themselves as building their civilization out of nature itself, as neither the analogue nor the translation of Natural Law but its direct expression."[8] In truth, I've never quite followed how the concept of natural law was supposed to provide the underpinning for human society. I know that when Jefferson in the Declaration of Independence claims that people are endowed with "certain inalienable Rights" he is alluding to the principle of "natural rights," and I know that he claims that "the Laws of Nature and of Nature's God" underlie the American urge for freedom, but I've never quite understood what nature has to do with it. Such self-evident truths derive from a deep understanding of *human* nature, yes—but where does the rest of nature enter into the equation? How, exactly, does a nation or a people follow nature?

The answer lies in the road. Where the mountain opens and the river leads, in the placid calm where "the eye ultimately composes itself . . . that way too the road happens actually to lead." But that is no coincidence. As Jehlen puts it, "Pleased to observe that the road to Fredericktown traced out the landscape's natural contours, Jefferson saw affirmed his conviction that the national destiny was inherent in the continent."[9] What he sees is the road of American civilization, a human construct that cannot help but follow the geologic path laid out for it. In the confluence passage we might take that road for just a literal road, but Jefferson later offered two important elaborations on the road's social significance. Harold Hellenbrand points out that both the Declaration of Independence and Jefferson's first inaugural address pick up on the image of the road as a path to order emerging from chaos, putting it in a social context. In the original draft of the Declaration, Jefferson's penultimate paragraph accused the British of fostering violence and tumult (like the rivers)—but the paragraph ends with a way out, along the "road to glory & happiness." In the inaugural he spoke of the nation's need to return to first principles, "to retrace our steps and to regain the road which alone leads to Peace, Liberty, & Safety." In each case, notes Hellenbrand, Jefferson's rhetorical road leads "out of chaos and into happiness. . . . out of tumult and into harmony." Like Jehlen, Hellenbrand contends that Jefferson's view of nature goes beyond representation: "The stability of nature's inmost order was, for Jefferson, more than just analogous with the basic laws of human nature; it was almost coincident."[10] In society as in geology, one principle, one law.

These days the notion of natural law seems a quaint archaism, important insofar as it influenced the nation's founders, but not any kind of lasting, self-evident truth. Doesn't this application of natural law to the human realm confuse unlike things? I suppose I could see some connection between, say, social organization in bees and in people, as in Denis Diderot's defense of monarchy. After all, both bees and people are living things. But rivers and revolutions? Geology and politics? Geography and history? Aren't we comparing apples and oranges? Not even that—apples and oranges are both living things. It's more like comparing apples and Mack trucks.

The truth is that today even those of us who would like to believe in some human connection to nature feel too keenly our dissociation from it. We have trouble seeing one principle at work in both the abstract constructions of history and the physical reality of a river rushing through a cliff-sided gap. At best we see them as two separate but equal realms, and that seems a world away from the sense of unity implicit in the assumption that all of creation follows the same laws. But we draw analogies from that other realm, and that too implies some sense of our connection to nature, or of nature's relevance to us. Jehlen says that Jefferson's passage of description on the passage of the rivers through the Blue Ridge presents a "meaningful landscape expressing inherent order and purpose," reflecting his view of nature in the New World as "incarnating the national spirit and ideology." Slotkin says the passage presents "a natural metaphor of the course of American history, from threatful present to promising future." [11] Incarnation or symbol, natural law or metaphor — is the difference really all that great? To draw analogies from nature is not the same as reducing nature to "mere" metaphor. There is nothing "mere" about it. If our understanding of social and cultural processes is drawn from our observations of natural processes, that is not so far from assuming that natural laws apply universally. When we speak of the "mainstream" of society or the "current" of history, we are imaging abstract concepts as natural phenomena, perceiving history as river, establishing a relationship between the two.

Critics who have argued for the literary merit of the *Notes* usually focus on Jefferson's placement of himself in such scenes as the confluence passage. In an analysis of the style of the *Notes*, Clayton Lewis claims that in the description of the rivers "Jefferson enacts his belief that there is no *fundamental* difference between human and natural processes, no separation of subject from object, observer from observed. Jefferson is observing nature and at the same time participating in its active processes." And since nature has a restorative power, leading us from tumult to composure, Jefferson recommends that sort of participation to all Americans. So he tries to include the viewer with a readerly appeal in the second person — "*You* stand on a very high point of land." But he also complains that there are "people who have passed their lives within half a dozen miles" of the confluence of the rivers who have never come to see this sight. [12] His point is that they, we, America, need to pay attention. Whether we regard nature as the source of universal law, or of useful analogy, or of language itself, it is by nature that we know the world.

❁   ❁   ❁

I descend the cliffs, following the walkway down steps of hand-carved rock, wandering the cobblestone streets. I see the reconstructed fort where John Brown made his stand, stop in at historical museums and the bookstore, pick up pamphlets and read signs that tell the story of John Brown's raid. Down by the river, the Shenandoah, I see buzzards circling overhead. I also see a family of geese, actually several families, eight adults and twenty-seven goslings, gliding upstream.

And of course I think of death when I see the buzzards, of John Brown, of the Confederacy. And the goslings make me think of rebirth, of the South, of the United States, of Harpers Ferry itself.

The town of Harpers Ferry changed hands eight times during the war. Both sides feared that it could serve as a gateway to invasion, south through the Shenandoah Valley or east via railway lines to Washington. The town was a hotbed of military activity. In April of 1861 Union forces set fire to the armory and arsenal to keep weaponry out of southern hands. But the machinery was intact, and when the Confederates arrived they shipped the weapon-making equipment south. Then they burned the factory buildings and blew up the railroad bridge. If those disruptions were not enough to chase away the citizens of Harpers Ferry, the flood of 1870, and numerous floods since then, added impetus to the exodus. But now it's a beautiful bucolic town, a national historic site that represents something important about our past, oozing history from every cobblestone, every shale boulder on the steps up to Jefferson Rock.

I cross the footbridge over the Potomac, climb Weverton Cliffs, the A.T. roughly following the route that a few of Brown's men took to escape. Two were later captured and executed, but five made their way north to freedom. Next day I'm at Gathland, the former estate of George Alfred Townsend, a journalist and novelist in the era of Reconstruction. The name of the place comes from his pen name, Gath, formed by his initials plus an "H." Some of the buildings are falling over, some are just walls covered with ivy. Others have been renovated, and his bizarre memorial to Civil War correspondents, erected in 1896, still stands. A square tower and ramparts and a weather vane crown the stone memorial, about fifty feet high. At the bottom is a horseshoe-shaped arch, to each side a woman's head, one over the word *Speed*, the other over *Heed*. Above are three arches, representing, according to a nearby sign, "Depiction," "Description," and "Photography." Below the tower is a statue of Mercury in the act of either drawing or sheathing a sword. A couple of horse's heads protrude from the wall above the arches. On one side is a plaque praising the work of war correspondents for their toils, which "cheered the Camps, Thrilled the Fireside, Educated Provinces of Rustics Into a bright nation." On the back of the memorial is a list of war correspondents and artists, including Townsend himself and the famous Union photographer Matthew Brady.

What most moves me at Gathland is the empty mausoleum. A sign next to it explains that Townsend had the tomb built for himself, but when he died in New York City in 1914, penniless after his fortune dissipated, his remains never made it back to Gathland. Now, says the sign, "Gath's empty tomb mutely symbolizes the uncertainties of Life, Fame and Fortune and the certainty of death."

Symbols. A Rock. Rivers, mountains, birds, Harpers Ferry. A monument, a tomb.

I remember—lying under Jefferson rock, I could see the drizzle silvery against the cliffs across the river. Looking down at the river, though, I could see no sign of the falling rain. Eventually, as rain collected on the rock, streamlets of water made their way down grooves in the slate. I took a picture, hoping to get the rock, the rivers, and the cliffs, and, yes, hoping too somehow to capture the spirit of Thomas Jefferson. Here's the irony: that grand panorama has stayed the same from Jefferson's time to ours, but its meaning has changed—from portent of the future for Jefferson to symbol of the past for me. From evidence of an inland sea bursting through the mountain for a late eighteenth-century natural historian to an example of successful "river piracy" for contemporary geologists. On the trail the next day, I was noticing small, transient things—the song of a wood thrush, a peewee, a jay; some crown vetch, the tiny wood sorrel just coming into flower, and the jack-in-the-pulpits that (according to a hiker writing in a register near Gathland) were blooming by the millions just a few weeks before but were now evident only by one sad, sagging flower-pod, withered and browning. The evanescent, the ephemeral—these, I imagine, remain constant. Jefferson might have heard and seen all these and thought of time and change, and so too John Brown, maybe while he awaited the rebelling slaves who never came and the soldiers who did.

I dwell on these things, too, appreciating their quiet, magnificent beauty. It is no disparagement of what they are, in and of themselves, to see in a withering flower and the squawk of a jay that somehow these things tell us something about ourselves and our place in the world. Whether they are symbols or illustrations of natural law, they may come and go, but they last forever.

8

From Wind Gap to Water Gap:
On the Trail of *Edgar Huntly*

DOES NATURE EXIST? An absurd question, of course. Just ask my col-
league's six-year-old daughter, who after being stung by a bee this past
summer refused to leave the house for two months, or did so only under
vociferous protest. Just ask any Appalachian Trail hiker in the process of ex-
periencing firsthand (and -foot) the boot-busting, ankle-wrenching, blister-
building rocks of Pennsylvania. Remnants of the most recent ice age, when
glaciers came this far and deposited the rocky rubble they'd scraped up farther north before retreating — every one of those rocks seems deliberately
placed on edge. Does nature exist? Look for it under your boot sole. Feel it
deep in the sole.

I recall Samuel Johnson's response to biographer James Boswell's discussion of Bishop Berkeley's "ingenious sophistry to prove the non-existence of
matter." Boswell didn't want to believe Berkeley's theory, but was unable to
disprove it. Said Johnson, "I refute it *thus*," and he kicked a rock.[1]

❧ ❧ ❧

So maybe it's a stupid question, the kind of deconstructionist musing that
comes from spending too much time penned up in the concrete walls — or
are they abstract walls? — of a library. As it happens, the question comes to
me while I'm temporarily liberated from the stacks, hiking what is reputed
to be the very rockiest section of the rockiest state on the trail, the fifteen-
mile stretch from Wind Gap to the Delaware Water Gap in eastern Pennsylvania. Underfoot are the rocks, in my mind is Charles Brockden Brown's
1799 novel *Edgar Huntly; or Memoirs of a Sleep-walker*. In a preface to an
excerpt published in the *Monthly Magazine* a few months before the book
came out, Brown asserted that "those who have ranged along the foot of the

Blue-Ridge, from the *Wind-gap* to the *Water-gap,* will see the exactness of the *local* descriptions."[2] What has me pondering absurdist notions about the materiality of the wild is the discrepancy between the nature I see and the nature I'm reading about. They are so different as to be from two different worlds. Not that things have changed so drastically in the two hundred years since Brown wrote about this place, not in geologic terms. If Brown were here today, he'd recognize it as the same place he wrote about—the Delaware River in its place, crashing through the Kittatinny Ridge, the forested mountains, a few cleared valleys in the distance. But what he described in writing I cannot recognize in the place around me. Granted, the book is fiction, but it's fiction that Brown claims is set in a verifiably real place. So I'm wondering if *Edgar Huntly* demonstrates the claim of those poststructuralist theoreticians who claim that nature, like everything else we have a word for, is purely a social construct. There may be a nature out there, but we can never know it or truly perceive it because we can see the world only through the conceptual lenses available to us through our cultural conditioning.

That conditioning pervades even the stuff of life that we consider outside of culture, the stuff that we mean to refer to by the word *nature.* Quick definition: Nature is that which is not human or created by humans. Neil Evernden says nature is a "word-cage" devised to separate the human from the nonhuman, putting us in the position of "the detached observer" looking in at something that is devoid of human qualities.[3] But it's not always so easy to distinguish the two. Sea, desert, forest, mountain, OK, clearly not human constructs. But what about a garden? Or a potted plant hanging in your living room? Or a reservoir? Or the hill wrapped in a ribbon of highway on a Lexus commercial? Is anything in "nature" really free of human influence? Not any more, according to Bill McKibben in *The End of Nature.*[4] Problem number one, then, is that we can't separate nature and culture. Problem two is that, even if we could, we don't know what we mean by that which is not culture. How can we speak of nature as an entity when, to different people at the same time, or to the same people at different times, the word means not only different things but opposite things? To some it is the ultimate source of moral virtue—to be natural is to be good—and to others it is that which must be overcome in order for us to behave well—to revert to nature means to become bestial, savage. "Nature" seems to be an abstraction, an empty ideological vessel into which we pour whatever prejudices and cant we want as it serves our purposes of the moment. But isn't nature supposed to be the essence of the concrete, the antithesis of the abstract?

❁   ❁   ❁

To a great extent, nature is the chief determinant of plot in *Edgar Huntly*. In the first half of the book the titular hero engages in a quest of sorts, into the wilderness, and in the second half he seeks to escape a prison of sorts, out of the wilderness, and in both parts his progress is hindered by natural obstacles. The quest begins with Edgar seeking the murderer of his friend Waldegrave. He suspects one Clithero Edny, whom Edgar has seen mysteriously digging under the elm tree where Waldegrave was killed. Edgar follows Edny on a difficult journey into the wilderness, realizes that his prey is sleepwalking, and loses him when Edny enters a cave. When he confronts Edny with his suspicions, Edny confesses . . . to a different murder. Back in England, Edny had killed, in self-defense, Arthur Wiatte, the father of his fiancée, Clarice, and the twin brother of his benefactress, Mrs. Lorimer. To spare Mrs. Lorimer the pain of the news, a torment sure to be heightened by her long-held belief that her death must accompany that of her twin, Edny decides to stab her in her sleep. It turns out that he is about to stab not Mrs. Lorimer but his fiancée, and when he is discovered in the act, he flees to America, convinced that Mrs. Lorimer has indeed keeled over dead as a result of seeing him about to kill her niece. But really, though Edny does not know this, she just fainted.

End of Clithero Edny's story. Edgar is full of sympathy for poor Clithero, and when he disappears, Edgar searches for him. He explores the cave where Edny disappeared on his first visit, finds his way from the cave to a precipice, sees Edny across an abyss before he disappears again. Edgar returns the following day with an ax to fell a tree across the abyss, finds Edny asleep, and leaves food for him. On his fourth trek into the wilderness, Edgar is caught in a storm, and almost caught by a panther. He escapes only because the tree-bridge across the chasm collapses just after Edgar gets across. The panther leaps after Edgar, falls just short, and plunges to its death. Then things really get exciting.

Edgar awakes one night in a pit in a cave. He has no idea how he got there, but apparently he too has taken up sleepwalking. What follows is a sequence of out-of-the-frying-pan-into-the-fire adventures in the woods. Edgar escapes from the pit, only to meet another panther. He kills it with a tomahawk and, ravenous, eats its flesh raw—and then nearly dies from the revolt of his digestive system. He recovers, then finds his way out of the cave by following the distant hiss of water—only to blunder upon a small war party of Delaware Indians. He kills the lookout, rescues a helpless captive maiden, then flees with her. They find a decrepit cabin, but before long so do the rest of the Delaware warriors. Edgar kills three more Indians, but is wounded and passes out. Friends find him but leave him for dead. When he awakes he wanders some more, kills another Indian, finds a house and is given directions, then tries to cross the ridge in order to make his way home. Gets lost. In the dark someone — his friend and mentor Sarsefield, he finds out later — mistakes him for an Indian and shoots at him. To escape, Edgar dives into the river from a ridiculous height. He survives the plunge, avoids the fusillade of gunfire that greets him when he surfaces, and crosses the river, but nearly drowns before he can clamber out. On the other side of the river, he finds a couple more corpses strewn about, one Delaware, one white, recrosses the river, finds a house to rest in and meets up with Sarsefield, who, as it happens, is also former friend and mentor to Clithero Edny and (wonderful coincidence) newly married to Mrs. Lorimer, whom Edny had tried to kill.

Edgar learns that Indians and not Edny killed Waldegrave. Against Sarsefield's wishes, Edgar tries once more to save Edny, by telling him that Mrs. Lorimer is alive. But when Edny finds that out, he threatens to complete his mission of murderous kindness. Sarsefield has Edny taken by the authorities, but he escapes by diving into the river, where he is presumed drowned. We are left with the impression that Edgar is going to marry Edny's ex-fiancée, despite the fact that the whole story is written in the form of a lengthy letter to Waldegrave's sister, to whom he is already affianced.

Confusing? Yes, as confusing as the obstacle-laden maze of the wilderness setting, full of precipices, vertiginous summits, plunging waterfalls, deep chasms, dark pits, tortuous caves, and rugged thickets. It's a landscape of the negative superlative, where Edgar must "pierce into the deepest thickets, . . . plunge into the darkest cavities, . . . ascend the most difficult heights, and approach the slippery and tremulous verge of the dizziest precipices"—and that description is from the early going, before he has delved into the heart of the dark wilderness he calls Norwalk (23). In Norwalk the descriptions are even more exaggerated, with "craggy eminences and deep dells," hollows as steep as wells where snow lasts into midsummer, where cascades disappear in mists and chasms, and the air is alive "with the reverberations of the torrents and the whistling of the blasts" (96).

Except for the caves and thickets, it sounds like the setting for the hunting scenes in the film *Deer Hunter*, which was supposedly set in Pennsylvania. But the rounded Appalachians evidently did not suit the producers' preconceived notions of what mountains ought to look like, so they filmed in the Washington Cascades, which, yes, does have the requisite precipices, chasms, and cascades. So I cannot say that the wilderness in *Edgar Huntly* is not real—but it sure doesn't seem like it's from eastern Pennsylvania.

Why, then, does Brown boast about the "exactness of the local descriptions"? And if his version of nature did not come from the area between Wind Gap and Water Gap, where did it come from?

❦   ❦   ❦

A few critics have taken Brown at his word and celebrated *Edgar Huntly* as an early example of American realism. Dennis Berthold claims that "any Philadelphian . . . in 1799 would instantly recognize the setting," soon to be one of the most famed examples of American sublime scenery as celebrated by the Hudson River School painters. Ursula Brumm likewise attests to the novel's realism: "*Edgar Huntly* is not a gothic romance according to English models; nor is Brown's nature simply a haunted forest transplanted to America." Rather, says Brumm, the landscapes of *Edgar Huntly* derive from first-hand knowledge.[5]

Brumm is furthering the argument made by Brown himself in his preface to the *Monthly Magazine* excerpt, and then in the preface to the completed novel, where he promised to "exhibit a series of adventures, growing out of the condition of our country," and to reject the typical novelistic conventions of "puerile superstition and exploded manners; Gothic castles and chimeras" in favor of "the perils of the western wilderness" depicted "in vivid and faithful colors" (3). Brumm also has in mind the arguments of numerous critics who believe that in *Edgar Huntly* Brown has simply taken what are in essence European conventions of landscape description and placed them in a setting only ostensibly American. Some contend that Brown's modes of landscape description derive from the conventions of the Gothic novel. So his mountains are more like the German Alps than the Appalachians, and even more than that like haunted castles, with summits for turrets and caves for dungeons.[6]

Other critics contend that Brown relies mainly on the aesthetics of the sublime and the picturesque as derived from British sources. Brown's use of this aesthetic tradition appears most obviously in Edgar's constant search for summit prospects and in the language of the sublime that flavors his descriptions of Norwalk. Kenneth Bernard comments, "He is not describing any real landscape. The fantastic cliffs, gloomy hollows, rushing streams, dangerous chasms, dead trees, moss, storms, mazes, and so on were all commonplaces of eighteenth-century prose and poetry. He is describing sublime or picturesque landscapes according to principles laid down by such writers as Edmund Burke and William Gilpin, depicted by certain painters like Salvator Rosa and Claude Lorrain, and used by such writers as Ann Radcliffe." Alan Axelrod suggests that the language of the sublime and picturesque doesn't so much govern landscape description in the novel as actually *replace* it. Considering how much of the novel takes place amid a mountainous wilderness, surprisingly little descriptive detail surfaces. Axelrod speaks of Brown's "failure to render the concrete and particular in the American landscape." Instead, Brown is interested in the "'effect' of the landscape," which we get through Huntly's morose consciousness.[7]

So if Brown's wilderness is not real, what's it there for? Most critics agree that it serves as an analogue to Edgar's mental state. The maze of precipices, caverns, chasms, cliffs, and trails that lead to the brink of numerous abysses, is, in George Toles's words, "the immense enlargement of a diseased condition originating in the narrator's psyche." Donald Ringe calls it "an extended symbol of mind . . . a symbolic projection into the inner reaches of Huntly's mind." Norman Grabo speaks of the "obvious reciprocity between Edgar's mental state and external conditions," but he points out that we can't be sure if the landscape merely reflects or actively influences the state of mind: "The reciprocity is such that each seems to inform and symbolize the other, and we never quite know whether nature is being internalized or his emotional and mental states are being externalized."[8]

Edgar himself draws the parallel between setting and mind. In his first venture to "the verge of a considerable precipice," where "a dreary vale was discoverable, embarrassed with the leafless stocks of bushes and encumbered with rugged and pointed rocks," he says, "This scene reminded me of my situation" (19). He is on the brink—and in terms of the plot, he plunges in, deciding to pursue Edny further. What a fall (from innocence, perhaps?) lies therein. Edny too sees some connection between the world and his mood when he expresses his affection for the deepest recesses of the Norwalk wilderness: "This scene is adapted to my temper. Its mountainous asperities supply me with images of desolation and seclusion" (89). Setting is a means of characterization, then, that in turn validates much of the plot movement. Because they find something that appeals to their psyches in the gloomy woods, Huntly and Edny spend a lot of time there, and so they know the woods well enough to find their way around, even in the dark. Even, evidently, in their sleep. When the landscape becomes disorienting, it both reflects and causes Edgar's mental confusion.

So nature in *Edgar Huntly* is a plot device and, inasmuch as it serves as an index to the protagonist's state of mind, a character reference. Perhaps too it is a key to the book's theme. What we learn from the book about human interaction is that benevolence to others can backfire. The more good Edgar tries to do, the more harm he does, until eventually his efforts to save Clithero bring about his death. On that level, Brown was critiquing the notion, much vaunted in the late eighteenth century, of what was called the "power of sympathy," and he was exposing the fallibility of American optimism, our naive, hopeful delusion that we can change the world for the better.[9] Brown's implicit commentary on nature follows the same pattern from innocence to disillusioning experience. He learns that the woods are not just the tame setting for the exercise of his moral and aesthetic faculties. In an article subtitled "The Picturesque Traveler as Sleepwalker," Beth Lueck points out that Brown demonstrates the picturesque appeal of American scenery at the same time as he satirizes the picturesque practice of evaluating landscapes for their painterly appeal. As an afficionado of the picturesque, Edgar constantly puts himself in danger by lingering to admire scenery when he ought to be more concerned about saving his skin.[10] On one of his early visits to Norwalk in pursuit of Edny, Edgar pauses to delight in the prospect: "A large part of this chaos of rocks and precipices was subjected, at one view, to the eye. The fertile lawns and vales which lay beyond this, the winding course of the river, and the slopes which rose on its farther side, were parts of this extensive scene." Huntly climbs to a still higher point, hoping that "its greater elevation would extend my view and perhaps furnish a spot from which the whole horizon was conspicuous." He gets so wrapped up in the "desolate and solitary grandeur" of the scene that he is shocked to catch a glimpse of Edny on the rocks across a chasm—so shocked that, Edgar confesses, "I forgot for a moment the perilous nature of my situation" (102–3). As a result he almost falls to his death.

On his next trip he is caught in a storm, but, says Edgar, "instead of lamenting the prevalence of this tempest, I now began to regard it with pleasure. It conferred new forms of sublimity and grandeur on this scene" (122). While he is lost in reverie, a panther is stalking him and his bridge to safety is slipping into the gorge. By the end of the story, after encountering and killing five hostile Indians and two hungry panthers, and after overcoming an endless number of impediments raised by the land itself, Edgar has made some progress in terms of becoming more practical about viewing the landscape. When he crosses the ridge to find the road home, he tarries at the summit and looks around at the Water Gap, the pictorially famous scene where cliffs rise high above the Delaware River. Edgar is temporarily—but only temporarily—distracted: "I pondered for a while on these stupendous scenes. They ravished my attention from considerations that related to myself; but this interval was short, and I began to measure the descent, in order to ascertain the practicability of treading it" (214).

Lueck concludes that Edgar has learned nothing about either nature or human nature, remaining foolishly naive about both to the end. That would make sense in the context of Enlightenment beliefs about the intertwining of moral and aesthetic sympathies. Quite simply, aesthetic taste and moral virtue were considered linked, arising from the same innate "common sense," which referred not to native intelligence but to an innate sensibility that made possible appreciation for the beautiful and the good. So if Edgar remains a moral blunderer, committed to saving Edny even as his philanthropy consistently backfires, then perhaps we are to take Edgar as an aesthetic blunderer as well, committed to aesthetic valuing of the wilderness no matter how inappropriate to the circumstances. Lueck says Edgar "has not yet understood . . . the true nature of the American wilderness: its inherent hostility to man and the necessity of knowledge and precaution when setting forth into the wilds."[11]

Lueck's argument is fascinating, but I don't see that Edgar's perceptions of nature consistently reflect aesthetic appreciation. The impression given by the story as a whole, and especially the second half, where he tries to make his way home, is precisely that the wild is hostile, and we are getting that perception in Edgar's words. So he has indeed "learned" that nature is more than a series of pretty pictures—but is hostility indeed the "true nature of the American wilderness," or of any wilderness? Is that realism? Or could it be that the hostility, sterility, and danger that Edgar sees are just a different view of nature than that held by adherents of the picturesque—a different cultural construct?

❁   ❁   ❁

A few miles northeast of Wind Gap the trail leaves Blue Mountain, the ridge it has followed for over a hundred miles, and crosses a shallow saddle onto Kittatinny Mountain. On a drizzly day, the rain rinses the leaves clean and the sky's gray background highlights the autumn leaves' carnival of color. The leaves are about half fallen, and I'm wondering which is the palette, which the canvas, ground or trees? There are those colors to look at, the delicious scent of downed leaves in the early stages of rot and the patter of rain on the leaves, the feel of rocks underfoot and pack on back to attend to—but somehow, before I know it, I've slipped out of my senses and into my mind. I'm dwelling, unconsciously at first, on a nonsense rhyme that, adapted to my pace, the jingly-jangly melody lost as each phrase is measured to the length of a step, takes on the intellectual dimensions of a zen koan:

> The bear went over the mountain,
> The mountain, the mountain,
> The bear went over the mountain
> To see what he could see.
> And all that he could see,
> And all that he could see,
> Was a bear going over the mountain,
> The mountain, the mountain,
> A bear going over the mountain
> To see what he could see.

Maybe I've got too much time on my hands, but the longer I think on these lines, the more profound they become. The initial repetition of "the mountain" suggests to me its solidity, its unmistakable presence, its thereness. Why does the bear go there? Not to satisfy any kind of mating or survival or homing instinct, but out of curiosity, suggesting a thought process on the bear's part, allowing us to empathize with it, and thereby obliterating the usual distinction between animals and humans, nature and culture. Then there's the second repetition, about the "all" that the bear could see. While the repetition of "mountain" seems to reiterate single-minded awareness of something prominent in the world demanding our attention, the repetition of the "all" leaves room for alternate readings. Is the "all" that the bear could see synonymous with "only"? Or is it a suggestion of amplitude—he could see *all*, everything. And what is it he could see all of, or what is the only thing he could see? A bear going over the mountain. Perhaps that is indeed all—a living thing interacting with the world, exploring the world, being in the world. Just like us. Or perhaps the point is that the only thing we ever see in the world is ourselves.

And Edgar Huntly—was the only thing he saw in the wilderness himself, his situation, his culturally formed preconceptions? Or was there a there there?

❁   ❁   ❁

I'm giving credence to the idea of nature as a cultural construct because in *Edgar Huntly* I can see more of the social and historical context in which the book was written than I can see images of the actual landscape in which it was set. The aesthetic conventions of the picturesque and the sublime are only part of that context. The historical moment is also relevant to the picture — or creation — of nature in *Edgar Huntly*. Alan Axelrod sees the "wildering maze" of *Edgar Huntly* as an analogue to Brown's aesthetic dilemma as an American writer in 1799, caught between civilized Old World models of fiction and the uncharted territory of American fiction. The aesthetics of the sublime and the picturesque may themselves be a product of history. Kate Soper argues that the rise of the sublime in eighteenth-century England is a product of the "scientific Enlightenment, the growth of industry and the increasing domestication of nature. . . . It is only . . . a culture that has commenced, in some sense, to experience its alienation from nature as the negative consequence of its industrial achievement that will be inclined to 'return' to the wilderness or to aestheticize its terrors. . . . The cultivation of the sublime is the expression of anxiety, but also the aesthetic 'luxury,' of a culture that has begun to experience its power over nature as a form of severance from it."[12]

Charles Brockden Brown knew of the picturesque and the sublime because he was publishing articles by and about William Gilpin in magazines that he edited. In *Edgar Huntly* he was importing English aesthetics and testing their applicability to the American landscape, and finding, perhaps, that despite his desire to celebrate the natural scenery of the New World, here human civilization had not yet attained sufficient control over the environment to make it possible for him or his protagonist or, by implication, the American public to "aestheticize its terrors." Or to put a more positive slant on it, Americans were not yet sufficiently alienated from the natural world to reduce it to a matter of mere aestheticism. But in rejecting aesthetic conventions of the sublime and picturesque, Brown was not getting beyond cultural constructivism. By suggesting that nature is hostile — a *rugged, sterile desert*, with *precipices* yawning at every other step, to use some of his most common descriptors — Brown is simply reverting to the most common cultural stereotype about nature prevalent before the rise of sublime aesthetics. As it happened, historical events of the late eighteenth century in eastern Pennsylvania kept that negative preconception viable long after English aesthetic traditions were suggesting other possible views of nature.

Edgar Huntly is set in the 1780s, when there was a late flurry of raids by the usually peaceful Delawares against small frontier communities. In 1781 two attacks occurred in the terrain of Brown's book, one incident where an old man was killed and three prisoners were taken somewhere along the

Delaware, and another, near Stroudsburg, just a few miles from the Water Gap, where a man and his son were shot and scalped, another son was wounded, and "the man's wife and infant . . . were carried off and the child's brains were dashed out." [13] Edgar's family met a similar fate. He says that his parents and an infant sibling were "murdered in their beds" on the edges of the Norwalk wilderness by Indian "assassins" (173). In short, the territorial disputes of recent history might justify Edgar's sense of unease on the Pennsylvania frontier. The land seems to him as hostile as the "savages," as he calls them, so closely associated with it.

But the historical context might also serve to make us and Brown's original readers sympathetic to the Indians, and less so toward Edgar. The raids of the 1780s were sparked by Delaware resentment of white land grabs dating back to the infamous Walking Purchase Treaty of 1737. According to an earlier treaty negotiated by William Penn, white settlement was to extend as far as a man could walk in a day and a half, or about forty miles as traversed by William Penn himself. A large elm tree along the Delaware River near Philadelphia gained renown as the "Treaty Elm," a symbol of peace and harmony between native peoples and the colonial Quakers. But then Thomas Penn, William's unscrupulous son, reinterpreted the treaty by hiring trained runners to do the "walking," one of whom covered about sixty-five miles. Then Penn drew the boundary line to the whites' advantage, angling northeastward to the Delaware River, rather than due east. As a result, the Delawares were forced off land as far north as the Forks of the Delaware, near what is now Easton, and beyond.

All of this history is called to mind by *Edgar Huntly.* Edgar lives near the Forks of the Delaware, on disputed ground. In fact, we learn that his uncle's land occupies the site of a former Lenni Lenape village. Further, an elm tree plays a central role in the book—but as Sydney Krause points out, the parallel is ironic: "Under Penn's tree the transaction was for peace and friendship, under Brown's for vengeance and murder," symbolizing "the triumph in time of racial enmity over amity." Perhaps the tree even provides the motive for Waldegrave's murder. Krause suggests that the killing was intended as a reminder of the broken promises made under Penn's elm. The Delawares may have been "exacting retribution at the foot of a counterpart Elm, the whole point of the murder being for whites to realize the violation that occasioned it." [14]

Though Edgar remains, consciously at least, committed to his view of Indians as savage and depraved, his language at times seems to take their side. When he first encounters the warriors in the cave, Edgar the Indian-hater admits that "a long course of injuries and encroachments had lately exasperated the Indian tribes" (173). When he introduces the character of Old Deb, the Lenni Lenape woman who refused to leave Norwalk with the rest of her people, Edgar says, "She declared her resolution to remain behind, and maintain her possession of the land which her countrymen should impiously abandon" (207). She is a figure of ridicule in the area for her pretensions to the land, tolerated because she is old and seemingly harmless. But in presenting her claims, Edgar's language is not completely dismissive: "She conceived that by remaining behind her countrymen she succeeded to the government, and retained the possession of all this region. The English were aliens and sojourners, who occupied the land merely by her connivance and permission, and whom she allowed to remain on no terms but those of supplying her wants" (208–9). In all these examples, the phrasing could be Old Deb's, her inflections infiltrating Edgar's language as his narrative voice enters her "character zone." This is a classic example of what Mikhail Bakhtin calls "heteroglossia," a blending of language styles that, in Bakhtin's view, distinguishes the novel as a superior form of narrative. In contrast to forms like the essay and the poem, where the author's monologic voice dominates, usually to the exclusion of all other voices, the novel allows for inclusive dialogue even within a single narrative voice, the language shifting to adopt the perspectives of narrator, other characters, and even readers.[15]

It may be that the dialogics here result from Brown slyly interjecting a counterargument to Edgar's anti–redskin racism, a subtext suggesting the ambiguities of the territorial disputes in frontier America, or hinting at a subconscious ambiguity in Edgar's mind about his right to this particular piece of wilderness. If the Delawares have legitimate claims to Norwalk, perhaps Edgar's savagery in regard to the Indians is one more way in which his character is questionable. Perhaps too it explains Edgar's sense of displacement in Norwalk, his unceasing anxiety. The landscape of Norwalk becomes increasingly hostile when native Americans make their appearance—perhaps they remind Edgar of his cultural and familial guilt, since he has grown up on land that is not rightfully his or his family's or his culture's. To see the land as hostile is to sense, on a subconscious level at least, that he does not belong there. Perhaps that guilt is one of the things bothering his subconscious so much that he takes to sleepwalking.

These are all possible explanations for *Edgar Huntly*'s subtext of sympathy for the Delawares. Or, more likely, in Bakhtin's view at least, it could be just the novel doing its customary work, inevitably allowing into the narrative a variety of perspectives in dialogue with one another, and the narrative itself in dialogue with other related narratives. Which is to say, the form of the novel itself is a cultural construct, as is every other genre that Brown borrowed narrative elements from. The sublime landscape and atmosphere of foreboding owe something to the Gothic novel, transported to American soil. The image of the landscape as a hostile place associated with the indigenous peoples of the Americas owes much to the tradition of the Indian captivity narrative. These genre conventions, as well as the prevailing aesthetic modes of the sublime and picturesque, as well as the historical situation—all these helped create the nature of *Edgar Huntly*. They gave Brown a context in which to create and, to a great extent, the language he had to work with.

Was Brown aware of all this? No—but that's the point. In attempting to recreate nature, he is blinded, or at least his vision is bounded, by historical and cultural contexts. The point is not that Brown chose to ignore the real world of nature in order to privilege culturally available ideas about nature but that all he could see were those culturally available ideas. It's the old story of the Inuit's twenty-eight words for snow. It's not just that our language is impoverished for having only the one word *snow*, but that our culture, in terms of that one phenomenon of nature, at least, is impoverished. We have no cultural need or desire for the Inuit's degree of sensitivity to wintry precipitation. But the Inuit need to know snow better than we do. Their culture has created a necessity that is addressed by language, and so their language gives twenty-eight possibilities for describing white stuff falling from the sky. We see only one—snow is snow, not one of twenty-eight different things. But who is to say that the twenty-eight names for snow cover all the possibilities for what can fall from above in winter?

Charles Brockden Brown had more than one option available to him in describing the natural world. Perhaps he had as many as twenty-eight. But no matter how many he had, they were all constructions of some sort, words and concepts that arise from particular historical and social necessities. In attempting to describe the real world, those words and concepts end up constructing it.

      ❀   ❀   ❀

But let's get real. Nobody, not even a radical constructivist (which, interesting irony, is a kind of deconstructionist), denies that there are such things as oak trees, black bears, quartzite cliffs, and running water. Clearly the phenomena of nature exist. Just because we end up talking about nature in human terms, as we cannot help but do whenever we use language, which is very much a social construct, that does not mean that nature is a fantasy. Environmentalists fear that if nature is perceived as merely a cultural construct, nobody's going to care much if we despoil it, or replace it with another kind of cultural construct, like a highway. Soper cautions, "It is not language that has a hole in its ozone layer." She urges us to distinguish between "those forms of being (bodies, geographical terrain) that are culturally transmuted and those kinds of things (telephones, aeroplanes) that are indeed culturally 'constructed.'" [16] When we perceive nature (as opposed to pave it and build on it), we don't construct it, we don't make it. Even to say nature is "transmuted" by our acts of conceptualization may be a bit much. We don't change nature either, at least not by thinking and talking about it. But if not transmute, then what is it we do to nature — trans*mit*? trans*late*? I prefer these terms, since the change is not in nature itself but in the concept as it is transferred from the world to our consciousness.

Let's consider what sorts of translations nature undergoes in the process of entering our minds. The most basic kind of cultural construction is the use of a singular term, nature, to reflect (or reflect upon) what is out there. The singular implies that all the discrete phenomena of the woods and fields and so on somehow coalesce into a unified entity. In Neil Evernden's words, "Nature is, before all else, a category, a conceptual container that permits the user to conceive of a single, discernible 'thing.'" [17]

I remember a junior high science project that I called "The Balance of Nature." I put some snails and some ferns and mosses in an aquarium and covered it with Saran Wrap. The idea was that the ferns and mosses would give off oxygen, which the snails would take in, in turn giving off carbon dioxide, which the plants would take in, in turn giving off oxygen, and so on ad infinitum. It was my first introduction to the idea of an ecosystem, and it seemed to show the symbiotic interrelationship between all living things. Granted that my aquarium was very much constructed by me, was it not a microcosm of the world that demonstrated that there is indeed a kind of unity to it all, a unity that can be studied via the precepts of ecology? What's socially constructed about that?

I'd still like to believe in "The Balance of Nature" — everything connected with everything else in a perfect system, an ideal community where the checks and balances, life and death, predator and prey, plant and animal, all work together to create a perfect ongoing cycle, perpetual motion, equilibrium. But there's an awful lot of ecological science to suggest that all that is a fiction.[18] An ecological community is not a closed system that maintains itself. Predators come and go, the community changes. Forests do not evolve into a static, self-sustaining climax forest. There is no climax, there is no original state. Fire, disease, insect infestations, climatic change, old age, predation, and undoubtedly chance — all of these can alter the makeup of even the longest established habitat. Change is the only constant.

In short, the widely held view of ecology is, to some degree, a fiction, just another cultural construct. We speak of an "ecological community," as if the hawk drops in on the mouse for a cup of midmorning coffee, and the bobcat offers to help turtle shovel the driveway. Competition, not cooperation, may be the norm in nature — but those are human constructs, too, metaphors by which we translate nature into terms, social concepts, that are familiar to us, as if we are trying to decide if nature is run as a capitalist society, the ultimate in laissez-faire, or a commune. In fact, we should recognize that what Donald Worster calls "a new ecology of chaos" is itself another cultural construct, a product of a particular historical and cultural moment. The recent ecological emphasis on competition can be seen as part of the Reagan-era reaction against socially concerned politics, a defense of the principle of self-interest, a manifestation of the-end-of-the-twentieth-century sense that disorder reigns.[19]

So it appears that at times even the findings of science are cultural constructs — or culturally translated visions of nature. Science's vaunted objectivity is itself a fiction, for the observer is always a part of the observation, affecting it. Is light a particle or a wave? It's whichever one you look for. Is nature orderly or chaotic? Whichever you want to find. According to Katherine Hayles, a literary critic who once worked as a research chemist, "The most pernicious aspect of the objectivist view is the implicit denial of itself as a representation." All observations are somehow positioned, and that position changes the perspective. In a fascinating article called "Searching for Common Ground," Hayles notes that scientists frequently object to notions about nature's cultural construction by invoking the law of gravity. She points out that there are several explanations for gravity, scientific and otherwise. According to Newton, gravity is caused by "mutual attraction between masses." According to Einstein, it is caused by the "curvature of space." According to a native American, it could be caused by "Mother Earth call[ing] out to kindred spirits in other bodies." All of these could account for the phenomenon of gravity. Hayles does not say that all interpretations are valid. She rejects absolute "cultural relativism" and calls for a "constrained constructivism," whereby we do a reality check before accepting a theory. But we should be willing to recognize the validity, particularly within its own cultural context, of any reasonable construction that accurately accounts for the phenomena of experience.[20]

The way to get at the truth of gravity or any other matter, says Hayles, is by recognizing that "each construction is positioned and local, covering only a tiny fraction of the spectrum of possible, embodied interactions. How then does one reach toward the world's totality? By imaginatively bringing together the different knowings that all the diverse parts of the world construct through their interaction with it."[21] She goes on to say that we should imaginatively attempt to see "how other creatures experience the flux" of the world—but perhaps another place to start would be to see the possibilities suggested by other cultural and historical and individual constructs, those of other places and times—or in the case of Charles Brockden Brown's *Edgar Huntly*, the same place in a different time and a different cultural context.

Hayles says that true objectivity requires something else, though, too—incorporating awareness of subjectivity. True objectivity means recognizing your own position, turning "inward to look at how one's own assumptions are constructed" before "turning outward to know more about the world."[22] So here's my position—one who believes that we are products of our environment far more than our environment can be said to be a product of our culture—at a historical moment when nature is rare and under constant threat of becoming ever rarer, and as a result all the more precious, to some of us at least—a moment when we're ever more aware of our effects on earth, though some of us are in deep denial about this—a postromantic, posttranscendental, postmodern moment—when the version of ecology that evinces faith in balance and community is the reigning metaphor by which we seek to understand nature—and I'm in a shelter facing southeast, into the wind, along the ridge from Wind Gap to Water Gap, my down bag getting soaked by rain angling in, so in the middle of the night I'm setting up my tent inside the shelter.

About my science project on "The Balance of Nature": it didn't work. After a few days condensation built up on the Saran Wrap, and the ferns started wilting. I couldn't tell if the snails were still alive, but they weren't moving. In short, my aquarium world did not seem to be a sustainable system. It was no prototype for Biosphere 2. Maybe if we'd had a compost heap my project could have been reincarnated as an interactive part of some other natural system . . . but, no, we had no garden, no compost heap. I dumped the ferns and the moss and the snails in the trash. Tried to keep fish in the aquarium, but they died too. Then gerbils. Same story.

❁   ❁   ❁

For all the critical debate about the verisimilitude of Brown's landscape descriptions, nobody seems to have conducted an obvious test: to venture into the woods between Wind Gap and Water Gap and see for themselves if the terrain fits the textual description. Not that critics of Charles Brockden Brown need be singled out in this regard—literary critics in general have neglected fieldwork. If the evidence they seek is not in the library, they don't want to know about it. Perhaps the neglect is part of the critic's fear of the first person. It wouldn't be objective, would it, to tell how you actually respond to something or to confess that what you've seen or experienced may be relevant to your reading, even if that information will help resolve a critical problem.

Culturally loaded backpack on, I've decided to take the radical step of checking original sources, the forest stuff out of which *Edgar Huntly* is made—by which I mean not the trees that were turned into paper but the place that inspired the story. This too is a kind of research, involving a different kind of "foot notes" than most literary scholars are used to.

The first problem to be resolved is whether Brown even intended to describe this area. He says so in that first preface, and Edgar says he lives north of the Forks of the Delaware, which is consistent with the apparent setting of much of the action on and near the ridge from Wind Gap to Water Gap. But Krause, in the Historical Essay accompanying the bicentennial edition of *Edgar Huntly*, claims that "the action of the novel never ranges anywhere near *that* far north or west." [23] His argument is based largely on his identification of Huntly's home town of Solebury, a real town in Bucks County about fifty miles south of the Water Gap, near the Delaware River. Krause doesn't mention it, but another piece of evidence supporting his claim is Brown's statement that Norwalk is full of caves because the area is underlain by limestone (22). The ridges between Wind Gap and Water Gap are actually made up of Silurian rocks—quartzite, sandstone, and conglomerate. But south of the ridges is the former continental shelf, older Ordovician and Cambrian rocks, shale, sandstone, and, yes, limestone. If we can trust Brown's geology, Krause's case for the setting is plausible.

Krause has a hard time, though, explaining away Brown's explicit statement that his story takes place between Wind Gap and Water Gap. Dennis

Berthold makes the case for this setting, pointing out that the sublime descriptions fit the physical facts and the psychological effects of the Water Gap.[24] Besides, since elsewhere in the novel Brown fictionalizes place names (like Norwalk), isn't it possible that Brown lifted the name of Solebury for its symbolic implications and geographically transplanted it? The impetus for the novel's action is Waldegrave's buried soul, and both Edny and Huntly at some point are buried souls trapped in caves. I note too that in the *Monthly Magazine* preface Brown speaks of these mountains as the Blue Ridge. Actually the Blue Ridge ends in south central Pennsylvania, about 175 miles from the Water Gap. Perhaps, though, Brown was confusing the Blue Ridge with Blue Mountain. Brown's description of Norwalk as a "rugged and rocky vein [that] continues upwards of 50 miles," opening into the Indian territories to the west, is compatible with the geological facts about Blue Mountain — and not at all with any of the small mountains, hills really, in the area farther south (172).

All in all, I take it that Brown can be taken at his word that his setting is indeed intended to be the ridge and environs between Wind Gap and Water Gap. But what about his claim that his descriptions will be instantly recognizable to anyone who has been here?

I've come here in October, the same time of year Edgar Huntly was here. And I can't help but think about the rocks. On his sleepwalking adventure Edgar is out here shoeless, marching thirty miles in the dark. He complains most about brambles and thickets, but he does mention the "sharp fragments of stone" covering the soil (181). Once I hiked with a guy who walked the trail in Pennsylvania in sneakers, so I guess Edgar's "feat" is possible, if unlikely, and if possible, one more indicator of his heroic endurance on his marathon excursion in the dark. But one thing about the book absolutely does not ring true. It's October in a hardwood forest. The first thing that strikes one in a Pennsylvania hardwood forest in October, also the second, third, and ultimate thing that strikes one in a Pennsylvania hardwood forest in October, is color. Lots of it, the vivid red of maple leaves, the gold of hickory, the orange of oak, dripping off the trees and splattering the ground. It's the kind of scene that makes you wonder if God took design lessons from Jackson Pollock. (Or maybe it was the other way around.)

The leaves are also covering those wretched rocks, making it even harder on the feet and ankles and knees. And yet, in *Edgar Huntly,* no mention of autumn foliage, no trees tinged with any kind of hue. And Brown was writing, remember, about a time when the area was still wilderness, before the ridges were cleared in the nineteenth century.

What Edgar does mention are all those precipices, chasms, pits, dizzying heights, and depressing depths. Of these, at least in the first ten miles, I see nary a one. On Wolf Rocks there's a drop of about seventy-five feet. Looking to the west, I see a valley in the distance when the clouds part a bit. A few streaks of sun even filter through in-between rain drops. But somehow the view doesn't quite inspire vertigo.

So—Edgar Huntly wasn't really here. And even as I say that I see the absurdity of my argument. Of course he wasn't *really* here. He wasn't *really* anywhere! He's a fictional character! Created by Charles Brockden Brown!

Just as, maybe, the landscape was created by Charles Brockden Brown.

I'm reminded of one more set of culturally constructed conventions that might be governing the landscape description—the conventions of fiction. Krause suggests that Brown's boast that his local descriptions will be instantly recognizable may be no more than the conventional claim that early fiction always makes to realism—a claim that is so clearly part of the convention that readers may not even have been meant to take it seriously.[25] Other fictive conventions may also be at work, mainly the novel's traditional preoccupation with the problems of the individual in society, commonly presupposed to be its very subject. In fiction, character is of the essence, usually in relation to society, and the natural world, if it exists at all in a story, is called "setting," the place where something happens to someone, an adjunct to character, plot (what happens to the main character), and theme (what it all means in terms of the human condition or some social problem). But it is not of interest in and of itself.[26] Here is one critic's comment on *Edgar Huntly*: "Nature functions as an external reality, to be sure, but *more important* [italics mine], it serves as a model of man's inner reality—his subconscious mind."[27] There you have it—even if nature exists, it is only worth noticing insofar as it reflects the hero's state of mind. That is the world's purpose, and the question of its reality is beside the main point. Is this mere anthropocentrism or out-and-out solipsism?

But characters are fictional creations too, authorial constructs, and yet they are meant to express something real and recognizable. Doesn't Brown create Huntly in order to convey something about the human character? Brown is interested in real psychic phenomena, like sleepwalking and guilt, and real social phenomena, like the dangers of sympathy or incurable optimism, or the shortcomings of rationalism in coping with something as potentially disordered as the human mind, or human existence, or the American landscape.

In short, Brown is getting at something real through Edgar, and Edgar's story presents a possibility—here's what can happen to someone with these characteristics, in this kind of situation. In the same way, perhaps his vision of nature, his version of it, is also a possibility, one of many possibilities, one translation of the world, not necessarily universal, no more so than sleep-walking, but grounded in some sort of tangible reality. In Bakhtinian terms Edgar is engaged in a particular dialogue with nature, and his language will inevitably take on the inflections of its language as he enters what we might call its "setting zone." Its language? Yes, the language that speaks to us without words, the language we humans invented our languages for in order to translate the world into human terms.

It's midnight. I leave the shelter, tiny flashlight in hand, and walk into the woods, just far enough to be out of sight of the shelter. I turn off the flash-light. No moon, no stars. Wind blowing hard, rain lashing the side of my face under my hatbrim. I wait several minutes for my eyes to adjust. It's thickly dark, murky, but not pitch dark. Still, I'm afraid to take even a few steps without my flashlight on, afraid I'll not be able to find my way back. Without benefit of light, or a trail, yes, I guess these woods would be like a maze. I'm seeing credence in the nature of *Edgar Huntly*.

The next day, descending to the Water Gap, I'm caught in torrential rain, soaked through and through. But I still stop at overlooks, rocky outcroppings where I can look down at the river and across to Mt. Tammany. Supposedly the cliff face on Mt. Tammany looks like an Indian chief. I don't see it myself, but for some people I guess it's really there. I consider where I'm standing, think of *Edgar Huntly*. Yes, I suppose these do qualify as precipices. I wouldn't quite call them dizzying, but then again I don't get too close to the edge.

But I'm back to the same old catch-22: Am I seeing the land as Edgar did because these possibilities inhere in the land itself, or because I've read *Edgar Huntly* and am mentally prepared to see it in this way?

I suppose I can never know. But the idea of nature as a realm of multitu-dinous possibility—that I can live with.

9

Where the Open Road Meets Howl

THE COYOTE PACES along a wall of his chain-link cage, his toenails clicking on concrete. He stops at the corner of the cage, his ears tilt forward, his silvery eyes find mine. Then his brows drop and he turns away, toenails clicking, moving back and forth along that one wall, pausing each time to stare at me.

❁　　❁　　❁

Even before I got to the coyote cage, I thought that Bear Mountain, part of the Palisades Interstate Park Commission in New York, was a zoo, in the same way that people call Yankee Stadium the "Bronx Zoo." It's a hectic, crowded place, maybe two hundred people on the summit by midday on a bright Sunday in May. There's an observation tower on top, with panoramic views. A road winds its way up here, and looking to the west, out to New Jersey, I hear behind me some motorcycles grring, a helicopter in front of me whirring. To the south-southwest, about forty miles away, lies New York City. Even on a clear day, the view is hazy. The city looks like some barely discernible range in the distance, an outcropping of cliffs. Only when I look steadily for more than a few seconds do I see that the shapes are too evenly rectangular to be natural.

Heading down the mountain, toward Bear Mountain Inn, I see a man, woman, and child hiking up. The little boy is engrossed by something he sees in a stream; the man looks away from me as I approach. His T-shirt, emblazoned with the name of a motor oil, bulges at the belly. The woman is wearing cut-off jeans and lacy leotards. When I say Hi, accustomed as I am to the camaraderie of the trail, she looks at me suspiciously, as if she thinks I've mistaken her for someone I know.

Around Hessian Lake at the bottom of the mountain, thousands of people are picnicking. There's some sort of dog competition underway, and dogs of all sorts are wandering around, leashed, many with bandanas around their necks. (I've got one there, too, kept handy to mop up sweat rolling into my eyes on uphill climbs, or to be doused in streams so I can carry their coolness with me. Apparently, I'm au courant in dog fashion.) Radios are playing salsa, lighter fluid and charcoal briquettes scent the air, I hear people speaking Spanish and Chinese. New York City has come to the woods.

The trail follows an asphalt walkway through the park, leading past a statue of Walt Whitman, with an excerpt from "Song of the Open Road" engraved on a rock next to the statue. The lines give a good indication of what all these people, including me, are looking for here:

Afoot and light-hearted I take to the open road
Healthy, free, the world before me,
The long brown path before me leading wherever I choose.

. . . . .

Henceforth I ask not good fortune, I myself am good fortune.
Henceforth I whimper no more, postpone no more, need nothing,
Done with indoor complaints, libraries, querulous criticisms,
Strong and content I travel the open road.

. . . . .

Camerado, I give you my hand!
I give you my love more precious than money,
I give you myself before preaching or law;
Will you give me yourself? Will you come travel with me?
Shall we stick by each other as long as we live?

More than anything I've ever read, these lines capture, I think, the essence of what the trail has to teach, the sense that the world lies before us, leading us wherever we choose, nothing to fear. While a long hike can be psychically as well as physically demanding, once they adjust to life on the trail many thru-hikers discover that the hike is a joywalk. In part that may be because they are in such good physical shape that they're on an endorphin high. In part it's because they are living a simple life that consists of hiking from point A to point B, with nothing more stressful weighing them down than deciding where to plot tomorrow's point B. But somehow the effects last a lifetime. Whatever lies ahead in life, thru-hikers move on confident that they can get there. And if worse comes to worst, well, you can always go hiking. The trail teaches us to see life as an open road and to hike it "strong and content," to appreciate each step along the way and to anticipate without trepidation the next step, the next turn in the trail.

That's the sort of lighthearted assurance conveyed by Whitman's poem. And Whitman's long, irregular lines, breaking out of the confining boundaries of traditional meters, sprawling across the page, enact the themes of the poem, each line finding its own end point, determining its own rhythm, flaunting its liberation from constraint and conformity, boldly moving into the open spaces beyond the usual margins. Elsewhere in "Song of the Open Road" Whitman proclaims, "I think heroic deeds were all conceiv'd in the open air, and all free poems also. . . . From this hour I ordain myself loos'd of limits and imaginary lines." [1] The shifting meters of Whitman's poetry are akin to the rhythms of hiking, which is itself songlike, joyfully melodic, kept to the beat of footstep and pulse, at times allegro, at times adagio, making your heart beat hard and fast on an uphill climb, or, on the flat stretches, encouraging the streamlike meanderings of barely conscious meditation, with the luff of boots on earth repeating the mantra. Terra profundo.

Maybe New Yorkers find the open road on the Thruway heading north to Bear Mountain. But I'm not so sure. Even if a highway is part of the open road, we can't see it or feel it because we're going too fast, or because the impetus that projects our senses onto the world is something other than our own bodies. Maybe Bear Mountain is just one of many places where highways intersect the open road. You can see it from there, but all you can do by car is cross it.

The part of "Song of the Open Road" that's not contained on the plaque by the monument specifies that the open road leads through, or is one with, the natural world:

Now I see the secret of the making of the best persons,
It is to grow in the open air and to eat and sleep with the earth.

. . . . .

The efflux of the soul is happiness, here is happiness,
I think it pervades the open air, waiting at all times,

. . . . .

The earth is rude, silent, incomprehensible at first, Nature is rude and
    incomprehensible at first,
Be not discouraged, keep on, there are divine things well
    envelop'd. (110–11)

Recalling the pantheism of the transcendentalists, Whitman contends that the "divine things" of nature exist behind their surfaces, in spiritual meaning that is represented by the physical world, in an existence in the transcendental realm that can be better apprehended through intuition than intellect: "Paths worn in the irregular hollows by the roadsides . . . are latent with unseen existences," he writes; "Objects" in nature "call from diffusion my meanings and give them shape"—they are symbols that clarify meaning by representing moral and spiritual values in physical terms (108).

Among the moral values of nature celebrated by Whitman is democracy. The road to the natural world is open and equally available to all:

> Here the profound lesson of reception, not preference nor denial,
> The black with his woolly head, the felon, the diseas'd, the illiterate
>   person, are not denied;
> The birth, the hasting after the physician, the beggar's tramp, the
>   drunkard's stagger, the laughing party of mechanics,
> The escaped youth, the rich person's carriage, the fop, the eloping
>   couple,
> The early market-man, the hearse, the moving of furniture into the town,
>   the return back from the town,
> They pass, I also pass, any thing passes, none can be interdicted,
> None but are accepted, none but shall be dear to me. (108)

By the end of that stanza Whitman is not just celebrating the open road but seeming to speak for it. His poem has become the open road, welcoming all, invigorating all with a taste of the freedom of the open road, imparting its spirit, singing this song on the page.

Whitman's invitation to all his readers to join him on the open road leads to the poem's conclusion, the other stanza preserved on the plaque, in those lines addressed to a "Camerado." The spirit of companionship and community that those lines evoke are evident whenever hikers meet or walk together on the trail. But they are what seemed sorely lacking amid the crowds atop Bear Mountain or around Hessian Lake or in my encounter with the family on my way down the mountain. Whitman warns in the poem that "He traveling with me needs the best blood, thews, endurance" and "courage and health." Then he adds a warning note: "Come not here if you have already spent the best of yourself."

It seems that the crowds around Hessian Lake brought something less than the best of themselves on their search for the open road. They are oblivious to the hand that Whitman offers, unwilling even to make eye contact with a stranger. They have brought their fear and isolation with them on their journey, and so, for all the miles of pavement under their wheels, they have yet to take their first step on the open road.

❧ ❧ ❧

Below the engraved lines on the rock, Whitman's name is inscribed, the "Walt" half-covered by earth. Every autumn, I surmise, leaves pile up in the crevice where the rock meets the ground, and every winter the leaves decompose, building soil. With a twig I scrape away at the dirt, several decades' worth, enough to make the whole name visible. Behind me, Walt watches.

The statue of Whitman stands about eight feet high, atop a boulder that big all around. Walt holds his hat in his right hand, is just setting his weight onto his right foot, his left hand forward as he strides. His beard is full and flowing to the right, his eyes level, looking slightly left, over the head of an admirer of the statue. The tarnished bronze of the statue is green and black, Walt's forehead and left sleeve especially green. The statue was presented to the Park Commission in 1940 by William Averell Harriman as a memorial to his mother, Mary Williamson Harriman, on the thirtieth anniversary of her gift of ten thousand acres of land and one million dollars to establish the Bear Mountain and Harriman State Park sections of Palisades Park. That land contains the first stretch of trail designated as part of the A.T. In the hour that I spend at the statue, taking notes, nobody stops to look—not at the statue, at least.

The poet Louis Simpson must have sat about where I am. In a 1960 poem entitled "Walt Whitman at Bear Mountain," and addressed to Walt, Simpson writes: "As for the people—see how they neglect you! / Only a poet pauses to read the inscription." Even in 1960 Simpson saw here the sort of tawdry suburbanization that troubles me. "The Open Road goes to the used-car lot," he complains to Walt. "Where is the nation you promised?" Among the signs of our decay, writes Simpson, are "the realtors, / Pickpockets, salesmen, and the actors performing / Official scenarios" who have "contracted / American dreams"—in the process either ignoring or co-opting Whitman's visions of what America ought to be, and could be. Simpson ends the poem with a note of hope, though—an optimistic vision of "The clouds . . . lifting from the high Sierras, / The Bay mists clearing."[2] I move on past the statue, still following the white paint blazes marking the Appalachian Trail, into the zoo.

❧ ❧ ❧

In separate cages, in various stages of boredom are a bobcat, a red fox, three black bears, an osprey, several red-tailed hawks, a bald eagle, a turkey buzzard, some owls, and a deer. But what catches my attention most is the eastern coyote, *canis latrans*. He's big—not fox-sized, as I'd always imagined, but about the size of a mature German shepherd. A sign on the cage says that eastern coyotes are larger than western ones. They may have returned east from the west to thrive on lush eastern vegetation, or they may be natives that dwindled when forests of the eastern United States were cleared for farm and pasture land in the nineteenth century, but have flourished anew as the woods have returned. This one's fur is a mixture of gray and white and tawny, with some thin patches. Except for his regular pauses to stare back at me, he paces incessantly. And fast. He manages to sustain a quick trot even within the twenty-foot-square confines of his cage.

I can see more diverse wildlife here in the Bear Mountain Zoo than I'd see in several weeks of hiking in the woods. And I must admit that I'm fascinated. But it's a guilty pleasure I feel. A zoo is worse than a prison—it's like a concentration camp, for the inmates have committed no crime. They are incarcerated for being different, for being something other than *homo sapiens*. But still I'm curious, and I look. And the coyote paces.

The paved path leads out of the zoo, past the reptile house and a historical museum and onto the Bear Mountain Bridge. Used to be that hikers had to pay a ten-cent toll, but now the trail enters the bridge just past the toll booth. Walking across, heading east, you can see pleasure boats and commercial liners. Downstream is Manhattan, upstream is West Point.

On my first hike on this portion of the trail, when I was with three friends, we'd heard that hikers could stay for the night at Graymoor Monastery, about five miles or so up the trail. Mark and I were moving fast, well ahead of Bob and Joe Dunes, and we got to the monastery around dinnertime. We knocked at a building on the monastery grounds, asked if this was the place where hikers could sleep, and a guy wearing jeans and a plaid shirt—very unmonklike attire, we thought—said, "Sure, I suppose so, come on in." Turns out that we were in a drying-out place for homeless people from New York City. The monks drove into the city in a van, offered meals and a bed to the homeless, and brought them back to the monastery. The man in charge said we should lock up our packs in a closet. We were assigned bunks but slept little, kept awake by the groans and shouts of men suffering from delirium tremens. Bob and Joe never showed up.

The sound of piped-in electronic church bells woke us in the early morning. Mark and I were led into a cafeteria, seated at a long table, and served a breakfast of pancakes, corn flakes, and coffee. The homeless men were somber, but sobered-up and kind. All of them seemed to know about us and added to our allotted portions of breakfast. After breakfast Mark and I got our packs and hit the trail early, still wondering what had happened to Bob and Joe. We left a note tacked to a tree, telling them where we were headed for that night, figuring they'd catch up to us. The trail that day followed lots of dirt roads. The only people we met were a couple of middle-aged women out for the day bird-watching. We helped them pinpoint their position on their county map. They were amused by Mark's T-shirt—"cunning linguist," it read, though he was no language specialist. Later we ran into some threatening domestic dogs that we fended off with our hiking sticks. That night we slept under the clouds (Joe had the tent in his pack) on a grassy spot by Canopus Lake and woke up to a drizzle, then walked eight miles, getting soaked more by the wet brush than by the rain itself, to a lean-to with a galvanized tin roof. We got there by midday. Then the storm hit in earnest. A few hours later Bob and Joe arrived, happy and wet. They had stopped at a different building at the monastery and had been welcomed into the monks' residence, pampered with a private room with a shower, a hot dinner of thick stew, and a bacon-and-egg breakfast. They were having such a good time scrubbing at weeks-old sweat and grime in the showers and talking with the monks—who looked *very* monklike dressed in dark robes—that they didn't set out on the trail until the afternoon. One of the monks they talked with kept feeding them chocolate chip cookies, which he stored in the cowl behind his head.

We shared stories of our stay in the monastery, then settled down in the lean-to to wait out the storm, the tapping of rain on tin drifting in and out of our consciousness. Sometime in the dwindling light of late afternoon, Joe took from his pack a slim volume of poetry, a City Lights "Pocket Poets" edition of Allen Ginsberg's Beat Generation classic, *Howl and Other Poems*. We took turns reading, Joe, Mark, and I reading the three parts of the title poem. First the "who" part, a catalog of the calamitous sorrows of America's disaffected seekers—"who vanished into nowhere Zen New Jersey leaving a trail of ambiguous picture postcards of Atlantic City Hall." Then the "Moloch" part, a catalog of the materialist forces of modern society which, like the angry Old Testament god, demand human sacrifice—"Moloch whose mind is pure machinery! Moloch whose blood is running money! Moloch whose fingers are ten armies! Moloch whose breast is a cannibal dynamo! Moloch whose ear is a smoking tomb!" Then the address to Carl Solomon, a catalog of empathic woe for Ginsberg's friend confined to a mental institution—"I'm with you in Rockland / where we hug and kiss the United States under our bedsheets the United States that coughs all night and won't let us sleep." Finally, Bob read the "Footnote to Howl," the "everything is holy" part, a catalog of beatific, democratic inclusion—"Holy the solitudes of skyscrapers and pavements!"[3] Ginsberg's poem is the howl of someone or something wounded deep in the soul, of something trapped. Its setting—and target—is urban America. But somehow on that wet day, the reading fit our mood, even as we believed ourselves to be afoot and lighthearted and free-spirited out on the open road of the Appalachian Trail.

Perhaps it was the accompanying percussion of the rain on the roof, perhaps it was the company, perhaps it was the events of the past two days, perhaps it was relief at seeing my friends were okay—whatever it was, that reading of *Howl* was the most moving encounter with a literary work that I've ever had. Moreso even than when I heard Ginsberg himself read the poem several years later to a packed ballroom of scholars at the Modern Language Association's annual conference in New York City. There in the dripping lean-to, I was awash with sadness for the institutionalized—Ginsberg's friend Carl Solomon locked up in an insane asylum, the homeless men shrieking and crying out their alcoholic woes in the monastery, even the city dwellers rushing from their desperate work all week to their desperate picnics at Bear Mountain on the weekend and then back to the city. Perhaps my pity was patronizing and misplaced. After all, Ginsberg asserts in the "Footnote" that "The bum's as holy as the seraphim! the madman is holy as you my soul are holy!" (134) But my sympathy grew out of some sense of connection. I wanted all the mad, the desperate, the unhappy to fit with us under the pinging, leaking roof of that lean-to, and I wanted them to walk a mile or two with us on vibram souls down a gloriously muddy trail.

I wanted to share the open road. I wanted them to look up and realize that they were standing right on it and all they needed to do was start walking. But maybe I was wrong. Surrounded by walls of steel and glass and concrete, forced there by necessity, by responsibilities, by circumstances, by all that they'd never seen or even read about of the world around them—perhaps they were as securely caged as the coyote behind chain-link in the Bear Mountain Zoo.

❧   ❧   ❧

Using the same long line as Whitman, Ginsberg makes that line not so much a means of conveying expansiveness and freedom as it is a vessel for pouring out vast internal anguish. In *Howl* he defines his poetics as the attempt "to recreate the syntax and measure of poor human prose and stand before you speechless and intelligent and shaking with shame, rejected yet confessing out the soul to conform to the rhythm of thought in his naked and endless head" (130–31). Any expansiveness, it seems, is contained by the skull. Ginsberg took his epigraph for *Howl* from Whitman's *Song of Myself*: "Unscrew the locks from the doors! / Unscrew the doors themselves from their jambs!" But in Ginsberg's poem those lines seem more like a plea than a fait accompli. Throughout, images of containment predominate. Seedy apartments and dingy hotel rooms, alleyways, railroad yards, bathhouse partitions, cardboard boxes that serve as shelter under dark bridges — that is the claustrophobic geography of *Howl*. Ginsberg speaks of the disaffected of his generation "who chained themselves to subways for the endless ride from Battery to holy Bronx on benzedrine until the noise of wheels and children brought them down shuddering mouth-wracked and battered bleak of brain all drained of brilliance in the drear light of Zoo" (126). Not only is their mad rush for experience conducted while bound by constraint, it ends in containment. In the second part of *Howl* Ginsberg calls the monster-god of modern America "Moloch the incomprehensible prison! Moloch the crossbone soulless jailhouse and Congress of Sorrows!" (131) In the final section the images of confinement are most explicit, as Ginsberg expresses his empathy with Carl Solomon, locked up in an insane asylum, screaming in a straitjacket. As wide-ranging as the poem is, depicting scenes from across America, again and again the horrors of contemporary American society are presented in images of containment. The most geographically expansive line, where the montage moves beyond the borders of the United States, ends in the ultimate state of confinement, the coffin: Ginsberg writes of his friends "who retired to Mexico to cultivate a habit, or Rocky Mount to tender Buddha or Tangiers to boys or Southern Pacific to the black locomotive or Harvard to Narcissus to Woodlawn to the daisychain or grave" (130).

On the rare occasions when *Howl* moves to the great outdoors, the images of openness are either unappealing or equally terrifying. He speaks for those "who lit cigarettes in boxcars boxcars boxcars racketing through snow toward lonesome farms in grandfather night" (127). The moon casts a "wartime blue floodlight," the sky is "tubercular" (128–29). In his madness Carl Solomon's soul has gone adrift someplace outside himself: "I'm with you in Rockland / where fifty more shocks will never return your soul to its body again from its pilgrimage to a cross in the void" (133). Loneliness, violence, sickness, emptiness — that's how *Howl* describes open space. It's no wonder that the poem ends with an image of retreat to cozy containment: the poet says to his friend, "in my dreams you walk dripping from a sea-journey on the highway across America in tears to the door of my cottage in the Western night" (133). De-

spite the anxieties about imprisonment that the poem has expressed, ultimately confinement offers refuge from the terror, the exposure, of openness.

❁   ❁   ❁

The road from Whitman to Ginsberg had led us from Bear Mountain to
Graymoor Monastery to the comforting confinement of tin-roofed Farmer's
Mills Shelter. But it hadn't been just the journey of a couple of days. In a
sense we'd traveled the path of American culture over the space and time of
a century. Whitman and Ginsberg are kindred spirits—they even look alike,
with long flowing beards, and both give open expression to their homo-
sexuality in their poems, and both rely on long, rhythmic lines structured
around the anaphoric catalog. Those long lines are declarations of freedom,
from both poetic tradition and social constraint. But the emphasis must
have been different for the two poets. Whitman could still feel himself part
of the mainstream of American society, celebrating its virtues and its progress, no matter how revolutionary his poetic line. Ginsberg, on the other
hand, no matter how out of step with American society he and his fellow
Beats may have felt, could still feel himself part of a poetic tradition. His
long poetic line owed something to jazz rhythms, and something to Hebrew
prayer, and to William Blake, and mad Christopher Smart, and most of all
to Whitman, an influence Ginsberg acknowledges in "A Supermarket in
California," addressed to Whitman. There Ginsberg calls Whitman "dear
father, graybeard, lonely old courage teacher." [4]

But if "A Supermarket in California" pays poetic tribute to Whitman, in
its perspective on American society it measures Ginsberg's distance from
Whitman every bit as much as *Howl* does when compared to "Song of the
Open Road." It's the distance of a century—with Civil War and the "triumph" of the Industrial Revolution and Darwinism and Freud and two
world wars, mustard gas and the hydrogen bomb, the advent of the techno-
logical era, Vietnam, and IBM, and "plasticwasp9to5america" all marked on
the measuring stick. It's the distance from nineteenth-century American optimism to twentieth-century ennui. In "A Supermarket in California," Whitman is pictured not as some heroic poetic pathfinder but as a "childless,
lonely old grubber, poking among the meats in the refrigerator and eyeing
the grocery boys." He seems a pathetic figure, a decline stemming more
from the change in the American setting than in the poet or the man. Ginsberg is accompanied in his imagination by his friend and mentor, and the
two poets "stroll dreaming of the lost America of love past blue automobiles
in driveways, home to our silent cottage"—the shelter of containment, akin

to the cottage refuge he dreams of offering Carl Solomon at the end of *Howl*. On the way there, Ginsberg and Whitman travel a road that has been paved over, the pedestrian making way for the Buick and the Chevy. Tellingly, the cars they see remain parked in driveways in front of the indistinguishable houses of suburbia. Ginsberg's friends among the Beats at least pulled out of the driveway and took to the highway, looking to get *somewhere*, they knew not where. But Jack Kerouac's version of *On the Road* is a far and frenzied, desperate cry from Whitman's contented vision of the open road.

What I found at Bear Mountain, from the motorcyclers whining their way to the summit to get a glimpse of the city they'd come from and would return to, to the crowds dousing themselves in the incense of charcoal briquettes and sealing themselves off from their neighbors with the sound-boundaries emitting from their radios, to the lonely statue of Walt Whitman to the cages of the zoo—that was the spirit of *Howl*. But amid the howls of the homeless being squeezed and shaken by the d.t.'s, and amid the clink of spoons on plain porcelain bowls of corn flakes within the walls of Graymoor Monastery, and under the storm-drummed tin roof of Farmer's Mills Shelter where four friends read aloud to one another and maybe to a couple hundred million or so people well out of earshot—there I felt the spirit of the open road.

The storm let up in the morning, though we were splattered with intermittent rain most of the day. The trail, heading northeast toward Connecticut, wound through some nice open meadows and tall hemlock woods with bracken and Christmas ferns lining the path of mossy ground—"as soft as you could want to walk on," said Bob. The next night we stayed in another leaking lean-to. Falling asleep, I thought of the coyote, of his silent pacing, and of the city, too.

10

Greylock and the Whale

On August 5, 1850, Herman Melville met Nathaniel Hawthorne on a climb of Monument Mountain, in the Berkshires of northwestern Massachusetts. Hawthorne had just moved to nearby Lenox, and Melville was vacationing with relatives in the town of Pittsfield, about six miles north of Lenox. Within a couple of months after meeting Hawthorne, Melville bought a house in Pittsfield, an estate that he named Arrowhead because he found some Indian relics on the property. On their hike to Monument Mountain, Melville and Hawthorne were accompanied by several members of the nation's literary establishment. Evert Duyckinck, editor of the *Literary World* and later coeditor of one of the first and most influential anthologies of American literature, was there, as were James T. Fields, Hawthorne's publisher and, a few years later, publisher of Henry David Thoreau's *Walden*; Cornelius Mathews, a little-remembered but prolific writer who frequently contributed articles to the *Literary World*; and Oliver Wendell Holmes, poet, essayist, and renowned conversationalist and one of Melville's Pittsfield neighbors. As recorded in letters by Duyckinck and published accounts by Mathews and Fields, the story goes that the group sought shelter from a thunderstorm in some rocks just below the summit. When the weather cleared, they reached the top, Melville clambering out on a rock jutting over the cliff, as if it were the bowsprit of a ship, and Hawthorne looking about for the "great carbuncle," the fictional jewel of the mountains featured in one of his short stories. Then they listened to Mathews recite William Cullen Bryant's 1824 poem about a legend of Monument Mountain. The story, source of the mountain's name (and kin to numerous similar legends that underlie "Lover's Leaps" up and down the Appalachians), is about an Indian maiden in love with her cousin. Caught between the proverbial rock and hard place of love and conscience, she throws herself, after a losing struggle with melancholia, off a cliff, landing on a literal rock and hard place. On the spot where she died a pile of stones has risen, each "Hunter, and dame, and virgin" who passes by contributing a rock to the primitive monument. After Mathews's recitation in 1850, the party descended and dined together. The conversation naturally turned to literature, and Melville defended the honor of American literature against disparaging comments made by the Anglophilic Holmes.[1]

Bryant's poem and Melville's side of the argument were both part of a nineteenth-century attempt to develop an American literature that was distinct from its English ancestry. One way to do that was to celebrate the vast expanses of still-wild land in America, a contrast to the tamed and fenced-in landscapes of Europe, and to "story" the land by recounting legends associated with it. In essence, Bryant's poem makes the mountain itself into a monument of sorts, evoking the legend whenever it is viewed. But for me, and apparently for the Melvilleans who every summer trek up Monument Mountain on the first Sunday of August, the mountain has become a monument not to star-crossed Iroquois lovers but to the meeting of Hawthorne and Melville. Starting the easy hike up Monument Mountain on a sunny day in May, I hatch a scheme to come up here on the first *Saturday* of August, the day before the annual jaunt of the Melvilleans, to leave love notes from "Herman" to "Nathaniel" tacked on trees—just a little something to titillate the literati.

I've got a copy of Bryant's poem in my pack, emulating the 1850 party's activities. Walking up, I close my eyes and try to feel the sunshine finding its way through cloud cover and leaf shadow to dapple my skin. And I try to put myself in Melville's hiking shoes. What could he and Hawthorne have talked about as they were just getting acquainted?[2]

At the top the answer seems obvious. Rocky outcrops offer vista-commanding seats just recessed enough to block the breeze while I read and contemplate and take in the views. The most prominent landmark on the horizon is Mt. Greylock, about thirty miles to the north. I venture to say that Greylock was also, or was soon to become, the most prominent landmark in the mind of Herman Melville. While he was staying with his relatives in Pittsfield, at an estate called Broadhall, Melville's favorite writing nook, according to a letter he wrote to Duyckinck eleven days after the Monument Mountain excursion, was an upstairs "garret way" with only a "little embrasure of a window"—a site chosen because it commands "so noble a view of Saddleback," to this day another name for Greylock.[3] Once he moved into

Arrowhead, Melville set up his writing quarters in an upstairs room facing the mountain. While he was working on *Moby-Dick*, then, every time he looked up from his desk, he was looking at "Saddleback," which, yes, as viewed from Arrowhead looks something like a whale. It's a wonder that the white whale isn't a humpback. In fact, Hawthorne made mention of the connection between mountain and whale in his *Wonder Book for Boys and Girls*; writing in midsummer of 1851, he speaks of Melville "shaping out the gigantic conception of his white whale, while the gigantic shape of Greylock looms upon him from his study window."[4] That spring Melville had built a porch, commemorated in an 1856 story called "The Piazza," on the north side of the house, under his study, away from the sun but facing Greylock. A year later he dedicated *Pierre*, another book written under the influence of the same view, to "Greylock's most excellent majesty," in gratitude for "his most bounteous and unstinted fertilizations."

Given his burgeoning admiration for Greylock, on the top of Monument Mountain Melville must have commented on the view. And that might readily, perhaps inevitably, have prompted Hawthorne to mention Thoreau. Hawthorne had just moved to the Berkshires from Concord, and it would have been natural for the sight of Greylock to evoke some comment about the local kook from his old neighborhood—the guy who lived by himself in a cabin out in the woods and who had, in fact, written about Greylock in his only published book as of 1850, *A Week on the Concord and Merrimack Rivers*. Hawthorne, after all, had a very direct interest in *A Week*, not just because he had lived in the same town as Thoreau, in an "Old Manse" right on the banks of the Concord River, and not just because he had spent some time with Thoreau and had expressed grudging admiration for his outdoorsmanship, his unyielding but intriguing character, his intellect, and his writing—but because he had bought from Thoreau the boat that Henry and his brother had used to travel the Concord and Merrimack rivers. Thoreau had called it the *Musketaquid*, after the Indian name for the Concord; Hawthorne renamed the boat the *Pond Lily*. Duyckinck too knew of *A Week*; he had printed, and probably written, a review of it in the *Literary World* in 1849, and he had been asked by Ralph Waldo Emerson in 1847 to recommend publication of *A Week* to the firm of Wiley & Putnam as part of their "Library of American Books" series—the series in which Melville's *Typee* and Hawthorne's *Mosses from an Old Manse* first appeared.

So what did Hawthorne and Melville talk about on the day they met? Winds sweep up the western slope of Monument Mountain and engage leaves in long-drawn whispers. I think I hear the name of Thoreau.

❀ ❀ ❀

Leaning against rock, I read Bryant's poem, lifting my eyes from the page every so often to scan the horizon and compare Bryant's word pictures with the reality. Then I close my eyes to imagine Hawthorne and Melville, a century and a half ago, hearing from the mouth of Cornelius Mathews the same words I am reading now. And I think of the repercussions of that meeting of Hawthorne and Melville in August of 1850.

The usual accounts of the effects of that fortuitous day go something like this: after he met Hawthorne, which was just a few weeks after his aunt had given him a copy of Hawthorne's *Mosses from an Old Manse*, Melville immediately dashed off a laudatory (though anonymous) review expressing admiration for Hawthorne's "power of blackness" in *Mosses* and daring to compare him to Shakespeare. At the same time, of course, he was claiming something for himself — that it was indeed possible to speak of an American writer, one who probed the dark secrets of the human psyche or who questioned the workings of the universe, in the same breath as one spoke of the greatest of all writers. Duyckinck, who was visiting Melville at Broadhall, apparently took the review with him when he returned to New York City on August 12. The first installment of the review appeared in the *Literary World* just five days later, the second and last installment a week after that. Though the review was ascribed to "a Virginian spending July in Vermont," Hawthorne quickly learned that Melville was the author, perhaps when Melville and Hawthorne visited each other on September 3 and 4. Then ensued a friendship that so inspired Melville that he entered his most creative phase as a writer. Critical wisdom has it that Melville's writing of *Moby-Dick* took a dramatic turn once he met Hawthorne, that it changed from another seagoing adventure along the lines of his previous best-sellers *Typee* and *Omoo* to the penetratingly philosophical tome that led some contemporary reviewers to believe that Melville had gone insane, but that has since made it a recognized classic.[5] If my conjectures are correct, though, other influences besides Hawthorne's began wending their way into Melville's mind and work that day on Monument Mountain — the influences of Mt. Greylock and of Thoreau, specifically Thoreau's description of his ascent of Greylock in *A Week on the Concord and Merrimack Rivers*.

❀ ❀ ❀

The Appalachian Trail follows the ridgeline of the Berkshires to the east of Monument Mountain (which is technically in the Taconic Range), ascends the Greylock massif from the town of Cheshire to the southeast, climbs to the top of Saddleball Mountain, and then follows Saddle Ridge north to the summit of Greylock. On a moonlit night in May, my friend Duane and I stay in a lean-to on the southeast side of Saddleball. We spend much of the night standing in our underwear cussing at porcupines. They have been trying to eat the wood walls of the lean-to, and their persistent scratching and crunching has kept us awake. Anything salty, anything that's been touched by human hands, they'll munch on. All night.

I poke under the lean-to with my hiking stick, nervous at the thought that my porky target might come out running right at me, quills tilting at my nakedness. Perhaps he'll hurl those quills with devastating and painful accuracy, like some crazed animal acupuncturist. Actually I'm well aware, intellectually at least, that it's a myth that porcupines can throw their quills, but I'm feeling vulnerable enough to wonder if folklore is not a valid source of information about the world. I mean, am I not being excessively logocentric to believe that only knowledge caged in the form of printed words or frozen in the laboratory of a page is *real* knowledge?

Duane pursues the safer course of chucking rocks at the porkies, and he seems more purposeful—and effective—in his efforts. Evidently he is not distracted by any sort of absurd philosphical inner monologue about what constitutes a valid source of knowledge. After a few hits from Duane's throws, the porcupines scramble out from underneath the lean-to and amble off into the woods, looking back at us reproachfully as we call them undignified names. Or perhaps that's a look of sneering insouciance on their faces, as if to say, like the Arnold Schwarzeneggers of the rodent world, "We'll be back!"

They are true to their unspoken words. Within the hour, not long after Duane and I have fallen asleep, we hear again the impressive variety of sounds that porcupines make—their kittenlike mews, their babylike coos and whines, their occasional squirrelly chatter and scoldings. Most of all we hear their infuriating gnawing and chomping. When we yell at them, they don't even bother to raise their quilled hackles. Insolent bastards, like rats carrying knives, they have no healthy fear of us.

I've heard of some hikers who dissuade porkies by smacking them across the snout with a hiking stick. Sometimes it's dissuasion with extreme prejudice—that is, the hikers kill them, and seem to enjoy it. I've even heard of a guy who slit one open in the soft underbelly, then skinned, roasted, and ate it.

When I first encountered porcupines I was enthralled. Few wild creatures will get so close to people. They're night critters, like raccoons, and they've learned to associate campers with food. That first time I saw one, I followed its progress with a flashlight as it climbed a slim spruce and checked me out from a limb not ten feet above my head. That night I became acquainted with the porcupine's repertoire of sounds. I also discovered that porcupines' coats vary quite a bit in color — one sat chewing on bark within the bright circle of my flashlight beam, his delicate-featured face surrounded by a blond leonine ruff. I've seen others graying, some with whitish patches, some all black.

They're after our food, of course, but they'll settle for our boots if they can get them, or for any other sort of camping paraphernelia that they can find. Once, in the Catskills, I left a metal canteen on a picnic table outside a lean-to. A porky chewed on it all night — a most annoying sound — and took off one whole side and the bottom of the canteen. Nailed to my apartment wall spout-side down, right next to the light switch, it made an excellent candle holder. But a lousy canteen. I've been lucky, though. The only other thing I've lost to porcupines is sleep.

Duane and I venture out in pursuit one more time, feeling ridiculous standing around in our underwear, our skin phosporescent in the moonglow. To the east we see the lights of the town of Adams. Looking north we see a sloping shoulder of Saddleball, and beyond it a red light from the radio tower atop Mt. Greylock. Because of the intervening ridge of Saddleball, we can't see Greylock itself, just the tower lights reaching above the ridgeline. From the privy, just up the trail, Duane announces that he can see another light, a white one, on top of Greylock. We wonder if, since we're awake anyway, we could hike up at night, guided by those lights, our path lit by the moon. But we're starting to shiver, and besides, I need daylight on our ascent so I can look for some 150-year-old literary tracks.

Sufficiently moon-bathed, we snuggle back into our sleeping bags and do our best to ignore the porcupines. I light a candle and read for a while. Then we actually get some sleep. Somewhere between consciousness and sleep, between nighttime and daylight, I wonder: did Thoreau and Melville have any trouble with porcupines when they were up here?

❀   ❀   ❀

Our route the next day follows the path of Melville's sightline from his house in Pittsfield, the view he wrote about in "The Piazza." The narrator of that story is fascinated, beguiled by a light shining up on the slopes of Greylock. He envisions a romantic soul living up in those Valhallan regions, and he sets off on a journey thither, like some epic wanderer or a knight on a quest. Melville compares the narrator's piazza to the deck of a ship and the landscape to a sea:

> For not only do long ground-swells roll the slanting grain, and little wavelets of the grass ripple over upon the low piazza, as their beach, and the blown down of dandelions is wafted like the spray, and the purple of the mountains is just the purple of the billows, and a still August noon broods upon the deep meadows, as a calm upon the Line; but the vastness and the lonesomeness are so oceanic, and the silence and the sameness, too, that the first peep of a strange house, rising beyond the trees, is for all the world like spying, on the Barbary coast, an unknown sail.[6]

On our ascent I tell Duane of Melville's conceit that the landscape is like a seascape. Duane gets into the spirit, saying that the haze makes hills on the eastern horizon look like distant cresting waves, and that outcrops of white marble along the trail are like sea foam bubbling up from below, gushing over earth's geologically billowing surface. He points out too that looking east from Saddle Ridge we can see a town called Cheshire *Harbor*. When we get to the summit, we find that the source of last night's white light atop Greylock is a bona fide lighthouse, originally intended for the Charles River estuary in Boston but instead built here in 1932 as a memorial to Massachusetts' war dead.

When the narrator of "The Piazza" finds the source of the light he had admired from afar, he is disappointed. It's a shack on one of the lesser peaks to the south of Greylock—perhaps Saddle Ball or, just a mile or so toward Arrowhead, a promontory called Jones Nose. Perhaps the setting is a bit to the west, for the narrator speaks of passing through a "hopper-like valley," and the steep decline just west of the summit is called The Hopper. The shack is sad home to a woman named Marianna, who ekes out a living by sewing while her brother cuts wood and burns coal. The sunlight that had made the windows glimmer from the narrator's perspective in the valley serves mainly to stir up flies and wasps. Marianna spends her days envying the inhabitant of a gleaming house off in the distance—the narrator's, of course. The lesson, I suppose, is that the grass is always greener on the other side of the fence, and that fence is the boundary line between civilization and wilderness. The romantic luster of nature is a mirage. Life in the woods is no picnic when you have no choice but to live there. In some ways "The Piazza" retraces some of the themes of *Moby-Dick*. Greylock is a version of the white whale—the object of a quest, the vastness and sublimity of nature personified, though best admired from afar, for it has its dark side. Just as the white whale challenges Ishmael's naive impressions of nature's beneficence, so too the reality of Marianna's life on the mountain falls short of the narrator's romantic expectations. Nature is the setting not for some adventurous lark or pastoral idyll but for tragedy, whether dramatic or sadly muted.

❀   ❀   ❀

On the summit I read Thoreau's account of his climb, part of the "Tuesday" chapter from *A Week on the Concord and Merrimack Rivers*. Thoreau ascended in 1844 via a notch called the Bellows Pipe, on the northeastern side of the mountain. On the way up he stopped at a house for supplies and met a woman whom he apparently admired. In what must be the most erotic passage that he ever wrote (not that that's saying much), Thoreau describes the "mistress" of the house as "a frank and hospitable young woman, who stood before me in a dishabille, busily and unconcernedly combing her long black hair while she talked, giving her head the necessary toss with each sweep of the comb, with lively sparkling eyes, and full of interest in the lower world from which I had come, talking all the while as familiarly as if she had known me for years. . . . I had thoughts of returning to this house, which was well kept and so nobly paced, the next day, and perhaps remaining a week there, if I could have entertainment."[7]

This may not seem like very titillating stuff, but it's as overtly sexual as Thoreau ever gets, the most attentive and suggestive description of a woman's physicality in all of Thoreau's writing. But perhaps the attraction was only subliminal. He concludes the description by saying that the woman "reminded me of a cousin of mine." As William Howarth points out, "If her attire, her loose hair, and her reference to [some wild] students were meant as provocations, then Thoreau missed the point" (70). Subliminal though the sexual attraction may have been, clearly something about the woman appealed to Thoreau, enough so to tempt him to stay for a week—if he could find "entertainment" there. Perhaps Thoreau was moved by the simplicity of her life, or the unabashed and refreshing directness of her manner, or the admirable situation of her home high up the valley. He suggests that there is a necessary correlation between geographic height and moral elevation: "It seemed as if he must be the most singular and heavenly-minded man whose dwelling stood highest up the valley," writes Thoreau, just before he meets the woman who lived in "the last house but one" as he ascended (69). Perhaps he saw her as a "heavenly-minded" woman, one who had taken on the spirit of the mountain. I ponder the irony, that Thoreau expresses such rare

(for him) earthly desire for a woman he associates with the spiritually as well
as physically higher realm of a mountaintop. In the woman of Greylock,
perhaps Thoreau saw the possibility of marrying the earthly and the transcendental.

Thoreau climbed Greylock a few months after he unwittingly started a
forest fire around Concord and was, according to Howarth, in "public dis-
grace." On Greylock, says Howarth, Thoreau "described how space and solitude on a mountain journey restored his dignity and self-confidence. . . .
Eventually *Walden* repeated this story, that exile can clear away the 'quiet
desperation' of life spent at home" (56). Thoreau spent a cold night on the
summit, covering himself with boards left over from some construction work
done to improve the observation tower three years earlier. (The tower was
originally built by students from Williams College in 1830.) In the morning,
with clouds rising to his feet, Thoreau felt that he was "a dweller in the
dazzling halls of Aurora," surrounded by "such a country as we might see in
dreams, with all the delights of paradise" (76). Howarth calls the description
a "Transcendental *aubade*," or morning song, a "visual climax to his story
[that] verified its central theme, that greatness abides in 'trivial places' and
people, that physical challenge rewards the mind and spirit" (78).

❀   ❀   ❀

Lying in new spring grass on the top of Greylock, reading about Thoreau's
climb, with Melville's "The Piazza" still fresh in my mind from last night's
read, I appreciate the literary vista. The themes of two of the greatest works of
American literature, *Moby-Dick* and *Walden*, are encapsulated by works set
on this mountain. And those Greylock-inspired words tell virtually the same
story, but in reverse. A man ventures up the mountain on a quest, apparently
trying to revive a restless, dissatisfied spirit. He meets a woman. For Thoreau,
the woman represents all that is good in the world, in nature; for Melville,
the encounter with the woman leads only to disillusionment. Since Thoreau's account came first, I wonder if Melville read Thoreau's account and
deliberately used it as the basis for his antitranscendentalist story.

A few weeks later, following the path of my thought through the stacks of
the library, I find that I am hardly exploring uncharted intellectual territory.
Richard Moore convincingly demonstrates that Melville in "The Piazza"
picked up several plot elements from Thoreau's account in *A Week*: the encounter with the lone woman, her curiosity about the world below, a description of a ruined mill. He does not note other key similarities, perhaps other
borrowings—the references in both accounts to Spenser's *Faerie Queene*,

which in Melville's story become ironic, or Thoreau's Marianna-like description of the buildings of Williams College "gleaming far down in the valley." Moore also has at least a couple of facts wrong—he claims that Melville's narrator visits the summit and that Thoreau and Melville's narrator ascend Greylock along the same route. In fact, the narrator of "The Piazza" seems to have come up the western side of the mountain, through the Hopper—almost directly opposite Thoreau's route. That seems appropriate since Melville's narrator and Thoreau reach opposite conclusions about the value of the wild and its effect on us. As Moore points out, Melville's story is "calculated to disparage" Thoreau's account: Marianna's sad life is a "counterargument" to Thoreau's defense of self-sufficiency, and the narrator's visit to Greylock "exposes realities inimical to transcendental optimism."[8]

I'm puzzled by the apparent contradiction between Melville's fascination with Greylock and his challenge to the transcendentalist assumption that nature is benevolent and knowable. I wonder if he was ultimately disappointed in his love affair with the mountain, an affair consummated shortly after *Moby-Dick* had gone to press. On August 11, 1851, just about a year after the Monument Mountain excursion, he climbed Greylock with Evert Duyckinck and nine other friends and relatives, including Sarah Morewood, an indefatigable organizer of nature hikes who, with her husband John, had purchased Broadhall just after Melville had stayed there. Both Morewood and Duyckinck described the Greylock excursion in letters, and Duyckinck wrote up an account for the *Literary World*. The group hiked up from Williamstown and down to North Adams, which would suggest that they went up via the Hopper (like the narrator of "The Piazza") and down via the Bellows Pipe (where Thoreau came up). Duyckinck claims that their routes were the other way around, but he may have the names confused, since the Hopper does not lead to North Adams. According to Moore, Thoreau may have been a topic of conversation, for in his account of the climb in the *Literary World* Duyckinck quotes from Thoreau's description of Greylock.[9] In at least one particular Melville emulated Thoreau. Sarah Morewood wrote that Melville climbed a tree to holler to some lagging members of his party;[10] Thoreau too had climbed a tree on the way up, though his purpose in doing so was to take a compass bearing on the summit.

Like Thoreau, and unlike the narrator of "The Piazza," Melville and his group camped overnight on top, but they stayed inside the observatory. Duyckinck reported in letters to his wife that "the sun rise was a failure. . . . no fiery edged mountains of the sun's lightning flash"—quite a contrast to Thoreau's ecstatic aubade. But Duyckinck and Melville apparently saw cloud formations as striking as those witnessed by Thoreau. The clouds, says Duyckinck, were "rolling in smoking masses, through their looped raggedness disclosing the lower world. The full moon rose as it never rose before & when it reached our level appeared in broken spots of fire or girt with a ring of cloud." In his next letter he says that in the morning "mountains and clouds . . . rolled away from each other with the sublimity with which mountains are invested in the N. Testament. It was worth while to see that." [11] Whereas Thoreau's trip to Greylock culminated in sunrise breaking through a solid bank of clouds, Melville's party found themselves disappointed by the sunrise and most struck by the moon and by the shifting, ambiguous shapes of clouds. It's the difference between day and night, between transcendental optimism and brooding uncertainty. It's the difference between *A Week* and "The Piazza," or between *Walden* and *Moby-Dick*.

❁   ❁   ❁

Tired after a night engaged in battle with the porkies, I try to fall asleep in the summit grass. I wonder how Melville could have resisted the euphoria that always seems to accompany a summit vista. It is true that in our rush to romanticize the wild we fail to appreciate the hardships that would surely come with living there, but from this vantage point—where I can see the White Mountains of New Hampshire, the Green Mountains of Vermont, and the Catskills of New York; where the wind clears the clouds and keeps the bugs away—what's not to romanticize? I wonder if Melville's decision to have the narrator of "The Piazza" not ascend to the summit was part of an attempt to keep the grandeur of the mountain to a minimum. Then again, I bet Thoreau would have remained thoroughly convinced that nature is our means of access to higher realms even if he had never reached the top. Perhaps even if the two were hiking together, they would still record divergent impressions of their experience. When Thoreau was climbing Greylock, he almost seems to have anticipated the opposing viewpoint Melville would offer. When a local farmer volunteered the opinion that he would never reach the top before dark, Thoreau shrugged off the farmer's pessimism: "Even country people . . . magnify the difficulty of travelling in the forest, especially among mountains. They seem to lack their usual common sense in this. . . . It is very rare that you meet with obstacles in this world, which the humblest man has not faculties to surmount. . . . So far as my experience goes, travellers generally exaggerate the difficulties of the way. Like most evil, the difficulty is imaginary" (70). On top, looking over the clouds, Thoreau complained that "the inhabitants of earth behold commonly but the dark and shadowy under-side of earth's pavement" (77). Undoubtedly Melville would strike Thoreau as one of those who sees only the "dark and shadowy under-side" of clouds, one who exaggerates the "evil" and "difficulty" of travel in the mountains, or through life.

Years later Thoreau would still consider mountains a touchstone for separating the nature-lovers from the nay-sayers. In an 1857 journal entry Thoreau describes a recurring dream of a mountain that he climbs through "a dark and unfrequented wood . . . along a rocky ridge half clad with stinted trees, where wild beasts haunted." He says that the summit "can never become familiar; you are lost the moment you set foot there." In short the mountain of his dreams is a spooky, bleak-sounding place, and yet he calls it "the face of a god turned up," a "thoroughly purified" place. He descends through pleasant meadows, and concludes:

> There are ever two ways up: one is through the dark wood, the other through the sunny pasture. That is, I reach and discover the mountain only through the dark wood, but I see to my surprise, when I look off between the mists from its summit, how it is ever adjacent to my native fields, nay, imminent over them, and accessible through a sunny pasture. Why is it that in the lives of men we hear more of the dark wood than of the sunny pasture?
>
> A hard-featured god reposing, whose breath hangs about his forehead.
>
> Though the pleasure of ascending the mountain is largely mixed with awe, my thoughts are purified and sublimed by it, as if I had been translated. (Howarth, 11–12)

In their writings, it is clear which routes up the mountain Melville and Thoreau choose to follow.

❁   ❁   ❁

It's breezy up here, amid the gusty breath hanging about the forehead of Greylock. I wrap my heavy sweater and down vest more tightly around me, put on a wool hat. I can't believe Thoreau spent a night up here with no sleeping bag, with just a bunch of boards over him. In *Walden* Thoreau says that a big box is all we really need for housing. Howarth calls his blanket of boards on Greylock "a makeshift coffin," anticipating his "experiment with poverty" at Walden (75). Too cold to nap, I reread Thoreau's account of his night on top. In the morning, in what he calls "the pith of this long digression" (for the whole description of Greylock is something Thoreau supposedly remembers during a misty dawn on his rowing trip up the Merrimack

River),[12] he says, "I discovered around me an ocean of mist, which by chance reached up exactly to the base of the tower, and shut out every vestige of the earth, while I was left floating on this fragment of the wreck of a world, on my carved plank in cloudland" (75–76). Sea imagery. Perhaps another of Melville's borrowings for "The Piazza"? And then it comes to me, like a view from a high place, the summit euphoria of the researcher: Thoreau on the top of Greylock—alone amid an "ocean" of mist, protected from the elements by a "coffin" of boards, "floating on this fragment of the wreck of a world," a carved fragment, no less—essentially describes the ending of *Moby-Dick*. Call him Ishmael.

My scholarly curiosity is aroused. Is it possible that Melville was reading Thoreau's account of Greylock while he was writing the epilogue to *Moby-Dick*? Sitting on the deck of his piazza, perhaps, or by his study window, might he have found in Thoreau's description the image that would provide the ending of his greatest book, with the *Pequod* whale-sunk and Ishmael floating atop Queequeg's coffin—with no "vestige of the earth" to be seen?

The voices in the mountain winds have no answers to my questions. I've followed in Melville's footsteps up Monument Mountain and Greylock, and glimpsed some tantalizing possibilities. But whatever proof I can find of Melville's acquaintance with Thoreau's work is going to come not from long-faded footprints but from the still-legible print under thin layers of dust in the scholarly texts of a good library.

❁   ❁   ❁

I approach my research in a spirit of adventure, vowing to follow the trail I'd begun on Greylock, guided now by the alphanumeric signposts of the Library of Congress cataloging system. I tell myself that the library stacks are, after all, just forest in a different state. I journey into the land of the lexical vista, the wilderness of words where mountain landscapes sprawl within the typeset confines of the page.

The subject of Thoreau's influence on Melville has provoked spirited debate among literary critics. Most notably, Egbert S. Oliver claims in a series of articles from 1945 to 1948 that Thoreau is the model for the absurd and ridiculous transcendentalists in "Bartleby the Scrivener," "Cock-a-Doodle-Doo!," and *The Confidence Man*.[13] And Moore is convincing in demonstrating that "The Piazza" is an antitranscendentalist reworking of Thoreau's account of his Greylock climb. The problem in accepting these stories as evidence of Melville's persistent satire of Thoreau is that Thoreau was not a famous or even a highly esteemed writer at the time, so some critics have wondered, as Sidney P. Moss puts it, "*why* a well-known author like Melville would wish to satirize an obscure passage in an obscure book by an unknown writer . . . and *who* was to understand the point of his satire, for what value has satire if the object of its ridicule is unknown?" [14] Moss is referring to Melville's story "Cock-a-Doodle-Doo!," but the point could apply as well to "The Piazza." Moss may underestimate Thoreau's reputation in mid-nineteenth-century New England among writers — as a crackpot hermit associated with Ralph Waldo Emerson even if not as a writer of note in his own right — but his questions bring up a key issue. If my conjectures are correct, then the answer to Moss's question about how Melville would have known of Thoreau concerns a certain conversation on Monument Mountain.

No scholar has suggested that Thoreau's *Week* had any influence on Melville's work before the mid-1850s — and yet Melville certainly read *A Week* much earlier, borrowing it from Evert Duyckinck in mid or late July of 1850. Brian Higgins and Hershel Parker suggest that Melville may have borrowed *A Week* out of interest in the Greylock description, since he knew that he would shortly be in the area. [15] If it is true that Melville was acquainted with *A Week* before he ever met Hawthorne or reached the top of Monument Mountain, then perhaps Hawthorne and Duyckinck were not telling Melville anything new if they brought up Thoreau as a topic of conversation once Greylock hove into view. It is also possible, though, that Melville did not read *A Week*, or the Greylock portion of it, until after the Monument Mountain trip in August. But we can safely say that he was acquainted with it by the following spring, for during a March visit to Arrowhead, Hawthorne apparently joked with Melville about Thoreau's book. According to an entry in Theodore F. Wolfe's *Literary Shrines*, "The pair spent most of the week in smoking and talking metaphysics in the barn, — Hawthorne usually lounging upon a carpenter's bench. When he was leaving, he jocosely declared he would write a report of their psychological discussions for publication in a book to be called 'A Week on a Work-Bench in a Barn,' the title being a travesty upon that of Thoreau's then recent book, 'A Week on Concord River.'" [16]

If Melville had read *A Week* before the spring of 1851, it would seem that he had not yet gotten to the epilogue of his whale story, which he finished in the summer of 1851. But on the previous August 7, two days after the Monument Mountain excursion, Duyckinck had reported in a letter to his brother that Melville's whale tale was "mostly done," terming it "a romantic, fanciful

& literal & most enjoyable presentment of the Whale Fishery." [17] Obviously, that description does not quite accord with the finished novel, but it is likely that Melville was indeed near the end of a draft of the book in the late summer of 1850. James Barbour and Leon Howard contend that the final thirty chapters of *Moby-Dick* reflect Melville's reading of *Sartor Resartus* in the summer of 1850; several plot elements in that concluding section have parallels in Carlyle's work.[18] So if Melville was reading *Sartor Resartus* as he wrote the final chapters, it is quite possible that he was reading Thoreau's *Week*, which he borrowed *after* he borrowed *Sartor Resartus*, as he was writing the epilogue to *Moby-Dick* — in late summer or fall of 1850, perhaps, not mid-1851.[19]

Barbour and Howard point out that what Melville likely added to *Moby-Dick* from the autumn of 1850 till he finished the book the following July was much of the book's philosophical suggestiveness. And they say that Carlyle may have been the source for much of that, since Ahab's claim that "all visible objects, man, are but as pasteboard masks" is akin to Teufelsdroch's contention in *Sartor Resartus* that "all visible things are emblems. . . . Matter exists only spiritually, and to represent some Idea, and body it forth." But that transcendental philosophizing could also have been influenced by Melville's acquaintance with the work of Emerson (Melville had attended a lecture of Emerson's in 1849) and his reading of Thoreau. Like a transcendentalist, Ishmael ponders the symbolic significance of natural objects, like white whales. In fact, one of the early criticisms of *Moby-Dick* was that it was too much in the transcendentalist vein.[20] But as would be the case in the later works in which Melville takes issue with the transcendentalists, like "The Piazza," he is far less sanguine than Thoreau about nature's virtues or even about our ability to identify nature's meaning and value. Just as "The Piazza" is an inversion of Thoreau's ascent of Greylock, a rebuttal of sorts, so too is Ishmael an anti-Thoreau. Ishmael's musings in *Moby-Dick* constantly make use of the transcendental method, the reading of things in nature as physical representations of spiritual matters, but they are devoid of transcendental optimism. Ishmael tries to read nature symbolically, but he is never sure just what is being represented. What does the white whale stand for? Purity? Innocence? Evil? God? Nature? Is it hellish or divine? Good, bad, or indifferent? The only thing Ishmael is sure of is the Hawthornian (and un-Thoreauvian) lesson that we — people, that is — must depend on one another. We are anything but self-sufficient. The unpardonable sin is to set yourself off from your fellow men, as Ahab does; that way madness lies. We are all connected to one another as surely as Ishmael and Queequeg are linked by a lifeline when Ishmael enters the sperm whale. To be alone and floating on a fragment of the wreck of a world is cause for despair, not celebration.

❧   ❧   ❧

I want to be Thoreauvian, a lover of nature, one who finds meaning, sense, value, in the natural world, one who is at ease with himself amid nature and who sees nature's purposes. But the porcupines have me wondering. A porcupine would be an unexceptional creature were it not for those quills. From the Thoreauvian perspective, there's much to admire about the porcupine. Those quills enable him to get by in a world where there are such things as predators. And I've got to admire the porcupine's self-assurance, a quality that makes him so unafraid of large, loud, obscenity-spewing, rock-chucking mammals that he is willing to get close enough for us to observe him at our leisure. I've got to admire, too, nature's creativity in conceiving of such a creature. And I suppose that I could learn something from porcupines, though my wife tells me that I'm defensive enough as it is, hackles always ready to rise.

But for all my admiration for even such a thing as a porcupine, there is something to be said for the Melvillean view of the natural world, too. I'm not having dreams about a great white porcupine or anything like that, but I wonder about the mystery, the unknowability of creation, and, yes, the ambiguity of our feelings about nature. Why was I so uncomfortable about sharing a little space on the mountain with the porcupines? What drove me, Ahab-like, to embark on a vengeful hunt for the blood of the porcupine when all I'd lost was a little sleep?

What would Thoreau and Melville have done, I wonder, about the problem of the porcupines? Thoreau might have eaten one, as he eats the woodchuck, as he dreams of eating fried rats, in *Walden*. But I doubt that he would have eaten one out of some sense of revenge. More likely he'd seek only to feed his hunger for the wild or satisfy his curiosity. Probably he would have followed one, tried to find out where and how it lives. Melville might wonder what kind of world has such hurtful things in it. What kind of God would create such a creature? But there is no less a sense of awe in such ponderings as there is in outright appreciation. And perhaps I underestimate Melville's appreciation for nature. I mean, it's only from a limited anthropocentric perspective that *Moby-Dick* is tragic. From the point of view of a Greenpeace activist—or more to the point, from a cetacean perspective—the ending is triumphant: a whale is saved.

Surely there is some lesson in those porcupines. I'm just not sure what it is.

   ❁   ❁   ❁

I sit here tapping at a keyboard, books and photocopied articles spread over my desk. It's an untidy landscape in which to sum up some kind of meaning from my wanderings over the geological print of the Berkshires, my meanderings through a forestful of old books and dusty academic articles. I don't want to claim too much here. Critics have identified over one hundred sixty published sources for *Moby-Dick* — "more than a source for every chapter," point out the editors of the Northwestern-Newberry edition.[21] Perhaps all I'm doing is adding one more to the list. In fact, claims have been made for at least three other sources for the epilogue alone: Robert Southey's *Commonplace Book*, which has a story about a coffin used as a boat; Thomas Campbell's "Death Boat of Heligoland"; and Thomas Hope's *Anastasius*, in which the only two survivors of a shipwreck escape on a floating hencoop.[22] I do not believe that Thoreau's influence on Melville was as great as that of Hawthorne, or Carlyle, or Shakespeare, all of whom seemed to feed Melville's tragic vision in a way that Thoreau did not. What Thoreau did feed was Melville's enthusiasm for Mt. Greylock.

Atop those mountains in the Berkshires, I felt something of the nationalistic pride, the sense of artistic possibility that writers felt about their land in the nineteenth century. It used to be that Americans felt that their character had been formed by their land. The American landscape was the very image of freedom, wilder than the tamed landscapes of Europe, vast and expansive like our unbounded future. The land, our artists and writers and even literary critics once believed, could be the source for distinctly American art forms. Perhaps it's in the nature of the bookish beasts of the academic world, but I sense that attachment to the land, that faith in the power of the land, all too little in literature and literary criticism these days. Scholars do influence studies that go no further than an author's reading — as if the land did not exert its own influence.[23] I venture to say that Greylock was the inspiration for whatever interest Melville had in Thoreau. In fact, Melville's reading of Thoreau may have gone no further than the description of Greylock in *A Week*. But let us not underrate the value of a landscape. Hiking on Mt. Greylock and Monument Mountain, I felt myself in sacred places — sacred to me in part because great writers whom I admire wrote about those places, but sacred too because they had inspired the work of great writers, had made the writing possible. My claims that Thoreau's work may have influenced the ending of *Moby-Dick*, or that Hawthorne and Melville may have talked about Thoreau on the day they met, can indeed be supported (if not proved) through an examination of the evidence contained in a good library. But everything I learned in libraries about Melville's reading of Thoreau did no more than reinforce what I sensed the moment I read their words while reclining in summit meadows and nestling amid sheltering rocks atop the mountains where they'd rambled. Sharing their geographic perspectives, I felt that I understood their views. To overhear literary conversations over a century old, to follow the trail of an influence, I went to the source, where leaves still whisper with the wind on the slopes of Monument Mountain and Greylock.

11

Synecdoche and Ecology:
Frost in the Greens and Whites

Down in tennessee I shared a shelter on a stormy night with Indigo, Trail Mix, and Just Jane. While our noodles boiled on hissing stoves, we looked out the open front of the lean-to to see slivers of rain, lit by jolts of lightning, slant down at sharp gust-driven angles. After dinner, by shivering candlelight, with our pots soaking under the runoff from the eaves, we took turns leafing through a paperback collection of Robert Frost poems that someone had left in the shelter. In the morning Indigo remarked that he had been an English major at Dartmouth, which Frost briefly attended, and I confessed to being an English professor, and so we commenced class over our granola. What I like about Frost, I said, is the way he makes his language seem so natural and free even as he's working within very tight constraints of form. A Frost poem, I opined, is like a shelter—"a rigid structure that gives the illusion of openness."

Trail Mix crawled out of his sleeping bag and checked his pack where it had been hanging from rafters at the front of the shelter. "*Illusion* of openness! Man," he said, "my stuff is *soaked* from rain blowing in through that illusion of openness."

I stood corrected. It's real openness, real naturalness, within the solid structure of a Frost poem.

❀   ❀   ❀

At present I am hiking in Vermont, still thinking about the idea of Frost poem as shelter. In Tennessee I'd been thinking about the *form* of a Frost poem, but it seems to me now, entering Frost country, that the comparison is thematically apt as well. A Frost poem invariably faces out into the natural world, and from inside the poem you can feel the elements blowing, insinuating their way in. The structure may be log-solid, but the outside air wafts in. Not like a tent, where the walls separating human space from natural are clearly visible and present, albeit thin, all the way around.

I'm carrying in my pack a copy of Frost's first Pulitzer Prize–winning collection *New Hampshire*. The book is arranged in three parts: the discursive essaylike title poem (which I'm saving to read once I reach New Hampshire), a section of "Notes" consisting mainly of narrative poems featuring human protagonists, and then a section called "Grace Notes," lyric poems focused primarily on the natural world. I am particularly interested in this collection on the assumption that it most reflects Frost's acquaintance with the terrain of the Appalachian Trail in Vermont and New Hampshire. His first two volumes, *A Boy's Will* and *North of Boston*, grew out of his experience at his Derry farm, in southeastern New Hampshire. Frost moved to Franconia, in the White Mountains, in 1915, a setting that surely helped inspire the title and content of the volume he published a year later, *Mountain Interval*. But still many of the poems there were written before 1915. In 1920 he moved to South Shaftsbury, Vermont, just west of the main ridge of the Green Mountains; *New Hampshire* was published three years later, containing mostly poems composed since 1916. His later volumes seem more consciously "universal"; they take life in New England as their starting point but are not so much *about* life in New England. As the title of his 1938 collection has it, Frost was exploring *A Further Range*. But in *New Hampshire* the poems are still very much connected to the places where he lived in the mountains, his homes in the Whites of New Hampshire and the Greens of Vermont.

In Vermont the A.T. joins with the Long Trail for about a hundred miles. Just past Route 9, the trail crosses City Stream, flowing down the mountains westward toward Bennington. I pause there to fill up a water bottle and read "A Brook in the City," about a stream that's been forced underground, "thrown / Deep in a sewer dungeon."[1] But the speaker (call him Frost) has known the stream in its wilder state. I look around for a flower to toss in, "to try its currents where they crossed," as Frost had. I settle for a twig and a leaf, neither of which gets very far before it disappears in silver swirling rapids. I hold a finger in the current, to see if the water will indeed "leap my knuckle." Yes, though at the same time the current also coils itself around my finger.

I admire the detailed observations in the poem and appreciate the childlike curiosity of Frost, watching flowers get carried downstream, noticing what water does to a finger, a finger to water. The poem ultimately offers a complaint about human disregard for nature and a conjecture about what

we do to ourselves when we so fanatically "control" nature as to remove it
from our lives. In its absence, perhaps, is the germ of the dis-ease of modern
civilization:

> I wonder
> If from its being kept forever under
> The thoughts may not have risen that so keep
> This new-built city from both work and sleep. (231)

City Stream. A Brook in the City. Is this the brook Frost had in mind?
After all, just a few miles north of where this stream enters the Bennington
city limits is the stone cottage in South Shaftsbury that Frost moved into in
1920. Over a hill from there, heading toward the mountains, is the Gully
Farm, which he bought in 1928, a place (now owned by television producer
Norman Lear) with wonderful views toward Mt. Equinox, with open fields
and stands of birch. In the woods stands an enormous red oak, reputed to be
the largest tree in Vermont.

Frost once said that his brook in the city is "partially based" on a stream
in Greenwich Village.[2] But perhaps City Stream up here in the Green
Mountains is another part of the inspiration. "A Brook in the City" suggests
to me that Frost is more a celebrator of the wild than he is usually given
credit for. Most Frost critics have traditionally sought to praise him by insist-
ing that nature was not that important to him; human concerns were. Nature's main significance in Frost's work, they say, is symbolic. It is a text we
read in order to glean moral lessons. Perhaps this stance says more about the
traditional biases of literary criticism than about Frost's actual work. Literature, after all, is considered one of the "humanities," as if the human realm
were its only concern. But even the recent critics who take more interest in
literature of the natural world seem to accept the argument that Frost is not
much of a nature poet. Among ecocritics, Frost is either ignored or dispar-
aged (in passing) for his excessive anthropocentrism. Whether in praise or
blame, critics seem to accept that nature is of secondary importance to Frost.
At most, he is reputed to be a pastoral poet, someone who writes of nature as
a tamed, domesticated, agrarian middle ground between civilization and
wilderness.

But "A Brook in the City" decries the taming of "an immortal force" of
nature, its imprisonment "for nothing it had ever done / Except forget to go
in fear perhaps." Much of New Hampshire, in fact, at least in the section of
lyric poems called "Grace Notes," has a wilderness feel, with Frost entertain-
ing the possibility that nature does something more than serve as a conve-

nient set of metaphors for human understanding. Many of the poems explore a concern central to his work—"The line where man leaves off and nature starts," as he expresses it in the title poem of *New Hampshire* (171). That line typically forms the border of Frost country. *New Hampshire* is the place where he's most willing to venture across the line into the realm of nonhuman nature.

I am inclined to attribute Frost's wild edge in *New Hampshire* to the influence of his recent excursion, a few months before the book appeared, along a certain road less traveled, a white-blazed line he followed afoot. In August of 1922 he joined his children Lesley, Marjorie, and Carol and a couple of friends on a hike of the Long Trail. From South Shaftsbury they crossed Bald Mountain to pick up the trail in Hell Hollow, then headed north, crossing Glastenbury and Stratton Mountains. On the fourth day, a thunderstorm drove them to seek shelter in the town of Peru, where Frost, suffering from blisters, curtailed his hike. From there he walked to Manchester, took a train to Rutland, spent a couple of days recuperating in a hotel, then tried, unsuccessfully, to catch up to the others by walking on valley roads. The Frost children continued on the trail to Smuggler's Notch in Johnson, Vermont. Afterward, Lesley wrote an account of the trip for the Bennington *Banner*. The headline hailed them as the first to complete the Long Trail. Though her father made it only part of the way on the trail, still it was the most extensive hike he ever undertook.[3]

❦   ❦   ❦

As I lean over from streamside and midstream boulders, Hell Hollow Brook moves too fast for me to see my reflection. I take pictures of cascades gushing white. Where the water runs clear, I see quartz stones on the streambottom. I read some poems, and I think I see truth.

In "For Once, Then, Something" Frost describes himself peering over the edge of a well and seeing himself "Looking out of a wreath of fern and cloud puffs" (225). That's what most of us see when we look into nature, reflections of ourselves. And that's what critics have assumed Frost's poems are all about—seeing ourselves in nature. To whit, according to John Lynen in *The Pastoral Art of Robert Frost*: "In the end, Frost's rural world is interesting because it symbolizes the world we ourselves know." The "central fact of his regionalism [is] that it presents the world of rural New England, not for its own intrinsic interest, but as a symbol of the whole world of human experience." And again: "Though he writes about a forest or a wildflower, his real subject is humanity." In a poem called "The Woodpile," "The woodpile itself is unimportant. It is meaningful only because it leads to a revelation of human nature." In other words, Frost doesn't really care about the "merely natural" world, he cares about the human realm, which Lynen characterizes as "the great world," the "larger world."[4] To which I say, "Bunk."

I don't mean to pick only on Lynen's book, but it has been an influential study, and it is representative. A book I admire much more, George Bagby's recent *Frost and the Book of Nature*, offers the same emphasis: "For Frost, as for so many other American nature writers, natural phenomena are almost never purely physical or random; they seem to have been 'put there' as signs or messages for the human observer." In what he calls Frost's "emblem poems," Bagby says Frost "first describes the partial, physical vehicle of the synecdoche that constitutes the poem, and then comments on the larger — spiritual, epistemological, psychological, or ethical — tenor of the figure."[5] Bagby is trying to clarify Frost's claim that he was the "poet of synecdoche," putting his artistic faith in that figure of speech in which the part is taken to represent the whole. Or, as Frost put it, "Always, always a larger significance. A little thing touches a larger thing."[6] What I don't get is why everybody supposes that nature is the little thing, human spirit or psychology or ethics the larger thing. How is it that we live on the earth and are larger than it is?

Frost looking into the well sees down deep "a something white, uncertain." Then a drop falls from a fern to blot out the image. "What was that whiteness?" he asks. "Truth? A pebble of quartz? For once, then, something." Critics have universally read that closing line as a choice between something grand or something trivial — the "truth that would validate the artist's quest as a heroic seeking" versus "the merely material," says one.[7] I see it differently. In the whiteness of the quartz we need not see metaphor in order to find something remarkable. It is not a matter of the humanly significant versus the trivial, but of the significantly metaphysical, the spiritual, or the cultural, the truth we discern from reading nature symbolically, as a good transcendentalist should, versus the equally significant physical world, the concrete, matter. Not "just" a pebble, or "nothing more than some gleaming stone,"[8] but nature's own self, unadorned and unmagnified by our own readings or expectations or shapings of it. Either way — Truth or A Pebble of Quartz — it was *really* something.

Some critics have considered Frost's pebble a small geolyric version of Melville's white whale. We can't be quite sure what it represents. But *Moby-Dick* is misread in much the same way as Frost's poem is. The cetological chapters of *Moby-Dick* (the parts I've heard English professors disparage as "all that crap about whales," worth skipping so as to get to "the good stuff," the metaphysics) are precisely about the whale as whale, as opposed to the whale as symbol. Either way, suggests Melville, and as Ishmael comes to discover, the whale is really something.

I'm reminded of another literary work, touching on a similar theme, by a much more obscure writer — in terms of publication, completely obscure. Driving up to the trailhead at Route 9, I detoured to South Shaftsbury to see Frost's Stone Cottage and the Gully Farm. At first I drove past the Stone Cottage, and pulled in just down the road at a shack. Painted on white clapboard, fading black letters read "Art Museum." Inside, the place was crammed with canvases painted by the proprietor, a man named Frank Howard. I fancied him a typical Yankee codger, his angular face grizzled with white stubble, his frame gnarled and lean. To say his attire was unfashionable is radical understatement — yellow sweatpants rose several ludicrous inches above the waistband of his thick trousers. I asked about mountain pictures, and he showed me paintings of some local scenes, of the Adirondacks, and Katahdin, and some imaginary landscapes. And a portrait of John Muir. When I reacted with interest, he told me he also had one of Henry Thoreau, up at the house. We walked together up a dirt lane. The yard and the porch were overgrown with knee-high weeds, the kitchen piled high with crushed-up tin cans. Though it was June, water gushed from the kitchen sink, to keep the pipes from freezing. More paintings lined the hallways and upstairs bedrooms.

We chatted. As a kid Frank used to play with Frost's grandson, Prescott. Once they played at a little stream with a waterwheel that Robert had made for Prescott. But theirs was a difficult friendship, for Prescott was bossy, and, said Frank, "I don't take to being bossed." Given Robert Frost's reputation, Prescott's assertiveness may have been an inherited trait.

After the requisite dickering over price, I bought the painting of Thoreau. Then Frank showed me a box overflowing with his poems, each written in a careful, neat hand. One was about trees, appreciating them for providing poetic inspiration and preventing mudslides. Another was about a wading pool. It said something about people seeing the pond as a kind of mirror, which amounts to a rather "shallow" understanding. For they see "naught but themselves there" — and what they see is "not even fair." I commented on the clever allusion to the "mirror, mirror on the wall" fable.

Now, sitting by Hell Hollow Brook, it occurs to me that Frank's poem is kin to Frost's "For Once, Then, Something." We think that to see nature as

pure nature is to see only its surface. But maybe the truth is that the surface
is the symbolic level where we see ourselves. Deeper down, there's something else. Maybe it's something more.

❦   ❦   ❦

Near the top of Glastenbury Mountain, cold water, so cold my palms ache,
pours from a piped spring. A shelter faces south over the edge of the mountain. Breezes keep the black flies down, and clear sky drops to a horizon
below eye level, giving a gorgeous view as far as Greylock. Time for a long
lunch break, watching for buntings or spring azures or violets or lapis la-
zuli — fragments of blue, none of which I find, to go with the sky. My search
is initiated, of course, by a poem, "Fragmentary Blue":

> Why make so much of fragmentary blue
> In here and there a bird, or butterfly,
> Or flower, or wearing-stone, or open eye,
> When heaven presents in sheets the solid hue? (220)

Frost's answer to his question is that heaven is so far from earth that "It only
gives our wish for blue a whet." I enjoy the pun — whet/wet — knowing that
the sky is our source for things other than blueness, and the forecast calls for
rain. I'm thinking too about small things and large things, about synecdoche.
If we read this poem symbolically, then we read "heaven" in all its religious
overtones, think of it as the place up there above the sky, of eternal spiritual
rest on pillowdown clouds and angels playing elevator music on golden
harps. Down here on poor earth we get just small tastes of that heaven, doled
out in natural images. Nature is the small, and the human significance, the
spiritual significance suggested by "heaven," is the large — that would be the
usual reading.

But to use the physical object, the detail from nature, to represent the
metaphysical or the human meaning seems more like symbolism than synecdoche. A symbol suggests one thing, often something abstract, in terms of
another, usually something concrete. Synecdoche uses a part of something
to suggest the whole of it. Deliberately differentiating himself from the sym-
bolists and imagists of his day, Frost made a point of calling himself a synec-
dochist. Was he simply confused?

I'm willing to take Frost at his word and assume that he knew what he was
talking about in reference to the guiding figure of his art. In the first stanza
of "Fragmentary Blue" Frost offers three images from nature (bird, butterfly,

flower), one that partakes of both nature and the human (the wearing-stone), and one that seems to refer to human physicality (the open blue eye). Then he brings up the topic of heaven. Is he moving, then, from the natural to the human, from the physical world to, as Bagby puts it, the "*larger* realm of spiritual fulfillment"? From "observation of a specific natural fact . . . to a recognition of the *larger* imaginative reality implicit in it," a "*larger* human insight of which the observed phenomenon is the partial embodiment"? (italics mine).[9] Only if we read the second stanza to refer strictly to a metaphorical heaven, as the place where God lives and good people go. I don't necessarily take it that way, especially in light of a comment Frost once made: "I think there's probably nothing 'up there' but stockpiles of nature observations that came from earth."[10] Not something spiritual or metaphysical, in other words, but more of the physical world, more nature. If we take the second stanza of "Fragmentary Blue" as one of those observations from earth, we see blue sky that is not there just to represent something metaphysical—but which is still pretty heavenly. The poem is "about" the natural world, which includes the human realm (and our concern about the afterlife) but is not limited to it, which includes the physical and metaphysical realms but is not limited to either one. As I see it, Frost is not primarily interested in the human or metaphysical realm; I don't see that he's using the natural world solely or even mainly as a means to that greater end. Both are means, both are end. But if one, nature or human, has to be "whole" and the other "part," it makes sense that nature is the whole that contains the human part of nature, and the physical contains the metaphysical.

Many of the nature lyrics in the "Grace Notes" include references to the human or metaphysical realms without being dominated by those realms. In "The Onset" Frost begins with a natural image, a description of the first snow of the season "hissing on the yet uncovered ground." The second half of the first stanza shifts to suggest the human lesson. Stumbling, he is

> As one who overtaken by the end
> Gives up his errand, and lets death descend
> Upon him where he is, with nothing done
> To evil, no apparent triumph won,
> More than if life had never been begun.

If the poem were to end here, it would fit the pattern critics have attributed to Frost—from observation to lesson, image to moral. The fall up into abstraction, I've heard the process called. But the poem does not end there. The second stanza returns to nature, as Frost describes the "precedent" he knows so well, of life returning when winter's done: "the peeper's silver croak" and the

> water of a slender April rill
> That flashes tail through last year's withered brake
> And dead weeds, like a disappearing snake.
> Nothing will be left white but here a birch,
> And there a clump of houses with a church. (226)

Yes, the poem returns to mention human concerns and constructs at the end. Yes, we get the moral lesson that winter is a kind of death, but spring and life always return. In things white there is still life, is the idea, and death too is part of life. Why is this synecdoche and not symbolism? Because the principle of passing on and coming back applies not exclusively or even mainly to humanity, but to all of life. We can read this as a lesson not just about human existence, but about existence in general. Frost, in fact, is careful *not* to give undue emphasis to the human over the natural. To illustrate what's left of white after winter, Frost gives the comforting examples of a birch and a clump of houses and a church. Though the houses and church get the last word, they are equated with a simple birch, which we would usually consider an insubstantial thing next to a living village. And notice the word choice "clump"—as if the houses amounted to some eye-catching but indeterminate mass of foliage found in the woods.

The other thing Frost does in this poem, and in fact in most of his nature poems (and not just in *New Hampshire*), is to devote the bulk of the lines to nature. In "The Onset," ten of the second stanza's twelve lines give very precise, detailed natural imagery. We do a disservice to the poem to focus only on some lesson about life after death as we understand that concept in human (religious) terms, because much of the poem has nothing to do with that, like the peepers croaking and the snowmelt running downrill. The process is similar in poems like "Nothing Gold Can Stay." Five lines describe the gold of early leafbuds in spring, which is soon consumed, leaf by leaf, by green. Then Frost gives two one-line examples, followed by a synopsis of the overarching principle being demonstrated:

> So Eden sank to grief,
> So dawn goes down to day.
> Nothing gold can stay. (222–23)

That is a wonderfully succinct comment on things ephemeral, including in that category material wealth and glory, as evoked by the metaphoric implications of "gold," and human youth and innocence, as evoked by the line about Eden. But the Eden reference is only one of three examples, and it is embedded in the middle of a series of examples, getting the least emphasis. And the gold of the last line is not just a symbol of wealth and earthly reward, it is also the color of impermanence in the natural world. The poem does not build through natural images in order to deliver a punch line about material wealth being transient. Rather, that line is one example, one part of a larger pattern that includes but also extends beyond the social realm. The metaphoric implications of the word *gold*, or of *heaven* in "Fragmentary Blue," should certainly be part of a good reading of the poem—but they should not be mistaken for the whole. The lesson is not just observable in nature so that it can be rendered applicable to human civilization. It is observable in both, applicable in both.

Carol Adams has coined the phrase "the absent referent" to convey a sense of what happens in much metaphoric use of nature imagery. Often, she says, as the image "becomes metaphor, its meaning is lifted to a 'higher' or more imaginative function. . . . Metaphorically, the absent referent can be anything whose original meaning is undercut as it is absorbed into a different hierarchy of meaning. . . . The absent referent is both there and not there. It is there through inference, but its meaningfulness reflects only upon what it refers to because the originating, literal, experience that contributes the meaning is not there. We fail to accord this absent referent its own existence."[11]

Adams uses the term as part of her scholarly defense of vegetarianism. Her chief example is of a rape victim saying she "felt like a piece of meat," a phrase that may express the human victim's pain but leaves out what is only implied in the metaphor: the suffering, the existence even, of animals slaughtered in the name of dinner. But the idea of the absent referent has wider implications, pertaining to the linguistic appropriation of nature as a storehouse for handy metaphor.

An example of the absent referent can be found in Frost's "Misgiving," a poem that devotes three quatrains to a description of leaves refusing to fly with the wind, "choosing" instead to rest by a "sheltering wall" or giving "at utmost a little reluctant whirl / That drops them no further than where they were" (236). Though there is some close observation of the behavior of leaves in an autumn wind, the natural image is subsumed by the moral drawn in the final quatrain, where Frost expresses the hope that when he has the chance to pursue "knowledge beyond the bounds of life" (like a leaf off a tree?), he won't choose to rest instead. The poem relies on extensive (and unconvincing) anthropomorphizing of the leaves promising to follow the wind and then seeking shelter, and the description seems preamble for the moral lesson, which is so heavy-handed and prominently placed as to leave readers thinking of human desires and not the leaves.

Generally, though, the natural world in Frost's work is anything but an absent referent. It is always there, and much of the time it constitutes the very subject of the poem. This is not to deny that humanity is there as well. But to say that the human "hierarchy of meaning" contains the "point" of a Frost poem is to ignore nature as an emphatically present referent. Nature is not the "little thing" touching some larger human or moral thing. More often the point applies to, and encompasses, both nature and humanity, the physical as well as the metaphysical, the moral, the metaphoric. In his essay "Education by Poetry," Frost wrote that "the philosophical attempt to say matter in terms of spirit, spirit in terms of matter, to make the final unity" constitutes "the height of all poetic thinking." [12] Note the lack of hierarchical order in his statement—both spirit and matter are required, and neither is of a higher order of things.

In this sense Frost's synecdoche is an implicitly ecological tactic. We don't just read nature as text. We're right there in the book with it, all part of the same story. Or poem. The point of a Frost poem is not primarily a moral lesson about human existence but a "larger" observation about all of existence, all of life, where nonhuman and human life, the physical and the metaphysical realms, are all parts of a whole called nature.

❁   ❁   ❁

On the third day of my hike I cross Stratton Mountain, see six toads, a spring peeper, and a good-sized garter snake on the way up. Near the top I think I hear someone hammering, and it takes me a while to realize that what I hear is a woodpecker doing his thing. What kind of wood, I wonder, makes that resounding a sound when pecked?

At the summit I climb the first flight of stairs up the firetower, getting about as high as the treetops. It was from a Stratton Mountain treetop, in 1900, that Benton MacKaye first envisioned a long-distance trail running the length of the Appalachian chain. Sounds like that woodpecker is still building it.

Rain urges me off the firetower and down the mountain. At Stratton Pond the rain and the black flies struggle for control of the atmosphere. The far shore appears and disappears as the murk does magic tricks. The pure, haunting notes of a white-throated sparrow carry across the pond. Birders say

that its two-toned call sounds like "Old Sam Peabody, Peabody, Peabody."
Doesn't sound like that to me, it sounds like, well, a whistle that I can't put
into words. If only this page could sing. . .

But of course pages can't sing and words can't whistle and humans can't
ever really step into the heart or mind or larynx or stamen or ecological niche
of other living things, and our attempts to do so are rendered in the distinctly
human medium of language. There are lines we can't cross, even — or especially — following the squiggly isoalphabetic lines we put down on paper.

So how in the world, goes the objection, can human beings ever see the
world or talk about the world in anything other than human terms? In other
words, how can we be anything but anthropocentric? To which I answer,
using language to take us on a journey into some other consciousness is
precisely what literature does. It allows us, at least for the space of a story, a
poem, a song, to try on other lives, to experience other existences, to identify
with someone else, or something else.

New Hampshire is Frost's survey of the borderlands of his poetic realm,
and many of the poems describe glimpses of what lies on the other side of
the line between anthropocentrism and biocentrism. The book's famous final poem, "The Need of Being Versed in Country Things," traces that shift
in perspective. The first four stanzas draw a desolate picture of a burned
farmstead going to ruin, only the chimney left standing, birds flying in and
out of broken windows, their singing "like the sigh we sigh / From too much
dwelling on what has been." But the final two stanzas correct the impression
of desolation by giving a birds'-eye view of the scene:

> Yet for them the lilac renewed its leaf,
> And the aged elm, though touched with fire;
> And the dry pump flung up an awkward arm;
> And the fence post carried a strand of wire.

> For them there was really nothing sad.
> But though they rejoiced in the nest they kept,
> One had to be versed in country things
> Not to believe the phoebes wept. (242)

"To be versed in country things" means to reject the pathetic fallacy, our
tendency to project human emotions onto nature. It also means getting the
facts of life straight, the facts of other lives, that is. Once a cliff-dwelling
species, phoebes have expanded their range in recent centuries by finding
an abundance of nesting sites in the detritus of human civilization.[13] A ruined farm, to a phoebe, is an opportunity, and it is home.

The movement from romantic preconception to a corrected realistic perception also appears in "A Boundless Moment." Walking in the woods on a fair day in early spring, Frost and a companion see a gleam of something pale in the maples—"the Paradise-in-Bloom." In point of fact, no such flower grows in New England, and even if it did, "such white luxuriance" would not be abloom in still-wintry March. In the final stanza, Frost admits "his own pretense" and then corrects his identification with "the truth": "A young beech clinging to its last year's leaves" (233–34). As in "For Once, Then, Something," I take the title to impart dual meaning. The "boundless moment" may not be just the one where he stood "in a strange world" seeing some exotic flower appear in the wrong time and place. It may also be the moment of truth, where fact replaces fancy and the "flower" turns out to be last year's leaves on a beech tree. The facts matter to Frost, and he generally gets them right. Beech trees do grow among maples, and they do hang on to their leaves through the winter, and it is in March that the leaves' tannin decomposes and they turn white.

But "to be versed in country things" is not just a matter of knowing about other things and understanding the facts about their lives—it is also an act of imagination. The anthropocentric poet sees things only from a human perspective. The biocentric poet tries other perspectives as well, perhaps one from which a ruined farmhouse may not be worth crying over, like a phoebe's. Yes, it is true, as Frost once stated, that few of his poems are devoid of a human presence.[14] It is also true that even fewer are devoid of a natural presence, and in many that presence is the point. Frost's poems remind us of the "boundless moments" of pleasure that the natural world can give us. In "Dust of Snow" it's snow falling off a crow-shook hemlock bough. In "Looking for a Sunset Bird in Winter," it's a cold winter evening and a leaf on a tree where once he heard a bird sing—"that was all there was to see" (and that all was really something)—and this haikulike boundless moment:

> A brush had left a crooked stroke
> Of what was either cloud or smoke
> From north to south across the blue;
> A piercing little star was through. (233)

In "Evening in a Sugar Orchard" it's sparks tangling with "bare maple boughs" and forming constellations and the moon just

> moon enough to show
> On every tree a bucket with a lid
> And on black ground a bear-skin rug of snow. (234)

And in "A Hillside Thaw" it's the day the sun makes "silver lizards out of snow," all running downhill, until the moon casts a cold silent nightspell that holds them still, "One lizard at the end of every ray" (237–38).

These are essentially moments of transcendental unity, but of a different sort from those that arise when we suddenly perceive a spiritual lesson inherent in some natural object or event, when a natural image transforms into moral message. These are things we find outside ourselves, the moments we are granted when we cease to be just ourselves and allow the world in.

         ❧   ❧   ❧

By the side of Little Rock Pond, a garter snake lifts its head and freezes, then doubles back over himself and heads off in the direction I least expect him to go; the pink of a lady's slipper turns almost translucent as its bloom fades; scudding ripples on the pond make a breeze visible before it arrives to blow the bugs away (temporarily); sitting on a rock a few feet from shore I dip my feet and am coolly content; minnows come to investigate until a toe twitch sends them shooting for cover and a small burst of silt explodes underwater; up on Green Mountain crows squawk excitedly over something dead and delicious—these are some of the boundless moments on the trail in Vermont.

These moments come to us through our senses, which are the routes we take to get out of ourselves. That is often the role of the human observer/perceiver in a Frost lyric—to serve as recorder of the senses at work and at play in the world. Is this what Frost meant when he called himself "a sensibilitist" and "an environmentalist" (166)?

The trail, that avenue of the senses, turns east at Sherburne Pass, leaving the ridgeline of the Green Mountains, entering a more pastoral landscape, offering views of quaint white houses in green valleys that invite imaginative habitation, crossing open fields and young woods where whatever it is that doesn't love stone walls pulls them apart with tendrils and time. The trail in eastern Vermont touches much of what ecologists call "edge effect," the biologically rich and diverse territory at the margin between fields and woods. That margin is called an "ecotone," a kind of line between zones. Like a bit of Frostian poetry, like a trail, negotiating the borders between the human and the wild. A trail is our gateway out of the human realm, our entryway to the wild, following contours implicit in the land. But it's also a human construct, the Appalachian Trail coming into creation, perhaps, the moment Benton MacKaye, nestled in a Stratton Mountain treetop, first envisioned it running along the Appalachian ridgeline, built anew whenever we go to the mountains and walk there, both following a line in the earth drawn by others and reinscribing it with our boot soles.

I'm thinking about the trail as a kind of line as I walk and as I read, for *New Hampshire* is full of lines about lines. In "Two Look at Two" a couple, a human couple, come to "a tumbled wall" in the woods blocking their "onward impulse," and they see first a doe, then a buck (229). The wall seems like a barrier of sorts, separating the human and the natural. But what follows is another boundless moment, where imaginatively we cross not just the wall but the line between anthropocentrism and biocentrism:

> Two had seen two, whichever side you spoke from.
> "This *must* be all." It was all. Still they stood,
> A great wave from it going over them,
> As if the earth in one unlooked-for favor
> Had made them certain earth returned their love. (230)

As in "For Once, Then, Something," ambiguities abound. The phrase "It was all" both delimits ("It was all" meaning there's no more) and expands ("all" meaning everything, all boundaries exploded). The title suggests an equivalency between the deer couple and the human couple, and it confounds the boundaries between subject and object—who's doing the looking, the two deer or the two people? Which set of lovers is the subject of the poem, which is the perceiver and which the observed object? For once, then, for that boundless moment, those boundaries disappear. We cross the line into another consciousness.

At times Frost shows how the lines we seek to draw between ourselves and nature cannot be clearly or precisely drawn. In "Blue-Butterfly Day" he describes butterflies in early spring resting in road ruts "Where wheels have freshly sliced the April mire." That line might seem like a critique of human effects on the land—after all, the word *sliced* seems violent, and the word *mire* makes it sound like the wheels have made a mess of the land. But the poem as a whole stresses the beauty of the scene. The butterflies are described as "sky-flakes" and "flowers that fly and all but sing." The context makes clear that the wheel tracks, far from desecrating the biosphere, offer welcome respite at the season of rebirth. The butterflies in the ruts "lie closed over in the wind"—a lovely and precise description of their wings folded up—after "having ridden out desire"—which I take to mean they've recently mated (225). The road offers similar succour in "Our Singing Strength," where a snowfall in early spring covers all the surrounding fields, while "The road alone maintained itself in mud." The birds, both natives of the area and those caught in mid-migration on their way back north, flock to the road, exhausted with trying to find a dry perch in trees. They move "like ripples over rocks" in front of the narrator walking along the road (239–40).

Along the lines where man leaves off and nature starts, there we are most likely to encounter a rich diversity of other living things, there we find that human presence and natural rhythms can be compatible with one another. Following those lines, on the earth and on the page, we sometimes look up and find ourselves on the other side.

❀   ❀   ❀

Frost wrote that the biggest difference between Vermont and New Hampshire is that Vermont's mountains "stretch extended straight" while New Hampshire's "curl up in a coil." But otherwise the two states are "Yokefellows" matched thick end to thin like complementary wedges, alike enough that his praise of New Hampshire "Will serve almost as well about Vermont" (164–65). The trail crosses the border into New Hampshire at the Connecticut River, then cuts through the campus of Dartmouth College in Hanover. Heading northeast, it climbs Smarts Mountain and Cube, Moosilauke and the Kinsmans, skirts Lonesome Lake, then descends to Franconia Notch, renowned (if nothing else via its silhouette on New Hampshire highway signs) for the geologic feature known as the Old Man of the Mountain, a series of granite ledges on Profile Mountain that look like a human face.

Before he moved to Vermont, Frost lived in Franconia, just a few miles north of Franconia Notch. His front windows and porch faced the Franconia Ridge, a line of mountains including Liberty, Little Haystack, Lincoln, and Lafayette. In an upstairs bedroom (the house is now open to the public) there's a picture of Frost, with family and friends, on the summit of Lafayette.

In "New Hampshire" Frost wishes that these mountains were higher. One reason he proposes for this desire to elevate the mountains is his mistaking "the solid moulding of vast peaks of cloud" for the "pitiful reality" of the mountains themselves (169). The image reminds me of mountain paintings of the Hudson River School, where clouds echo the shapes of the mountains in an attempt to make visual the transcendentalist faith in correspondence between the natural and spiritual realms, the clouds representing the intangible realm of the spirit. Clearly the illusion tempts Frost, as it does the many critics who want to look past the physical reality of Frost's natural facts to the spiritual echoes that form around them.

But Frost goes on to say, no, that's not it, he wants the mountains higher

because he once saw an early map that exaggerated their height, and he
wishes to taste cool mountain air: "To tap the upper sky and draw a flow / Of
frosty night air on the vale below" (169). The appeal is not to the spirit, which
feeds on meaning, but to the imagination and senses, which feed on images
drawn from books and the physical world. "The more the sensibilitist I am,"
says Frost, "the more I seem to want my mountains wild." In explaining
further what he means by that, Frost tells a story of a logger freeing a logjam,
dodging a log that threatened "to break his back for him," then "dancing,
skipping, with his life / Across the roar and chaos," and crowing with glee at
the fun of it all (170).

In contrast to the logger is the "prude afraid of nature":

> He had a special terror of the flux
> That showed itself in dendrophobia.
> The only decent tree had been to mill
> And educated into boards, he said. (170–71)

Funny stuff. This prude is also the source of the line about "The line where
man leaves off and nature starts," a reference to Matthew Arnold's sonnet "In
Harmony with Nature"—an ironic title since Arnold argues that harmony
with nature is neither possible nor desirable. Not desirable because nature is
the realm of cruelty, human civilization the realm of mild compassion. Not
possible because humanity and nature are distinct and separate realms:
"Man must begin," says Arnold, "where Nature ends." The prude's problem,
according to Frost, is knowing "too well for any earthly use" just where that
line between humanity and nature lies. Too well for earthly use, but not
perhaps for human use. Out of fear comes arrogance, as in Arnold's assertion
that "man hath all which Nature hath, but more, / And in that more lies all
his hopes of good." And out of arrogance comes the logic of domination.
Frost's Arnoldian prude would be quick to convert nature into manufactured
object, the stuff of civilization. But the raw material of nature the prude will
shy away from, all too aware of the borderline at nature's edge, a line which
he's "never over-stepped . . . save in dreams" (171).

In his fear, the prude sees nature as dark and oppressive, a view not entirely foreign to Frost's poems—think of the ominous tree scratching at the
window in "The Hill Wife." But in "New Hampshire" Frost stakes out a
different kind of territory for himself, or sets himself up as someone who will
take a different approach to nature. Unlike the prude, he is not so definite
about where the line between man and nature lies—that is, he is not so sure
of our absolute distinction and separation from nature. But even to the extent

that he accepts or recognizes some barrier between man and nature, he's willing to cross it, to explore the wild, the flux and roar and chaos where nature exists on some terms other than those by which they are appropriated or ordered into a human scale of reference—whether educated into boards or shaped into moral messages.

The other role that the persona of "New Hampshire" rejects is that of the "puke," who commits the sin of Ahaz. That sin is usually read as the simplistic idolatry of nature worship. But Frost hedges in his condemnation of nature worship, conceding that "Nothing not built with hands of course is sacred" (171). So if nature may in fact be sacred, then what distinguishes him from Ahaz? The sin of Ahaz, as I read it, is not just that he worshipped nature, setting up shrines in the hills, but that he made sacrifices to those shrines, including his own sons (see 2 Kings 16 and 2 Chronicles 28). His sin, perhaps, in Frost's eyes, was to love nature above people as well as God. These are all parts of the whole, none of which should be sacrificed in the name of another.

Prude or puke. These terms define opposite extremes of the roles we play in trying to establish a right relationship with the natural world. At different times Frost tries on these roles, and at times he rejects that sort of either-or thinking as a means of viewing the world. Prude versus puke, fear versus worship, natural versus human, physical versus spiritual—can't nature, large and multitudinous, contain all these?

"Me for the hills where I don't have to choose," says Frost (170).

❧   ❧   ❧

Throughout "New Hampshire" Frost sprinkles footnotes referring readers to poems in the "Notes" section that elaborate on themes or situations brought up in the title poem. This was his way of poking gentle fun at the elaborate appendixes of scholarly footnotes in T. S. Eliot's *The Waste Land* (a prude's view of the world?), published the year before *New Hampshire* appeared. The footnote to the line about heading for the hills directs the reader's attention to "An Empty Threat," where Frost gives his most explicit recognition of his attempt to move beyond anthropocentrism. The poem is about his pipe dream of "getting away from it all" (which I somewhere once heard rendered as the wonderful verb "to gafiate") by running off to Hudson's Bay, described as a place of incomprehensible blankness:

Give a head shake
Over so much bay

Thrown away
In snow and mist
That doesn't exist,
I was going to say
For God, man or beast's sake,
Yet does perhaps for all three. (211–12)

Plato and others have said the poet speaks for God, many have claimed to
write on behalf of humanity, but not many poets have considered the beast's
perspective. Or, as Frost does elsewhere in *New Hampshire*, the bird's.

The line about "The line where man leaves off and nature starts" refers
the reader to "A Fountain, a Bottle, a Donkey's Ears and Some Books," a
narrative poem set in the area around Kinsman Mountain. In the poem Frost
asks a friend named Old Davis to show him a fountain built by Mormons on
Kinsman. Together they "made a day of it out of the world, / Ascending to
descend to reascend"—which is a fine concise description of the rigors of
hiking in the Whites. They don't find the fountain, but they do find a cliff
where vegetation has stained the rock in the shape of a bottle—"A likeness
to surprise the thrilly tourist," something akin to the Old Man of the Mountain. Davis offers to take Frost to another tourist attraction, converging rock
slides that "look like donkey's ears" (214). When Frost is unimpressed, the
guide accuses him of liking only books and not nature. But already the line
between human construct and the natural is blurred. What is a fountain but
an imitation of nature? What is that bottle on the cliff but the exercise of
human fancy, seeing a design in vegetative whimsy? What are the donkey's
ears but an attempt to perceptually reduce a powerful geologic force into an
image of domestication? These are all images of nature envisioned as human
or at least domesticated objects, seen from a solely human perspective.

Davis takes Frost to the abandoned home of a dead poet, Clara Robinson,
a crippled woman who was confined to her bed and wrote verses about "The
posies on her inner window sill, / And the birds on her outer window sill"
(215). The window is a kind of dividing line between inside and outside.
Now, with no one to care for the place, the outside has come in—shattered
glass sequins the floor, and rain has swollen and stained the books spilled on
the floor, multiple copies of the same book really, written by her. "Boys and
bad hunters" have shot out the windows, but they haven't harmed the books,
just dropped them on the floor after reading a line or two (216).

What's in those books, one presumes, is supposed to be what's outside, the
world beyond the window, that now-broken line between the natural and the

human. Frost envisions liberating one of the books, hoping "To send it sailing out the attic window / Till it caught the wind." It might fly momentarily, "Only to tumble like a stricken bird" (216). He seems to want to send the books back to nature, but he's all too aware that her poems don't soar. Nature too has been "shut-in," inside the cover of a book (215). But if a book can't fly, it can at least walk away, in the hiker-poet's back pocket.

Frost does not quite praise the poet's work, but he seems more impressed with the discovery of her books than with the views of the bottle or the donkey's ears. Though her poems may not have quite captured what's out there beyond the window, there is at least something of nature in them. Despite all the limitations of her life and her art she has at least made an attempt to imaginatively get outside herself.

The "Fountain" poem is typical of the "Notes" in picking up ideas and situations from "New Hampshire" and turning them into stories and in introducing themes that are further developed in the "Grace Notes." "The Census Taker," like "The Need of Being Versed in Country Things," takes as its subject an abandoned homestead. But here the speaker is less sanguine about both the absence of a human population and the area's return to nature. The farmstead here stands "in a waste cut over / A hundred square miles round it in the mountains" (174). The place has been decimated by clear-cutting:

> every tree
> That could have dropped a leaf was down itself
> And nothing but the stump of it was left. (175)

It will not be so easy for nature to return here. The census-taker closes with the comment, "It must be I want life to go on living" (176). This is another one of those lines that has implications for both human and nonhuman life, the speaker's sympathies lying with both. There is no recrimination regarding the objectionable logging practices of the former inhabitants, just a sad picture of what the place is like once they're gone — with their own absence contributing to the gloom. As in "A Brook in the City," mistreatment of the natural world becomes the harm we do ourselves.

Many of the "Notes," like the "Grace Notes" about lines, stress our ability to achieve some kind of integration with nature, telling stories about how nature enters our lives, becomes part of our lives, is part of our reason for being, suggesting that the lines of separation between us and nature are easily crossed. "The Star-Splitter" opens with an image of Orion approaching by "Throwing a leg up over our fence of mountains," making it seem close and neighborly (176). The story suggests that if the stars don't come to us, we can go to them. A neighbor of Frost's who is curious "about our place among the infinities" burns his house down for the insurance money, which goes to buy a telescope, visual transport to infinity (177). In "A Star in a Stone-Boat" a piece of the sky, in the form of a meteorite, becomes part of a stone wall, resting on the line between us and nature, not far beyond it.

Though the protagonists of the "Notes" narratives are human, nature is not quite relegated to background. Many of the poems involve human characters interacting with nature. In "Paul's Wife" Paul Bunyan finds a snake-skinlike thing in an evergreen, dips it in water and it comes to life as a woman whom he falls in love with and who becomes his life's companion. In essence, he marries nature.

The lesson of integration, of following the line where the human and the natural meet and are one and inseparable, seems to apply especially to art. In "The Ax-Helve" a neighbor explains to Frost that the art of carving a good tool handle is to follow nature:

> the lines of a good helve
> Were native to the grain before the knife
> Expressed them. (187)

In a study of the ecological thrust of Frost's poems, Michael McDowell has pointed out that "in Frost no one ever conquers nature. Conquest is never even an intention." [15] Instead, Frost's protagonists learn to go with nature, to follow it, or to let it in, whether they're building walls, ax-helves, poems, trails, or a life.

❀   ❀   ❀

Climbing Lafayette, I'm caught in a swirl of clouds. Patches of clear sky occasionally open up to give glimpses of Franconia Notch, of Cannon Mountain and the Kinsmans, but not enough to give anything like a panoramic view. No view of the Old Man's profile, but perhaps the angle is wrong from here.

At the summit, the sky lifts to the south and west. I look back over the ridgeline toward Lincoln, Little Haystack, and Liberty, and it's a clearly demarcated line, clouds shrouding the eastern side of the ridge, crashing against it and dissolving upwards like surf-spray over a rock jetty. On the other side, it's clear for about twenty minutes, until clouds surge up from the notch like a mile-high tide washing in.

The trail follows rugged Garfield Ridge above Hawthorne Falls, over Mt.

Garfield, South Twin, and Guyot, along Zealand Ridge and down to Crawford Notch past Zealand Falls and Thoreau Falls, Ethan Pond, and Ripley
Falls. On Zealand Ridge a grouse with a red slash above each eye flaps clum-
sily off the Trail to perch in a low-hanging branch. He cocks his head as I
approach, but he doesn't fly away. It's a spruce grouse, tame enough that
people used to "harvest" them by knocking them out of trees with walking
sticks.

At Ethan Pond I stay in a shelter, glad to be out of an all-day drizzle. In
the late afternoon I'm reading "The Aim Was Song," one of the "Grace
Notes." It's about man teaching the wind how to whistle so as to make a song:

> He took a little in his mouth,
> And held it long enough for north
> To be converted into south,
> And then by measure blew it forth.

No more of nature's free verse. Frost's "Man" imposes metrical order upon a
force of nature so as to show it, "word and note, / The wind the wind had
meant to be." And the wind comes to understand: "The aim was song — the
wind could see" (224).

At first I find the poem's anthropocentrism unsettling and out of keeping
with the tone of the rest of *New Hampshire*. Is Frost saying that nature is
somehow deficient until we arrange it into some sort of artistic expression?
And what's that about the wind coming to "see" what it is supposed to be? As
if it is nature's purpose or intention or desire to become art. As if nature *has*
something we'd recognize as purpose or intention or desire. And as if we
could instruct it as to the proper expression of its purposes, intentions, or
desires. The whole thing reminds me of a line from Hawthorne's "The Great
Stone Face": "Creation was not finished till the poet came to interpret, and
to complete it."[16] Didn't that artist-is-God stuff go out with the romantics?

But of course Frost is a poet writing about poetry, defending his brand of
tightly structured poetry, his concern for both "word" and "note," or sense
and sound. As a poet, naturally he's aware of his own role in shaping nature
into metrical form. That's not such a bad role for the human part of creation
to play — like Thoreau's suggestion that "a writer a man writing is the scribe
of all nature — he is the corn & the grass & the atmosphere writing."[17] The
artist as nature — and only part of nature, at that. It's not like he does it all by
himself. "Man" is not the original source of the energy that goes into the
artistic creation. In the act of whistling, the man *converts* the wind into
song — but he doesn't create the song from nothing. Man is the creator not

of nature itself, but of the song that takes something from nature and in turn gives it expression. Frost's song begins in nature and returns to it.

A white-throated sparrow calls from somewhere in the spruces surrounding the shelter. I take out my pennywhistle, key of C, and imitate the call, then add grace notes and improvise, returning to the sparrow song as a base melody.

The sparrow calls back.

12

Democracy and Ecology:
Hawthorne's White Mountain Stories

Early june in new england: most hikers know better than to risk their sanity on trails still boggy from the spring melt, still buggy from the spring hatch. Tired of feeding my blood to too many black flies, hungry for someone to talk to—I'm delighted to be reaching New Hampshire's White Mountains, where I know there will be hikers galore to show pictures of the kids to and where the stretches of trail above tree line shouldn't be too buggy. I stay in several of the high-country huts run by the Appalachian Mountain Club, a bit pricey but very convenient and very social.

At Greenleaf Hut on the western slope of Mt. Lafayette I play Scrabble with a banker from Connecticut, an engineer from New Jersey, and a couple of nurses from Massachusetts who call themselves "The Living Goddesses." When my opponents find out my profession, I am tabbed a ringer. I sit out the second game and serve as official dictionary and adjudicator: "wen," sure, like a pimple, not a reference to time; "veals," plural of veal, ok; "zincs," I don't think so. The game-winning play is on "en"—you mean like the letter N, I say, dubiously; well, it *is* in the Scrabble dictionary.

In the bunkroom after lights-out, somebody's snores provoke occasional snickers building to giggles and guffaws and reaching a crescendo of widespread hilarity. The laughing more than the snoring keeps everybody else awake.

Through the Whites I hike alone but at camp and at the huts I meet a variety of people—a financial analyst out with his son, a massage therapist, a retired mechanic out botanizing, a woman in sales, a recent college graduate who turned down a job in business in order to spend a summer doing trail work, a couple of guys from Georgia who have never been north before and drove all day to get here. I make a pest of myself asking them all the same questions: Why do you come to the mountains? What value do you find here? I get a lot of answers that contain the words *peace, harmony, oneness,* and *serenity.* I also get these:

"What am I looking for? Ten dollar bills."

"Me, I'm looking for twenties."

"I happen to love screwing up my knees. Doesn't everyone?"

"Why do I come here? Because it's here. Of course."

"Why would anyone want to go anywhere else?"

❁   ❁   ❁

Nathaniel Hawthorne came to the Whites in September of 1832, traveling through what was then called the Notch of the White Mountains (now Crawford Notch) and staying for several days at Ethan Allen Crawford's Inn. The details of his trip are recorded in "The Notch of the White Mountains" and "Our Evening Party among the Mountains," both parts of his 1835 "Sketches from Memory." In "Our Evening Party" Hawthorne remarked upon the woodsy decor of Crawford's Inn, the deer antlers, foxtail, bear's paw. And he remarked upon Ethan Crawford, a mountain man of legendary strength. Hawthorne describes him blowing a five-foot trumpet, setting off reverberating echoes that "found a thousand aerial harmonies in one stern trumpet-tone." The other guests at Crawford's that night included two young married couples, a physician, a mineralogist, a trader, and a foppish poet, whose "Sonnet to the Snow on Mount Washington" Hawthorne deemed "as cold as [its] subject."[1]

The next morning, starting at 4 A.M., Ethan guided the party through the Ammonoosuc Ravine and up to the summit of Mt. Washington, which Hawthorne said "looked near to Heaven" (424). After his stay at Crawford's, Hawthorne continued on his journey to the Green Mountains, then up to Burlington, Vermont, on Lake Champlain, and over to Niagara Falls. His return trip took him to Fort Ticonderoga and the Erie Canal.[2] Hawthorne apparently did not see the White Mountains again, at least not up close.[3] But for the next couple of decades, the Whites seemed to stay with him, forming the setting not just for two of his "Sketches from Memory" but for three of his stories, "The Ambitious Guest" (1835), "The Great Carbuncle" (1836), and "The Great Stone Face" (1850). In the stories, Hawthorne adheres to the nationalist literary agenda of his day, seeking to create a distinctly American literature out of native materials, to story the landscape with legends and history associated with natural landmarks. Hawthorne also creates a distinctly American hero, characterized by virtues that mark the influence of a democratic society. As it happens, those same virtues seem compatible with an ecologically sustainable society as well.

❀   ❀   ❀

"Out here people are at their best."

"I have a thing about trees. I can't explain it. But I love to stand next to trees, or under them. And to touch them. There's something about them — the way they breathe in what we breathe out, as if they're our other half. Does that make any sense?"

"I just love the constant surprises. Every time you come around a turn on the trail, there's something new, some kind of plant, or a tree, or a bug, or a neat rock, or a view."

"Everything's so . . . I don't know, *homogenous*."

❀   ❀   ❀

In Franconia Notch, the granite ledges of Profile Mountain form chin, nose, and forehead of a stony visage. The Old Man of the Mountain, it's called, although a roadside sign also credits Hawthorne's name for it, "The Great Stone Face." Hawthorne's story of that name explores the idea current in the nineteenth century that the American character must reflect the American landscape. The idea was given its pithiest expression in John Greenleaf Whittier's 1868 poem "Among the Hills," where he wrote that America must produce "a man to match his mountains." Whittier was speaking symbolically. Hawthorne's story takes the notion literally.

The story is about Ernest, who grows up in the valley below the Great Stone Face and hears from his mother the prophecy that, someday, from this valley will come the greatest man of the age, and his face will be in every particular that of the Great Stone Face. Several personages are hailed as he who fulfills the prophecy: Gathergold, a shrewd and wealthy trader; Blood and Thunder, an illustrious, iron-willed military commander; Old Stony Phiz, a statesman and orator of such eloquence he "could make a kind of illuminated fog with his mere breath." In every case, Ernest anticipates seeing the stone face rendered in flesh. But though the rest of the populace delude themselves into seeing a resemblance, Ernest sees none of the virtues that he has come to know, through long and familiar association, in the Great Stone Face. None of the "gentle wisdom," the "deep, broad, tender sympathies," none of the nobleness, grandness, sweetness, goodness, the "vast warm heart," peace, wisdom, sublimity, stateliness, "divine sympathy," "high purpose," beneficence, cheer, solemnity.[4]

Ernest meanwhile has grown up to become a simple husbandman, and gains a reputation for virtues that echo those of the mountain. He is helpful, loving, happy, calm, pensive, mild, quiet, unobtrusive, intelligent, tender, "industrious, kind, and neighborly," of "a hopeful and confiding nature," with a "gentle sincerity" and "tranquil and familiar majesty," who "neglected no duty," whose heart contains "wider and deeper sympathies than other hearts," who entertains "unworldly hopes for some great good to mankind," and is renowned for the "well-considered beneficence of his daily life" and the "pure and high simplicity of his thought" (33, 39, 42, 37, 38). Ernest becomes convinced that a certain poet is the man of prophecy. This poet bears some resemblance to the poet described by Emerson in his essay "The Poet," in that his "poetic faith" glorifies those "sordid with the common dust of life," demonstrates the ties that bind all humanity, and celebrates the beauty of the human spirit and of the world. The poet composes an ode in honor of the Great Stone Face that is "grand enough to have been uttered by its own majestic lips" (43).

Ernest is hopeful that, just as the poet's words reflect the spirit of the Great Stone Face, perhaps his face will reflect its physical features. But when they meet, Ernest must admit that no physical likeness is evident. The poet himself confesses that though he has been able to give verbal expression to his glimpses of the familiar truths that can be found in nature, at times he lacks faith in those truths, and "in the grandeur, the beauty, and the goodness, which my own words are said to have made more evident in nature and in human life" (46). In him there is no harmony of word and thought and life.

The poet perceives what readers have caught onto long before, that Ernest himself, a simple man whose life has been unadorned by material, martial, political, or aesthetic ambition or achievement, is the man of prophecy. But Ernest, ever humble, wishes it were not so, that there were someone more eminent who would qualify as the great man of the age. Hawthorne is saying that America's greatness lies not in its businessmen, its statesmen, its war heroes, not even in its artists, but in its simple citizenry. It's a surprising symbolic value to find in mountains, which are typically seen as emblems of magnificence and imperial stature. In "Sketches from Memory," Hawthorne himself makes the usual sort of symbolic association in celebrating the mountain as a monument to George Washington, whom he seems to claim as our greatest hero. "Mountains are Earth's undecaying monuments," says Hawthorne. "They must stand while she endures, and never should be consecrated to the mere great men of their own age and country, but to the mighty ones alone, whose glory is universal, and whom all time will render illustrious" (424). But in "The Great Stone Face," and in the other White Mountain stories that were written much closer to the time of his travels in the Whites, Hawthorne associates mountains with democratic rather than imperial virtues. The ordinary, the simple, the humble.

Throughout the story, Hawthorne stresses that the mountain has been Ernest's moral guide, source of "a better wisdom than could be learned from books, and a better life than could be moulded on the defaced example of other human lives" (33). The lesson is reminiscent of Puritan teachings that nature is a form of Scripture, created by God for man's edification. That was one reason to appreciate the American landscape right from the start of European settlement, for here in the wilderness (as the Puritans saw it) was God's unadulterated handiwork in plenty. But by the nineteenth century the theological lesson, intended to make us humble in the face of God's power, had been replaced by a nationalist impulse, intended to celebrate the middle station of life that most Americans occupied in the absence of an equivalent to English aristocracy.

Some hint of that democratic theme surfaces in "Sketches." In describing his stay at Crawford's, Hawthorne says it would be worth his while "to spend a month hereabouts, in sleighing time, for the sake of studying the yeomen of New England" (427). Of course, he never had a chance to do that. It is also possible that he never actually saw the Old Man of the Mountain. Neither "Sketches from Memory" nor his letters about his trip in the White Mountains mention the Stone Face. The idea for the story first appears in an 1839 notebook. Possibly the idea arose from a conversation with Ralph Waldo Emerson, for a letter from Emerson to Margaret Fuller in September of that year mentions his visit to the "pleasing wonder" of Profile Mountain, where "the grave old Sphinx gazes eastward with an expression that may be called great & natural." [5] Hawthorne may have been on his way to visit the Old Man when he died. Hoping to revive his health in 1864, Hawthorne was traveling north to the Whites with his old college friend, former President Franklin Pierce. They made it to the Pemigewasset Inn in Plymouth, about thirty miles south of Franconia Notch, when Hawthorne died in his sleep.

❧   ❧   ❧

After breakfast at Greenleaf, I wish my Scrabble partners well, climb Lafayette, follow the ridge to Mt. Garfield, break for lunch at the summit. Just below the summit and down off the ridge, my map tells of a "Hawthorne Falls," but a trailworker tells me you have to bushwhack to get there. Wet and tired, I save that side trip for another, drier day. I arrive at Galehead Hut in midafternoon and spend a couple of hours reading and warming up with hot coffee, looking forward to another Scrabble game. But right before dinnertime a woman slips on a rock and breaks her leg just a hundred feet down the trail. Fortunately, there's a doctor staying at the hut. He sets the bone. The hutmaster, Sara, makes radio contact with AMC headquarters, and the word comes that we should get the woman to a hospital quickly. Sara asks for volunteers to carry the woman down the mountain. It will take all night, she warns us. Though everyone is tired, and some are poorly equipped for bad weather, an impressive number volunteer. Some of us, though, think that a litter carry in the dark, in the rain, over slick and steep trails, at the risk of hypothermia, is a bad idea, especially when there's a doctor right here. The hutmaster talks further with headquarters, and finally everyone agrees we should wait for a rescue team. The team arrives in the middle of the night, and over hot coffee they decide to take the injured woman out at dawn.

I follow the trail over South Twin and Guyot, down through Zealand Notch, rest at Thoreau Falls, then stomp through swamp en route to the shelter at Ethan Pond. There's a caretaker there, a woman named Jessica with rings in her nose and left eyebrow. While I play my pennywhistle, imitating bird calls, she's building a fence around a tent site. With an ax, she shaves the bark from leg-thick poles and notches them. With the flat side of the ax-head she drives in the support posts and secures the ridgepole with six-inch nails. When she's done working and I'm done playing, we agree to make dinner together and share what we've got. That way we get variety— she's having noodles with tomato sauce and I'm having noodles with cheese sauce. But she's also got fresh vegetables. And I've got spices.

Over dinner I learn that she's recently graduated from college, working out here for the summer before getting a "real" job, or maybe going on to graduate school, she's not sure yet. Maybe that's something she'll figure out while she's out here. I ask my usual questions about the values she finds here.

"For me, it's not about knowing facts about nature, or being able to identify species. It's the beauty, the spirit of the place. I feel I belong out here. You know how some people have street smarts? I feel like I have woods smarts. Being out here—it just comes naturally to me."

From Ethan Pond, named for Ethan Crawford, the trail slabs the side of Mt. Willey and runs past Ripley Falls on the way down to Crawford Notch. The story goes that the notch was discovered by Timothy Nash while hunting a moose in 1771; the truth is that the route was an old Indian trail, and Nash was probably looking for it because he was a member of a Lancaster,

New Hampshire, committee appointed to seek out routes to improve the town's access to other areas. Abel Crawford settled about six miles north of the narrowest portion of the notch, the Gateway, in 1791, then moved six miles south of the Gateway a year later and turned the original homestead over to his father-in-law, Eleazar Rosebrook. Finding innkeeping more lucrative than farming, the Crawfords and Rosebrooks opened up inns and worked to improve the road through the notch. In 1816 Ethan, Abel's son, moved into the Rosebrook inn, and in 1828 Ethan's younger brother Thomas moved into a third Crawford inn right at the Gateway. Ethan cut two trails up Mt. Washington, the Crawford Path, which the A.T. picks up near Mt. Clinton and follows up to Washington, and the bridle path, which cuts through a valley to the Ammonoosuc Ravine and then up the west spur of Washington.[6]

The road through the notch is now called Route 302. About a mile up the road from the trail crossing is the site of the Willey House, where in August of 1826 a landslide wiped out the Willey family — husband and wife, five children, a hired boy and a hired man. Three of the bodies were never found. The others were found under a shelter where they had sought refuge. But because a boulder diverted the slide, the house they'd abandoned was untouched. Cruel irony — if the Willeys had stayed put, they'd have been safe.

A rock with a plaque marks the spot now, right next to a small store that sells sundries and ice cream. Across the road is a parking lot and the Saco River floodplain.

The Willey disaster had achieved a certain amount of renown even before Hawthorne exercised his fancy upon it in "The Ambitious Guest." It was the subject of numerous poems and sermons. One would think that the gist of many of the sermons would be something like, "Remember the Willeys, oh ye of little faith." But apparently the Willeys, who had providentially survived a landslide two months earlier, were held morally blameless, and the event was read as a reminder of the might of God, whose mysterious ways lie beyond the comprehension of puny men.[7] Hawthorne acknowledges that "the story has been told far and wide, and will forever be a legend of these mountains."[8] Small wonder, then, that he first published this as one of his *Twice-Told Tales*. But if the Willey disaster was so well known, why did Hawthorne feel obliged to tell it again? And why, if he intended in his White Mountain stories to celebrate the American landscape, does he choose for his topic such a horrifying bit of local history?

Some of the ideas for the story seem to have sprung from the seedbed of

"Sketches from Memory." In the first paragraph of "The Notch of the White Mountains," Hawthorne describes the "red path-ways of the Slides," and he imagines the notch to be cut by a "demon . . . or one of the Titans . . . elbowing the heights carelessly aside as he passed" (422–23)—a mountain god of the sort that could command the rockfalls of "The Ambitious Guest," which sound "something like a heavy footstep" taking "long and rapid strides." But whereas the titanic power in the sketch is merely careless, in the story it demands respect and turns into a cosmic ironist. The father identifies falling rock as the work of "The Old Mountain," a spiteful sort of spirit who hurls stones "for fear we should forget him" (326).

Early in the story, though, the family seems to have been able to accommodate themselves to the demands of the mountain. Theirs is a simple life, a contented life, one in which the mountain serves them well by providing them with a living. The opening scene shows the family gathered around a fire fueled by the mountain's detritus, "the drift-wood of mountain streams, the dry cones of the pine, and the splintered ruins of great trees, that had come crashing down the precipice" (324). The mountain provides stuff for sustenance, and the valley of the Saco and the notch funnel visitors, paying visitors, to their door.

The mountain offers psychological benefits as well. All are happy, having "found the 'herb, heart's ease,' in the blackest spot in New England" (324). Cold and windy as it might be, that spot seems to be responsible for the family's idyllic contentment. In the house the stranger finds "warmth and simplicity of feeling, the pervading intelligence of New England, and a poetry, of native growth, which they had gathered, when they little thought of it, from the mountain-peaks and chasms" (327). Like Ernest in "The Great Stone Face," they have absorbed the spirit of the mountain.

Into this idyllic existence the ambitious guest enters like a snake in a garden. His ambition is as yet obscure; he knows that he is foreordained to achieve some kind of distinction, but he knows not how. But in his ambition he commits the sin of pride. Speaking to the daughter he says, "You think my ambition as non-sensical as if I were to freeze myself to death on the top of Mount Washington, only that people might spy at me from the county roundabout. And truly, that would be a noble pedestal!" (328). The implication is that he is another Washington, one of those "whom all time will render illustrious." Besides the egotism implicit in comparing himself to Washington, there is hubris, too, in assuming that the mountain exists in order to commemorate any human.

The daughter at first resists the young man's temptations, defending the "comfortable and contented" — and unambitious — life they have been living (328). Ultimately, though, the guest's ambition affects the family, and discontentment sets in. The father, for example, wishes for "a good farm, in Bartlett, or Bethlehem, or Littleton, or some other township round the White Mountains; but not where they could tumble on our heads. I should want to stand well with my neighbors, and be called 'Squire, and sent to General Court, for a term or two; for a plain, honest man may do as much good as a lawyer" (329). Only the children seem immune to the infection of ambition. The smallest child's greatest wish is that they all take a midnight hike out to the flume for a drink of water. An easily satisfied desire, for something simple that would reinforce their connection to nature, an inspired whim that would have saved them all, but which the grown-ups dismiss as absurd. Then the story relies on the circumstances of history. The slide arrives, they all die. But Hawthorne never names either the family or the mysterious stranger. Perhaps he knows that posterity will remember the Willeys ("Who has not heard their name?" he asks). For the ambitious guest, the namelessness is more cruel irony. His name is buried with him and his ambitions.

This "Old Mountain" of the Willeys clearly is nothing like the kindly "Old Man of the Mountain" in Franconia Notch. The emphasis here is on the mountain's sublime power, a frightening force harking back to the "howling wilderness" of Puritan writings. Puritanical, too, in the sense of the dark wilderness as a punitive force, a means of divine retribution. In Michael Wigglesworth's 1662 *Day of Doom*, for example, straying from the path of moral righteousness is followed by an apocalypse in which "The Mountains smoak, the hills are shook, the earth is rent and torn."[9] But if the family and the guest are sinners in the hands of an angry mountain, what exactly is their sin? Hawthorne says they were ambitious (and Hawthorne is an honorable man), but since when is ambition a sin?

Perhaps it is a trinity of sins, against God, nature, and country. In failing to trust in Providence when the landslide arrives, the family earns the wrath of God, Old Testament style. In wishing to escape the mountain, the ambitious father fails to appreciate its gifts, and thus earns the wrath of the mountain titan. And in seeking a higher station in life and not appreciating his simple and contented life, the father is guilty of violating the democratic social order. If "The Great Stone Face" shows the heroism of the humble life, "The Ambitious Guest" issues a stern warning against the sort of restlessness that leads to a desire for material or social improvement. Stay put — that's the moral of both stories.

But what could be less American than a message like that? Aren't we a people always looking to improve ourselves, always on the move, forward? When Frederick Jackson Turner issued the classic statement of how the American landscape formed us in its image—the frontier hypothesis of 1894—his point was that the frontier, with lots of open land always available and promising new opportunities just beyond the horizon, made us expansive and forward-looking and ever optimistic. To this day, we assume that progress is an unalloyed good and that it is driven by the motor of ambition, fueled by our individual strivings to improve our social and economic lot in life. Isn't that what America is all about? Isn't this the land of opportunity?

Hawthorne's story reminds us that for much of American history, what America stood for, what was considered the prime virtue of this land and our character, what it meant to be an American, differed greatly from our current conception. Through the first half of the nineteenth century, those enterprising literary souls who sought to define the American character as something distinct from its European ancestry (they were not much concerned with our native American and African ancestry) emphasized our connection to wilderness.[10] In part we were defined as a kind of chosen people, closer to God because our land came straight from his hand. Our forests were natural scripture uncorrupted by human editing via the saw or plow. Socially, American writers boasted of our classlessness, the fact that here were no great extremes of wealth or poverty. Opportunity in America meant not the chance to accrue unlimited wealth but to have your own piece of land to make a living on. Hawthorne's version of the American dream looks back to the Jeffersonian agrarian ideal rather than forward to the concept of upward mobility, where everyone hustles to reach society's upper echelons. Hawthorne discourages his fellow citizens from seeking material improvement at the risk of moral debasement, promoting the virtues of honesty and hard work not because they lead to material success but because they are morally satisfying. It is only later in our history, in the post–Civil War era of Horatio Alger stories and the robber barons, that the dominant myth of American opportunity became the rags-to-riches story, and it was deemed that the purpose of virtue was to be rewarded.

Maybe Hawthorne was just a reactionary trying to maintain the status quo. But the lesson of humility has ecological as well as religious and social implications, and in that sense his moral system seems downright subversive. We think of economic growth, for ourselves and for the nation, as an automatic good. But growth feeds off something, and often that something is the natural world, which we call "natural resources." Bill McKibben points out in *The Age of Missing Information* that those who live in some way connected to the land accept the idea that growth has its necessary limits. A farmer knows that intensive and concentrated growth will exhaust the soil, and it will need fallow time to recover. Someone who spends time in the woods knows that a forest does not grow endlessly. Eventually it reaches a state of sustainable maturity.[11] The lesson applies at the personal level as well. As I approach middle age, it occurs to me that in our own lives we eventually reach a state of sustainable maturity, of satisfied acceptance, when we become more or less content with what we have, and less concerned about making our mark in the world.

I wonder: Is America Hawthorne's ambitious guest? In pursuing its land-grabbing, empire-extending policy of Manifest Destiny in the mid-nineteenth century, the entire nation was guilty of ambition. Today (and for that matter back in the nineteenth century, too) the lands we grab in the name of empire are within our own borders. After two hundred years, we are still like a restless, ambitious youth.

Hawthorne's story reminds us that we're not so old that God and nature can't sometimes still administer a good spanking.

❀   ❀   ❀

When I was hiking in Crawford Notch in 1977 with friends named Pesch and Joe Dunes, I remember resting by the side of the road, waiting for Dunes to return from his hitch into Bartlett for supplies. Pesch and I saw several teenaged boys cross the road and head up the trail to Webster Cliffs carrying a box of Triscuits and a bottle of Tango, a premixed vodka and orange drink. When we started up the trail, joined by Dunes and a thru-hiker named Peter, we found Triscuits lining the trail. At first we were amused, feeling like we were following Hansel and Gretel into the forest. Then we found the empty Triscuit box stashed under a log bridge, and we were no longer amused. Pesch picked up the box, and we all picked up our pace until we caught up to the teenagers.

We were an intimidating looking group, I imagine, all bearded and scruffy and very physically fit after a couple of months of hiking. Pesch, all five-and-a-half feet of him, marched up to the kids, holding out the empty Triscuit box, and said, "Hey, you guys dropped this." Before they could respond, he went on, "And I'll tell you something—if we find an empty bottle of Tango by the side of the Trail, we're gonna break it over your fucking heads!"

Behind him, Dunes and Peter and I nodded and muttered "Yeah."

The kids said, meekly, "Sorry."

Pesch said, "Don't apologize to me. Apologize to the mountain."

In retrospect, I'm not sure our strategy of confrontation was the most rhetorically effective way to bring about a change of attitude on the part of those kids. We didn't really teach them anything about respect for place or others, or about responsibility for what one consumes and what one leaves behind in the world.

But, damn, it felt good.

Now, climbing up Webster Cliffs, I ask myself, what were those kids looking for here?

Not beauty or purity or harmony or serenity—none of that idealistic crap. What they were after was a chance to get away from people telling them what to do, like teachers or parents or other meddlesome grown-ups. Maybe it *was* something idealistic—freedom.

And what were we finding here?

For a few moments at least, self-righteousness. And power.

❀   ❀   ❀

In "Our Evening Party among the Mountains," Hawthorne introduces the legend of the great carbuncle, the belief "that a gem, of such immense size as to be seen shining miles away, hangs from a rock over a clear, deep lake, high up among the hills." A spirit guards the jewel with befuddling mists, and deluded adventurers' lives are "worn away in the vain search for an unearthly treasure." Hawthorne mused that "on this theme, methinks I could frame a tale with a deep moral," a tale that followed the sketch within a year (428). The tale was "The Great Carbuncle," the moral a lesson on the meaning and value of mountains and wilderness.

The story relates the quest of eight obviously allegorical figures for a jewel hidden in the White Mountains. As I read the allegory, the characters, modeled on the guests Hawthorne encountered at Crawford's Inn, represent common modes of appreciating or valuing nature in American history—a history we can trace with reference to the White Mountains. The gem too is symbolic—it is the thing of value that we search for in nature.

A merchant named Ichabod Pigsnort seeks the gem for profit. If he finds it, he intends to sell it to the highest bidder. But Pigsnort never even catches a glimpse of the carbuncle's rays and, in fact, ends up losing the fortune that he started with. After he gives up the quest, Indians kidnap him and hold him for a fortune-depleting ransom. His long absence from business affairs further deteriorates his capital, and he ends a pauper. One critic sees "poetic justice" in Pigsnort's fate, reduced "to a material poverty that complements his spiritual bankruptcy." [12] Pigsnort represents all those who came to America dreaming of El Dorado — and didn't find it. That motivation and that sort of disillusionment surfaced early in the history of European acquaintance with the Whites. After Darby Field made the first recorded ascent of Mt. Washington in 1642, John Winthrop, governor of the Massachusetts Bay Colony, noted that "the report he brought of shining stones, &c. caused divers others to travel thither but they found nothing worth their pains." The same greed motivated those who prized America mainly as a gateway to the riches of the Orient — with the same result. Hawthorne suggests that the mountains possess value that will frustrate those who can measure worth only in dollars and cents. [13]

The conceited aristocrat Lord de Vere hopes to bring the gem home to his ancestral castle, to "make it a symbol of the glories of our lofty line," suggesting some relationship between the merits of his family history and the would-be family jewel. [14] But de Vere's appreciation for the jewel does not extend to the mountain scenery for which the jewel serves as emblem. De Vere arrogantly claims that the mountains are an inadequate setting for the carbuncle: "Never, on the diadem of the White Mountains, did the Great Carbuncle, hold a place half so honored, as is reserved for it in the hall of the de Veres" (156). But Lord de Vere returns home with nothing. In place of the carbuncle, he settles for a "wax-lighted chandelier" to adorn his castle. When he dies and is placed in the family burial vault, "funeral torches" in lieu of the Great Carbuncle serve "to shew the vanity of earthly pomp" (164). In terms of the values he finds in nature, de Vere echoes the colonial writers who saw America only as a symbol of imperial magnificence, the glories of the American landscape representing the virtues of British nobles who laid claim to those lands. (See, for example, George Seagood's "Expeditio Ultramontana" in chapter 6).

De Vere's story reminds us of the fate of the European colonial powers in America, who valued the land mainly as territory to extend their imperial reach. The Whites were an early prize in battles for dominion in the New World. The French and their Indian allies fought to keep English settlers to the south and east of the mountains in the seventeenth century. But Massachusetts and New Hampshire militia occupied the Whites during Queen Anne's War (1702–13) and Lovewell's War (1723–25); one unit climbed Mt. Washington in 1725. Ultimately, of course, the British too lost control of their American colony. The English people who settled in the newly claimed territory eventually ceased to be English; their loyalties were to the territory, the country, that formed them and that they cared for. Not that the

imperialist urge ended with the British relinquishment of the land. Given
Hawthorne's rhapsodies on the imperial greatness symbolized by Mt. Washington, the highest peak in the Whites, it is useful to consider that one man's
patriotism is another man's imperialism. The mountain was named in 1784,
when George Washington was still General Washington and not yet our first
president. It has been a long time since anyone referred to Mt. Washington
as "Agiocochook."

The poet in "The Great Carbuncle" hopes to sneak the jewel back to his
garret in London. There he hopes to imbibe inspiration and hence gain
fame from the jewel: "My soul shall drink its radiance — it shall be diffused
throughout my intellectual powers, and gleam brightly in every line of poesy
that I indite. Thus, long ages after I am gone, the splendor of the Great
Carbuncle will blaze around my name" (155). Unfortunately, the poet ends
up mistaking a chunk of ice for the Great Carbuncle. Hawthorne, repeating
the joke he made about the poet in "Our Evening Party among the Mountains," wryly notes that "if his poetry lacked the splendor of the gem, it retained all the coldness of the ice" (164). This poet is like those of the early
period of nationhood, focusing on American scenery as one way to form an
indigenous poetry, but borrowing the shopworn language and style of English descriptive poetry, ill-suited to the New World.[15]

The scientist Dr. Cacophodel also fails to appreciate the mountains and
their representative gem for what they are, seeing them only as means to
scientific ends. He intends to take the carbuncle back to his lab in Europe
and spend his life "reducing it to its first elements" — crushing some of the
stone to powder, dissolving some in acid, and burning or melting the rest in
order to "gain an accurate analysis" (154). In regarding the stuff of mountains
as the ingredients for an experiment, Dr. Cacophodel seems like a caricature
of the Age of Reason. In the history of the Whites, the age of scientific exploration was sparked by a 1784 expedition mounted by Jeremy Belknap and
Manasseh Cutler. (It was on this trip that Agiocochook was dubbed "Mt.
Washington.") Though Belknap himself was too fat (by his own admission)
to join his companions in ascending to the top of Washington, his reports of
the trip were enormously popular. The account in his *History of New Hampshire* seems very much in the vein of Dr. Cacophodel in its privileging of
scientific values above all others. Though Belknap raves that "nature has,
indeed, in that region, formed her works on a large scale," he cautions that
"when amazement is excited by the grandeur and sublimity of the scene
presented to view, it is necessary to curb the imagination, and exercise judgment with mathematical precision: or the temptation to romance will be

invincible."[16] Resisting "the temptation to romance," Belknap explained away the legends that would inspire Hawthorne's story. The sightings of sparkling jewels, decided Belknap, result from sun glinting off snowfields or wet rocks.

Like the poet, Dr. Cacophodel seems motivated less by a concern for humanity than by his thirst for fame. He regards the carbuncle as a "prize . . . reserved to crown my scientific reputation" (154). And like the poet, he deludes himself in ultimately considering his quest a success, finding a hunk of granite to perform his experiments upon. Despite their lack of success, the poet and the scientist, contentedly deluded, fare better than the merchant and the aristocrat. Hawthorne rewards, at least minimally, their devotion to beauty and truth; if ego also plays a part in their pursuits, it pales compared to the selfishness of Pigsnort and de Vere. But all intend to take the carbuncle away from the White Mountains and America, and none comes close to finding the real thing. Maybe their failures are a kind of punishment for their lack of concern about preserving America's natural resources, an unpatriotic as well as ecologically unsound plundering.

The other four seekers succeed, but their success does not necessarily bring happiness. The seeker, "weather-beaten" and "clad in the skins of wild animals," is driven by a "peculiar madness," an "inordinate lust," and a "passionate dream" (150). He terms his search "the vain ambition of my youth" and "a fate upon me, in old age" (153–54). The quest itself means more to him than the object of the quest. "The pursuit alone is my strength," he says, "the energy of my soul — the warmth of my blood, and the pith and marrow of my bones! Were I to turn my back on it, I should fall down dead" (154). Should he find the stone, he expects no profit, spiritual or material, from it. He would only take it to a secluded cave and die with it in his arms. The seeker comes close to fulfilling his ambition, for he dies within sight of the carbuncle, and in a secluded spot at that. But he never possesses or touches the gem. The seeker seems a type of the American frontiersman who has long had the hero's role in American mythology — Daniel Boone, Natty Bumppo, Davy Crockett.[17] Perhaps these are the rough-hewn models for the legends in the Whites built around men like Darby Field, Timothy Nash, or Ethan Crawford. The seeker/frontiersman is the restless explorer driven to discover wilderness not for what might be made from it, but, as the mountaineer's credo goes, "because it's there." But once he opens up the wilderness, civilization follows, and the wilderness is no more. To succeed in the quest means the end of the seeker's reason for being.

The cynic's fate is harsher still, for his motive in seeking the carbuncle is the most "vain," "foolish," and "impious." Looking at the world through dark glasses that "deform and discolor the whole face of nature," he is willfully blind to *any* value in the mountains. He denies that the carbuncle even exists, terming it "The Great Humbug" (162). Hawthorne suggests that the cynic's inability to detect anything of value is related to a moral deficiency: "He was one of those wretched and evil men, whose yearnings are downward to the darkness, instead of Heavenward" (157). Alone among the party, he commits Hawthorne's unpardonable sin: he is "so estranged from natural sympathies . . . as to acknowledge no satisfaction at the sight of human faces, [even] in the remote and solitary regions whither they had ascended" (140). Even in the presence of the carbuncle he denies its existence, until he takes off his glasses, is stunned by "a single flash of so glorious a phenomenon," and is blinded — a literal blindness to match his earlier aesthetic and moral blindness (163). Later he roams the world in search of light and dies in the London fire, the sort of hell-on-earth deserved by those who are blind to nature's beauty and value. The cynic's attitude harks back to the first responses Europeans had to the American wilderness. They felt disorientation, fear, and disapprobation, as when John Josselyn described the Whites in 1672 as "a rude heap of massie stones piled one upon another. . . . daunting terrible, being full of rocky Hills, as thick as Mole-hills in a meadow, and cloathed with infinite thick Woods." [18]

These failed questors represent typically American landscape aesthetics, mostly from the literary past, that Hawthorne deems deficient. The two successes in the quest, the newlyweds Matthew and Hannah, differ in important ways from their competitors. First of all, they share their pursuit, reinforcing the importance, particularly to Hawthorne, of communication, connection, communion with fellow humans. Their motive in seeking the carbuncle combines aesthetic and practical motives; their appreciation is not the aesthete's elitist indulgence in art for art's sake but the homemaker's appreciation for utility as well as beauty, function as well as form. They "need its light in the long winter evenings; and it will be such a pretty thing to show the neighbors, when they visit us" (156–57). Their willingness to share what they hope to get, with each other and with the neighbors, reveals their generosity and kindheartedness where others demonstrate greed and selfishness.

The simplicity of their lives also contributes to Matthew and Hannah's success, which they achieve because they have the proper attitude to the quest and its object. They are not consumed, figuratively, by the quest; on the ultimate day of the search, they sleep late, their bridal bed of pine boughs representing the values of love and home and family. Nor are they consumed literally by the quest; while the seeker dies within sight of the carbuncle and the cynic is blinded by it, Matthew and Hannah drink in its radiance, tremble at its power, and wisely conclude that such awful magnificence is not compatible with their simple lives. Their home will be lighted and warmed with "blessed sunshine," "quiet moonlight," and "the cheerful glow of [the] hearth" (163). The stone they leave where it is.

❀   ❀   ❀

At Mizpah Hut on another drizzly day, socked in by clouds, no views, I talk with a man in his seventies who has come up here to look at alpine plants. He's enthusiastic about his field guide to wildflowers and points out some of the nuances of the drawings. I also talk with a family from Maine and a couple from Long Island. In the early evening, a group of college students comes in, wet and happy. They're tenting outside the hut, but they come in to dry out and write in their journals. Their field trip here is part of a University of Michigan program for the study of New England literature. Four other groups from the program, each with about eight students and two leaders, are camped in the Whites, and tomorrow they'll all meet at the summit of Washington.

The students are affectionate with each other, scratching each other's backs, brushing each other's hair. Several of them, music majors, play in a band together, and one has a backpacker's guitar. The hutmaster also has a guitar, and in the evening we make music. Spoons and pots and pans serve as percussion.

When the music's over, I ask my usual questions.

"What value do I find here? A sense of wonder, I guess."

"Being out here brings me joy."

"I love the feeling I get after a long day of hiking, sort of giddiness, release. Even if I have to make dinner in the rain."

"I like traveling with everything I need on my back, being totally self-sufficient."

"The most important thing is that it takes me back to myself."

"I love the whole metaphor of climbing the mountain, the way it relates to my life. On a mountain, I feel overwhelmed. I think I can't do it. But then I find out I can. I've always been able to get where I'm going. That's a valuable lesson, one I bring home with me. Every time I'm faced with a decision that seems huge, I know I can just take my time and I'll get there."

Interesting, I think. Their search for value seems to look inward. Which makes sense for college students, certainly, since young adulthood is precisely the time in our lives when we become preoccupied with finding ourselves. But I'm surprised at their apparent concern with self-improvement since in watching them what impresses me most is their togetherness, their reliance upon one another.

In the late evening, it's time for their class. They take turns reading aloud "The Great Carbuncle."

❀   ❀   ❀

Next morning I'm off into the clouds above tree line early, excited to be entering the terrain of Hawthorne's story. Though the rain has stopped, the trail is wet, a fast clear stream. I keep an eye out for red garnets, reputedly one source of the carbuncle legend, and mica chips, source of an earlier name for these mountains — the Crystal Hills. On the trail below the summit of Mt. Monroe, a flat sliver of mica on a marble-sized pebble shines underwater. I pick it up, inspect it, and (with a twinge of guilt) put it in my pocket. It'll make a nice gift for my little boy.

Matthew and Hannah, the seeker, and the cynic find the carbuncle on a cliff by the side of a high tarn. That's got to be one of the Lakes of the Clouds, I think. I imagine taking pictures of the lakes, themselves a couple of glittering jewels in the sun. But of course when I get there the lakes are enshrouded with clouds and I can see only about twenty feet — from shore, not even to the other side. A snowbank slants down into the water, turns into molar-colored ice underwater. I take some pictures, knowing that what will turn out is a bunch of indefinite white shapes, snow, ice, water, fog all blending together.

This is the place. Somewhere around here, there's some kind of treasure.

❀   ❀   ❀

Climbing higher into the clouds over the sharply angled boulder fields, I think back to the Scrabble game at Greenleaf Hut, and my initial questions about the value of mountains. Allen, a loan officer about my age who was up here hiking with an old friend from high school, listened to some of the answers I was getting. He thought a bit and said, "You know, I don't think you can really explain what it is that we find here. It's something we can't describe, something inside us that just likes being out here. Have you heard of some biologist, at Harvard, I think? He's got a name for it."

Oh, yeah, I said, Edward Wilson. Biophilia. Love of living things. The innate, ineffable thing, an instinctive response, that draws us to nature. In fact, the reason I'm asking everyone about nature's meaning and value is that I've been reading Stephen Kellert's *The Value of Life*, an attempt to better understand and define Wilson's biophilia hypothesis. Kellert says our appreciation for nature can be categorized into nine basic values. What strikes me about Kellert's list is the extent to which the values he speaks of are personified by the characters of "The Great Carbuncle." The utilitarian, based on "material exploitation"—that's Pigsnort. The naturalistic, the desire to experience and explore nature in order to satisfy our curiosity or our urge for discovery—that's the seeker. The ecologistic-scientific, expressed via the "systematic study of structure, function, and relationship in nature" in order to satisfy our desire for knowledge and understanding—Dr. Cacophodel. The aesthetic, the search for beauty, inspiration, and harmony in nature—the poet. The dominionistic, the drive for "mastery, physical control, dominance of nature"—the imperialist Lord de Vere, the English aristocrat interested in bringing home a piece of America as a colonial bauble. The negativistic, "fear, aversion, alienation from nature"—the cynic. The humanistic, based on "strong emotional attachment and 'love' for . . . nature," emerging from our need for "bonding, sharing, cooperation, companionship"—Matthew and Hannah. Count them too as representatives of the moralistic value, based on "spiritual reverence and ethical concern for nature," fruit of our search for "order, meaning, kinship, altruism." Only one of Kellert's motives or values is not accounted for in Hawthorne's story: the symbolic, the "use of nature for language and thought." [19] But might not that be Hawthorne himself, using these characters and the carbuncle as symbols to illustrate his ideas about nature's meaning and value?

Kellert creates no hierarchy of values. All are reasons why we need nature in our lives. Even the negativistic is, in a way, a positive valuing since to fear nature is also to respect it, hold it in awe. That's part of the point of "The Ambitious Guest." But in "The Great Carbuncle," Hawthorne does create a hierarchy of values, condemning most of the ways we appreciate nature and holding up as ideals the moralistic and humanistic. The whole story is about the search for order and meaning (the moralistic), and Matthew and Hannah's sense of the proper order of things (and of their place and the carbuncle's place in that order) leads them to leave the carbuncle in the mountains. They choose not to disrupt the natural order. That decision arises from a variety of moral virtues, the same set of virtues recommended in "The Great Stone Face" and "The Ambitious Guest," among them reverence for nature and humility. Contentment comes when we accept the limits on our capacity or desire to convert nature into a possession or resource. Without that acceptance we may be consumed by our strivings to tame the untamable, to possess what cannot be possessed.

Matthew and Hannah's connection to others, the humanistic motive, also contributes to their decision. For Hawthorne the ultimate sin is always to distance oneself from others, to live in isolation, whether out of pride or ambition or desire or monomania. Early in "The Great Carbuncle" there is a moment where all the adventurers share a kind of communion. When they all meet in the valley, they need each other. The woods are vast, the "roar of the Amonoosuck . . . too awful for endurance if only a solitary man had listened"—and so they share a shelter that they've all pitched in to make, "where each man was the host, and all were the guests of the whole company" (150). They even share their food around the fire. But in the morning, while Matthew and Hannah sleep late, cuddling with each other, the others are off, each "impelled by his own selfish and solitary longing" (149). At the end, Matthew and Hannah renounce whatever selfish motives they may have had, and the carbuncle remains where it can be rediscovered by the next set of adventurers—in essence, shared with them. By renouncing possession, Matthew and Hannah also serve the needs of nonhuman living things who will thrive best if the natural order is left intact.

Clearly the actions of Matthew and Hannah show their capacity to care for others. But Kellert claims that nature not only gives us a suitable outlet for our innate need to *express* our connection to other living things, it actively *develops* our "emotional capacities for attachment, bonding, intimacy, and companionship."[20] Up on the mountain, when they are weary and threatened by storms, Matthew and Hannah recognize their mutual dependence on each other. They find that their deepest needs are satisfied not by possessions but by each other and nature. Most thru-hikers say that what they cherish most about their experience on the trail is the people they have met—the folks who live near the trail and have offered rides, food, and cheer, and the hikers with whom they have shared campsites and stories and aches, pains, weariness, and joy. Maybe it's because nature is a neutral ground, where there are no power relations established. Here we are both guest and host, says Hawthorne. As guests, we are on equal footing, properly respectful of what is not ours. We would never dream of being so presumptuous as to rearrange the furniture. As hosts, we have come to feel pride in a place where we have been able to make ourselves at home for a while. It may not be elegant, this home away from home, but its unpretentious simplicity is part of its charm, and the grounds are quite lovely, and we've done wonders with it, we know, though at times, to be sure, it's more than we can manage.

❊   ❊   ❊

Headed up the cone of Washington, over boulders of metamorphic rock, I'm thinking of Allen again. His own take on the kind of categorization offered by Kellert or Hawthorne is that they're trying to contain something fluid in wire cages. Biophilia is something we cannot put a name to, and it is something that comprises all of Kellert's nine values at once. What Hawthorne has done in "The Great Carbuncle" is use allegory to have a character represent one particular value. In truth, all are part of us. I suppose Hawthorne has a point in denigrating some of the values we find in nature—the arrogance of dominion, the false sentimentality of aestheticism, the cold and mechanical logic of science, the obsessive and isolating demands of the quest, the spiritual emptiness of utilitarianism. But we all savor the arm-raising rush that accompanies the last step of an ascent—a conquest of the self if not of the mountain—and if we're at all alive and awake of course we take deep pleasure in nature's beauty, and we're (naturally) curious about the facts of nature, and we know the thrill of discovery, and, yes, anyone who's ever carved a handle on a walking stick knows the satisfaction of making something useful out of a natural object. In the history of the Whites we could find very positive examples of all the traits Hawthorne objects to. I know my life would be emptier if I didn't have on my living-room wall one particular expression of the aesthetic valuing of the Whites, a poster-print of Thomas Cole's *Notch of the White Mountains*, with clouds moving in over steep hills of autumnal gold. Cole was just one of the hordes of nineteenth-century American landscape painters loosely designated as the Hudson River School who found aesthetic inspiration in the Whites.[21] Looking at the map around Mt. Washington, I see reminders of another kind of passion for this place, the scientific: Boott Spur, Bigelow lawn, Oakes Gulf, Tuckerman Ravine—all named after botanists of the first half of the nineteenth century.[22]

These names and pictures are reminders of people who loved this place, for all kinds of reasons, and that affection, and those reasons, become part of the place. It is not just that history gives us names by which we know a place (though that's something), or ways to see and value what is there (though that's something too). I see the mountain, I see a sliver of mica—and they are worth admiring for what I can see of them. But I know too that the rock is a container for time, its core is the past underlying the surface of the present, and it is flecked through with passion, where for all kinds of reasons it has been esteemed.

So, no, these other means of valuing nature do not deserve condemnation. But Hawthorne reminds us that excess of any particular sort of regard for nature has its costs, and they are costs incurred by ourselves as well as the land. And he reminds us of the humanistic and the moral motives that we tend to ignore. These are not the values that change the course of history, and those who live up to those values are not likely to go down in history, commemorated by place-names or legends. But humility, acceptance, connection, communion — these are the values that make us happy and that make us see our way to saving the world. For our own good.

At the end of "The Great Carbuncle" Hawthorne says that when Matthew and Hannah tell their story later in life, nobody believes them. For once they renounced their claim to it, the carbuncle, it is said, lost its luster. To the extent that "the jewel which would have dimmed all earthly things" represents pride and wealth and ambition, perhaps its splendor wanes because Matthew and Hannah have conquered its lure. Others say the carbuncle fell into the lake. The suggestion is that we have become modern-day cynics, believing there may have been something of value here once, but now it is gone, lost. Hawthorne, though, concludes that "some few believe that this inestimable stone is blazing as of old," and they've seen it shine, and he himself is the "latest pilgrim" who has sought it (165).

Clouds whip across the mountain, but a few patches of high sky begin to show through, the first I've seen for days. I pass a couple who ask, "Hey, what's that blue stuff up there called?" Soon the ceiling lifts enough that I can see the radio tower on the summit. Excited at the prospect of sunshine, knowing the summit is near, I push uphill. At the top I find a parking lot, a road, a railroad track, an observatory, a shop, a restaurant, and scattered other buildings. As I step onto the pavement two guys who have been watching me climb give a small cheer, say I must be in pretty good shape "for a guy your age." At the summit signboard a woman with an English accent agrees to take my picture. In the restaurant I find a phone and call home. Then I lounge about at a picnic table, munching my gorp and snapping pictures of the northern Presidentials when the clouds shift. A train arrives, hissing loudly, the steam engine canted so as to remain level on the steep slopes. I'm reminded of another Hawthorne story, "The Celestial Railroad," about pilgrims who try to get to the Holy City by train. As if you could buy a ticket to salvation.

A lot of hikers hate the summit of Washington, despising those who have driven or ridden to get up here, many of whom in turn think hikers must be idiots to walk up. William O. Douglas, a former thru-hiker and the Supreme Court justice who once considered the proposition that trees may have legal standing, complained that the people who get up here without walking "represent the America that had grown soft and flabby and overfed and perhaps a bit callous." [23] For a moment I wonder why people would even bother driving or riding up. It's the climb that makes the summit what it is. The journey, not the destination, is the goal. I spend a moment in quiet detestation of a fresh bumper sticker boasting "This Car Climbed Mt. Washington." (Big deal—you're staking ego gratification on some internal combustion engine that you didn't even make?) Then I realize I'm falling into one of the traps Hawthorne warned about. The seeker's, I guess.

There is more than one reason to go to a mountain. At least these people are out here looking. They see my backpack and stop to chat, ask where I came from, where I'm headed. Someone asks what I'm reading. Someone else asks about my camera, shows off his. A middle-aged guy tells me about his hike up here twenty years ago. An elderly couple ask if my gaiters are intended to protect me from snakebite. No, snow, I say. They look at me like I'm nuts since the day is now sunny and warm and it's decidedly unsnowy up here. I congratulate myself for not bursting into laughter at their question about poisonous snakes on the top of Mt. Washington. But I also take off my gaiters.

Early in the afternoon the students from the University of Michigan arrive at the summit from several different trails. They all have friends, and a few have lovers, from groups that were camped elsewhere in the mountains. They are happy to see one another again, also ecstatic and proud about getting to the top. Hugs, kisses, cries of delight, shouts of laughter, high fives all around. They congregate at the summit signboard, over forty of them, for pictures.

The trail heads north then east past Mts. Jefferson, Adams, and Madison before shifting south down to Pinkham Notch. I take a shortcut to Pinkham, headed east over Lion Head, above Tuckerman Ravine. My boots slush across a softening snowfield, the sound melting into the snow, as if it can't resist the heavy downward pressure of the afternoon sunlight. In my pocket I feel the mica-sided pebble tapping on my thigh. I hold it up, catching the sun, then let it drop into the snow, knowing I've got stories to bring home instead.

13

Contact! Contact!
A Walk to Thoreau's Ktaadn

In THE FALL OF 1995 I put out an e-mail call inviting ecocritics on-line to join me the following summer on a hike through Maine's Hundred Mile Wilderness, the longest roadless stretch on the Appalachian Trail, to the trail's end point on Mt. Katahdin. The occasion is the sesquicentennial of Henry David Thoreau's climb of Katahdin in September of 1846, a trip he took during the second year of his stay at Walden Pond. His account of the journey, written up as "Ktaadn," was first published in the *Union Magazine* in 1848 and later revised as the first of three chapters in *The Maine Woods* (1864).

I envision our hike as a sort of symposium in the field, an ambulatory commemoration of Thoreau's hike. I warn about bugs and muddy trails, but promise moose sightings and loon calls. And can't you just imagine, I say, the scintillating fireside chitchat:

"Ow! Damn black flies."

"Ah, quit your complaining. After all, we all know that nature is only a cultural construct."

"Is not!"

"Is too!"

"Deconstructionist dog!"

"Essentialist insect!"

"Hey, you guys, quit disparaging the biota. Remember what Emerson says. . . ."

"Oh, don't talk to me about Emerson. Emerson wouldn't know the biota from a bottle."

"Aren't you thinking of Wallace Stevens? You know, 'I placed a jar in Tennessee. . . .'"

And so on.

At first about a dozen people are interested. But one by one they drop out. One's got a book deadline. Several are low on cash. One "has" to get ready for a conference in Hawaii (academic life is tough, isn't it?). One confesses that he's not in good enough shape. I lose a couple of e-mail addresses. At the end it's down to me and my friend David, who accepts the role of official symposium respondent. David, now teaching in South Carolina, wrote a dissertation on Thoreau's natural history essays, but his most eminent qualification for the position of respondent is compatibility. We hiked together in the Smokies and found that we both wake up early, we walk at the same pace, and we enjoy each other's company.

In early July I pick up David at the train station in Wilmington, Delaware, and we drive north, noticing roadside woods change from beech and maple and oak to birch and hemlock and pine. In Monson, Maine, southern end of the Hundred Mile Wilderness, we stay at Shaw's, a boardinghouse with a reputation for being friendly to hikers. In the evening we visit the town's general store to pick up last-minute supplies and a couple of beers to drink by the side of Lake Hebron. David gets "Black Fly" stout, a local brew. Our first taste of the Maine woods. Our version of the black spruce beer Thoreau tried on his trip to Katahdin. Of his brew, Thoreau wrote, "It was as if we sucked at the very teats of Nature's pine-clad bosom in these parts . . . the topmost most fantastic and spiciest sprays of the primitive wood, and whatever invigorating and stringent gum or essence it afforded, steeped and dissolved in it—a lumberer's drink, which would acclimate and naturalize a man at once—which would make him see green, and, if he slept, dream that he heard the wind sough among the pines."[1]

Now that's good beer. Henry should have been a copywriter.

We suck at Nature's pine-clad bosom, twelve ounces' worth, waiting to feel acclimated and to see green. At dusk, we think we hear the wind soughing, but it turns out to be mosquitoes.

❀   ❀   ❀

Next morning, after a hearty breakfast of cheese-filled scrambled eggs, blueberry pancakes, sausage, and hashbrowns at Shaw's, we hit the trail. Within a quarter mile we see loons on Spectacle Pond. The trail is etched like skate tracks through mossy woods, all silvered from last night's rain.

It will take us about a week to reach Baxter State Park, then another day or two to reach Katahdin. Approaching from the west, we are not really walking in Thoreau's footsteps; he came by stage, foot, and bateau from the southeast, through Millinocket. We will not touch ground he trod until we are through the Hundred Mile Wilderness.

Our conversation the first day dwells on the similarities between reading and backpacking. Both progress linearly, both require patience as you follow along. Sometimes what you encounter seems like something you've seen before, but you know there could always be some surprise right around the next turn. And everyone packs for the excursion a little differently, but no matter what stuff you bring along, you can't take too much baggage, or you won't get far. In the case of a book, the excess baggage consists of stuff like too much emotional weight or too solid and unmalleable an ideology.

Another similarity: both the reader and the hiker set their own pace. Every A.T. hiker travels the same terrain, but some move fast and with dogged determination, some slowly and with serene deliberation. By controlling the pace, you create your own narrative in a way that differs from our lives in civilization, where we get caught up in a pace that is not of our own making. There we are more like watchers of TV, following someone else's story.

David says both reading and backpacking require imagination.

That stops me. Doesn't backpacking put you in the here and now, not some other time and place long ago or faraway? Isn't that the antithesis of imagination?

David says something about landscape shaping your perceptions, but you need imagination to let it do that. I begin to understand. It requires imagination too to perceive the invisible webs of life in a place, the ecological connections. That means being able, in Benton MacKaye's phrase, to "see what you see," which means seeing not just the tangible objects you can actually see but seeing as comprehending, seeing how everything fits together *here*, belongs *here*, in this particular place, with this particular climate and geology and supporting these particular kinds of plant and animal life.[2]

But is it not possible for a backpacker to miss those connections, to fail to see how other things fit in the landscape one sees? Well, yes, just as an unimaginative reader misses most of what goes on between the lines. Some hikers never get beyond their preoccupation with their own physical and psychological indices, asking themselves how is this affecting me now. But most who have been out in the woods for a while progress toward a state of receptive attention to what is around them. That movement requires an act of imaginative projection out of yourself, out of your own perspective, into a perspective that includes but is not limited to the self. That is essentially what happens when you get caught up in a story, too—you try on other lives, experience the life and identity and mindset of someone who may be very different from yourself, from a different culture or time or place or maybe even species.

And that is the path Thoreau follows in "Ktaadn," a movement out of himself, a loss of self not just so that he could find himself again but so that he could discover the world.

❀   ❀   ❀

We reach Wilson Valley Lean-to just before the rain. A short day of hiking, so there is plenty of time before nightfall to think of where we're headed, and to read.

"Ktaadn" to my mind is the most misunderstood of Thoreau's writings. The usual reading is that Thoreau was scared spiritless by the mountain. It was too wild and inhospitable for Thoreau to "interpret" in his customary way, and so he retreated, shaken out of his transcendental wits, to the pastoral world of Walden. According to the traditional reading, Thoreau encountered on the mountain a "forbidding . . . stark, inhuman nature" by which he was "positively repelled," an "alien, hostile nature" that he found "frightening."[3]

This judgment derives from two famous passages, dual climaxes of the essay. The first comes at the height of Thoreau's ascent, on the Table Land, which seemed to Thoreau "an undone extremity of the globe," where the mountain "had rained rocks," a place "such as man never inhabits," where "vast, Titanic, inhuman Nature has got him at disadvantage, caught him alone, and pilfers him of some of his divine faculty. She does not smile at him as in the plains. She seems to say sternly, why came ye here before your time? This ground is not prepared for you. Is it not enough that I smile in the valleys? I have never made this soil for thy feet, this air for thy breathing, these rocks for thy neighbors" (143–44).

The second climax, even more powerful rhetorically, comes on the descent, as Thoreau and his party passed through the "primeval, untamed, and forever untameable *Nature*" of the Burnt Lands. There Thoreau elaborates on the ways in which the mountain seems inhospitable to humanity:

> It is difficult to conceive of a region uninhabited by man. We habitually presume his presence and influence everywhere. And yet we have not seen pure Nature, unless we have seen her thus vast, and drear, and inhuman, though in the midst of cities. Nature was here something savage and awful, though beautiful. I looked with awe at the ground I trod on, to see what the Powers had made there, the form and fashion and material of their work. This was that Earth of which we have heard, made out of Chaos and Old Night. Here was no man's garden, but the unhandselled globe. It was not lawn, nor pasture, nor mead, nor woodland, nor lea, nor arable, nor waste-land. It was the fresh and natural surface of the planet Earth, as it

was made forever and ever,—to be the dwelling of man, we say,—so Nature made it, and man may use it if he can. Man was not to be associated with it. It was Matter, vast, terrific,—not his Mother Earth that we have heard of, not for him to tread on, or be buried in,—no, it were being too familiar even to let his bones lie there—the home this of Necessity and Fate. There was there felt the presence of a force not bound to be kind to man. It was a place for heathenism and superstitious rites,—to be inhabited by men nearer of kin to the rocks and to wild animals than we. We walked over it with a certain awe, stopping from time to time to pick the blueberries which grew there, and had a smart and spicy taste. Perchance where *our* wild pines stand, and leaves lie on their forest floor in Concord, there were once reapers, and husbandmen planted grain; but there not even the surface had been scarred by man, but it was a specimen of what God saw fit to make this world. What is it to be admitted to a museum, to see a myriad of particular things, compared with being shown some star's surface, some hard matter in its home! I stand in awe of my body, this matter to which I am bound has become so strange to me. I fear not spirits, ghosts, of which I am one,—*that* my body might,—but I fear bodies, I tremble to meet them. What is this Titan that has possession of me? Talk of mysteries!—Think of our life in nature,—daily to be shown matter, to come in contact with it,—rocks, trees, wind on our cheeks! the *solid* earth! the *actual* world! the *common sense! Contact! Contact! Who* are we? *where* are we? (150)

For the life of me, I don't see how anybody can read that and hear anything other than ecstasy. I look at the language of these passages, and I see very few words that carry negative connotations. "Drear," OK. "Savage" and "awful"? Thoreau admired the savage, and "awful," a standard descriptor of sublime appreciation, means to be full of awe, which is precisely the emphasis of the rest of that sentence, and, it seems to me, of the rest of the passage; after all, he repeats the word *awe* three times. Another lexeme of the sublime is *terrific*, which, yes, has an etymological connection to terror, but it is the terror that excites. "Chaos and Old Night"? Well, maybe, except Thoreau loved the night, and the phrase comes from Milton's *Paradise Lost*, where "Chaos and Old Night" is the realm of Satan, who seems to enjoy an awful lot of authorial sympathy, and who certainly wins the admiration of most readers.

No, the key word here, the one that has led so many critics astray, I think, is *inhuman*. Both passages dwell on the ways in which Ktaadn is a place "such as man never inhabits." But would that not serve to recommend it to Thoreau? To see it otherwise is to underestimate both his misanthropic strain and his commitment to the wild. "Inhumanism" in fact is the guiding principle of American literature's other great wilderness prophet, Robinson Jeffers. What Jeffers means by "inhumanism" is nonanthropocentrism, the attempt to see the world from some perspective other than the human. It is only their anthropocentric bias that has led critics to see "inhuman" as a synonym for "bad" or "scary." But Thoreau flat out says that Ktaadn, though not made for us, is "beautiful," "fresh and natural," "a specimen of what God saw fit to make this world." Ktaadn is "pure Nature," he says. It is even a good place for picking blueberries that have "a smart and spicy taste." This is revulsion?[4]

Something else about this passage that seems to have thrown off critics is their sense that at the end Thoreau seems to be losing it. And the "it," I guess, is his mind. Or his self. He doesn't know who or where he is, and he feels himself possessed by some Titan. He is in awe of his body, and his senses seem to register pure physical sensation, matter, "rocks, trees, wind on our cheeks! the *solid* earth! the *actual* world!" Those are the things he's coming into "Contact! Contact!" with.

The prose rhythm alone suggests that Thoreau's tone here is far from negative. A student of mine once said that this passage reminded him of body surfing, where you lose control as you're carried away by some force larger and more powerful than ourselves, but in that loss of self there's also a sense of oneness with the wave (or in Thoreau's case, with the world). The experience may be disorienting, and yes, maybe even frightening, but most of all it is exhilarating.[5] Maybe literary critics need to get out more often, to rediscover that there's a life of the body as well as a life of the mind. And a world that's bigger than our consciousness.

In truth, the experience Thoreau describes is not so unusual. Encountering the wild, don't most people feel themselves moved by it, maybe even carried away, much as Thoreau was on Ktaadn? That's why we go — to the mountains and the rivers and the rest of the solid earth and actual world. Even in literature there are precedents for what Thoreau describes. When Robinson Crusoe hits his lowest point, recovering from a fever, just before he comes to accept God and his lot in life, he experiences the kind of disorientation Thoreau felt on Ktaadn: "What is this Earth and Sea of which I have seen so much, whence is it produc'd, and what am I, and all the other Creatures, wild and tame, humane and brutal, whence are we?" ("*Who* are we? *where* are we?") For Crusoe, losing his sense of self and his sense of certainty about the world is the first step toward finding God.[6] He begins by going back to first principles, the origins of things, the mystery of existence. So too Thoreau. But Thoreau doesn't find God in the Bible. He finds God lurking behind the bare rocks of Ktaadn.

Closer to Thoreau's transcendental home is Ralph Waldo Emerson's classic statement on the loss of self: "Standing on the bare ground,—my head bathed by the blithe air, and uplifted into infinite space,—all mean egotism vanishes. I become a transparent eyeball. I am nothing. I see all. The currents of the Universal Being circulate through me; I am part or particle of God."[7] Where better than a fog-enshrouded mountaintop above tree line to enact this idea? On bare ground, head bathed by air and uplifted into infinite space, Thoreau loses all trace of egotism and becomes nothing. That is precisely when the currents of universal being can circulate through him, where he can become part and particle of the world.

But I'm getting ahead of my story. Katahdin is still a hundred miles away. In every step I expect that I'll leave a piece of myself—this one in mud leaving an imprint of my sole—this one where water seeps slowly into the fresh print—another splattered by rainfall—one washed away by streamflow before it can even form—this one leaving no discernible trace on a slab of granite. Here I go.

       ❁   ❁   ❁

Day two: Approaching Katahdin by water, Thoreau expressed endless admiration for the boatmen poling the bateau up and down rapids. I have seen hikers who move with that sort of grace and skill, finding toeholds on slanted sides of rocks or roots, skipping across boggy trail, gliding from foot to foot to walking stick. An adept hiker seems to move like water flowing downhill, holding hands with gravity.

Thoreau took a turn at poling the bateau and promptly got it stuck, twirling in a whirlpool, "doing doughnuts," as the river-runners say. I empathize with his ineptitude. On our first couple of days of hiking I have taken several spectacular falls, legs flying up and the rest of me plopping down. On one I pitch forward and bury my watch in mud. On another I slip off a log bridge and land with my butt up on the bridge and the rest of me down in a bog. When I try to heave myself up, the stitching in my hip belt tears out. I sew it up, but I don't have any heavy duty thread. Can only hope it holds.

Atop Barren Ledges we have a terrific view of the surrounding countryside—an "archipelago of lakes," Thoreau called the Maine woods. A hundred and fifty years after he was up here, Thoreau's impression of Maine's wildness still holds. "No clearing, no house," said Henry. "It did not look as if a solitary traveller had cut so much as a walking-stick there" (145). We cross no roads, see no towns from the ledges. No cottages line the shores of endless lakes, no motorboats throttle across their surface. We do, though, see dark lines drawn by logging roads slicing through the forest green, and on distant slopes we see clearcuts. But even in his day Thoreau complained about the beaverish enthusiasm of loggers.

Other impressions hold true as well. Thoreau visited Maine in early September, but he notes that "in the summer myriads of black flies, mosquitoes, and midges, or, as the Indians call them, 'no-see-ums,' make travelling in the woods almost impossible" (87). In early July we are just about at the end of black-fly season, and we haven't seen any no-see-ums. Or felt them, which I guess is more to the itchy point. But the mosquitoes are bad. I notice the backs of knees and thighs of hikers headed south, almost through the Hundred Mile Wilderness. They look like burn victims, with swollen red welts covering their legs.

In one more regard, too, our experience echoes Thoreau's. "The best shod," he said, "for the most part travel with wet feet" (102) The trail is muddy in places, pure streambed in others. And there are the fords. No footbridges cross the streams up here, and the high water has buried the boulder-hopping routes across. We wade through waist-high, fast-moving streams. After a while we don't even bother wringing out our socks afterward.

Our conversation gets progressively less literary. I wonder aloud why Thoreau doesn't mention most of the stuff that dominates our thoughts—David's tendinitis, my equipment failures (in addition to the torn hip belt, torn stitching on my boots and a broken tent zipper), sore spots on our toes (and accompanying worries about blisters), an uncomfortable rash between my butt cheeks, David's bout of diarrhea. My guess is that Thoreau did not want to individualize his experience too much, so that he could serve as a representative self. David says Henry was trying to preserve a heroic image. I object that when he shows his incompetence at poling the bateau, getting stuck in a whirlpool, that's hardly heroic. Then again, what he does there is use himself as foil in order to show the expert boatmen, Uncle George and Tom Fowler, in a heroic light. *He* does not have to be the hero, but he is interested in the idea of heroism. And heroes don't sweat the small stuff, like malfunctioning zippers on four-hundred-dollar tents.

We stay in a shelter at Cloud Pond. In the night a hellacious thunderstorm hits. Lightning flashes nonstop, like a loose light bulb on God's front porch. Thunder rumbles constantly, interrupted only by sharp cracks that arrive simultaneously with shocks of lightning that seem to suck the air out of our bellies. I expect to see a tall spruce outside the shelter burst into flame. In case that happens, and it falls on us, I plan an escape route to the pond, see myself swimming with the leeches. Later I realize that the image of the tree on fire came from my reading. While Thoreau was camped on Katahdin, "in the very nest of a young whirlwind," he was awakened by the shouts of one of his companions, who was "startled in his dreams by the sudden blazing up to its top of a fir-tree" and woke up "thinking the world on fire" (141).

In the storm at Cloud Pond, at first little rain patters down, then it pounds on the shelter's tin roof with a fury. Though I am safely ensconced, I feel the sheer power of the storm, I see why we speak of a *force* of nature, and I understand Thoreau's message from Ktaadn, that the universe is not made for man, that it is much bigger than we are, and that there are times and places we are afterthoughts, with no more power to exert our wills or make our presence felt than a no-see-um in a storm.

And, yes, I am afraid.

❧   ❧   ❧

Day three: Over the Chairbacks today. I hear a moose—a ruckus in the woods, then a snort. Don't see it, though. I do see a big brownish garter on the ledges climbing out of Chairback Gap and pitcher plants in the bog before Fourth Mountain. Legless locomotion. Carnivorous vegetation. What a world. We are surprised to see pitcher plants this far north. David is working on a collection of writings by early southern naturalists, and shares with me the tidbit that the first person to describe the pitcher plant in print was Alexander Garden in 1776.

David is also working on a review of Lawrence Buell's *The Environmental Imagination*, from which I recall descriptions of Thoreau as "environmentalist prophet" and "the patron saint of ecologism." I go further, call Henry the ultimate ecohero, he who blazed the trail from egocentrism to ecocentrism.[8] That trail leads to Ktaadn, I say, where Thoreau seems to lose all sense of his identity as something separate from the world. Or maybe that's where the trail started.

I'm expecting confirmation from David, since Thoreau was his dissertation subject. But David says he's tired of Thoreau, wants to open up the canon of nature writing to other writers, doesn't like Thoreau's position of unquestioned dominance among nature writers. At which point I elevate my rhetoric and claim that Thoreau is not just ecohero or "environmentalist prophet" but nature writing's ultimate authority, spirit of the druidic divinity, Pan of the pen. Ecogod.

Maybe at first he was just trying to get my goat, but now David gets serious. The problem with worshiping Thoreau, he says, or with setting up his kind of writing as the ideal or standard by which other nature writers are judged, is that we thereby exclude other kinds of writers. I object that Thoreau's writing is wonderfully varied—that's part of his appeal. At times he's moralistic, applying the transcendental method. At times he's scientific, interested in facts for their own sake. Always he's observant, but in a variety of ways, about human nature, and nonhuman nature, and about books. David agrees in part, acknowledging that Thoreau tries out a variety of language styles in *The Maine Woods*, but he says that the shifts are part of an ultimately unsuccessful attempt to find an appropriate language. Thoreau tried latinate scientific terminology, but found it boring; he tried native American language, but found it inauthentic since of course he wasn't native American (and in his view neither were the native Americans any more, having been corrupted by contact with Anglo-American culture). Perhaps the language of transcendentalism was too anthropocentric. So he resorted, on the Table Land of Katahdin, to no words, the inability to describe.

I argue that the shifts in language styles indicate not a series of failed attempts but the much-esteemed dialogics of heteroglossia, the opening up of Thoreau's narrative to a variety of language styles and the worldviews associated with them. Among those languages and worldviews is the sublime, whose ultimate claim is that in the presence of the awesome power of nature, words fail.

Words fail us, too, by the time we get to camp by the side of the West Branch of the Pleasant River. We bathe in the river, cook dinner, swat at black flies, retreat into the tent, and read ourselves to sleep, listening to the river.

❃   ❃   ❃

Day four: First thing in the morning we ford the West Branch, go through the straight and tall white pines of the Hermitage, a part of the "arrowy Maine forest" that somehow avoided being converted into mainmasts. In colonial times all white pines in America were considered the king's property, and chopping one was a capital offense. Those pines were reserved for the tall masts of the Royal Navy. In Thoreau's day, their fate was somewhat less glorious. En route to Katahdin, Thoreau despaired at the thought of Maine's forests being converted into matchsticks (89). He does not, however, bemoan the destiny of pines made into pencils, perhaps out of consideration for the Thoreau family business.

We hike along Gulf Hagas Brook, up Gulf Hagas Mountain and West Peak. At a lunch break, while I read more of "Ktaadn," David confesses that he is having trouble getting psyched to do his reading of southern naturalists. I say he should have brought *The Maine Woods*. Nah, he says, all three parts are the same story: "Going to Maine. Sure is wild!" True enough, I suppose — but that's a story I don't mind being part of.

We talk of Thoreau's humor. David says that somewhere Thoreau speaks of tea made from the needles of arbor vitae (Latin for the "tree of life") as the "tea of life." And he says that William Ellery Channing, in his biography of Thoreau, says that when Thoreau made puns like that he would "laugh heartily." I always thought of Thoreau's puns as more clever than ha-ha funny. Maybe you had to be there.

The sun is out, but ominous clouds start to blur the horizon. We have some climbing to do, over Hay and Whitecap. "Let's get going," I say. Only later, too late, on the other side of the mountain, do I think of what I should have said: "Let's make Hay while the sun shines." Though the moment is long gone, I try out the pun on David. He grunts in response. I laugh heartily.

Southbound hikers pass the word about Hurricane Bertha, sweeping in from the Atlantic and due to hit the Carolina coast tomorrow. Nobody knows what the consequences might be up here. One guy, an ex-forest ranger, warns that if the storm hits here the trails will be impassable. A trailworker says southern Maine will likely get tropical storms, but up in the mountains we might have fine weather.

Once again, the lesson of connection. What is happening off the Carolina coast, over a thousand miles away, affects us here. I've been worrying about what could stop us from getting to Katahdin — equipment failure, blisters, maybe a torn muscle, or aging bones, or (in the face of all of the above plus the harassment of mosquitoes) a faltering spirit or loss of nerve. But those are all things over which we exert some control. Thoreau on Ktaadn lets us know that some places on this earth are beyond our control. We could be stopped by a hurricane, or a thunderstorm that knocks trees down across the trail, or floods it, or that warns with lightning and thunder that only the forces of nature will visit the mountaintop today.

On Whitecap we see rainclouds scudding by to the west of us, get sprinkled by a few wind-driven drops. On the way down the mountain we marvel at our first views of Ktaadn, off across the lake country. It looks so big, so close. Often when we see our next climb, a mountain a few miles away, we are surprised at how far away it looks. Ktaadn, over seventy miles distant, looks like it's a few steps away. On his first view of Ktaadn, Thoreau wrote that it looked "like a dark isthmus . . . connecting the heavens with the earth" (114). As he approached over the next couple of days, the mountain seemed to retreat. In our case, the mountains will retreat behind clouds, and we won't see it again for several days.

❧   ❧   ❧

Day five: July 12—Henry's birthday. From Logan Brook down to the East Branch of the Pleasant River, to Mountain View Pond, over Little Boardman Mountain, skirt Crawford Pond, to Cooper Brook. In the morning, a ruffed grouse startles us and does her wounded mother routine, one wing hanging limply as she crosses the trail in front of us then circles around back to her nest, moaning pitifully all the while. Grossly overacted, in the opinion of these reviewers. Though it worked.

On the trail David confesses that he does respect Thoreau more than any other writer for his commitment to an idea and his willingness to live it. What Thoreau does that a natural history writer like Alexander Garden fails to do, says David, is explore the big questions. He doesn't just observe nature. He ponders its meaning. Why, then, I ask, shouldn't Thoreau be held up as the ideal for nature writers? David's reply: Because too many nature writers too readily accept Thoreau's solutions—following him up the symbolic path from natural fact to spiritual significance, as if that's all you can do with nature, and adopting and celebrating solitude as the means of dealing with social problems. Even an admirer like Buell charges Thoreau with being "escapist."[9]

We spend the afternoon swimming and washing clothes. Cooper Brook cascades into a lovely deep pool right in front of the lean-to. We dive upstream off rocks jutting into the pool and let the current carry us back. The water is cold but not chilling. Patches of sun break through the clouds and haze, and we wash shirts and socks and underwear, lay them out to dry on the rocks. We lay ourselves out to dry too. The black flies are just plentiful enough to coax us back into the brook for respite every so often. It's a delicious day, a "washing day" Thoreau would have said.

Tomorrow we head down into the lake country, where we hear the trail is a swamp and the mosquitoes are relentless. And the rain approaches.

Still no moose.

❧   ❧   ❧

Day six: we hike twenty-two miles today, mostly in the rain. First an easy eleven to Potaywadjo Spring, an enormous liquid eye fifteen feet across where the water percolates up through bubbling sand. The rain starts before noon, but for the first hour doesn't penetrate the tree canopy. In the afternoon, though, along Nahmakanta Stream and Nahmakanta Lake, we get drenched. No discussion of Thoreau, just slogging through the water, thinking wistfully about families and home. We're bushed when we reach the shelter at Wadleigh Stream. A camp group of a dozen Quebecois teens is tenting nearby. So is a newlywed couple from Idaho out on a six-week honeymoon hike. David and I share the shelter with Blue Iggy, Sweet Pea, Tradja, and Gotta Go, thru-hikers doing twenty-milers every day, ready to finish the trail in a couple of days.

At dusk, we hear guitar sounds coming from a blue tent. I take out a pennywhistle to drop a shrill hint that the guitar should come to the lean-to. The couple from Idaho show up, Jeff and Tristan, trail-named the Von Trapps because they are musicians and she looks like Julie Andrews. They play in a band in Idaho, and he's carrying a small, cheap guitar. To the rain's rooftop percussion, we play music, some originals by the Von Trapps, some songs by the Bare Naked Ladies, Cat Stevens, the Eagles — good trail names all, we decide. The thru-hikers, starved for music after four months on the Trail, applaud and thank us.

✿   ✿   ✿

Day seven: The rain stops this morning. Up Nesuntabunt first thing, nice views of Nahmakanta Lake and the shadowy lower slopes of Ktaadn beneath low-lying clouds. Down to Crescent Pond, then along Pollywog Stream, or rather *in* Pollywog Stream since the stream has flooded with the rain and the trail is knee-deep. We wade through about a quarter mile of that, then dry out our socks on a bridge as the sun starts to come out. Back on the trail, several brooks to ford, thigh-high in torrential current, then up along the banks of Rainbow Stream, which is absolutely thundering. Churning whitewater, not a patch of clear-flowing stream. I feel like we're hiking on the rim of a washing machine, looking into the suds around the agitator, except that this isn't just swirling around but crashing downhill. In my fear of slipping into the maelstrom, I suppose I would even call that current hostile. And yesterday's pouring rain was none too friendly either. But that rain made the current, and I know even as I'm looking at it that the boiling whitewater of Rainbow will be one of the moments I'll carry home from this trip.

I said before that I cannot understand how literary critics have so often, as I see it, misread "Ktaadn." It's not just, I think, that they don't get out enough, and so fail to recognize that fear and danger, rather than tainting our experiences in nature, add sense-tingling spice. (And a different seasoning for every season.) They have also been misled by the literary traditions they are steeped in. The classic tradition for appreciating nature is pastoral, where the natural ideal is a comfortable middle ground between civilization and wilderness. The dominant literary tradition for appreciating nature in early nineteenth-century America is the transcendental, whereby nature is viewed as a data bank of physical facts from which moral lessons can be withdrawn. But Thoreau's description of Ktaadn falls into neither category. He says the mountaintop is "not lawn, nor pasture, nor mead, nor woodland, nor lea, nor arable"—in a word, not pastoral. It offers no meditative solace, repose, or renewal to its human visitor. And it is pure matter, seemingly devoid of spirit, so it does not lend itself to the sort of transcendental philosophizing whereby we read the moral meaning inherent in a natural fact. Most critics have assumed, it seems, that if Thoreau values nature on Ktaadn, he would express his appreciation in pastoral or transcendental terms. Finding neither, they've concluded, somewhat hastily, that he does not value Ktaadn's nature at all.

There are, of course, other literary traditions in which nature can be valued, and the one most conducive to valuing raw wilderness is the sublime. Ronald Hoag, the first critic to reassess the tone of "Ktaadn," argues that Thoreau's rhapsodic language in the Burnt Lands section constitutes "a breathtaking apprehension of the sublime." And counter to most other critics, he asserts that the description is compatible with transcendentalism. As he explains it, "It is precisely because the matter atop Katahdin is so intense and so pure that it is, therefore, so perfectly spiritual . . . a paradigm of correspondence." [10]

Hoag's perception that awe as opposed to despair or disillusionment governs the tone of the essay strikes me as sound. In the sublime he has found a literary context that seems compatible with the truth of the matter Thoreau encountered on Ktaadn. But even Hoag is still trying to fit Thoreau's description into traditional conceptual boxes. And so he ends up arguing that since Thoreau, as we well know, is a transcendentalist, then of course the Ktaadn experience must exemplify transcendentalist ideas—despite the fact that Thoreau admits to being unable to trace any correspondences between the natural facts of Ktaadn and any spiritual facts of human import, and he denies feeling transcendent over anything.

What all these critics have lacked is an ecological context, one that does not assume that human concerns are the be-all and end-all of nature. Only recently have some sensitive readers provided that ecocritical context. Ning

Yu, for instance, argues that "Ktaadn" constitutes "a reflective critique of the anthropocentric interpretation of nature." He finds in Thoreau's Ktaadn trip, traveling upwater from bay to river to lake and pond to stream to cascade and rill to mist and cloud, "a metaphoric journey in reverse order of the hydrological cycle, to the source of all lives, where he discovers a 'Titanic' nature that has ontological priority over the self-centeredness of human beings." Ktaadn snags clouds in its granite grasp. The clouds drop liquid ballast. The water dances down, shaping mountains, resting in ponds, feeding oceans, from which clouds arise. Spring streams nurture black-fly larvae, which grow up to feed trout and discourage civilization's inroads into the Maine woods. Thoreau traces water back to where it is "source of [all] life," says Yu, rather than "material resource" for human consumption.[11]

Other ecocritics similarly looking beyond the borders of anthropocentrism find the tone of "Ktaadn" more uplifting than did earlier critics. John Tallmadge notes that Thoreau may have perceived the mountain as alien and indifferent, but suggests that that perception only exposed the inadequacy of "received modes of representation . . . to compass the experience." And that hardly constitues rejection or retreat. John O'Grady argues from his experience among mountains that Thoreau's loss of self is no "cowardly retreat" but a "prelude to enlightenment." Don Scheese, after retracing Thoreau's routes on New England's mountains, concludes that Thoreau's experiences above tree line suggest that he had no reason to "freak out" on Ktaadn. Thoreau's rejection of anthropocentrism amounts to an appreciation that values the "mystery" of nature over our "mastery" of it.[12]

Is ecocriticism just another conceptual box to cram a work like "Ktaadn" into? If so, it is a box big enough to hold more than just the perspective of a certain culture or even of a whole species. It holds the world's stories.

We get to Rainbow Stream Lean-to by lunchtime, an easy eight-mile day. The thru-hikers are there, planning an afternoon marathon. Sweet Pea and Tradja unload the heaviest stuff from their packs and give it to Blue Iggy and Gotta Go. They're all headed for Hurd Brook Shelter, twelve miles from here, but Sweet Pea and Tradja are going to hike three more miles to a store at Abol Bridge at the end of the Hundred Mile Wilderness. There they'll get snacks and beer to bring back to their friends at Hurd Brook. In other words, they'll do twenty-six miles today, much of it at a near-jog through mud and wet trail. I say we're staying here at Rainbow Stream, but I ask Sweet Pea, a young woman who must weigh all of ninety-eight pounds, to bring us back a six-pack. What the hell, it would only be another twelve miles. I'm joking, of course.

At night David and I play more tunes with the Von Trapps. Rainbow Stream sings on as we turn in for the night.

Tomorrow we leave the Hundred Mile Wilderness. Three days to Katahdin.

❦   ❦   ❦

Day eight: Today the Trail goes along Rainbow Stream to Rainbow Deadwaters and Rainbow Lake, up Rainbow Ledges, where we are relieved to be out of the muck and onto rock again, and then down to Hurd Brook. Waiting for us there, to our surprise and delight, is a six-pack of Katahdin Red Ale, compliments of Sweet Pea and Tradja. Attached is a note in which Sweet Pea apologizes for not making it all the way back to Rainbow Stream. Marveling at their generosity (they had to carry that six-pack three and a half miles!), David and I have one each, leave the rest for the Von Trapps.

On Rainbow Ledges David asks if I've gotten what I needed from the Hundred Mile Wilderness. Yes, I say. The thunderstorm at Cloud Pond, our worries about the hurricane, the swollen roaring waters of Rainbow Stream—these are moments when I grasped Thoreau's point that nature is not "made for man." I suppose we always realize, no matter how smug or concerned we get about the effects of human civilization, that nature is ultimately in control of the world. But we do not often feel that that dominion extends to and includes us. Accepting that it does might require readjusting, downward, our sense of our own significance, but that might also be what it takes for us to feel part of the world. And in that absorption there is certainly no cause for despair. We come out here to get in touch with a power greater than ourselves, or at least to see and sense it and be impressed.

At times on our trip, like when we made it through some of the fords, we have delighted in our control and mastery over nature, our conquest of it. That conception of a contest between humanity and nature underlies much of the rhetoric of American literary treatments of nature through the nineteenth century. David points out that the contest is often a means of self-definition for Americans. Exactly. Which is why Thoreau's experience on Ktaadn has been so hard for us to make sense of, because what he does up there is give up the contest, the whole attempt at self-definition through the encounter with the natural world. Maybe it's not that he "loses it" (or himself) up there, but *relinquishes* the self. To Buell that sort of relinquishment—"to give up individual autonomy itself, to forgo the illusion of mental and even bodily apartness from one's environment"—is not just the plot but the point of American environmental writing.[13] The moment of relinquishment is zenlike, beyond reason and understanding, where the self disappears into the all. We call that kind of thing mystical oneness.

David asks, so if the lesson is letting go, giving up the contest, why should a thru-hiker even go up Katahdin? I've heard of some who choose not to, leaving the journey openended, unended, never-ending, forever to be continued. True, most do go up the mountain, but that climb is no renunciation of what they may have learned from the trail, a lesson akin to what Thoreau learned from Ktaadn. Yes, they have gained confidence in both their physical abilities and their ability to accept and overcome whatever the natural world throws in their way. But few think of their success as "beating" nature. They come to see a summit, especially a magnificent one like Katahdin, not as something they've won, or earned, or bagged, but as a gift, something freely given to those who have prepared themselves. It's the gift of the world, and to receive it you must first give something of yourself. So maybe an ascent involves neither losing nor relinquishing the self, not giving *up* but giving *of* the self.

And now I think I understand why so much nature writing is written in the first person. It may seem peculiar that writers groping toward an understanding of the world around them have so much to say about their own place in it — a preoccupation that might seem more egocentric than ecocentric. But maybe the ecological imagination virtually requires the presence of the first person. Near the end of *A Natural History of the Senses*, Diane Ackerman writes that the senses "bridge the personal and the impersonal, the one private soul with its many relatives, the individual with the universe, all of life on Earth." [14] The senses connect us to the world, and the "I" functions in nature writing as the perceiving self that makes those connections. It is through our senses that we get close to the world, come to know it, take it in. It is not just that the first person brings a sense of immediacy, as opposed to the distancing effect of the third person's pose of objectivity. The first person makes possible the encounter with the otherness of the world. And the first person also makes possible what is often the climax of the story in nature writing — the gift of the self to the world.

❁   ❁   ❁

Coming out of the Hundred Mile Wilderness, we follow a road to the West Branch of the Penobscot, cross on Abol Bridge. Thoreau camped a quarter-mile upstream, where Abol Stream and Katahdin Stream enter the river. We load up on junk food at a small store, then camp along the river amid a stand of birch. Hiding out from a drizzle, we read a day-old newspaper. It may as well have been a week old — nothing new, really, to report. Better we'd read the eternities. We hear logging trucks rumble by, out the tent window see rafters paddle downriver.

I ask David if he got what he wanted out of the Hundred Mile Wilderness. He expresses regret about not seeing a moose. That might make a good trail name, I say: No Moose. Actually, Thoreau didn't see one either.

Thoreau spent his time at camp fishing in the Abol, catching trout that "swallowed the bait as fast as we could throw in." He rhapsodized about the glistening tints to their scales, calling them "bright fluviatile flowers . . . made beautiful, the Lord only knows why, to swim there." Thoreau's frying pan sizzled with fish after fish until, "luckily for the foolish race, and this particularly foolish generation of trout, the night shut down at last, not a little deepened by the dark side of Ktaadn, which, like a permanent shadow, reared itself from the eastern bank" (133). Thoreau awoke before dawn to catch more fish.

We go to the store for microwaved pizza for dinner and greasy doughnuts and hot coffee for breakfast. In the morning we backtrack to Abol Bridge, to see if the mountain has shucked its cloud cover, but it's still socked in. Then we're off on our approach to Ktaadn.

❁   ❁   ❁

Day nine: Wild roses edge the dirt road that takes us across Abol Stream. The sun fights its way through the clouds as we ford waist-high, tannin-hued Katahdin Stream. We hike up along Nesowadnehunk, which Thoreau renders "Sowadnehunk," "signifying 'running between mountains'" (132), then face a daunting ford of the Lower Nesowadnehunk. Five times we try to cross upstream, where the flow seems a bit tamer. But we can't do it. The current is too strong, tugs at our boots as we try to find some solid footing, pushes at our hips. David gets knocked in, but climbs out right away and retreats. Finally, we cross right where the trail comes to the stream. The water foams angrily there, but it's not as deep, and we get across.

Upstream we cross the Upper Nesowadnehunk on a fallen log, pass Big Niagara and Little Niagara Falls—and there, the day clearing, we have a view of part of the Katahdin massif. Shortly after noon we reach Daicey Pond. Across the pond looms Baxter Peak, top of Katahdin. We swim, rent a canoe, chase loons on the pond. David, in the bow, takes to calling me Joe Polis, after the Indian hero of "The Allagash and East Branch." Which would make David Henry.

I ask to switch positions.

When we return the canoe, the Von Trapps have arrived, and we all swim together. David and I hike on to Katahdin Stream. In the late afternoon we meet Sweet Pea, Blue Iggy, Tradja, and Gotta Go, down from the mountain, done with the trail. Happy but subdued, not sure what to think about their hike being over, they warn us to wear warm clothes heading up and to bring lots of water.

Tomorrow we climb.

❀   ❀   ❀

In 1846 Thoreau, as the most experienced climber in his party, took the lead, heading up along Abol Stream, crossing to the south side of the stream and then, keeping Abol Slide to their left and aiming for what appeared to be the highest peak (probably South Peak), he bushwhacked across open country and over a spur to the south (possibly Rum Mountain). From there they could see Ktaadn, which, says Thoreau, "presented a different aspect from any mountain I have seen, there being a greater proportion of naked rock, rising abruptly from the forest; and we looked up at this blue barrier as if it were some fragment of a wall which anciently bounded the earth in that direction" (137). At noon, they roasted more trout over a fire, then climbed till four in the afternoon. They camped by what Thoreau took to be the headwaters of Murch Brook, now called Katahdin Stream, but those who have studied Thoreau's route insist it must have been Abol Stream.[15] Thoreau took advantage of the remaining daylight to try for the summit, climbing over the spreading tops of krummholz spruce, ending at "the skirt of a cloud," where the rocks were like "the flocks and herds that pastured, chewing a rocky cud at sunset." Another pun there, perhaps. Many New England mountains, sculpted by glaciers, slope gently on their north side and drop precipitously to the south. That geological feature is called a *roche moutonnée*, or sheepback, and Thoreau, coming up steeply from the south, may have taken Ktaadn for one. After watching the rocks grazing, Thoreau returned to camp, set in a ravine.

The next day he climbed higher, into the clouds, and reached the Table Land before he felt "compelled to descend" (145).

❀   ❀   ❀

Day ten: In the night I see stars, making me hopeful about clear skies for our climb. But at dawn an ominously dark cloud engulfs Ktaadn. We leave our packs at the ranger station, carry snacks and water and extra clothes in fanny packs and shoulder-slung stuff sacks. At Katahdin Stream we fill our bellies with water, then hike up past Katahdin Falls. A few minutes later David realizes he left his new "Mt. Katahdin" cap, purchased at Abol Bridge, back by the stream. He runs back to get it, the Von Trapps pass us, we start up again, and then David realizes he left his glasses back where he'd put his stuff down when he ran back to get his cap. This prompts a story: of the time he took his wife on a winter day hike in the Smokies, lost the trail, and ended up on the North Carolina side instead of in Tennessee — a whole mountain range away from their car. That story sparks recollections of the many times he has wandered off-trail in the past week. And so, on the last day of our hike, on the last few miles of the A.T., he earns his trail name: Pathfinder.

Above tree line the trail winds up and around boulders, calling for lots of scrambling and twisting through crevices and crannies. The conditions must be typical of Katahdin, much like what Thoreau describes: windy, cloudy, cold. We move up the Gateway, a sharply angled line of rocks. Pulling ourselves up exposed boulders, unable to see anything off to the sides, we feel like we're suspended in midair, the wind trying to pluck us off the rocks and into the moving white void. It's like a Lower Nesowadnehunk of the air. We meet a couple who had come up the Abol Trail and decided to come right back down via the Hunt Trail, without trying for the summit. "It's too cold and windy up there," they tell us, "twice as bad as here. You can't do it."

Their words accentuate our fears — that the wind is too strong, the clouds too threatening, the ridge too steep and exposed and narrow. Maybe we should stop.

In the lee of a boulder the Von Trapps are waiting for us to discuss the situation. Should we go on?

I'm thinking of course of Thoreau — who did not get to the top. But at least he reached the Table Land. We decide that it might be smart to turn back up there. But we are not at our limit now, so we may as well go on, together, until we cannot safely go any further.

More scrambling in the wind — then up on the Table Land we find the wind really no worse than below. Just as Thoreau describes it, occasionally a light spot in the clouds appears, a dim bruise in the sky hinting at the sun, and at times we can see around us for about forty yards. But mostly we see only twenty feet, and our companions are silver shadows, vague ghostly silhouettes in the mist. Ktaadn is a "cloud-factory," said Thoreau, and we traverse the smokestack's rim (143).

We get to the top, David, the Von Trapps, and I. "Northern Terminus of the Appalachian Trail," reads the summit sign. The End. Much celebration, congratulations, and picture taking. But it's too cold to hang around for long.

Coming down, at the Gateway, the clouds thin out, a vista opens up, and

I feel a quick flash of vertigo. If I had known how steeply the ravines fall away on each side, I would have been less bold in clambering for hand and foot-holds on the way up. Now I do know, and it gives me pause.

The cloud bank is rising, and below us we see more of what Thoreau describes — the map of Maine spread out before us, with lakes scattered like fragments of a broken mirror. Once again, Thoreau's essay surprises me by being, still, a reliable guide to the Maine woods.

And the next minute I see that even more the Maine woods have been my guide to Thoreau's essay. Coming down the mountain Thoreau describes a sparrow flitting past him, "unable to command its course, like a fragment of the gray rock blown off by the wind" (145). I look around for wind-tossed sparrows, listen for them. And then, a gust of realization. I am the sparrow, catching a wave, riding the currents, blown away, and I am a fragment of the mountain.

And the wind, soughing, calls my name.

❀   ❀   ❀

Afterward: Further down the Gateway we meet a boy scout troop lounging among the rocks and would-be thru-hikers climbing up, preparing to take their first southbound step off Katahdin, headed for Georgia. Rocks bake in the sun, and we peel off hats, jackets, and wool shirts, zip off pant legs. If it stays sunny, the summit this afternoon will be more like a picnic ground in a city park than the "untamed and untameable nature" that Thoreau de-scribes, and that I think I encountered. But when we're below tree line the clouds move back in, bringing a rain squall.

Those critics who think Thoreau had a terrible time up on Ktaadn dis-agree about the extent to which his "failure" stayed with him. Leo Stoller argues that on Ktaadn "the universe pantheistically informed with a benign godhead had suddenly dissociated into its parts. For the rest of his life he was to strive in vain to reunite them." Other critics contend that although he may have been momentarily thrown for a loop, Thoreau recovers even within the space of the essay.[16] Though I dispute the notion that Thoreau's experience on Ktaadn was negative, I'll hold with the camp that says its ef-fects were long-lasting. Thoreau was profoundly moved by Ktaadn. That's why, on his two later trips to Maine, in 1853 and 1857, he hoped to return to the mountain. It is the place that for him embodied the wild.

Thoreau's memories of Ktaadn crop up again and again in his writing. In the final chapter of *Walden* the language and theme of the "Contact" pas-sage reappear: "We can never have enough of Nature. We must be refreshed by the sight of inexhaustible vigor, vast and Titanic features. . . . We need to witness our own limits transgressed, and some life pasturing freely where we never wander." In an 1857 letter to a friend, Harrison Blake, the echoes are even stronger. "You must ascend a mountain to learn your relation to matter, and so to your own body, for *it* is at home there, though *you* are not." Referring to the White Mountains, he asks, "*Who* am I? What are they? — those little peaks — call them Madison, Jefferson, Lafayette. What is *the matter?*" Earlier that year in his journal Thoreau referred to a mountain in his dreams as "unhandselled, awful, grand."[17]

But the lasting influence of Ktaadn went beyond the descriptive language he exercised upon it. In his letter to Blake about the matter of mountains, Thoreau writes, "Going up there and being blown on is nothing. We never do much climbing while we are there. . . . It is after we get home that we really go over the mountain, if ever. What did the mountain say? What did the mountain do?"[18] What the mountain said to Thoreau percolates through his perceptions of nature for the rest of his life. When he returned to Walden Pond he was working on drafts of both *A Week on the Concord and Merrimack Rivers* and *Walden*. At that point he apparently inserted into *A Week* the Greylock episode that forms the book's centerpiece, perhaps its climax.[19] And *Walden?* Lawrence Buell traces in Thoreau's most famous work a "conspicuous movement . . . away from egocentrism, as indexed by how often the 'I' appears." Buell notes that Thoreau's use of the first person gradually diminishes in *Walden*, from an average of 6.6 times per page in the first two chapters to an average of only 3.6 in the last five. At the same time, references to "Walden," the "pond," and the "wild" increase from 1.8 to 2.3. Buell takes this as evidence of Thoreau's relinquishment of self — which requires not the "*eradication* of ego" but the "suspension of ego to the point of feeling the environment to be at least as worthy of attention as oneself" — and his progress "along a path from homocentrism toward biocentrism." Thoreau took his first step on that path descending from Ktaadn.[20]

Perhaps it is in Thoreau's *Journal*, though, his life's work, that we most see the influence of Ktaadn. In the last decade of his life, the journals become more and more preoccupied with the facts of nature, less and less reflective about the transcendental meaning of those facts. What is that transition but an increasing preoccupation with matter, the solid earth, the actual world?

❁   ❁   ❁

At Katahdin Stream Campground our car, delivered by a friend of the Shaws, is waiting for us. We drive out of Baxter Park, still searching in vain for our moose, take the Von Trapps back to Monson, say our good-byes, then head south. We stop at a diner for hot pastrami sandwiches, coffee, and Dutch apple pie. On into the night, we drive. We talk about going home to our families, and, since David's baby girl is named Kory MacKaye, our talk of family leads us to the subject of her namesake, Benton MacKaye.

In a 1927 lecture, when the Appalachian Trail was in the formative stage somewhere between idea and reality, MacKaye gave a talk on "Outdoor Culture," making it his occasion for explaining "'the why' of the Appalachian Trail." We need outdoor culture, said MacKaye, in order to restore the proper balance in our lives between "the natural and the artificial." We have become overcivilized, and to counter the influence of the "Civilizee," we need a dose of the "Barbarian." The Barbarians need to claim the high ground on the crest of the Appalachian Range, establish a Barbarian Utopia, and from there launch a Barbarian invasion. The Civilizee, said MacKaye, "sees in the mountain summit a pretty place at which to play at tin-can pirate and to strew the Sunday supplement; our Barbarian sees in the mountain summit the strategic point from which to resoundly kick said Civilizee and to open war on the further encroachment of his mechanized Utopia." [21] David and I are all for invading, but first we figure a hot shower is in order. We pull into a motel near Old Orchard Beach.

Next day we continue south, but detour off the interstate to visit Concord, Massachusetts. We yawn through a tour of Emerson's house, perking up only at seeing a chair with a drawer under the seat reputedly built by Thoreau to hold Emerson's oft-misplaced Sunday gloves. We also see pictures of a wild (but short-lived) summer house built by Thoreau and Bronson Alcott using irregularly shaped natural materials. Emerson said he wanted to call it "Tumbledown Hall."

We drive on to Walden Pond, now a state reservation. The day is sunny, and the parking lot full. At the pond a thousand or so people crowd the beach and the concession stand. We don't know whether to laugh or cry or wind our watches. From Thoreau's footsteps on Ktaadn to Henry's backyard—what a comedown. Olfaction of suntan oil overpowers the scent of pines. Of course, the suntan oil also overpowers the scent of deet (the active ingredient in bug dope) and the stench of armpit sweat that still permeates our clothes.

Walden's water is "remarkable for its purity," said Thoreau. Even more remarkably, it still looks pretty clear today, though a bit turqoise-hued, which David attributes to the blend of reflected blue sky and high urine content. We walk around the pond, people getting fewer the farther we go. Just down the trail from the site of Thoreau's cabin, a tremendously paunched man wearing headphones has laid claim to a sandy spit of beach, perhaps where Henry bathed every morning.

Farther along we find an opening in the brush, where rocks lead down to the water, and we swim. It's quiet, peaceful, quite removed from the hubbub of the public beach. A woman strolls by, pausing to listen to bird calls. In the shallows David tracks a couple of small perch. A tall purple wildflower leans over the pond's edge — giant hyssop, I later learn.

We continue our circumambulation, stop to peer down the railroad tracks where Henry walked to town. Nearing the public beach, we share our impressions of the place. Shocked at first at how much use Walden gets, sensing desecration, we are also impressed at how easy it is to slip away from the hordes just by walking to the far side of the pond. The water is delicious on the skin. I'm wondering, though, how to commence our barbarian invasion, how to continue climbing the mountain.

Maybe the pond itself has enough of the wild in it to bring a touch of the barbarian to the civilized world. Buell suggests that those who come to Walden to swim and "enjoy the pond" might be truer to the spirit of Thoreau than those who come to worship at the shrine of his cabin site.[22] Maybe so. But when David and I stood at the cabin site, adding stones to the memorial cairn next to it, a teenaged girl wearing a T-shirt over her bathing suit wandered over and read a nearby plaque. Printed there was the passage from *Walden* that reads "I went to the woods because I wished to live deliberately, to front only the essential facts of life." The girl read silently, looked at the chained-off outline of the cabin site, and walked back to the pond. Somehow I think that she and all the other sunbathers who stroll by and read a bit of Thoreau's story will go home with something more than a suntan.

So let the Civilizees come to Walden.

But let there also be a Hundred Mile Wilderness, and a Ktaadn.

NOTES

Introduction: Walking the Line

1. Bruce Chatwin, *The Songlines* (New York: Penguin, 1987).

2. Benton MacKaye, "An Appalachian Trail: A Project in Regional Planning," *Journal of the American Institute of Architects* 9 (1921): 325–30. For a good collection of MacKaye's writings, see *From Geography to Geotechnics*, ed. Paul T. Bryant (Urbana: Univ. of Illinois Press, 1968).

3. *Appalachian Trail Conference Member Handbook*, 13th ed. (Harpers Ferry: Appalachian Trail Conference, 1988), 4–6.

4. Dan Bruce, *The Thru-Hiker's Handbook* (Conyers, Ga.: Center for Appalachian Trail Studies, 1994)—a different edition appears annually; Earl V. Shaffer, *Walking with Spring: The First Thru-Hike of the Appalachian Trail* (Harpers Ferry: Appalachian Trail Conference, 1983); David Brill, *As Far as the Eye Can See: Reflections of an Appalachian Trail Hiker* (Nashville: Rutledge Hill, 1990); Robert A. Browne, *The Appalachian Trail: History, Humanity and Ecology* (Stafford, Va.: Northwoods Press, 1980); V. Collins Chew, *Underfoot: A Geologic Guide to the Appalachian Trail* (Harpers Ferry: Appalachian Trail Conference, 1988). David Emblidge, ed., *The Appalachian Trail Reader* (New York: Oxford Univ. Press, 1996).

5. The term *ecocriticism* was first used by William Rueckert in "Literature and Ecology: An Experiment in Ecocriticism," *Iowa Review* 9, no. 4 (1978): 71–86. For a fine collection of ecocritical theory and practice, see Cheryll Glotfelty and Harold Fromm, eds., *The Ecocriticism Reader: Landmarks in Literary Ecology* (Athens: Univ. of Georgia Press, 1996).

6. See SueEllen Campbell, "The Land and Language of Desire: Where Deep Ecology and Post-Structuralism Meet," *Western American Literature* 24, no. 3 (1989): 199–211. For the opposing view, holding that the abstractness of poststructuralist theory has rendered it irrelevant to ecocriticism, see Glen A. Love, "Revaluing Nature: Toward An Ecological Criticism," *Western American Literature* 25, no. 3 (1990): 201–15; and Karl Kroeber, *Ecological Literary Criticism: Romantic Imagining and the Biology of Mind* (New York: Columbia Univ. Press, 1994).

7. Scott Slovic, "Ecocriticism: Storytelling, Values, Communication, Contact"

(Paper delivered at Annual Meeting of the Western Literature Association, Salt Lake City, 5–8 October 1994).

8. Narrative scholarship is akin to the feminist practice of "autobiographical criticism," a defense of the subjective as a reaction against the disembodied voice of patriarchal authority. See, for example, *The Intimate Critique: Autobiographical Literary Criticism*, ed. Diane P. Freedman, Olivia Frey, and Frances Murphy Zauhar (Durham: Duke Univ. Press, 1993).

9. Kenneth Burke, "Literature as Equipment for Living," in *The Philosophy of Literary Form: Studies in Symbolic Action*, 3d ed. (Berkeley: Univ. of California Press, 1974), 293–304.

10. Simon Schama, *Landscape and Memory* (New York: Knopf, 1995), 24.

Chapter 1. Cherokee Myths and the Pleasures of Geopiety

1. James Mooney, *James Mooney's History, Myths, and Sacred Formulas of the Cherokees*, ed. George Ellison (Asheville, N.C.: Historical Images, 1992). Subsequent references, given parenthetically, are to this edition. References to the section on *Sacred Formulas*, paginated separately in Ellison's edition, are prefaced with SF.

2. John Kirtland Wright, "Notes on Early American Geopiety," in *Human Nature in Geography* (Cambridge: Harvard Univ. Press, 1966), 250, 256.

3. Ibid., 252.

4. Yi-Fu Tuan, "Geopiety: A Theme in Man's Attachment to Nature and to Place," in *Geographies of the Mind: Essays in Historical Geosophy*, ed. David Lowenthal and Martyn J. Bowden (New York: Oxford Univ. Press), 13–14, 33.

5. Keith H. Basso, "'Stalking with Stories': Names, Places, and Moral Narratives among the Western Apache," in *On Nature: Nature, Landscape, and Natural History*, ed. Daniel Halpern (San Francisco: North Point Press, 1987), 114.

6. Joseph E. Brown, "Modes of Contemplation through Action: North American Indians," *Main Currents in Modern Thought* 30, no. 2 (1973–74): 60; J. Baird Callicott, "Traditional American Indian and Traditional Western European Attitudes toward Nature: An Overview," in *Environmental Philosophy: A Collection of Readings*, ed. Robert Elliot and Arran Gare (University Park: Penn State Univ. Press, 1983), 231–59.

7. Basso, "Stalking," 101–2.

8. Joe Cook and Monica Cook, *The Appalachian Trail Companion*, 1974 (Harper's Ferry: The Appalachian Trail Conference, 1994), 7.

9. Charles Lanman, *Letters from the Alleghany Mountains* (New York, 1849), 73–74, quoted in Mooney, *Myths of the Cherokees*, 443–44.

10. Ann Sutton and Myron Sutton, *The Appalachian Trail: Wilderness on the Doorstep* (Philadelphia: Lippincott, 1967), 42.

11. Michael Frome, *Strangers in High Places: The Story of the Great Smoky Mountains* (Knoxville: Univ. of Tennessee Press, 1980), 85.

12. Lanman, *Letters*, 110.

13. Ibid., 113.

14. Frome, *Strangers*, 306.

Chapter 2. Puc Puggy in the Nantahalas:
The Turning Point of William Bartram's Travels

1. Charlotte M. Porter, "William Bartram's Travels in the Indian Nations," *Florida Historical Quarterly* 70 (1992): 449.

2. The essay has never been published, but Kerry Walters, in his article "The 'Peaceable Disposition' of Animals: William Bartram on the Moral Sensibility of Brute Creation," *Pennsylvania History* 56, no. 3 (1989): 173 n. 16, says he is working on a critical edition of the treatise.

3. William Bartram, *Travels through North and South Carolina, Georgia, East and West Florida, the Cherokee Country, the Extensive Territories of the Muscogulges, or Creek Confederacy, and the Country of the Choctaws*, intro. by James Dickey (New York: Penguin, 1988), 293. Subsequent references, given parenthetically, are to this edition.

4. Moonchild did not, of course, leave bibliographic documentation in the trail register, but I'd better: Wendell Berry, *The Unforeseen Wilderness: An Essay on Kentucky's Red River Gorge* (Lexington: Univ. Press of Kentucky, 1971), 34.

5. N. Bryllion Fagin, *William Bartram: Interpreter of the American Landscape* (Baltimore: Johns Hopkins Univ. Press, 1933), 128–76.

6. Ibid., v.

7. Dickey, "Cerulean Ixea, The Exuberant Fields, Gnaphalium, the Absolute Crocodile and the Wondrous Machine," in Bartram, *Travels*, x.

8. Frances Harper, ed., *The Travels of William Bartram: Naturalist's Edition* (New Haven: Yale Univ. Press, 1958): 391.

9. Frome, *Strangers*, 47.

10. Robert Arner, "Pastoral Patterns in William Bartram's *Travels*," *Tennessee Studies in Literature* 18 (1975): 138, 142, 137–38.

11. Ibid., 143.

12. The word *ecology* was first used by the German zoologist Ernst Haeckel in 1866. According to Robert P. McIntosh, ecology did not develop as a recognized science until the 1920s, and it attained its popularity outside scientific circles only in the 1960s (*The Background of Ecology: Concept and Theory* [Cambridge: Cambridge Univ. Press, 1985], 2).

13. Pamela Regis, *Describing Early America: Bartram, Jefferson, Crèvecoeur and the Rhetoric of Natural History* (DeKalb: Northern Illinois Univ. Press, 1992), 5–25.

14. Ibid., 60.

15. Walters, "The 'Peaceable Disposition,'" 157.

16. Bruce Silver, "William Bartram's and Other Eighteenth-Century Accounts of Nature," *Journal of the History of Ideas* 39 (1978): 605.

17. L. Hugh Moore, "The Aesthetic Theory of William Bartram," *Essays in Arts and Sciences* 12, no. 1 (1983): 29.

18. L. Hugh Moore, "The Southern Landscape of William Bartram: A Terrible Beauty," *Essays in Arts and Sciences* 10, no. 1 (1981): 41.

19. See Arner, "Pastoral Patterns," on Bartram's use of pastoral imagery and themes; Moore, "The Aesthetic Theory of William Bartram," on the beautiful, the picturesque, and the sublime; and Fagin, *William Bartram*, for a review of Bartram's influence on romanticism.

20. Charles Adams, review of *Describing Early America,*, by Pamela Regis, *American Literature* 65 (1993): 149.

21. Charles Adams, "William Bartram's *Travels*: A Natural History of the South," in *Rewriting the South: History and Fiction*, ed. Lothar Honnighausen and Valeria Gennaro Lerda (Tübingen: Francke, 1993), 118.

22. Murray Bookchin, "What Is Social Ecology?" in *The Modern Crisis*, 2d ed. (Montreal: Black Rose Books, 1987), 59, 72, 58.

23. Qtd. in Porter, "William Bartram's Travels," 448.

24. Josephine A. Herbst, *New Green World* (New York: Hastings House, 1954), 253; Linnaeus qtd. in Philip G. Terrie, "Tempests and Alligators: The Ambiguous Wilderness of William Bartram," *North Dakota Quarterly* 59, no. 2 (1991): 19; Larry R. Clarke, "The Quaker Background of William Bartram's View of Nature," *Journal of the History of Ideas* 46 (1985): 445.

25. Bartram, *Observations on the Creek and Cherokee Indians*, Transactions of the American Ethnological Society 3, no. 1 (1853): 41.

26. Ibid., 42.

27. Regis, *Describing*, 74–75.

28. Christopher Looby, "The Constitution of Nature: Taxonomy as Politics in Jefferson, Peace, and Bartram," *Early American Literature* 22 (1987): 259.

29. See Neil Evernden, "Beyond Ecology: Self, Place, and the Pathetic Fallacy," *North American Review* 263, no. 4 (1978): 16–20.

30. Looby, "The Constitution of Nature," 252–73; Douglas Anderson, "Bartram's *Travels* and the Politics of Nature," *Early American Literature* 25 (1990): 3–17.

31. Frome, *Strangers*, 82.

32. Mooney, *Myths of the Cherokee*, 118.

Chapter 3. Mary Noailles Murfree: Ecofeminist of the Great Smoky Mountains

1. Elaine Showalter, "Toward a Feminist Poetics," in *The New Feminist Criticism: Essays on Women, Literature, and Theory*, ed. Showalter (New York: Pantheon, 1985), 129.

2. Charles Egbert Craddock [Mary Noailles Murfree], *In the Tennessee Mountains*, ed. Nathalia Wright (Knoxville: Univ. of Tennessee Press, 1970).

3. Durwood Dunn, *Cades Cove: The Life and Death of a Southern Appalachian Community, 1818–1937* (Knoxville: Univ. of Tennessee Press, 1988), 144.

4. Charles Egbert Craddock [Mary Noailles Murfree], *In the Clouds* (Boston: Houghton Mifflin, 1887). For information on Murfree's acquaintance with the Smokies and geographic identifications of her fictional place-names, see Durwood Dunn, "Mary Noailles Murfree: A Reappraisal," *Appalachian Journal* 6 (1979): 198–200.

5. Ecofeminist theory began with Sherry Ortner's seminal 1974 article "Is Female to Male as Nature Is to Culture?" in *Woman, Culture, and Society*, ed. Michelle Zimbalist Rosaldo and Louise Lamphere (Stanford: Stanford Univ. Press, 1974), 67–87. For a fine review of ecofeminist books, see Linda Vance's "Remapping the Terrain: Books on Ecofeminism," *Choice* (June 1993): 1585–93.

6. Charles Egbert Craddock [Mary Noailles Murfree], *Prophet of the Great Smoky Mountains* (Boston: Houghton Mifflin, 1885), 129, 284. Subsequent references, given parenthetically, are to this edition.

7. Barbara Welter, *Dimity Convictions: The American Woman in the Nineteenth Century* (Athens: Ohio Univ. Press, 1976), 84; Grimke quoted in Blanche Glassman Hersh, "The 'True Woman' and the 'New Woman' in Nineteenth-Century America: Feminist-Abolitionists and a New Concept of True Womanhood," in *Woman's Being, Woman's Place: Female Identity and Vocations in American History*, ed. Mary Kelley (Boston: G. K. Hall, 1979), 275.

8. Carol Gilligan, *In a Different Voice: Psychological Theory and Women's Development* (Cambridge: Harvard Univ. Press, 1982).

9. William Dean Howells, "Editor's Study," *Harper's* 72 (Jan. 1886): 322.

10. Richard Cary, *Mary N. Murfree* (New York: Twayne, 1967), 172–74.

11. Ibid., 86; Horace Scudder, "Recent American Fiction," *Atlantic* 64 (July 1889): 125, 123.

12. Harry R. Warfel, "Local Color and Literary Artistry: Mary Noailles Murfree's *In the Tennessee Mountains*," *Southern Literary Journal* 3 (1970): 160. For synopses of early reviews, see Reese M. Carleton, "Mary Noailles Murfree (1850–1922): An Annotated Bibliography," *American Literary Realism, 1870–1910* 7 (1974): 293–378.

13. Elizabeth Ammons, "Going in Circles: The Female Geography of Jewett's *Country of the Pointed Firs*," *Studies in the Literary Imagination* 16 (1983): 84.

14. Horace Scudder, "Recent American and English Fiction," *Atlantic* 69 (May 1892): 697.

15. Karen Warren, "The Power and Promise of Ecological Feminism," *Environmental Ethics* 12 (1990): 125–46.

16. Ynestra King, "Feminism and the Revolt of Nature," *Heresies* 4, no. 13 (1981): 12; Vance, "Remapping," 1585. See also Susan Prentice, "Taking Sides: What's Wrong with Eco-Feminism," *Women & Environments* 10, no. 3 (1988): 9–10. Prentice says that the feminist movement has worked to establish the idea that gender is a social

construct, while ecofeminism buys into the patriarchal assumption that "biology is destiny."

17. Patrick D. Murphy, "Sex-Typing the Planet: Gaia Imagery and the Problem of Subverting Patriarchy," *Environmental Ethics* 10 (1988): 157.

18. Allen W. Batteau, *The Invention of Appalachia* (Tucson: Univ. of Arizona Press, 1990), 195, 38–56.

19. Stephen Trimble, "A Land of One's Own: Gender and Landscape," in *The Geography of Childhood: Why Children Need Wild Places*, by Stephen Trimble and Gary Paul Nabhan (Boston: Beacon Press, 1994), 53–75.

20. Ibid., 63.

Chapter 4. Horace Kephart's "Man's Game" and the Community of Our Southern Highlanders

1. Jim Chase, *Backpacker Magazine's Guide to the Appalachian Trail* (Harrisburg, Pa.: Stackpole Books, 1989), xiv.

2. Gary Snyder, *The Practice of the Wild* (San Francisco: North Point Press, 1990), 7.

3. Biographical information about Kephart comes from George Ellison, Introduction to Horace Kephart, *Our Southern Highlanders: A Narrative of Adventure in the Southern Appalachians and a Study of Life among the Mountaineers* (Knoxville: Univ. of Tennessee Press, 1976), ix-xlviii; and Jim Casada, Introduction to Kephart's *Camping and Woodcraft: A Handbook for Vacation Campers and for Travelers in the Wilderness* (Knoxville: Univ. of Tennessee Press, 1988), vii-xxxiii. Subsequent references to Kephart, given parenthetically, including volume number for the two-volume *Camping and Woodcraft*, are to these editions.

4. Frome, *Strangers*, 145–47.

5. Ibid., 152; Casada, Introduction to *Camping and Woodcraft*, xxvi.

6. Batteau, *The Invention of Appalachia*, 90; Ellison, Introduction to *Our Southern Highlanders*, xlvi, xlii.

7. Quoted in Larry Luxenberg, *Walking the Appalachian Trail* (Mechanicsburg, Pa.: Stackpole Books, 1994), 9.

8. Nina Baym, "Melodramas of Beset Manhood: How Theories of American Fiction Exclude Women Authors," in Showalter, ed., *The New Feminist Criticism*, 71–72.

9. Carter Martin, "Found Fiction: Horace Kephart's 'A Bear Hunt in the Smokies,'" *Ball State University Forum* 27, no. 1 (1986): 53–58.

10. Henry B. Wonham, "In the Name of Wonder: The Emergence of Tall Narrative in American Writing," *American Quarterly* 41 (1989): 289.

11. Frome, *Strangers*, 155.

12. Gary Snyder, "Why Tribe," in *Earth House Hold: Technical Notes & Queries to Fellow Dharma Revolutionaries* (New York: New Directions, 1969), 115, 116.

Chapter 5. Pilgrim at Tinker Cliffs

1. Annie Dillard, *Pilgrim at Tinker Creek* (New York: HarperPerennial, 1985), 62. Subsequent page references, given parenthetically, are to this edition.

2. For assessments of Dillard's connections to and differences from the transcendentalists, see C. D. Albin, "A Ray of Relation: Transcendental Echoes in Annie Dillard's *Pilgrim at Tinker Creek,*" *Journal of the American Studies Association of Texas* 23 (1992): 17–31; John E. Becker, "Science and the Sacred: From Walden to Tinker Creek," *Thought* 62 (1987): 400–413; Marc Chenetier, "Tinkering, Extravagance: Thoreau, Melville, and Annie Dillard," *Critique* 31, no. 3 (1990): 157–72; Mary Davidson McConahay, "'Into the Bladelike Arms of God': The Quest for Meaning through Symbolic Language in Thoreau and Annie Dillard," *Denver Quarterly* 20, no. 2 (1985): 103–16; and Gary McIlroy, "*Pilgrim at Tinker Creek* and the Social Legacy of *Walden,*" *South Atlantic Quarterly* 85, no. 2 (1986): 111–22.

3. Margaret Loewen Reimer, "The Dialectical Vision of Annie Dillard's *Pilgrim at Tinker Creek, Critique* 24, no. 3 (1983): 182, 188.

4. Scott Slovic, *Seeking Awareness in American Nature Writing: Henry Thoreau, Annie Dillard, Edward Abbey, Wendell Berry, Barry Lopez* (Salt Lake City: Univ. of Utah Press, 1992), 3, 5–6, 8.

5. Karla Hammond, "Drawing the Curtains: An Interview with Annie Dillard," *Bennington Review* 10 (April 1981): 32. For elaboration on Dillard's use of the *via positiva* and *via negativa*, and their resolution in the *via creativa*, see Linda L. Smith, *Annie Dillard* (New York: Twayne, 1991), 17–41.

6. Sandra Humble Johnson, *The Space Between: Literary Epiphany in the Work of Annie Dillard* (Kent, Ohio: Kent State Univ. Press, 1992), 52.

7. Ibid.

8. Snyder, *Practice*, 101–2.

9. Ibid., 103.

10. Dolores LaChapelle, "Mountains Constantly Walking," interview in Jonathan White, *Talking on the Water: Conversations about Nature and Creativity* (San Francisco: Sierra Club Books, 1994), 177.

11. Paul Bryant, "Nature as Picture / Nature as Milieu," *CEA Critic* 54, no. 1 (1991): 22–34.

12. Michelle Murray, "Ms. Dillard: In Her Creek a Sense of How Things Are," *National Observer*, 23 March 1974, 27.

Chapter 6. From Imperialism to Nationalism: The Knights of the Golden Horseshoe Cross the Blue Ridge

1. John Fontaine, *The Journal of John Fontaine, an Irish Huguenot Son in Spain and Virginia, 1710–1719*, ed. Edward Porter Alexander (Williamsburg, Va.: Colonial

Williamsburg Foundation, 1972). Subsequent page references, given parenthetically, are to this edition.

2. For a fuller description of the golden horseshoes, see Curtis Carroll Davis, "The Virginia 'Knights' and their Golden Horseshoes: Dr. William A. Caruthers and an American Tradition," *Modern Language Quarterly* 10 (1949): 490–507. Davis notes that the inscription may have read "Sic jurat transcendere montes," or, "Thus does he *swear* to cross the mountain" (505–6).

3. Robert Beverley, *The History and Present State of Virginia*, ed. Louis B. Wright (Chapel Hill: Univ. of North Carolina Press, 1947), 127–28.

4. George Seagood, "Expeditio Ultramontana. From the Latin of Arthur Blacka-more," in *Colonial American Poetry*, ed. Kenneth Silverman (New York: Hafner, 1968), 317–22; William A. Caruthers, *Knights of the Golden Horseshoe: A Tradition-ary Tale of the Cocked Hat Gentry* (1841; rpt. Chapel Hill: Univ. of North Carolina Press, 1970). Subsequent page references, given parenthetically, are to this edition.

5. Marjorie Hope Nicolson, *Mountain Gloom and Mountain Glory: The Rise of the Aesthetics of the Infinite* (Ithaca, N.Y.: Cornell Univ. Press, 1959).

6. For the accounts of Lederer and Batts and Fallam, see Clarence W. Alvord and Lee Bidgood, *The First Exploration of the Trans-Allegheny Regions by the Virginians, 1650–1674* (Cleveland: Arthur H. Clark, 1912). For a summary of early exploration and settlement of the Blue Ridge Mountains, see Thomas Perkins Abernethy, "The First Transmontane Advance," in *Humanistic Studies in Honor of John Calvin Met-calf* (Charlottesville: Univ. of Virginia Studies, 1941), 120–38.

7. Delma R. Carpenter, "The Route Followed by Governor Spotswood in 1716 across the Blue Ridge Mountains," *Virginia Magazine of History and Biography* 73 (1965): 405–12. For a succinct review of the controversy over the route (and a defense of the claims for Swift Run Gap as the site of the crossing), see Edward Porter Alex-ander, "John Fontaine and His Journal," in Alexander's edition of Fontaine's *Journal*, 13–19.

8. Robert Spiller, "The Cycle and the Roots," in *Toward a New American Literary History: Essays in Honor of Arlin Turner*, ed. Louis J. Budd, Edwin H. Cady, and Carl L. Anderson (Durham: Duke Univ. Press, 1980), 3–28.

9. Silverman, *Colonial American Poetry*, 6–7; Eugene R. Huddleston, "Topograph-ical Poetry in the Early National Period," *American Literature* 38 (1966): 303, 321.

10. Spiller, "The Cycle," 8–9.

11. Ralph Waldo Emerson, "The American Scholar," in *Nature, Addresses, and Lectures*, vol. 1 of *The Collected Works of Ralph Waldo Emerson*, ed. Robert E. Spiller and Alfred R. Ferguson (Cambridge: Belknap Press of Harvard Univ. Press, 1971), 52. For a complete study of the rise of American literary nationalism, see Benjamin Spencer, *The Quest for Nationality: An American Literary Campaign* (Syracuse: Syracuse Univ. Press, 1957). For references to American nature as a source for a distinctly national literature, see especially pages 10–14, 47–51, and 164–67.

12. Caruthers also mistakenly says the expedition took place in 1714. For a complete discussion of Caruthers's use and abuse of historical facts, see Davis, "Virginia 'Knights,'" 493–500.

13. See, for example, Richard L. Morton, *Colonial Virginia, vol. 2: Westward Expansion and Prelude to a Revolution, 1710–1763* (Chapel Hill: Univ. of North Carolina Press, 1960), 449–53.

14. Davis, "Virginia 'Knights,'" 500.

15. Cooper describes and defends the landscape of the future in his 1828 *Notions of the Americans—Picked Up by a Travelling Bachelor* (New York: Frederick Ungar, 1965). His spokesman, Cadwallader, tells a European companion, "The moral feeling with which a man of sentiment and knowledge looks upon the plains of your hemisphere, is connected with his recollections; here it should be mingled with his hopes" (1:250).

16. For a discussion of the influence of the Scottish commonsense school on American life and literature, see Terence Martin, *The Instructed Vision: Scottish Common Sense and the Origins of American Fiction* (Bloomington: Indiana Univ. Press, 1961).

17. Alexander, "John Fontaine," 14.

Chapter 7. Confluences: The View from Jefferson Rock

1. Thomas Jefferson, *Notes on the State of Virginia*, ed. William Peden (Chapel Hill: Univ. of North Carolina Press, 1954), 19–20.

2. Lewis B. Simpson, "Jefferson and the Writing of the South," in *Columbia Literary History of the United States*, ed. Emory Elliott et al. (New York: Columbia Univ. Press, 1988), 132; William Peden, Introduction to Jefferson, *Notes*, xxv.

3. William J. Scheick, "Chaos and Imaginative Order in Thomas Jefferson's *Notes on the State of Virginia*," in *Essays in Early Virginia Literature Honoring Richard Beale Davis*, ed. J. A. Leo Lemay (New York: Ben Franklin, 1977), 231; Wayne Franklin, *Discoverers, Explorers, Settlers: The Diligent Writers of Early America* (Chicago: Univ. of Chicago Press, 1979), 217 n. 20.

4. Gisela Tauber, "*Notes on the State of Virginia*: Thomas Jefferson's Unintentional Self-Portrait," *Eighteenth-Century Studies* 26 (1993): 635–48; Charles A. Miller, *Jefferson and Nature: An Interpretation* (Baltimore: Johns Hopkins Univ. Press, 1988), 106; Richard Slotkin, *Regeneration through Violence: The Mythology of the American Frontier, 1600–1860* (Middletown, Conn.: Wesleyan Univ. Press, 1973), 245–47; Stephen D. Cox, "The Literary Aesthetic of Thomas Jefferson," in Lemay, ed., *Essays in Early Virginia Literature*, 246. Virtually every commentator on the passage speaks of the triumph of order over chaos in Jefferson's description, usually implying some social dimension to the process. Many also note the same pattern in the other sublime setpiece of the *Notes*, the description of the Natural Bridge.

5. Qtd. in Miller, *Jefferson and Nature*, 46, 49–50.

6. Qtd. in Stephen B. Oates, *To Purge This Land with Blood: A Biography of John Brown* (New York: Harper & Row, 1970), 327.

7. Qtd. in Franklin B. Sanborn, *Memoirs of John Brown* (Concord, Mass., 1878), 94. The original note from Brown's last day is owned by the Chicago Historical Society.

8. Myra Jehlen, *American Incarnation: The Individual, the Nation, and the Continent* (Cambridge: Harvard Univ. Press, 1986), 3.

9. Ibid., 89.

10. Harold Hellenbrand, "Roads to Happiness: Rhetorical and Philosophical Design in Jefferson's *Notes on the State of Virginia*," *Early American Literature* 20 (1985): 5–7.

11. Jehlen, *American Incarnation*, 77, 60; Slotkin, *Regeneration*, 247.

12. Clayton W. Lewis, "Style in Jefferson's *Notes on the State of Virginia*," *Southern Review* 14 (1978): 674–75.

Chapter 8. From Wind Gap to Water Gap: On the Trail of Edgar Huntly

1. Qtd. in James Boswell, *Life of Johnson* (London: Oxford Univ. Press, 1953), 333.

2. Charles Brockden Brown, *Edgar Huntly; or Memoirs of a Sleep-Walker*, bicentennial ed., ed. S. W. Reid and Sydney J. Krause, vol. 4 of *The Novels and Related Works of Charles Brockden Brown* (Kent, Ohio: Kent State Univ. Press, 1984), 493. Subsequent references, given parenthetically, are to this edition.

3. Neil Evernden, *The Social Creation of Nature* (Baltimore: Johns Hopkins Univ. Press, 1992), 89.

4. Bill McKibben, *The End of Nature* (New York: Random House, 1989).

5. Dennis Berthold, "Desacralizing the American Gothic: An Iconographic Approach to *Edgar Huntly*," *Studies in American Fiction* 14 (1986): 130; Ursula Brumm, "Nature as Scene or Agent? Some Reflections on Its Role in the American Novel," in *Vistas of a Continent: Concepts of Nature in America*, ed. Teut Andreas Riese (Heidelberg: Carl Winter, 1979), 107–8.

6. On Brown's use of Gothic conventions in his landscape descriptions, see, in addition to Berthold's "Desacralizing the American Gothic," 127–38, Leonard Engel, "The Role of the Enclosure in the English and American Gothic Romance," *Essays in Arts and Sciences* 11 (1982): 59–68; and Elizabeth Jane Wall Hinds, "Charles Brockden Brown and the Frontiers of Discourse," in *Frontier Gothic: Terror and Wonder at the Frontier in American Literature*, ed. David Mogen, Scott P. Sanders, and Joanne B. Karpinski (Rutherford, N.J.: Associated University Presses, 1993), 109–25.

7. Kenneth Bernard, "Charles Brockden Brown and the Sublime," *Personalist* 45 (1964): 239; Alan Axelrod, *Charles Brockden Brown: An American Tale* (Austin:

Univ. of Texas Press, 1983), 29, 28, 31. On the lack of "expressive details" in Brown's nature descriptions, see also George Toles, "Charting the Hidden Landscape: *Edgar Huntly*," *Early American Literature* 16 (1981): 134. On Brown's use of the aesthetics of the picturesque and sublime, see also Dennis Berthold, "Charles Brockden Brown, *Edgar Huntly*, and the Origins of the American Picturesque," *William and Mary Quarterly*, 3d ser., 41 (1984): 62–84.

8. Toles, "Charting," 134; Donald Ringe, "Early American Gothic: Brown, Dana, and Allston," *American Transcendental Quarterly* 19, no. 3 (1973): 5; Norman Grabo, *The Coincidental Art of Charles Brockden Brown* (Chapel Hill: Univ. of North Carolina Press, 1981), 56. Almost every commentator on *Edgar Huntly* draws some connection between the landscape and Edgar's state of mind, a critical tendency Sydney J. Krause traces back to 1819, in a review by E. T. Channing (Historical Essay, *Edgar Huntly*, bicentennial ed., 392).

9. Sydney J. Krause, "*Edgar Huntly* and the American Nightmare," *Studies in the Novel* 13 (1981): 294–302.

10. Beth Lueck, "Charles Brockden Brown's *Edgar Huntly*: The Picturesque Traveler as Sleepwalker," *Studies in American Fiction* 15 (1987): 25–42.

11. Ibid., 37.

12. Alan Axelrod, "Irreconcilable Oppositions," in *Charles Brockden Brown*, 3–28; Kate Soper, *What Is Nature? Culture, Politics and the Non-Human* (Oxford: Blackwell, 1995), 226–27.

13. Krause, Historical Essay, 385.

14. Sydney J. Krause, "Penn's Elm and *Edgar Huntly*: Dark 'Instruction to the Heart,'" *American Literature* 66 (1994): 465, 476.

15. Mikhail M. Bakhtin, "Discourse in the Novel," *The Dialogic Imagination: Four Essays*, ed. Michael Holquist, trans. Caryl Emerson and Michael Holquist (Austin: Univ. of Texas Press, 1981), 259–422.

16. Soper, *What Is Nature?* 151, 137.

17. Evernden, *The Social Creation*, 89.

18. See, for example, S. L. Pimm, *The Balance of Nature?* (Chicago: Univ. of Chicago Press, 1991), and Donald Worster, "The Ecology of Order and Chaos," in *The Wealth of Nature: Environmental History and the Ecological Imagination* (New York: Oxford Univ. Press, 1993), 156–70.

19. Worster, "The Ecology," 162.

20. N. Katherine Hayles, "Searching for Common Ground," in *Reinventing Nature? Responses to Postmodern Deconstruction*, ed. Michael E. Soule and Gary Lease (Washington, D.C.: Island Press, 1995), 51–53.

21. Ibid., 58.

22. Ibid., 61. The phrase Hayles uses for this recognition of one's own position is "strong objectivity," a term she attributes to Sandra Harding, "After the Neutrality Ideal: Science, Politics, and 'Strong Objectivity,'" *Social Research* 59 (1992): 567–87.

23. Krause, Historical Essay, 386.

24. Dennis Berthold, "Charles Brockden Brown," 72–74; idem, "Desacralizing," 130–33, 138 n. 19.

25. Krause, Historical Essay, 297 n. 3.

26. Lawrence Buell makes similar observations, noting that the term *setting* "deprecates what it denotes, implying that the physical environment serves for artistic purposes merely as backdrop, ancillary to the main event" (*The Environmental Imagination: Thoreau, Nature Writing, and the Formation of American Culture* [Cambridge: Belknap Press of Harvard Univ. Press, 1995], 85).

27. Janet D. Pitman, "The Wilderness Experience in James Dickey's *Deliverance* and Charles Brockden Brown's *Edgar Huntly*," *Ball State University Forum* 23, no. 3 (1982): 73.

Chapter 9. Where the Open Road Meets Howl

1. Walt Whitman, "Song of the Open Road," in *Walt Whitman: Complete Poetry and Selected Prose*, Riverside ed., ed. James E. Miller Jr. (Boston: Houghton Mifflin, 1959), 109. Subsequent references, given parenthetically, are to this edition.

2. Louis Simpson, "Walt Whitman at Bear Mountain," in *At the End of the Open Road* (Middletown, Conn.: Wesleyan Univ. Press, 1963), 64–65.

3. Allen Ginsberg, *Howl*, in *Collected Poems 1947–1980* (New York: Harper & Row, 1984), 127, 131, 133; "Footnote to Howl," 134. Subsequent references, given parenthetically, are to this edition. We actually carried the slim original 1956 City Lights edition of *Howl and Other Poems*, but readers will find the *Collected Poems* more readily available.

4. Allen Ginsberg, "A Supermarket in California," *Collected Poems*, 136. Ginsberg explicitly acknowledges Whitman's influence in "Notes for *Howl* and Other Poems," in *The New American Poetry*, ed. Donald M. Allen (New York: Grove Press, 1960), 416; and "Allen Ginsberg on Walt Whitman: Composed on the Tongue," in *Walt Whitman: The Measure of His Song*, ed. Jim Perlman, Ed Folsom, and Dan Campion (Minneapolis: Holy Cow Press, 1981), 231–54.

Chapter 10. Greylock and the Whale

1. Duyckinck's account is quoted in Luther S. Mansfield, "Glimpses of Herman Melville's Life in Pittsfield, 1850–1851," *American Literature* 9 (1938): 26–48. See also Godfrey Greylock [James T. Fields], *Yesterdays with Authors* (Boston, 1872), 52–53; and Cornelius Mathews, "Several Days in Berkshire," *Literary World* 7 (31 August 1850): 166.

2. My attempt at sympathetic identification with Melville in order to discover a portion of his life story is akin to what Hershel Parker calls "narrative biography." It

is a practice he has found useful in the research for his two-volume biography of Melville. See his "Biography and Responsible Uses of the Imagination: Three Episodes from Melville's Homecoming in 1844," *Resources for American Literary Study* 21 (1995): 16–42. And for fuller descriptions of the events of Melville's life in 1850 and 1851, see volume 1 of Parker's biography: *Herman Melville: A Biography* (Baltimore: Johns Hopkins Univ. Press, 1996).

3. Jay Leyda, *The Melville Log: A Documentary Life of Herman Melville, 1819–1891*, 2 vols. (New York: Gordian, 1969), 1:389.

4. Ibid., 1:416.

5. The story of Melville's meeting with Hawthorne and its effect on his work has become almost standard in the numerous studies of the composition of *Moby-Dick*; for a summary of these studies, see section 5 of the Historical Note in the Northwestern/Newberry edition of *Moby-Dick*, ed. Harrison Hayford, Hershel Parker, and G. Thomas Tanselle (Evanston and Chicago: Northwestern Univ. Press and the Newberry Library, 1988), 648–59.

6. Herman Melville, "The Piazza," in *The Piazza Tales and Other Prose Pieces, 1839–1860*, ed. Harrison Hayford, Alma A. MacDougall, and G. Thomas Tanselle (Evanston and Chicago: Northwestern Univ. Press and the Newberry Library, 1987), 3–4. Subsequent page references, given parenthetically, are to this edition.

7. William Howarth, ed. with commentary, *Thoreau in the Mountains: Writings by Henry David Thoreau* (New York: Farrar, Strauss, Giroux, 1982), 69. Subsequent page references to Thoreau's account of his Greylock trip and Howarth's commentary, given parenthetically, are to this edition.

Stephen Adams identifies the woman as Rebecca Darling Eddy ("Looking for Thoreau's Dark Lady," *Thoreau Society Bulletin* 161 [1982]: 3–4).

8. Richard Moore, *That Cunning Alphabet: Melville's Aesthetics of Nature* (Amsterdam: Rodopi, 1982), 55–56. Moore's argument elaborates on the affinities between the two works first pointed out by Helmbrecht Breinig, "The Destruction of Fairyland: Melville's 'The Piazza' in the Tradition of the American Imagination," *ELH* 35 (1968): 254–83.

9. Moore, *That Cunning Alphabet*, 55; Evert Duyckinck, "An Ascent of Mount Saddleback," *Literary World* 9 (30 August 1851): 163.

10. Leyda, *Melville Log*, 1:424.

11. Quoted in Mansfield, "Glimpses," 43–46.

12. In truth, the "memory" of the Greylock climb during Thoreau's rowing trip on the Concord and Merrimack rivers is a fiction. The river trip was in 1839, the climb of Greylock in 1844. But Thoreau worked on the manuscript of *A Week* from 1842 until its publication in 1849. The Greylock episode was added late, no earlier than the fall of 1846, according to Linck C. Johnson, *Thoreau's Complex Weave* (Charlottesville: Univ. of Virginia Press, 1986), 228.

13. Egbert Oliver, "'Cock-a-Doodle-Doo!' and Transcendental Hocus-Pocus,"

New England Quarterly 21 (1948): 204–16; "Melville's Picture of Emerson and Thoreau in *The Confidence-Man*," *College English* 8 (1946): 61–72; "A Second Look at 'Bartleby,'" *College English* 6 (1945): 431–39.

14. Sidney Moss, "'Cock-a-Doodle-Doo!' and Some Legends in Melville Scholarship," *American Literature* 40 (1968): 193. See also Hershel Parker, "Melville's Satire of Emerson and Thoreau: An Evaluation of the Evidence," *American Transcendental Quarterly*, no. 7 (1970): 61–67.

15. Brian Higgins and Hershel Parker, Introduction to *Critical Essays on Herman Melville's Moby-Dick* (New York: G. K. Hall, 1992), 6. We know the approximate date of Melville's borrowing of *A Week* because he borrowed Tennyson's *In Memoriam* from Duyckinck at the same time, and Herman's sister Augusta wrote a letter to Duyckinck on July 20 thanking him for the Tennyson book. See Merton M. Sealts Jr., *Melville's Reading: Revised and Enlarged Edition* (Columbia: Univ. of South Carolina Press, 1988), 219.

16. Qtd. in Leyda, *Melville Log*, 1:407.

17. Ibid., 1:385.

18. James Barbour and Leon Howard, "Carlyle and the Conclusion of *Moby-Dick*," *New England Quarterly* 49 (1976): 214–24.

19. We can only conjecture when Melville wrote the epilogue. Mysteriously, it did not appear in the first English edition, which preceded by a couple of months the first American edition. According to the editors of the Northwestern/Newberry edition, it is a "theoretical possibility" that Melville had not yet written it when the proofs were sent to the London publisher, which would mean it was written in autumn of 1851. But it is more likely that the epilogue was simply misplaced when the first edition was typeset, for, according to Hayford, Parker, and Tanselle, "the body of the book gives evidence that the epilogue was not an afterthought" (Historical Note, 679) Critics of the English edition, printed without the epilogue, poked fun at Melville for apparently leaving no one alive to tell the story.

20. For a discussion of the early criticisms of *Moby-Dick* as excessively transcendentalist, see Perry Miller, "Melville and Transcendentalism," *Virginia Quarterly Review* 29 (1953): 556–75; rpt. in his *Nature's Nation* (Cambridge: Harvard Univ Press, 1967), 184–96.

21. On sources for *Moby-Dick*, see Mary K. Bercaw, *Melville's Sources* (Evanston: Northwestern Univ. Press, 1987); Hayford, Parker, and Tanselle, Historical Note, 646.

22. Thomas O. Mabbot, "A Source for the Conclusion of Melville's 'Moby-Dick,'" *Notes and Queries*, 26 July 1941, 47–48; Charles Duffy, letter in *Notes and Queries*, 15 November 1941, 278–79; and Luther S. Mansfield and Howard P. Vincent, eds., *Moby-Dick; or, The Whale* (New York: Hendricks House, 1952), 832.

23. One exception to the tendency of Melville scholars (like literary critics in general) to restrict their "influence studies" to reading matter is Hershel Parker, who suggests that "the most momentous effect on Herman Melville in the summer of 1850 may have come from the Berkshires, not from Nathaniel Hawthorne" ("Melville

and the Berkshires: Emotion-Laden Terrain, 'Reckless Sky-Assaulting Mood,' and Encroaching Wordsworthianism," in *American Literature: The New England Heritage*, ed. James Nagle and Richard Astro [New York: Garland, 1981], 65).

Chapter 11. Synecdoche and Ecology: Frost in the Greens and Whites

1. Robert Frost, "A Brook in the City," in *The Poetry of Robert Frost*, ed. Edward Connery Lathem (New York: Holt, Rinehart and Winston,1969), 231. Subsequent references, given parenthetically, are to this edition. As I mention, I actually carried in my pack the slim, original 1923 volume of *New Hampshire*, but readers will find the Lathem collection more readily available.

2. Jeffrey S. Cramer, *Robert Frost among His Poems: A Literary Companion to the Poet's Own Biographical Contexts and Associations* (Jefferson, N.C.: McFarland, 1996), 82.

3. For an account of the Frost family's Green Mountain hike, see chapter 14, "The Long Trail," in volume two of Lawrance Thompson's three-volume biography of Frost, *Robert Frost: The Years of Triumph, 1915–1938* (New York: Holt, Rinehart and Winston, 1970), 188–201.

4. John Lynen, *The Pastoral Art of Robert Frost* (New Haven: Yale Univ. Press, 1960), 49, 68, 146, 144, 5, 24, 25.

5. George Bagby, *Frost and the Book of Nature* (Knoxville: Univ. of Tennessee Press, 1993), 7, ix-x. Exceptions to the tendency of Frost critics to see his use of natural facts as representations of inner meaning are Darrel Abel, "'Unfriendly Nature' in the Poetry of Robert Frost," *Colby Library Quarterly* 17 (1981): 201–10, and Nina Baym, "An Approach to Robert Frost's Nature Poetry," *American Quarterly* 17 (1965): 713–23.

6. Qtd. in Elizabeth Shepley Sergeant, *Robert Frost: The Trial by Existence* (New York: Holt, Rinehart and Winston, 1960), 325.

7. Guy Rotella, *Reading and Writing Nature: The Poetry of Robert Frost, Wallace Stevens, Marianne Moore, and Elizabeth Bishop* (Boston: Northeastern Univ. Press, 1991), 84.

8. Ibid.

9. Bagby, *Frost and the Book*, 42, 45, 44.

10. Qtd. in Sergeant, *Robert Frost: The Trial*, 309.

11. Carol J. Adams, *The Sexual Politics of Meat: A Feminist-Vegetarian Critical Theory* (New York: Continuum, 1990), 42.

12. Qtd. in Edward Connery Lathem and Lawrance Thompson, eds., *Robert Frost: Poetry and Prose* (New York: Holt, 1972), 336.

13. Here, and in other observations on Frost's command of scientific fact in regard to nature, I am indebted to John P. O'Grady's "A Field Guide to Robert Frost," M.A. thesis, University of Maine at Orono, 1983.

14. "All but a very few have a person in them," said Frost of his poems (qtd. in

Sergeant, *Robert Frost: The Trial*, 26). And on another occasion: "I'm not a nature poet. There's always something else in my poetry. . . . There must be a human foreground to supplement this background of nature" (qtd. in Edward Connery Lathem, ed., *Interviews with Robert Frost* [New York: Holt, Rinehart and Winston, 1966], 26, 34). Of course Frost's dismissal of nature's importance in his work might well be a defensive reaction to the disparagement typically associated with the term *nature poet*.

15. Michael J. McDowell, "Since Earth Is Earth: An Ecological Approach to Robert Frost's Poetry," *South Carolina Review* 24 (1991): 95.

16. Nathaniel Hawthorne, "The Great Stone Face," in *The Snow-Image and Uncollected Tales*, vol. 11 of *The Centenary Edition of the Works of Nathaniel Hawthorne*, ed. William Charvat et al. (Columbus: Ohio Univ. Press, 1974), 43.

17. Henry David Thoreau, *Journal, vol. 4, 1851–1852*, ed. Leonard N. Neufeldt and Nancy Craig Simmons, in *The Writings of Henry D. Thoreau*, gen. ed. Robert Sattelmeyer (Princeton: Princeton Univ. Press, 1992), 28. The relevance of this journal entry of Thoreau's to Frost's poem is noted by Bagby, *Frost and the Book*, 38.

Chapter 12. Democracy and Ecology: Hawthorne's White Mountain Stories

1. Nathaniel Hawthorne, "Sketches from Memory," in *Mosses from an Old Manse*, vol. 10 of *The Centenary Edition of the Works of Nathaniel Hawthorne*, ed. William Charvat et al. (Columbus: Ohio State Univ. Press, 1974), 426–27. Subsequent references, given parenthetically, are to this edition.

2. For a discussion of Hawthorne's itinerary on his 1832 tour, see Alfred Weber, "Hawthorne's Tour of 1832 through New England and Upstate New York," in Alfred Weber, Beth L. Lueck, and Dennis Berthold, *Hawthorne's American Travel Sketches* (Hanover, N.H.: Univ. Press of New England, 1989), 1–23.

3. One source, however, claims that Hawthorne stayed at the Profile House in the early 1850s, after he wrote "The Great Stone Face" (Elizabeth Lathrop Chandler, *A Study of the Sources of the Tales and Romances Written by Nathaniel Hawthorne before 1853* [Menasha, Wis.: George Banta, 1926], 39). No record of that stay has been found.

4. Hawthorne, "The Great Stone Face," in *The Snow Image and Uncollected Tales*, vol. 11 of *Centenary Edition*, 38, 37, 41. Subsequent references, given parenthetically, are to this edition.

5. Ralph Waldo Emerson, *The Letters of Ralph Waldo Emerson*, vol. 2, ed. Ralph L. Rusk (New York: Columbia Univ. Press, 1939), 221.

6. Laura and Guy Waterman, *Forest and Crag: A History of Hiking, Trail Blazing, and Adventure in the Northeast Mountains* (Boston: Appalachian Mountain Club, 1989), 37–38.

7. John F. Sears, "Hawthorne's 'The Ambitious Guest' and the Significance of the Willey Disaster," *American Literature* 54 (1982): 347–48.

8. Hawthorne, "The Ambitious Guest," in *Twice-Told Tales*, vol. 9 of *Centenary Edition*, 333. Subsequent references, given parenthetically, are to this edition.

9. Michael Wigglesworth, *The Day of Doom*, in *Colonial American Writing*, ed. Roy Harvey Pearce (New York: Holt, Rinehart and Winston, 1950), 237.

10. This is a familiar idea in American literary and cultural history, receiving its classic formulation in Roderick Nash's *Wilderness and the American Mind*, 3d ed. (New Haven: Yale Univ. Press, 1982).

11. Bill McKibben, *The Age of Missing Information* (New York: Plume, 1993), 25–26, 119–20.

12. Patrick Morrow, "A Writer's Workshop: Hawthorne's 'The Great Carbuncle,'" *Studies in Short Fiction* 6 (1969): 162.

13. John Winthrop, *The History of New England, from 1630 to 1649*, ed. James Savage (New York: Arno, 1972), 2:89.

14. Hawthorne, "The Great Carbuncle," in *Twice-Told Tales*, 156. Subsequent references, given parenthetically, are to this edition.

15. For examples of the voluminous and forgettable landscape poetry of the early national period, see Eugene L. Huddleston, "Topographical Poetry in America: A Checklist, 1783–1812," *Bulletin of Bibliography* 25 (1966–67): 8–13, 35–36, 39.

16. Jeremy Belknap, *The History of New Hampshire* (New York: Arno Press, 1972), 3:40–41.

17. On the seeker as frontiersman, see Neal Frank Doubleday, *Hawthorne's Early Tales: A Critical Study* ((Durham: Duke Univ. Press, 1972), 148.

18. John Josselyn, *New Englands Rarities Discovered*, American Antiquarian Society, *Transactions and Collections* 4 (1860): 139–40.

19. Stephen A. Kellert, *The Value of Life: Biological Diversity and Human Society* (Washington, D.C.: Island Press, 1996), 38.

20. Ibid., 21.

21. For information on nineteenth-century art in the Whites, see *The White Mountains: Place and Perceptions* (Hanover, N.H.: Univ. Press of New England, 1980).

22. Waterman and Waterman, *Forest and Crag*, 47.

23. William O. Douglas, *My Wilderness: East to Katahdin* (Garden City, N.Y.: Doubleday, 1961), 218.

Chapter 13. Contact! Contact! A Walk to Thoreau's Ktaadn

1. Henry David Thoreau, *Thoreau in the Mountains*, ed. with commentary by William Howarth (New York: Farrar, Strauss, Giroux, 1982), 108. Subsequent references, given parenthetically, are to this edition. This is not the standard scholarly edition. That would be the Princeton edition of *The Maine Woods*. But Howarth's annotated collection is especially useful to those interested in retracing Thoreau's excursions to the mountain. Howarth relies on the Princeton edition for his text.

2. In response to a question about what the Appalachian Trail is for, MacKaye re-

sponded, "The ultimate purpose? There are three things: 1) to walk; 2) to see; and 3) to *see* what you see!" (qtd. in Glenn Scherer, "Benton MacKaye and the Birth of the Appalachian Trail," *Appalachian Trailway News* [November/December 1996]: 9).

3. John G. Blair and Augustus Trowbridge, "Thoreau on Katahdin," *American Quarterly* 12 (1960): 508–9; Stephen Adams and Donald Ross Jr., *Revising Mythologies: The Composition of Thoreau's Major Works* (Charlottesville: Univ. Press of Virginia, 1988), 65–66.

4. My argument here echoes that of John P. O'Grady, who notes that the "'standard' interpretation of the passage . . . is tenable only in a narrow . . . context, possible only if the reader denies the numerous, obvious counters to it in the text, not the least of which is the tone, which is not one of 'terror' but of *awe*" (*Pilgrims to the Wild: Everett Ruess, Henry David Thoreau, John Muir, Clarence King, Mary Austin* [Salt Lake City: Univ. of Utah Press, 1993], 39).

5. Michael Hopkins, English 265, Reading Nonfiction, Penn State Altoona, fall 1994.

6. Daniel Defoe, *Robinson Crusoe*, ed. Michael Shinagel (New York: Norton, 1994), 68.

7. Ralph Waldo Emerson, "Nature," in *Nature, Addresses, and Lectures*, vol. 1 of *The Collected Works of Ralph Waldo Emerson*, intro. and notes by Robert E. Spiller, ed. Alfred R. Ferguson (Cambridge: Belknap Press of Harvard Univ. Press, 1971), 10.

8. Buell, *The Environmental Imagination*, 365–66. In the chapter called "The Aesthetics of Relinquishment," Buell discusses Thoreau's progress toward ecocentrism in reference to *Walden*. For a definition of the ecohero as one whose "*ego*centric Self" is replaced by the "*eco*centric Self," see Tim Poland, "'A Relative to All That Is': The Eco-Hero in Western American Literature," *Western American Literature* 26 (1991): 195–208.

9. Buell, *The Environmental Imagination*, 389.

10. Ronald Wesley Hoag, "The Mark on the Wilderness: Thoreau's Contact with Ktaadn," *Texas Studies in Literature and Language* 24 (1982): 33, 38.

11. Ning Yu, "Thoreau and the New Geography: The Hydrological Cycle in 'Ktaadn,'" *ESQ: A Journal of the American Renaissance* 40, no. 2 (1994): 131, 123, 127.

12. John Tallmadge, "'Ktaadn': Thoreau in the Wilderness of Words," *ESQ: A Journal of the American Renaissance* 31, no. 3 (1985): 145–46; John P. O'Grady, *Pilgrims to the Wild*, 41–42; Don Scheese, *Nature Writing: The Pastoral Impulse in America* (New York: Twayne, 1996): 55–56.

13. Buell, *The Environmental Imagination*, 144.

14. Diane Ackerman, *A Natural History of the Senses* (New York: Vintage, 1991), 308.

15. Information on Thoreau's route up Katahdin comes from William Howarth, *Thoreau in the Mountains*, and J. Parker Huber, *The Wildest Country: A Guide to Thoreau's Maine* (Boston: Appalachian Mountain Club, 1981), 142–57. Personally, I'm skeptical as to these claims about Thoreau's route. I find it odd that Thoreau, an

experienced hiker, would confuse Abol and Katahdin streams. If he knew he had crossed to the south side of the Abol, why would he not realize, when they headed back to the west, that they'd be back at the Abol? I wonder if perhaps Thoreau neglected to mention a stream crossing or two, if maybe he really was camped by Katahdin Stream, or Murch Brook, several miles west of Abol Stream. According to the Howarth/Huber route, the trail that now most closely approximates Thoreau's route is the Abol, which follows the traditional nineteenth-century route up Abol Slide. But if indeed Thoreau was farther west, then the Hunt Trail, followed by the A.T., might be the current trail nearest to his route.

16. Leo Stoller, *After Walden* (Stanford: Stanford Univ. Press, 1957), 47. Similarly, John G. Blair and Augustus Trowbridge see Katahdin as a permanent "symbol in Thoreau's mind of the element in nature that defied his understanding" ("Thoreau on Katahdin," 514). For accounts of Thoreau's "recovery," see Frederick Garber, *Thoreau's Redemptive Imagination* (New York: New York Univ. Press, 1977), 94, and James McIntosh, *Thoreau as Romantic Naturalist: His Shifting Stance toward Nature* (Ithaca, N.Y.: Cornell Univ. Press, 1974), 207–15.

17. Henry David Thoreau, *Walden*, ed. J. Lyndon Shanley (Princeton: Princeton Univ. Press, 1971), 317–18; *The Correspondence of Henry David Thoreau*, ed. Walter Harding and Carl Bode (New York: New York Univ. Press, 1958), 497; *The Journal of Henry David Thoreau*, ed. Bradford Torrey and Francis H. Allen (Boston: Houghton Mifflin, Walden Edition, 1906), 10:142.

18. Thoreau, *Correspondence*, 497.

19. For an account of the influence of the Ktaadn experience on the writing of *A Week*, see Robert Milder, *Reimagining Thoreau* (New York: Cambridge Univ. Press, 1995), 38–41.

20. Buell, *The Environmental Imagination*, 168, 122, 178, 138.

21. Benton MacKaye, "Outdoor Culture—the Philosophy of Through Trails," in *From Geography to Geotechnics*, ed. Paul T. Bryant (Urbana: Univ. of Illinois Press, 1968), 176–79.

22. Buell, *The Environmental Imagination*, 385.

INDEX

Abenaki, 7
Abol Bridge, 240, 242, 243, 245
Abol Slide, 244, 268 n.15
Abol Stream, 242, 243, 244, 268 n.15
Absent referent, 189–90
Ackerman, Diane, 242
Adams, Carol, 189
Adams, Charles, 44
Adams, Mass., 167
Adams, Mt., 225
Adirondack Mountains, 185
Age of Missing Information, The
  (McKibben), 212–13
Age of Reason, 216
Agiocochook, 216. *See also* Washing-
  ton, Mt.
"Aim Was Song, The" (Frost), 201–2
Albert Mountain, 36
Alcott, Bronson, 248
"Alexander Spotswood Discovers the Val-
  ley of the Shenandoah" (Claytor),
  104–5
"Allagash and East Branch, The"
  (Thoreau), 243
Alps, the, 109, 135
"Ambitious Guest, The" (Hawthorne), 7,
  204, 209–13, 221
American Incarnation (Jehlen), 126–28
American Indians, 111–12, 117, 162–63,
  164. *See also* Abenaki, Apache, Chero-
  kee Indians, Creek Indians, Delaware
  Indians, Inuit, Iroquois, Lenni Le-
  nape, Meherrin Indians, Seminole In-
  dians, Sioux

"American Scholar, The" (Emerson), 111
Amicalola Falls State Park, 1
Ammonoosuc Ravine, 204, 209
Ammons, Elizabeth 65
"Among the Hills" (Whittier), 205
Anastasius (Hope), 178
Anderson, Douglas, 49
Anthropocentrism, 182, 197, 201, 235, 240;
  vs. biocentrism, 42, 191–92, 194; of literary criticism, 149, 177, 231
Apache, 18, 19
Appalachian Mountain Club (AMC),
  203, 208
Appalachian Trail, 1; as community,
  70–72, 78–79, 84–85, 154; in Georgia,
  9, 10–13, 16, 19–21, 70–71; history of,
  2–3; information about, 5; literature
  of, 6–7; in Maine, 226–28, 232–38,
  240–46; in Maryland, 129–30; in
  Massachusetts, 165–70, 172–73, 178–
  79; in New Hampshire, 195, 200–202,
  203, 205, 207–9, 213–14, 219–20,
  223–25; in New York, 151–53, 155–58,
  160–61; in North Carolina, 22–29, 31–
  34, 36–41, 49–50, 74, 78–79, 80, 84,
  87; in Pennsylvania, 131–32, 138–39,
  146, 148–50; purpose of, 70, 267 n.2;
  as story line, 1, 3, 4, 9, 67, 193–94;
  symbol of, 34; in Tennessee, 51–54,
  67, 74, 80, 84, 180; in Vermont, 180–
  83, 185–86, 190–91, 193, 195; in Virginia, 88–90, 93–94, 97–102, 104–5,
  107–8, 117–19; in West Virginia, 120,
  122, 124, 128–29

"Appalachian Trail: A Project in Re-
    gional Planning, An" (MacKaye), 2
Appalachian Trail Companion, 22–23, 24
Appalachian Trail Conference (ATC),
    2, 5; *Member Handbook*, 2
Argument from design, 43
Arner, Robert, 41
Arnold, Matthew, 196
Arrowhead, 162, 164, 168, 175
As Far as the Eye Can See (Brill), 5
Asheville, N.C., 73
Atlantic Monthly, 52
Attakullakulla, 40, 49
Autobiographical criticism, 252 n.8
Ax, John, 14
Axelrod, Alan, 136, 144
"Ax-Helve, The" (Frost), 200
Ayunini, 14. *See also* Swimmer

*Backpacker Magazine's Guide to the
    Appalachian Trail* (Chase), 70
Bagby, George, 184, 187
Bakhtin, Mikhail, 5, 45, 142, 150. *See also*
    Dialogics; Heteroglossia
Bald Mountain, 183
Barbour, James, 176
Barren Ledges, 232
"Bartleby the Scrivener" (Melville), 174
Bartram, John, 35, 46–47
Bartram, William: ecological under-
    standing, 36, 41–46, 47–48; *Observa-
    tions on the Creek and Cherokee In-
    dians*, 47; respect for other cultures,
    35–36, 46–47, 49; style, 44–45;
    Travels, 6, 36–50; unpublished essays
    by, 35–36, 253 n.2
Bartram Trail, 37
Basso, Keith, 18–19
Batteau, Allen, 67
Batts, John, 106
Baxter State Park, 227, 243, 247
Baym, Nina, 77–78
Bear Fence Mountain, 117–18
Bear Mountain, 151–56, 158, 160, 161
Bear Mountain Bridge, 156

Bear Mountain Zoo, 155–56, 158
Beat Generation, 157, 161
Belknap, Jeremy, 216–17
Bennington, Vt., 181, 182
Bennington Banner, 183
Berkeley, Bishop George, 131
Berkeley, Gov. William, 106
Berkshire Hills, 162, 165, 178, 264 n.23
Bernard, Kenneth, 135
Berry, Wendell, 37–38, 41, 70
Berthold, Dennis, 135, 148
Beverley, Robert, 104
Bible, 17, 23, 30, 59, 112–13, 232
Bigelow Lawn, 223
Big Meadows, 117, 119
Big Niagara Falls, 243
Biocentrism, 42, 191–92, 194, 247
Biophilia, 220–21
Blackamore, Arthur, 105
Blackwell Creek, 10
Blake, Harrison, 247
Blake, William, 160
Blood Mountain, 11, 12, 13
"Blue Butterfly Day" (Frost), 194
Blue Mountain, 138, 148
Blue Ridge Gap, 123
Blue Ridge Mountains, 88, 123; depic-
    tions of, by Brown, 132, 148; depictions
    of, by Caruthers, 111, 112, 113, 114; de-
    pictions of, by Dillard, 96; depictions
    of, by Jefferson, 120, 127; depictions of,
    by Seagood, 108, 109; early explora-
    tions of, 103, 104, 106, 258 n.6
Blue Ridge Parkway, 2
Bly Gap, 21
Bookchin, Murray, 45
Boone, Daniel, 75, 76, 77, 217
Booth, John Wilkes, 124
Boott Spur, 223
Boswell, James, 131
"Boundless Moment, A" (Frost), 192
Boy's Will, A (Frost), 181
Brady, Matthew, 129
Brill, David, 5
Broadhall, 163, 165, 171
"Brook in the City, A" (Frost), 181–82, 199

Brown, Charles Brockden, 131, 140; *Edgar Huntly*, 6, 131–43, 146–50
Brown, John, 124, 125–26, 128, 130
Brown, Joseph E., 19
Bruce, Dan "Wingfoot," 5
Bruchac, Joseph, 7
Brumm, Ursula, 135
Brushy Mountain, 91
Bryant, Paul, 94
Bryant, William Cullen, 162–63, 165
Bryson City, N.C., 73
Bucks County, Pa., 147
Buell, Lawrence, 234, 237, 241, 247, 249, 262 n.26, 268 n.8
Buffon, Georges-Louis Leclerc, Comte de, 121, 122
Bunyan, Paul, 200
Bureau of Ethnology, 14, 15
Burke, Edmund, 136
Burke, Kenneth, 8
Byrd, William, 108

Cades Cove, 52–53
Callicott, J. Baird, 19
Campbell, Thomas, 178
Camping and Woodcraft (Kephart), 73, 75–76, 77, 80, 85
Canaan, 17, 112
Cannon Mountain, 200
Canopus Lake, 157
Captivity narrative, 143
Carlyle, Thomas, 38–39, 176, 178
Carpenter, Delma, 107, 118
Caruthers, William, 105, 106, 119; *The Knights of the Golden Horseshoe*, 6, 105, 111–17
Carvin's Cove, 100
Carvin's Creek, 91
Cary, Richard, 62–63
Catskill Mountains, 167, 172
"Celestial Railroad, The" (Hawthorne), 224
"Census Taker, The" (Frost), 199
Chairback Gap, 234
Chairback Mountains, 234

Channing, William Ellery, 236
Charlie's Bunion, 74
Chase, Jim, 70
Chatwin, Bruce, 1, 4, 9
Chaucer, Geoffrey, 73
Cherokee, N.C., 31
Cherokee Indians, 9, 36; history of, 12, 29–31, 39, 40, 49–50; myths of, 11–16, 19–29, 31–33; territory of, 10–13, 19–32; William Bartram's encounters with, 36, 39–40, 47, 48, 49
Cheshire, Mass., 4, 165
Cheshire Harbor, Mass., 168
Chilhowee Mountain, 53
Chopin, Kate, 52
Christianity, 10, 23, 26, 29, 30, 58–59, 90–91, 98; geopiety in, 17–19. *See also* Bible, Canaan, Eden, New Testament, Old Testament
City Stream, 181–82
Civil War, 53, 124–26, 129
Cixous, Hélène, 65
Claytor, Gertrude, 104–5, 106, 117, 119
Clingman's Dome, 31–32, 53–54
Clinton, Mt., 209
Cloud Pond, 233–34, 241
"Cock-a-Doodle-Doo!" (Melville), 174, 175
Cold Spring, 37, 39
Cole, Thomas, 223
Coleridge, Samuel Taylor, 38
Commonplace Book (Southey), 178
Common sense, 115, 138, 259 n.16
Concord, Mass., 164, 170, 248
Concord River, 164
Confidence Man, The (Melville), 174
Connecticut River, 195
Cooke, Rose Terry, 52
Cooper, James Fenimore, 111, 114, 259 n.15; *The Pioneers*, 115
Cooper Brook, 237
Cosby Knob, 33
Cowkeeper, 38
Cox, Stephen, 123
Craddock, Charles Egbert. *See* Murfree, Mary Noailles

Crawford, Abel, 209
Crawford, Ethan Allen, 204, 207, 208, 209, 214, 217
Crawford, Thomas, 209
Crawford Notch, 201, 204, 208–9, 210, 213
Crawford Pond, 237
Creek Indians, 47
Crescent Pond, 238
Crockett, Davy, 7, 77, 217
Crystal Hills, 220
Cube Mountain, 195
Cumberland Mountains, 52, 56
Cummings, E. E., 70
Cutler, Manasseh, 216
"Cycle and the Roots, The" (Spiller), 110–11

Daicey Pond, 243
Damascus, Va., 4, 51
Dartmouth College, 180, 195
Davis, Curtis Carroll, 114
Day of Doom, The (Wigglesworth), 211
Dead Man Mountain, 91
"Death Boat of Heligoland" (Campbell), 178
De Beauvoir, Simone, 66
Declaration of Independence (Jefferson), 126–27
Deconstructionism, 131, 143, 226
Deep Creek, 74
Deep ecology, 5
Deer Hunter, 134
Delaware Indians, 134, 140–42
Delaware River, 132, 138, 141, 142, 150
Delaware Water Gap, 7, 131–32, 135, 137, 141, 146, 147, 148, 150
Democracy, 111, 114–15, 117, 154, 204–7, 211
Derrick Knob, 53–54, 74, 80
Derry, N.H., 181
Describing Early America (Regis), 42, 44, 48
Dialogics, 5, 45, 142–43, 150, 235. See also Bakhtin; Heteroglossia

Dickey, James, 39
Diderot, Denis, 127
Dillard, Annie, 89; Pilgrim at Tinker Creek, 6, 88–102; style, 88, 97
Doctrine of use, 110, 125
Dogen, 93
Dorson, Richard, 7
Doubletop Mountain, 118
Douglas, William O., 225
Douglass, Frederick, 125
"Drifting down Lost Creek" (Murfree), 56
Dunn, Durwood, 53
"Dust of Snow" (Frost), 192
Duyckinck, Evert, 162, 163, 164, 165, 171, 175–76, 264 n.15

East Branch of the Pleasant River, 237
Easton, Pa., 141
Ecocentrism, 234, 242, 268 n.8
Ecocriticism, 5–6, 7, 8, 182, 226, 239–40, 251 nn.5,6
Ecofeminism, 5, 54–55, 57, 59, 63, 66–69, 255 nn.5,16
Ecohero, 234, 268 n.8
Ecology, 146, 221; associated with democratic virtues, 205, 212; as cultural construct, 145; in ecocriticism, 5, 6, 239; history of, 253 n.12; inherent in Bartram's view of nature 36, 41–45, 47, 48; inherent in Frost's synecdoche, 190, 200; inherent in native American world views, 19; as science of interconnection, 6, 8, 45, 47, 48, 93, 144–45, 228, 242
Ecotone, 193
Eden, 17, 26, 112, 188–89
Edgar Huntly (Brown), 6, 131–43, 146–50
"Education by Poetry" (Frost), 190
Edwards, Jonathan, 7
Eliot, George, 51
Eliot, T. S., 197
Ellison, George, 73
Emerson, Ralph Waldo, 38, 164, 175, 207,

226, 248; "The American Scholar," 111; "The Poet," 206; as transcendentalist, 176, 232

"Empty Threat, An" (Frost), 197–98

End of Nature, The (McKibben), 132

Enlightenment, The, 121, 138, 140

Environmental Imagination, The (Buell), 234, 262 n.26, 268 n.8

Equinox, Mt., 182

Ethan Pond, 201, 208

"Evening in a Sugar Orchard" (Frost), 192

Evernden, Neil, 132, 144

Excursion, The (Wordsworth), 38

"Expeditio Ultramontana" (Seagood), 6, 105, 108–10, 215

Faerie Queene (Spenser), 170–71

Fallam, Robert, 106

Farmer's Mills Shelter, 160, 161

"Female Geography of Sarah Orne Jewett's *The Country of the Pointed Firs*, The" (Ammons), 65

Field, Darby, 215, 217

Field and Stream, 73

Fields, James T., 162

Fieldwork, 147

Fontaine, John, 103–4, 105, 108, 114, 115, 117, 119; biographical information, 106; *Journal*, 6, 103, 106–7, 110, 118–19; style, 106–7, 116

"Footnote to Howl" (Ginsberg), 158

Fork Mountain, 118

Forks of the Delaware, 141, 147

"For Once, Then, Something" (Frost), 183–85, 192, 194

Fothergill, John, 38

"Fountain, a Bottle, A Donkey's Ears and Some Books, A" (Frost), 198–99

Fourth Mountain, 234

"Fragmentary Blue" (Frost), 186–87

Franconia, N.H., 181, 195

Franconia Notch, 195, 200, 205, 211, 207

Franconia Ridge, 195

Franklin, N.C., 24

Franklin, Wayne, 123

Freeman, Mary Wilkins, 52

Frome, Michael, 50, 73

Frontier hypothesis, 212

Frost, Lesley, 183

Frost, Robert, 71; "The Aim Was Song," 201–2; "The Ax-Helve," 200; biographical information, 180–81, 195; "Blue Butterfly Day," 194; "A Boundless Moment," 192; *A Boy's Will*, 181; "A Brook in the City," 181–82, 199; "The Census Taker," 199; "Dust of Snow," 192; "Education by Poetry," 190; "An Empty Threat," 197–98; "Evening in a Sugar Orchard," 192; "For Once, Then, Something," 183–85, 192, 194; "A Fountain, a Bottle, a Donkey's Ears and Some Books," 198–99; "Fragmentary Blue," 186–87; *A Further Range*, 181; hike on Long Trail, 183, 265 n.3; "A Hillside Thaw," 193; "The Hill Wife," 196; "Looking for a Sunset Bird in Winter," 192; "Misgiving," 189–90; *Mountain Interval*, 181; "The Need of Being Versed in Country Things," 191–92, 199; *New Hampshire* (collection), 6, 181–202; "New Hampshire" (poem), 183, 195–97; *North of Boston*, 181; "Nothing Gold Can Stay," 188–89; "The Onset," 187–88; "Our Singing Strength," 194–95; "Paul's Wife," 200; "A Star in a Stone Boat," 200; "The Star-Splitter," 199–200; style, 180–81, 184, 186–90, 201; "Two Look at Two," 194; "The Woodpile," 183–84

Frost and the Book of Nature (Bagby), 184, 187

Fuller, Margaret, 207

Further Range, A (Frost), 181

Gainesville, Ga., 1, 9

Galehead Hut, 207–8

Garden, Alexander, 234, 237

Garfield, Mt., 201, 207

Garfield Ridge, 200
Gathland, 129–30
Geohistory, 3
Geopiety, 16–18
George I, King, 103, 107, 108–9, 114
Georgics, 51
Geotechnics, 2
Gilligan, Carol, 60
Gilpin, William, 136, 140
Ginsberg, Allen, 157–61; "Footnote to
    Howl," 158; *Howl*, 6, 157–61; influ-
    ence of Whitman upon, 158, 160,
    262 n.4; style, 158–59, 160; "A Super-
    market in California," 160
Glastenbury Mountain, 183, 186
Golden Horseshoe Expedition. *See*
    Knights of the Golden Horseshoe
Gothic novel, 135, 143, 260 n.6
Grabo, Norman, 136
Graymoor Monastery, 156–57, 160, 161
"Great Carbuncle, The" (Hawthorne),
    7, 162, 204, 214–24
Great Chain of Being, 42, 48
Great Smoky Mountains, 32–33, 51, 67,
    70, 78, 84, 227, 245; Cherokee in, 29–
    33, 50; in Murfree's stories, 51–54, 56–
    59, 255 n.4; Kephart in, 72–74, 76–77,
    80–84, 86
Great Smoky Mountains National Park,
    53, 74
"Great Stone Face, The" (Hawthorne),
    7, 114, 204, 205–7, 210, 211, 221, 266 n.3
Greenleaf Hut, 203, 207, 220
Green Mountain, 193
Green Mountains, 172, 181–83, 185–86,
    190–91, 193, 204
Greenwich Village, 182
Gregory's Bald, 53
Greylock, Mt., 162–74, 175, 178–79, 186,
    247, 263 n.12
Grimke, Sarah, 59–60
Gulf Hagas Brook, 236
Gulf Hagas Mountain, 236
Guyot, Mt., 201, 208

Haeckel, Ernst, 253 n.12
Hanover, N.H., 195
Harper, Frances, 39
Harpers Ferry, W.Va., 2, 4, 7, 130; in Civil
    War, 124, 126, 129; in Jefferson's *Notes*,
    120, 122, 123
Harriman, Mary Williamson, 155
Harriman, William Averell, 155
Harriman State Park, 155
Harte, Bret, 52
Hawthorne, Nathaniel, 3, 52, 176, 178; ac-
    quaintance with Thoreau, 164; "The
    Ambitious Guest," 7, 204, 209–13, 221;
    "The Celestial Railroad," 224; "The
    Great Carbuncle," 7, 162, 204, 214–24;
    "The Great Stone Face," 7, 114, 204,
    205–7, 210, 211, 221, 266 n.3; meeting
    with Melville, 162–65, 175, 179, 263
    n.5; *Mosses from an Old Manse*, 164,
    165; "The Notch of the White Moun-
    tains," 204, 210; "Our Evening Party
    among the Mountains," 204, 214, 216;
    "Sketches from Memory," 204, 206,
    207, 209–10; *Twice-Told Tales*, 209;
    visit to White Mountains, 204; *Wonder
    Book for Boys and Girls*, 164
Hawthorne Falls, 200, 207
Hayles, Katherine, 145–46
Hay Mountain, 236
Hazeltop Mountain, 117
Hebron, Lake, 227
Hellenbrand, Harold, 127
Hell Hollow, 183
Hell Hollow Brook, 183, 185
Henry Gap, 10
Hermitage, The, 235
Hessian Lake, 152, 154
Heteroglossia, 142, 235. *See also* Bakhtin;
    Dialogics
Higgins, Brian, 175
Hightop Mountain, 104, 107
"Hillside Thaw, A" (Frost), 193
"Hill Wife, The" (Frost), 196
History and Present State of Virginia
    (Beverley), 104

History, Myths, and Sacred Formulas of the Cherokee (Mooney), 11–16, 20–33
History of New Hampshire (Belknap), 216–17
Hoag, Ronald, 239
Hoagland, Edward, 7
Hogarth, William, 40
Hollins College, 89
Holmes, Oliver Wendell, 162–63
Hope, Thomas, 178
Hot Springs, N.C., 1, 4, 87
Howard, Leon, 176
Howarth, William, 169, 170, 173
Howells, William Dean, 61–62
Howl (Ginsberg), 6, 157–61
Huddleston, Eugene, 110
Hudson River School, 135, 195, 223
Human Nature in Geography (Wright), 16–18
Hundred Mile Wilderness, 226–28, 232–38, 240–46
Hurd Brook, 240–41

Icewater Spring, 74, 84
Images or Shadows of Divine Things (Edwards), 7
Imperialism, 105, 111, 118–19, 206, 216, 221; in Caruthers's *Knights*, 113–14; in Fontaine's *Journal*, 107; in Hawthorne's "The Great Carbuncle," 215, 221; in Seagood's "Expeditio Ultramontana," 108–10, 215
In a Different Voice (Gilligan), 60
Indian Removal Act, 30
Indians. *See* American Indians
"In Harmony with Nature" (Arnold), 196
Inhumanism, 231
In Memoriam (Tennyson), 264 n.15
Intentional fallacy, 18
In the Clouds (Murfree), 52, 53
"In the Name of Wonder" (Wonham), 81
In the Tennessee Mountains (Murfree), 52, 56
Inuit, 143

Invention of Appalachia, The (Batteau), 67
Iroquois, 19, 163
Itagunahi, 14

Jackson, Andrew, 29, 30
James, Henry, 52
Jeffers, Robinson, 231
Jefferson, Martha, 123
Jefferson, Mt., 225, 247
Jefferson, Thomas, 112, 212; biographical information, 121–22, 123; *Declaration of Independence*, 126–27; *Notes on the State of Virginia*, 6, 120–28, 130; style, 122, 128
Jefferson and Nature (Miller), 123
Jefferson Rock 120, 122, 124, 130
Jehlen, Myra, 126–28
Jewett, Sarah Orne, 52, 65
Johnson, Samuel, 131
Johnson, Sandra Humble, 92
Jonathan Draws the Long Bow (Dorson), 7
Jones Nose, 168
Josselyn, John, 218
Journal (Thoreau), 173, 247
Journal of John Fontaine, 6, 103, 106–7, 110, 118–19
Justus Mountain, 10

Katahdin, Mt., 7, 87, 185, 226, 227, 232, 241–49; end point of A.T., 1, 2, 4; Thoreau's account of, 228–32, 234–37, 239–47, 248, 268 n.15, 269 n.16
Katahdin Falls, 244
Katahdin Stream, 242, 243, 244, 247, 268 n.15
Kellert, Stephen, 221–23
Kephart, Horace, 72–77, 79–87; biographical information, 72–74; *Camping and Woodcraft*, 73, 75–76, 77, 80, 85; *Our Southern Highlanders*, 6, 73, 76–87; *Smoky Mountain Magic*, 74; *Sporting Firearms*, 81; style, 73–74, 80

Kephart, Mt., 74
Kerouac, Jack, 161
King, Ynestra, 66
Kinsman Mountain, 195, 200
Kittatinny Mountain, 138
Kittatinny Ridge, 132
Knights of the Golden Horseshoe, 3, 103–19, 258 nn. 2,7, 259 n.12
Knights of the Golden Horseshoe, The (Caruthers), 6, 105, 111–17
Krause, Sydney 141, 147, 149
"Ktaadn" (Thoreau), 226–47, 268 n.4, 269 n.16
"Kubla Khan" (Coleridge), 38

LaChapelle, Dolores, 93
Lafayette, Mt., 195, 200, 203, 247
Lakes of the Clouds, 220
Lambert's Meadow, 98
Lancaster, N.H., 208–9
"Land of One's Own, A" (Trimble), 68
Lanier, Sidney, 7
Lanman, Charles, 24, 30
Leatherstocking tales (Cooper), 111
Leclerc, Georges-Louis, Comte de Buffon, 121, 122
Lederer, John, 106
Lee, Robert E., 124
Lenni Lenape, 19, 141–42
Lenox, Mass., 162
Letters from the Alleghany Mountains (Lanman), 24, 30
Levelland Mountain, 13
Lewis, Clayton, 128
Lewis Mountain Campground, 107
Liberty, Mt., 195, 200
Licklog Gap, 37
Lincoln, Mt., 195, 200
Linnaeus, 42, 43, 44, 47, 48
Lion Head, 225
Literary criticism, 5–6, 7, 8, 18; deficiencies of, regarding nature, 147, 149, 178, 182, 231, 238–39, 264 n.23
Literary Shrines (Wolfe), 175
Literary World, 162, 164, 165, 171

Little Boardman Mountain, 237
Little Fork of the Sugar Fork of Hazel Creek, 73
Little Haystack Mountain, 195, 200
Little Niagara Falls, 243
Little Rock Pond, 193
Local color, 52, 64–65
Logan Brook, 237
Lonesome Lake, 195
Long Trail, 181, 183, 265 n.3
Looby, Christopher, 48, 49
"Looking for a Sunset Bird in Winter" (Frost), 192
Lorrain, Claude, 136
Lovewell's War, 215
Lower Nesowadnehunk Stream, 243, 245
Low Gap, 16
Lueck, Beth, 137–38
Lynen, John, 183–84

McAfee Knob, 88–89, 91
McDowell, Michael, 200
MacKaye, Benton, 2, 228, 267 n.2; "An Appalachian Trail," 2; idea for A.T., 2, 190, 193; "Outdoor Culture," 248
McKibben, Bill: The Age of Missing Information, 212–13; The End of Nature, 132
Madison, Mt., 225, 247
Maine Woods, The (Thoreau), 7, 226, 235–36
Manchester, Vt., 183
Manifest Destiny, 114, 213
Marbois, François, 121
Maryville, Tenn., 53
Mathews, Cornelius, 162–63
Max Patch, 78–79
Medicine Man, 20
Meherrin Indians, 103
"Melodramas of Beset Manhood" (Baym), 77–78
Melville, Herman: "Bartleby the Scrivener," 174; "Cock-a-Doodle-Doo!," 174, 175; The Confidence Man, 174; influence of Thoreau upon, 165, 170–71,

174–79, 263 n.8, 264 n.15; meeting with Hawthorne, 162–65, 175, 179, 263 n.5; *Moby-Dick*, 6, 164, 165, 168–73, 174–78, 184–85, 263 n.5, 264 nn.19,20; *Omoo*, 165; "The Piazza," 6, 164, 167–69, 170–72, 173, 174–75, 176; *Pierre*, 164; *Typee*, 164, 165

"Melville and the Berkshires" (Parker), 264 n.23

Merrimack River, 164, 173–74

Mexican War, 114

Middleton, Harry, 7

Milam Gap, 107, 117

Miller, Charles A., 123

Millinocket, Maine, 228

Milton, John, 230

"Misgiving" (Frost), 189–90

Mitchell, Mt., 2

Mizpah Hut, 219

Moby-Dick (Melville), 6, 171, 184–85, 264 n.20; composition of, 164, 165, 175–76, 178, 263 n.5, 264 n.19; influenced by Thoreau's *A Week*, 174, 176–79; themes of, 170, 172, 176–77

Mollies Ridge, 51

Monroe, Mt., 220

Monson, Maine, 4, 227, 248

Montesquieu, Charles, 121

Monthly Magazine, 131, 135, 148

Monument Mountain, 162–65, 171, 174, 175, 178–79

"Monument Mountain" (poem by Bryant), 162–63, 165

Mooney, James, 14–15, 50; *History, Myths, and Sacred Formulas of the Cherokee*, 11–16, 20–33; *Myths of the Cherokee*, 6

Moore, Hugh, 44

Moore, Richard, 170–71

Moosilauke, Mt., 195

Morewood, Sarah, 171

Moss, Sidney P., 175

Mosses from an Old Manse (Hawthorne), 164, 165

Mountain Gloom and Mountain Glory (Nicolson), 105

Mountain Interval (Frost), 181

Mountains and Rivers without End (Snyder), 94

Mountain View Pond, 237

Muir, John, 92, 185; *A Thousand Mile Walk to the Gulf*, 7

Murch Brook, 244, 268 n.15. *See also* Katahdin Stream

Murfree, Mary Noailles (pseud. Charles Egbert Craddock), 51–53, 55–68, 76; biographical information, 52; "Drifting down Lost Creek," 56; as ecofeminist, 66–67; *In the Clouds*, 52, 53; *In the Tennessee Mountains*, 52, 56; *Prophet of the Great Smoky Mountains, The*, 6, 52, 53, 56–62, 66; style, 62–66

Murfreesboro, Tenn., 52

Murphy, Patrick, 67

Myths of the Cherokee (Mooney), 6. See also *History, Myths, and Sacred Formulas of the Cherokee*

Nahmakanta Lake, 238

Nahmakanta Stream, 238

Nantahala Gorge, 26, 27, 28

Nantahala Mountains, 25, 26, 28–29, 36–41, 49–50

Nantahala River, 24, 26, 27, 37, 40

Narrative biography, 262 n.2

Narrative of the Life of an American Slave (Douglass), 125

Narrative scholarship, 7–9, 252 n.8

Nash, Timothy, 208, 217

National identity, 113–19, 126–28, 178, 205, 212

Nationalism, 106, 113–15, 116–17, 118–19, 178, 207, 216

Nationalism, Literary, 110–11, 163, 204, 216, 258 n.11

Native Americans. *See* American Indians

Native American Stories (Bruchac), 7

Natural Bridge, 121, 259 n.4

Natural history, 42, 68, 122, 237

Natural History of the Senses, A (Ackerman), 242

Natural law, 61, 126–28, 130
Natural scripture, 18, 105, 110, 207, 212
Nature: as cultural construct, 132, 138,
    139–40, 143–46, 149, 150, 226; defini-
    tion of, 132; as setting, 149; as symbol
    of national identity, 113–19, 126–28,
    178, 205, 212
Nature writing, 8, 94, 234–35, 237, 242
"Need of Being Versed in Country
    Things, The" (Frost), 191–92, 199
Neel's Gap, 13, 16
Neoclassicism, 41, 42, 44
Neohistoricism, 8
Nesowadnehunk Stream, 243
Nesuntabunt Mountain, 238
New Hampshire (collection by Frost), 6,
    181–202
"New Hampshire" (poem by Frost), 183,
    195–97
New Testament, 172
New York City, 151, 152, 156, 158, 165
Nicolson, Marjorie Hope, 105
North Adams, Mass., 171
North of Boston (Frost), 181
"Notch of the White Mountains, The"
    (sketch by Hawthorne), 204, 210
Notch of the White Mountains, The
    (painting by Cole), 223
Notes on the State of Virginia (Jefferson),
    6, 120–28
"Nothing Gold Can Stay" (Frost),
    188–89
Notions of the Americans (Cooper),
    259 n.15

Oakes Gulf, 223
Observations on the Creek and Cherokee
    Indians (Wm. Bartram), 47
Oglethorpe, Mt., 2
O'Grady, John P., 240, 265 n.13, 268 n.4
Old Man of the Mountain, 195, 198, 200,
    205, 207, 211
Old Testament, 19, 157, 197, 211; charac-
    ters from, 39, 101, 112, 197. See also
    Bible; Canaan; Christianity; Eden

Oliver, Egbert S., 174
Olympus, 109
Omoo, (Melville), 165
"Onset, The" (Frost), 187–88
On the Road (Kerouac), 161
On the Spine of Time (Middleton), 7
"Our Evening Party among the Moun-
    tains" (Hawthorne), 204, 214, 216
"Our Singing Strength" (Frost), 194–95
Our Southern Highlanders (Kephart), 6,
    73, 76–87
"Outdoor Culture" (MacKaye), 248

Palisades Park, 151, 155
Paradise Lost (Milton), 230
Parker, Hershel, 175, 262 n.2, 264 n.23
Parnassus, 109
Parson's Bald, 53
Pastoral, 123, 169, 182, 193, 229, 239,
    254 n.19
Pastoral Art of Robert Frost, The (Lynen),
    183–84
Pathetic fallacy, 48
"Paul's Wife" (Frost), 200
Penn, Thomas, 141
Penn, William, 141
Perrin, Noel, 7
Peru, Vt., 183
"Piazza, The" (Melville), 6, 164, 167–69,
    170–72, 173, 174–75, 176
Picturesque, 41, 135–36, 137, 140, 143,
    254 n.19
Pierce, Franklin, 207
Pierre (Melville), 164
Pilgrim at Tinker Creek (Dillard), 6,
    88–102
Pinkham Notch, 225
Pinnacle, the, 87
Pioneers, The (Cooper), 115
Pittsfield, Mass., 162, 163, 167
Plato, 198
"Plea for Captain John Brown, A"
    (Thoreau), 125
Plymouth, N.H., 207
Poe, Edgar Allen, 76

"Poet, The" (Emerson), 206
Pollock, Jackson, 148
Pollywog Stream, 238
Pope, Alexander, 41
Port Clinton, Pa., 4
Poststructuralism, 5, 132, 251 n.6
Potaywadjo Spring, 237
Potomac River, 120–21, 125–26, 129
Practice of the Wild, The (Snyder), 71,
    92–94
Prelude, The (Wordsworth), 38
Presidential Range, 224
Principle of indeterminacy, 94
Profile Mountain, 195, 205, 207
Prophet of the Great Smoky Mountains,
    The (Murfree), 6, 52, 53, 56–62, 66
Puc Puggy, 38. *See also* Bartram,
    William
Pulitzer Prize, 88, 181

Quakers, 40, 44, 48, 141
Quallah Reservation, N.C., 31
Queen Anne's War, 215

Rabun Gap, 37
Radcliffe, Ann, 136
Rainbow Deadwaters, 241
Rainbow Lake, 241
Rainbow Ledges, 241
Rainbow Stream, 238, 240, 241
Raynal, Abbé Guillaume, 121
Realism, 135, 138, 149, 192
Recluse, The (Wordsworth), 38
Regis, Pamela, 42, 44, 48
Reimer, Margaret Loewen, 90–91
Revolutionary War, 39, 49–50, 86, 121,
    125
"Rime of the Ancient Mariner"
    (Coleridge), 38
Ringe, Donald, 136
Ripley Falls, 201, 208
Robinson Crusoe, 72, 231–32
Rocky Mountains, 54
Rocky Top, 54

Romanticism, 44, 192, 201, 254 n.19
Rosa, Salvator, 136
Rosebrook, Eleazar, 209
Rum Mountain, 244
Rutherford, Gen. Griffith, 50
Rutland, Vt., 183

Saco River, 209, 210
Saddleback Mountain (Mass.), 163–64.
    See also Greylock, Mt.
Saddle Back Mountain (Va.), 107
Saddleball Mountain, 166–67, 168
Saddle Ridge, 166, 168
Sand, George, 51
Sartor Resartus (Carlyle), 176
Sawmill Brook, 98–99
Schama, Simon, 8
Scheese, Don, 240
Scheick, William J., 122–23, 124
Scorched Earth Gap, 97
Scott, Gen. Winfield, 30
Scott, Sir Walter, 111
Scottish Enlightenment, 115
Scudder, Horace, 63–64, 65
Seagood, George, 105, 106, 113, 114, 115,
    117, 119; "Expeditio Ultramontana," 6,
    105, 108–10, 215
"Searching for Common Ground"
    (Hayles), 145–46
Seattle, Chief, 71
Second Sex, The (De Beauvoir), 66
Secret History of the Dividing Line
    (Byrd), 108
Seminole Indians, 38
Sequoyah, 14, 29
Sermon on the Mount, 113
Setting, 64–65, 136, 149, 262 n.26
Shaffer, Earl, 5
Shakespeare, William, 165, 178
Shenandoah Mountains, 79, 87, 107,
    118–19
Shenandoah National Park, 7, 104
Shenandoah River, 103, 120–21, 123–24,
    125–26, 128–29
Shenandoah Valley, 104–5, 116, 129

Sherburne Pass, 193
Showalter, Elaine, 51
Siler Bald (in Nantahala Mountains), 36
Siler's Bald (in Great Smoky Mountains), 33
Silver, Bruce, 43
Silverman, Kenneth, 110
Simpson, Louis, 155
Sinai, Mt., 19
Sioux, 19
"Sketches from Memory" (Hawthorne), 204, 206, 207, 209–10
Skyline Drive, 107, 117–18
Slaughter Gap, 12
"Slavery in Massachusetts" (Thoreau), 125
Slotkin, Richard, 128
Slovic, Scott, 7, 91
Smart, Christopher, 160
Smarts Mountain, 195
Smith, Lee, 7
Smoky Mountain Magic (Kephart), 74
Smuggler's Notch, Vt., 183
Snyder, Gary, 71, 96; Mountains and Rivers without End, 94; The Practice of the Wild, 92–94; "Why Tribe," 84
Social ecology, 45–46, 47
Solebury, Pa., 147–48
Solomon, Carl, 157, 158, 159, 161
Songlines, The (Chatwin), 1, 4, 9
Song of Myself (Whitman), 159
Song of the Chattahoochee (Lanier), 7
"Song of the Open Road" (Whitman), 6, 152–54, 160
Soper, Kate, 140, 144
Southey, Robert, 178
South Peak, 244
South Shaftsbury, Vt., 181, 182, 183, 185
South Twin Mountain, 201, 208
Spectacle Pond, 227
Spence Field, 53–54
Spenser, Edmund, 170–71
Spiller, Robert, 110–11
Spirit of Laws, The (Montesquieu), 121
Sporting Firearms (Kephart), 81
Sports Afield, 73

Spotswood, Gov. Alexander, 103–5, 106, 107, 108, 109, 112–14, 115
Springer Mountain, 1, 2, 4, 9, 21, 78, 89
"'Stalking with Stories'" (Basso), 18–19
Standing Indian Mountain, 22, 24
"Star in a Stone-Boat, A" (Frost), 200
"Star-Splitter, The" (Frost), 199–200
Stevens, Wallace, 226
Stoller, Leo, 246
Stowe, Harriet Beecher, 71, 125
Stratton Mountain, 183, 190, 193
Stratton Pond, 190
Stroudsburg, Pa., 141
Stuart, J. E. B., 124
Stuart, John, 40
Sublime, 216; in Bartram's Travels, 37, 41, 44, 254 n.19; in Brown's Edgar Huntly, 135–36, 140, 143; in Caruthers's Knights, 114; development of, 105; in Hawthorne's "The Ambitious Guest," 211; in Jefferson's Notes, 123; in Thoreau's "Ktaadn," 230, 235, 239
"Supermarket in California, A" (Ginsberg), 160
Sutton, Ann and Myron, 24
Swift Run Gap, 104, 107, 258 n.7
Swim Bald, 27, 28
Swimmer, 14, 25
Synecdoche, 184, 186–90

Taconic Range, 165
"Tale of the Ragged Mountains, A" (Poe), 76
Tallmadge, John, 240
Tall tales, 7, 80–81
Tammany, Mt., 150
Tauber, Gisela, 123
Tennyson, Alfred, Lord, 264 n.15
Thomas, Will, 31
Thoreau, Henry David, 7, 70, 90, 164–65, 167, 169–79, 185, 201; acquaintance with Hawthorne, 164; "The Allagash and East Branch," 243; influence on Melville, 165, 170–71, 174–79, 263 n.8, 264 n.15; Journal, 173, 247; "Ktaadn,"

226–47, 268 n.4, 269 n.16; *The Maine Woods*, 7, 226, 235–36; "A Plea for Captain John Brown," 125; "Slavery in Massachusetts," 125; *Walden*, 54, 162, 170, 172, 173, 177, 246–47, 249; *A Week on the Concord and Merrimack Rivers*, 164, 165, 169–73, 175, 247, 263 n.12, 264 n.15
Thoreau Falls, 201, 208
Thousand Mile Walk to the Gulf, A (Muir), 7
Thru-hikers, 4, 89, 93–94, 99, 238, 240, 244, 246; attitudes of, 152–53, 222, 242; community of, 2, 70–72, 79, 84; descriptions of, 1, 2; generosity of, 241; motivations of, 1, 70, 72, 101
Thru-Hiker's Handbook, The (Bruce), 5
Thunderhead Mountain, 53–54, 80
Tiger Lilies (Lanier), 7
Tinker Cliffs, 88–90, 93, 99, 102
Tinker Creek, 88–89, 91, 95–96, 99, 100–102
Tinker Mountain, 88–89, 91, 96, 100, 102
Toles, George, 136
Townsend, George Alfred, 129–30
Trail names, 15
Trail of Tears, 29–31, 50
Trail registers, 70–71, 99
Transcendentalism, 125, 184, 193, 195; in Dillard's *Pilgrim*, 90, 257 n.2; Melville's reaction against, 170–71, 174, 176, 264 n.20; in Thoreau's works, 170, 229, 232, 235, 239, 247; in Whitman's "Song of the Open Road," 153–54
Travels (Wm. Bartram), 6, 36–50; influence of, 38–39; style, 44–45
Tray Mountain, 70
Treaty Elm, 141
Treaty of Tellico, 50
Trimble, Stephen, 68
Tsali, 30–31, 32
Tuan, Yi-Fu, 17–18
Tuckaleechee Cove, 80
Tuckaseegee River, 73

Tuckerman Ravine, 223, 225
Turner, Frederick Jackson, 212
Twice-Told Tales (Hawthorne), 209
"Two Look at Two" (Frost), 194
Typee (Melville), 164, 165

Uncle Tom's Cabin (Stowe), 125
Unforeseen Wilderness, The (Berry), 37–38
Union Magazine, 226
University of Michigan, 219, 225
Upper Nesowadnehunk Stream, 243

Value of Life, The (Kellert), 221–23
Vance, Linda, 66

Wadleigh Stream, 238
Walasi-yi, 13
Walden (Thoreau), 54, 162, 170, 172, 173, 177, 246–47, 249
Walden Pond, 226, 229, 247–49
Walking Purchase Treaty, 141
Walking with Spring (Shaffer), 5
Wallace Gap, 36
Walters, Kerry, 43, 253 n.2
"Walt Whitman at Bear Mountain" (Simpson), 155
Warfel, Harry, 64
Washington, George, 206
Washington, Mt., 2, 204, 209, 210, 215, 219, 223–25
Waste Land, The (Eliot), 197
Wayah Bald, 24–25, 37, 39–40, 41, 50
Wayah Gap, 23, 24, 36, 39–40, 49–50
Webster Cliffs, 213–14
Week on the Concord and Merrimack Rivers, A (Thoreau), 164, 165, 169–73, 175, 247, 263 n.12, 264 n.15
Welter, Barbara, 59
Wesser Bald, 39
West Branch of the Penobscot River, 242
West Branch of the Pleasant River, 235
West Peak, 236

Weverton Cliffs, 129
Whitecap Mountain, 236
"White Heron, A" (Jewett), 52
White Mountains, 172, 200–201, 203,
    205, 207–9, 213–20, 223, 224–25;
    in Frost's poems, 181, 195, 198; in
    Hawthorne's stories, 204, 205–7, 209–
    11, 214–19, 222, 224; in Thoreau's works,
    7, 247
Whitman, Walt, 152–55, 158–59, 160–61;
    influence on Ginsberg, 158, 160, 262
    n.4; *Song of Myself*, 159; "Song of the
    Open Road," 6, 152–54; statue of, at
    Bear Mountain, 152, 155, 160; style,
    153, 158, 160
Whittier, John Greenleaf, 205
"Why Tribe" (Snyder), 84
Wigglesworth, Michael, 211
Willey, Mt., 208
Willey family, 209, 211
Williams College, 170, 171
Williamstown, Mass., 171
Wilmington, Del., 1, 227

Wilson, Edward, 220–21
Wilson Valley Lean-to, 229
Wind Gap, 131–32, 135, 138, 146, 147, 148
Winding Stair Gap, 36
Wine Spring Bald, 36–37, 39–40, 41
Winthrop, John, 215
Wolfe, Theodore F., 175
Wolf Rocks, 149
Wonder Book for Boys and Girls
    (Hawthorne), 164
Wonham, Henry, 81
"Woodpile, The" (Frost), 183–84
Wordsworth, William, 38
Worster, Donald, 145
Wright, John Kirtland, 16–18

Yonaguska, 30–31
Yu, Ning, 239–40

Zealand Falls, 201
Zealand Notch, 208
Zealand Ridge, 201